WEBER BRAAI BIBLE

THE STEP-BY-STEP GUIDE TO EXPERT BRAAIING

BY JAMIE PURVIANCE

PHOTOGRAPHY BY TIM TURNER

First published as *Weber's Way to Grill* in the USA in 2009 by Weber-Stephen Products Co.

This South African edition published in 2014 by Struik Lifestyle
an imprint of Random House Struik (Pty) Ltd
Company Reg. No. 1966/003153/07
Estuaries No. 4, Oxbow Crescent, Century Avenue, Century City 7441
PO Box 1144, Cape Town 8000, South Africa
www.randomstruik.co.za

ISBN 978-1-43230-407-2

Copyright © in South African edition: Random House Struik (Pty) Ltd 2014
Copyright © in text: Weber-Stephen Products LLC 2009, 2014
Copyright © in photographs (except cover and pp 278—279): Weber-Stephen Products Co. 2009, 2014
Copyright © cover image (flames): Gallo Images/Getty Images/Hirusho Higuchi 2014

For Weber-Stephen Products LLC
Author: Jamie Purviance
Managing editor: Marsha Capen
Photographer and photo art direction: Tim Turner
Food stylist: Lynn Gagné
Assistant food stylists: Nina Albazi, Christina Zerkis
Photo assistants: Christy Clow, David Garcia, Justin Lundquist
Digital guru: Takamasa Ota
Indexer: Becky LaBrum

Colour imaging and in-house prepress: Weber Creative Services
Contributors: Patty Ada, Emily Baird, Gary Bramley, Neal Corman, Jerry DiVecchio, Ryan Gardner,
John Gerald Gleeson, Joyce Goldstein, Gary Hafer, Jay Harlow, Rita Held, Susan Hoss, Ellen Jackson,
Elaine Johnson, Carolyn Jung, Alison Lewis, James McNair, Andrew Moore, Merrilee Olson, Jeff Parker,
David Pazimo, Craig Priebe, Anne-marie Ramo, Justin Roche, Rick Rodgers,
James Schend, David Shalleck, and Bob and Coleen Simmons

Photography credit: Christy Clow, pages 278 and 279, used with permission
Design and production: Shum Prats, Elaine Chow
Weber-Stephen Products LLC: Mike Kempster, Global Chief Marketing Officer;
Brooke Jones, Vice President Corporate Marketing
Consulting Global Publishing Director: Susan J. Maruyama, Round Mountain Media

For Random House Struik (Pty) Ltd
Managing director: Steve Connolly
Publisher: Linda de Villiers
Managing editor: Cecilia Barfield
Design manager: Beverley Dodd
Editor: Gill Gordon
Typesetter: Randall Watson

Printing and binding: Toppan Leefung Packaging and Printing (Dongguan) Co., Ltd, China
Reproduction: Hirt & Carter Cape (Pty) Ltd

No part of this book may be reproduced in any form including, but not limited to, storage in
a retrieval system or transmission in any form or by any means, electronic, mechanical,
photocopied, scanned, downloaded, recorded, or otherwise, without prior written permission.

Weber, the kettle configuration, RapidFire, and the kettle silhouette are registered trademarks;
Smokey Mountain Cooker is a trademark; all of Weber-Stephen Products LLC, 200 East Daniels Road,
Palatine, Illinois 60067 USA. All rights reserved.

Weber-Stephen Products LLC is represented in South Africa by Weber South Africa,
141 Hertz Close, Meadowdale 1614, Johannesburg.
Dr. Pepper® is a registered trademark of Dr. Pepper/Seven Up, Inc., Plano, Texas.

www.weber.com
www.weber.co.za
www.randomstruik.co.za

AUTHOR'S ACKNOWLEDGEMENTS

The idea for this book emerged from the agile publishing minds of Mike Kempster, Susan Maruyama and Christina Schroeder. With the help of Jim Childs and Bob Doyle, they outlined an ambitious project and honoured me with the job of tackling it. I am grateful to each of them for their confidence and support.

When it came down to managing all the words and pictures here, Marsha Capen was a thoughtful and remarkably hard-working editor. She always found a gracious way to herd the flock of pigeons involved in this creative process.

The sheer quantity of photographs required for this book would strike fear into the hearts of many photographers, but Tim Turner, who is a master of light and lens (and quite a good griller, too), thrived on the challenge. He was assisted by a particularly talented crew, which included food stylists Lynn Gagné, Nina Albazi and Christina Zerkis, as well as photo assistants Takamasa Ota, Christy Clow, David Garcia and Justin Lundquist.

There is another excellent reason why the meat in this book looks so irresistibly fabulous. Almost all of it came from Lobel's of New York (www.lobels.com). Evan, Stanley, Mark and David Lobel, along with David Richards and all their colleagues, maintain standards so high for meat quality and customer service that whenever I open a box with Lobel's on the label, I am always delighted.

For the recipes, I relied on a sharp team of culinary minds. Many thanks to April Cooper, who handled most of the testing and tweaking, and thank goodness for the many other grillers involved, too. I especially want to acknowledge Patty Ada, Emily Baird, Gary Bramley, Neal Corman, Jerry DiVecchio, Ryan Gardner, John Gerald Gleeson, Joyce Goldstein, Gary Hafer, Jay Harlow, Rita Held, Susan Hoss, Ellen Jackson, Elaine Johnson, Carolyn Jung, Alison Lewis, James McNair, Andrew Moore, Merrilee Olson, Jeff Parker, David Pazimo, Craig Priebe, Anne-marie Ramo, Justin Roche, Rick Rodgers, James Schend, David Shalleck and Bob and Coleen Simmons.

I love what Shum Prats and Elaine Chow did with the design of this book, managing to strike a gorgeous balance between clear instructions and imaginative aesthetics.

I want to thank Weber's Creative Services department for improving the look of every page. Thank you, Becky LaBrum, for a very useful index.

For lots of good advice and generous support all along, I offer special thanks to Sherry Bale, Brooke Jones, Nancy Misch and Sydney Webber.

While working on this book, I referred to many other books for solid culinary information. I found the following ones very helpful: *The Complete Meat Cookbook* by Bruce Aidells and Denis Kelly; *The Cook's Illustrated Guide to Grilling and Barbecue* by the editors of *Cook's Illustrated*; *The New Food Lover's Companion* by Sharon Tyler Herbst; *The Barbecue Bible* by Steven Raichlen; and *How to Cook Meat* by Chris Schlesinger and John Willoughby.

In the final weeks of production, I had impeccable editing help from Sarah Putman Clegg and Carolyn Jung.

This book took me out of town for many days and nights, away from my wife, Fran, and our children, Julia, James and Peter. I missed some family vacations and quite a few weekends with the people that matter most to me. I owe them a lot for remaining patient and supportive throughout the whole process.

Finally, I want to thank a few mentors who gave a great deal of themselves to me early in my culinary career, Antonia Allegra, Esther McManus and Becky and David Sinkler. With selfless generosity, each one of them set me on the right course and encouraged me to get going.

Jamie Purviance
California

CONTENTS

CONTENTS

- BRAAI BASICS — 8
- RED MEAT — 32
- PORK — 94
- POULTRY — 132
- SEAFOOD — 176
- VEGETABLES — 228
- FRUIT — 264
- RESOURCES — 278
- INDEX — 312

INTRODUCTION

I wasn't born with a complete understanding and mastery of barbecue techniques. As a kid growing up in suburban America, I had to pick up the basics from my dad and other weekend grillers. Eventually, when it was my turn to grill, I had to imitate what I'd seen and I had to develop my own style by doing what so many others do. I had to improvise. I had to experiment. I had to wing it. Sometimes it worked, and other times… well, it didn't.

To be honest, I didn't really learn to barbecue until I was about thirty-years-old. That's when I tackled the subject in a much more methodical way. Obsessed with good food and frustrated by the limitations of winging it, I enrolled at the Culinary Institute of America. There I immersed myself in a rigorous curriculum of the hows and whys of topics like meat butchering, food chemistry, sauce making, and charcuterie. Under the supervision of demanding chefs, I learned serious science-based lessons like how heat affects the structure of meats and fats, how sauces are held together, and how marinades can unravel proteins.

Since my graduation some twenty years ago, I've focused my attention on how advanced culinary ideas relate to barbecuing. With the help of many experts at Weber, I've done extensive research on this particular way of cooking and I've written five books on the subject. Each book was an opportunity to learn more about what works on the grill and why some techniques work better than others. This book is a culmination of all the lessons I've learned.

So what is the right way to barbecue? Well, first of all, there isn't just one way to do it. It is not about

absolute right and wrong when it comes to issues like gas versus charcoal, direct versus indirect heat, or grilling with the lid on or off. This book includes and embraces any way to barbecue – as long as it works. And what works best, I've learned, is paying attention to culinary details. There is a big difference between winging it and paying attention.

Let me share a couple of examples of what paying attention can do. The first deals with the reason why most steaks turn out beautifully when grilled over direct high heat but most pork chops do not. Why should this be? High heat, of course, can char the surface of meat long before the centre is fully cooked. For a steak, that's a fine result, because you are left with a nicely caramelized outer crust and an interior that is dripping with rosy red juices. A pork chop is another matter. We don't like our pork chops raw in the middle, but if we barbecued most pork chops over direct high heat until the centres were properly cooked, the surfaces would be badly burned. That's why using medium heat is a better way to barbecue most pork chops. It allows the centres to reach an ideal degree of doneness without overcooking the surface. Simple enough, right? But back in my early days, when I was winging it, I threw every kind of meat over the same high heat. That's one reason things did not always work out.

Successful barbecuing is about paying attention to details as basic and significant as salt.

A second example about the importance of paying attention deals with something quite fundamental: salt. You might not give salt much thought, but did you know that, teaspoon for teaspoon, common table salt has about twice the sodium as some types of sea salt? So if you happened to use common table salt instead of the sea salt that I call for in almost every recipe in this book, I'm afraid your food will taste awfully salty (and a little metallic from calcium silicate found in common table salt). To take this topic one step further, I suggest that you pay attention to which brand of sea salt you use. They are not all the same. I recommend Maldon salt, because its crystals are hollow diamonds that dissolve easily on the surface of food, meaning the salt is less likely to fall off the food on the barbecue. On the other hand, there are sea salts on the market that are made of salt grains mixed with an anti-caking agent, which do not dissolve as well, and are high in sodium to boot. Read the labels carefully.

So, yes, culinary details matter. They explain why you would want to wrap barbecued ribs in aluminium foil during the final stages of cooking. They explain why you would grill fish fillets longer on the first side than the second. They explain why you would smoke a turkey with the breast side down.

That's why this book includes so many how-to photographs, explanatory captions and detailed recipes. The emphasis is on paying close attention. It's about learning how and why certain methods work well, so that you can move beyond the limits of winging it. Great taste lies in the details. Just pay attention and enjoy a new level of barbecuing success.

Jamie Purviance

BRAAI BASICS

Braaiing is so tightly woven into South African culture that almost everyone has something to say about the way to do it. All of us have had experiences that help us to be better braaiers. I think what separates the master braaiers from the beginners is really an understanding of the fundamentals. What follows here are the questions I hear again and again during my classes. The answers make the biggest difference in anyone's ability to braai.

STARTING A CHARCOAL FIRE

Q: WHAT'S THE DIFFERENCE BETWEEN COOKING OVER A WOOD FIRE VERSUS A CHARCOAL FIRE? IS ONE BETTER THAN THE OTHER?

A: It's all about ease and time management. A wood fire imparts a wonderful flavour, but has its drawbacks. Wood tends to create huge amounts of smoke and often requires waiting up to an hour or more for the flames to settle down and the embers to reach a manageable level of heat. Charcoal is essentially pre-burned wood, which means it reaches ideal cooking temperatures faster than wood and with much less smoke. It is made by slowly burning hardwood logs in an oxygen-deprived environment, like an underground pit or kiln. Over time, the water and resins are burned out of the logs, leaving behind big chunks of combustible carbon. These chunks are then broken into smaller lumps, hence the name lump charcoal (sometimes known as 'charwood').

Q: WHAT ABOUT BRIQUETTES? HOW ARE THEY DIFFERENT FROM CHARCOAL?

A: In South Africa, briquettes are more popular than charcoal. They are inexpensive and available practically everywhere. Most commonly, they are compressed black bundles of sawdust and coal, along with binders and fillers like clay and sodium nitrate. Some are presoaked in lighter fluid so that they start more easily, but they can impart a chemical taste to food if you don't completely burn off the lighter fluid before you begin cooking.

Standard briquettes don't burn as hot as charcoal and the amount of smoke produced is minimal at best. But they do produce predictable, even heat over a long period of time. A batch of 80–100 briquettes will last for about an hour, which is plenty of time to cook most foods without having to replenish the fire, whereas a pure charcoal fire may provide only half as much cooking time before it requires more coals.

Q: ARE THERE ANY OTHER CHOICES?

A: Pure hardwood (or 'all-natural') briquettes are a great option, if you can find them. They have the same pillow shape of standard briquettes, but they burn at higher temperatures, and with none of the questionable fillers and binders. Usually, they are made of crushed hardwoods bound together with nothing but natural starches. You'll probably pay more for these coals, but many serious braaiers and braai competitors consider them the gold standard of charcoal.

Q: IF SOMEONE IS ENTIRELY NEW TO CHARCOAL BRAAIING (AND MAYBE A LITTLE INTIMIDATED), WHAT'S THE BEST WAY TO GET STARTED?

A: My advice is to start by learning to light the charcoal safely and reliably using a chimney starter. This simple device consists of a metal cylinder with holes cut out along the bottom, a wire rack inside and two handles attached to the outside. Here's how to use the chimney. First, remove the top grate – or cooking grate – from your braai and place the chimney starter on the charcoal grate below. Next, place a couple of sheets of wadded-up newspaper under the wire rack, fill the upper chamber of the cylinder with charcoal, and light the newspaper through the holes on the side. (As an alternative, use firelighters in place of the newspaper.) The beauty of this method is that the chimney sucks the hot air up from the bottom and makes it circulate through the coals, lighting them much faster and more evenly than if you spread the coals out.

Lump charcoal will burn fast and be ready for cooking in about 15 minutes. Charcoal briquettes will take a little longer to light fully, generally 20–30 minutes.

When the charcoal is lightly coated all over with white ash (or lump charcoal is lit around the edges of all the pieces), it is ready to go. To empty it onto the charcoal grate, put on two insulated oven gloves. Grab hold of the heatproof handle in one hand and the swinging handle in the other. The swinging handle is there to help you lift the chimney and safely aim the contents just where you want them. For safety's sake, always wear insulated gloves when doing this. And never place a hot, empty chimney starter on the grass or on a wooden deck. Be sure to put the chimney starter on a heatproof surface away from children and pets.

If you don't have a chimney starter, build a pyramid of coals on top of a few firelighters, then light the firelighters. When the coals in the middle are lit, use tongs to pile the unlit coals on top. When all the coals are glowing bright orange and covered with ash, arrange them the way you want them on the charcoal grate.

Q: ARE YOU SAYING I SHOULDN'T USE LIGHTER FLUID?

A: That's right. Lighter fluid is a petroleum-based product that can really ruin the flavour of your food. I know there are some people who grew up with the stuff and think a hamburger is supposed to taste like petrol, but for the rest of us, we would never think of using it.

Q: HOW DO I KNOW HOW MUCH CHARCOAL TO USE?

A: That depends on the size of your braai and how much food you want to cook. Let's assume you have a classic 57 cm diameter kettle braai and you are cooking for four to six people. The simplest way to measure the right amount of coals is to use your chimney starter. (See, aren't you glad you got one?) Use it like a measuring cup for charcoal. Filled to the rim (with 80–100 standard briquettes), a chimney starter will provide enough charcoal to spread in a single, tightly packed layer across about two-thirds of the charcoal grate. That's usually enough charcoal to braai a couple of courses for four to six people. If you plan on cooking for longer than 45 minutes, you will need to add more charcoal.

Because lump charcoal comes in irregular shapes and sizes, it is harder to pack tightly in a chimney starter. So do yourself a favour; after you have spread the burning lump charcoal across the charcoal grate, fill in any gaps by adding a few more fist-sized lumps to the fire. The bed of coals should extend at least 10 cm beyond every piece of food on the cooking grate above, to ensure that everything cooks evenly.

Q: WHY WOULDN'T I FILL THE WHOLE CHARCOAL GRATE WITH BURNING COALS?

A: If you covered the entire grate with coals, then you would have only direct heat available to you. Everything on the cooking grate would be right on top of burning coals. That's fine for some foods, like burgers and hot dogs, but a lot of other foods do best cooked over both direct and indirect heat. Bone-in chicken pieces are a prime example. Have you ever seen what happens to them when they cook only over direct heat? They burn. The outside turns black before the meat along the bone has a chance to cook properly. The correct way to cook foods like this is to brown them for a while over direct heat and then move them over indirect heat to finish cooking.

Also, if the food being cooked over direct heat causes flare-ups, you have a convenient place to put the food while you figure out what to do next. At the very least, you can just close the lid and let the food finish cooking over indirect heat.

ARRANGING THE COALS

Q: WHAT EXACTLY IS THE DIFFERENCE BETWEEN DIRECT AND INDIRECT HEAT?

A: With direct heat, the fire is right below the food. With indirect heat, the fire is off to one side of the braai, or on both sides of the braai, and the food sits over the unlit part.

Direct heat works great for small, tender pieces of food that cook quickly, such as hamburgers, steaks, chops, boneless chicken pieces, fish fillets, shellfish and sliced vegetables. It sears the surfaces of these foods, developing flavours, texture and delicious caramelization while it also cooks the food all the way to the centre.

Indirect heat works better for larger foods that require longer cooking times, such as roasts, whole chickens and racks of ribs. As I mentioned, it is also just the right method for finishing thicker foods or bone-in cuts that have been seared or browned first over direct heat.

Q: DOES THE DIRECT METHOD COOK MY FOOD DIFFERENTLY FROM THE INDIRECT METHOD?

A: Yes. A direct fire creates both radiant heat and conductive heat. Radiant heat from the coals quickly cooks the surface of the food closest to it. At the same time, the fire heats the cooking grate rods, which conducts heat directly to the surface of the food and creates those unmistakable and lovely grill marks.

If the food is off to the side of the fire, or over indirect heat, the radiant heat and the conductive heat are still factors, but they are not as intense. However, if the lid of the kettle braai is closed, as it should be, there is another kind of heat generated: convective heat. This radiates off the coals, bounces off the lid, and goes round and round the food. Convection heat doesn't sear the surface of the food the way radiant and conductive heat do. It cooks it more gently all the way to the centre, like the heat in an oven, which lets you cook roasts, whole birds, and other large foods to the centre without burning them.

Q: ARE THERE ANY OTHER GOOD WAYS TO ARRANGE THE COALS?

A: The basic configuration I've described, with the coals to one side of the braai, is called a two-zone fire because you have one zone of direct heat and one zone of indirect heat. The temperature of a two-zone fire can be high, medium, or low, depending on how much charcoal is burning and how long it has been burning. Remember, charcoal loses heat over time.

You also can create a three-zone fire, which provides even more flexibility. On one side of the braai, pile coals two or three briquettes deep. Then, slope the coals down to a single layer across the centre of the braai, and place no coals on the opposite side. When the coals are completely ashen and have burned down for 10–20 minutes more, after being emptied from the chimney – voila! – you have direct high heat on one side, direct medium heat in the centre, and indirect heat on the opposite side.

There are also times when you might prefer a three-zone 'split' fire, where the coals are separated into two equal piles on opposite sides of the charcoal grate. This gives you two zones for direct heat (high, medium or low) and one zone between them for indirect heat. This works nicely for cooking a roast, such as pork loin or beef fillet, over indirect heat, because you have the same level of heat on either side of the roast.

Q: WHAT'S THE RING OF FIRE?

A: It's another way of arranging charcoal for both direct and indirect heat. The ring of coals around the perimeter provides direct heat while the empty centre of the ring provides an area of indirect heat.

Q: WHAT'S THE BULL'S-EYE?

A: The bull's-eye is the flip side of the ring of fire. With the coals piled in the centre of the charcoal grate, you have a small area of direct heat, but a lot of space around the perimeter for indirect heat. This is a convenient arrangement for slow cooking or warming several small pieces of food, such as bone-in chicken pieces.

Q: WHAT'S THE PURPOSE OF A DRIP TRAY ON A CHARCOAL GRATE?

A: The tray catches drippings, which helps to extend the life of your braai by keeping it clean. If you fill the tray with water, the water will absorb and release heat slowly, adding a bit of moisture to the cooking process.

JUDGING THE HEAT LEVEL

 HOW DO I KNOW I HAVE THE RIGHT LEVEL OF HEAT?

A: As soon as briquettes are lightly covered with gray ash (or lump charcoal is lit around the edges of all the pieces), and you've poured the coals onto the charcoal grate, you have very high heat, actually too high for almost any food to handle without burning quickly.

Spread the coals out the way you like, set the cooking grate in place, and close the lid. It's important now to preheat the braai. You should do this for 10–15 minutes, to make the cooking grate hot enough for searing and to make it easier to clean. The heat will loosen all the little bits and pieces clinging to the cooking grate, left over from the last time you braaied, and a braai brush will easily remove them.

There are two reliable ways to judge how hot a charcoal fire is. One is to use the thermometer in the lid of your braai, if there is one. With the lid closed, the temperature should climb past 260°C (500°F) initially. Then, once it has reached its peak, the temperature will begin to fall. You can begin cooking whenever the temperature has fallen into the desired range.

HEAT	TEMPERATURE RANGE	WHEN YOU WILL NEED TO PULL YOUR HAND AWAY
High	230°–290°C (450°–550°F)	2–4 seconds
Medium	180°–230°C (350°–450°F)	5–7 seconds
Low	130°–180°C (250°–350°F)	8–10 seconds

The second way is less technical but surprisingly reliable. It involves extending the palm of your hand over the fire at a safe distance above the charcoal grate. Imagine a beer can standing on the cooking grate, right over the coals. If your palm were resting on top of the can, it would be about 12 cm from the cooking grate. That's where you should measure the heat of charcoal.

If you need to pull your hand away after just 2–4 seconds, the heat is high. If you need to pull your hand away after 5–7 seconds, the heat is medium. If you need to pull it away after 8–10 seconds, the heat is low. Use common sense and always pull your hand away from the heat before it hurts – you don't want to get burnt.

Q: WHAT SHOULD I DO TO MAINTAIN THE HEAT FOR A LONG PERIOD OF TIME?

A: Under normal circumstances, a typical charcoal briquette fire will lose about 38°C (100°F) of heat over 40–60 minutes. A typical lump charcoal fire will lose heat even faster. To maintain the braai's temperature, you'll need to add new coals during cooking. If you are using standard briquettes, remember that they take 20 minutes or more to reach their highest heat, so plan accordingly. You'll have to add them 20–30 minutes before you need them. Alternatively, you can light the briquettes ahead of time in a chimney starter, keep them burning in a safe place, and add them when you need instant results. For me, adding lit coals is a much better way to cook because I find the taste of food suffers when it absorbs the aromas of partially lit (standard) briquettes.

Lump charcoal and all-natural briquettes light faster than most standard briquettes, so they require less lead time. Add them just 5–10 minutes before you need to raise the heat. Smaller pieces of lump charcoal will burn out quickly, so you will need to add them more often. Larger lumps will take a little more time to get hot, but they will last longer. Fortunately, lump charcoal and all-natural briquettes don't produce any unwanted aromas in the early stages of their burning.

For a fairly even fire, add about 10–15 briquettes, or an equivalent amount of lump charcoal, every 45 minutes to an hour.

Q: HOW SHOULD I WORK THE AIR VENTS ON MY KETTLE BRAAI?

A: The vents on the top and bottom of the braai control the airflow inside. The more air flowing into the braai, the hotter the fire will grow and the more frequently you will have to replenish it. To slow the rate of your fire's burn, close the top vent as much as halfway and keep the lid on as much as possible. The bottom vent should be left open whenever you are cooking so that you don't kill your fire.

All kinds of charcoal, especially briquettes made with fillers, will leave behind some ash after all the combustible carbon has burned. If you allow the ashes to accumulate on the bottom of the braai, they will cover the vent and starve the coals of air, eventually extinguishing them. So, every hour or so, give the vent a gentle sweep, to clear them of ashes, by opening and closing the bottom vent several times in a row.

STARTING A GAS BRAAI

Q: WHAT'S THE PROCESS FOR LIGHTING A GAS BRAAI?

A: There's nothing complicated about lighting a gas braai. However, gas braai operation does vary, so be sure to consult the owner's manual that came with your braai. To light a Weber gas braai, first open the lid so that unlit gas fumes don't collect in the cooking box. Next, slowly open the valve on your gas cylinder all the way and wait a minute for the gas to travel through the gas line. Then turn on the burners, setting them all to high. Close the lid and preheat the braai for 10–15 minutes.

Q: WHAT IF I SMELL GAS?

A: That might indicate a leak around the connection or in the hose. Turn off all the burners. Close the valve on your gas cylinder and disconnect the hose. Wait a few minutes and then reconnect the hose. Try lighting the braai again. If you still smell gas, shut the braai down and call the manufacturer.

DIRECT AND INDIRECT HEAT ON A GAS BRAAI

Q: HOW DO I SET UP MY GAS BRAAI TO COOK WITH DIRECT HEAT?

A: On a gas braai, simply leave all the burners on and adjust them for the heat level you want. For example, if you want direct medium heat, turn all the burners down to medium, close the lid, and wait until the thermometer indicates that the temperature is in the range of 180°–230°C (350°–450°F). Then set your food on the cooking grate right over the burners. If your braai does not have a thermometer, use the 'hand test' described on page 15.

Q: WHAT'S THE SETUP FOR INDIRECT HEAT?

A: On a gas braai, you can switch from direct to indirect heat almost immediately. Just turn off one or more of the burners and place the food over an unlit burner. If your braai has two burners, turn off the one towards the back of the braai. If your braai has more than two burners, turn off the one(s) in the middle. The burners can be set to high, medium or low heat, as desired. Whenever the food is over an unlit burner and the lid is closed, you're cooking over indirect heat.

BRAAIING KNOW-HOW

Q: DO I NEED TO CLEAN THE COOKING GRATES EVERY TIME I USE THE BRAAI?

A: You really should clean the grates every time, not only to be tidy, but also because any residue left on the cooking grates may cause your food to stick. You will find that food releases from the grates much more easily, and with more impressive grill marks, if the cooking grates are clean.

The easiest way to clean your cooking grates is to preheat the braai, with the lid down, to about 260°C (500°F). Then, while wearing an insulated braai glove or oven glove, use a long-handled braai brush to scrape off any bits and pieces that may be stuck to the cooking grates.

Q: WHAT ABOUT CLEANING THE REST OF THE BRAAI?

A: Once a month or so, you should do a more thorough cleaning of your braai. Be sure to read the instructions in your owner's manual beforehand. Wipe down the braai with a sponge and warm, soapy water. Scrape off any debris that has accumulated under the lid. Remove the cooking grates, brush the burners, and clean out the bottom of the cooking box and the drip pan. For full care and upkeep instructions, consult your owner's manual. With a charcoal braai, remember that ash naturally has a small amount of water in it. Don't leave ash sitting in your braai for a long period of time; it can rust some parts of your braai.

Q: DO I NEED TO OIL THE COOKING GRATES BEFORE I BRAAI?

A: I do not recommend it. Many braaiers do, and that's fine, but keep in mind that oil will drip though the cooking grates and may cause flare-ups on both charcoal and gas braais. You can avoid wasting oil and improve your chances of a food releasing more easily by oiling the food, not the grates.

Q: WHAT SHOULD I DO IF FLARE-UPS HAPPEN?

A: A certain number of flare-ups are to be expected. When oil and fat drip into a hot braai, especially a charcoal braai, they tend to produce flames. If the flames are barely reaching the surface of the food and then they subside, don't worry about it. If, however, the flames are rising through the cooking grates and surrounding your food, you need to act quickly. Otherwise, the foods will pick up a sooty taste and colour, and could burn.

On a charcoal braai, most flare-ups begin within a few seconds of putting food on the braai, or right after you turn food over. Your first reaction should be to put the lid on the braai and close the top vent about halfway. By decreasing the amount of air getting to the fire, you may extinguish a flare-up. You can check the status of the flare-up by carefully looking through the partially open vent. If the flames are still threatening, open the lid and move the food over indirect heat. That's one very important reason why you should always have an indirect heat zone available. After a few seconds, the oil and fat will usually burn off and the flare-up will subside. When the flare-up dies down, resume cooking your food over direct heat.

You are less likely to have flare-ups with a gas braai because many of them have a system that prevents fat and oil from falling directly onto the burners. For example, most Weber gas braais have angled steel bars on top of the burners. Not only do they prevent almost all flare-ups, they also transform dripping juices and fat into wonderfully aromatic smoke. The solutions to flare-ups on a gas braai are the same as they are on a charcoal braai. First, make sure the lid is closed. Then, if necessary, move the food over indirect heat.

Q: WHEN SHOULD I BRAAI WITH THE LID ON?

A: As often as possible. Whether using a charcoal braai or a gas braai, the lid is really important. It limits the amount of air getting to the fire, thus preventing flare-ups, and it helps to cook food on the top and bottom simultaneously. While the bottom of the food is almost always exposed to more intense heat, the lid reflects some heat down and speeds up the overall cooking time. Without the lid, the fire would lose heat more quickly and many foods would take much longer to cook, possibly drying out. Plus, using the lid keeps the cooking grate at a higher

temperature, giving you more conductive heat, which creates better searing and caramelization. Finally, the lid traps all those good smoky aromas inside the braai and surrounds your food with them. Otherwise, the smoke will drift away and serve no real purpose. One exception to this rule occurs when you are cooking very thin pieces of food, like bread slices and tortillas. They cook (and potentially burn) so quickly that it's wise to leave the lid off and watch them carefully.

Q: IS IT WORTH IT TO GET A ROTISSERIE ATTACHMENT FOR MY BRAAI?

A: If you want to cook large hunks of meat – like pork loins, whole chickens, turkey, duck and beef joints – a rotisserie attachment is a good investment. Any of those meats can be cooked right on the cooking grate over indirect heat, but the advantage of a rotisserie is that the food slowly self-bastes as it rotates and absorbs the flavours of the fire.

To ensure that the meat stays in place as it turns and cooks uniformly, use butcher's string to truss your food into a compact shape. Then secure the food on the spit, making sure it is centred as evenly as possible. This will put less strain on the motor. Always preheat the braai first. When ready to cook, set the spit in place, put a disposable foil tray underneath the roast to catch the grease, turn on the motor, and close the lid.

Q: SO WHAT SHOULD I BUY: A CHARCOAL OR GAS BRAAI?

A: That decision depends a lot on what kind of cook you are. There are some braaiers who put a high priority on enjoying the food as quickly, cleanly, and conveniently as possible. For them, a gas braai makes the most sense. The fire is ready in 10–15 minutes. The temperature stays right where you need it for as long as you need it, and cleanup is minimal. Then there are some braaiers who relish the opportunity to build their own fires and tend the coals. Glowing embers and wood smoke thrill them so much that cooking over charcoal is well worth the extra time and cleanup required. They believe with every last taste bud that the flavour of food cooked over a live fire is better. So, you tell me: which type of braaier are you?

SMOKING AND BRAAIING

Q: SUPPOSE I WANT TO TRY SMOKING FOODS. HOW DO I DO THAT?

A: Congratulations, you get a gold star. Every braaier ought to try smoking with hardwoods. Done right, it lends food an irresistible flavour.

Smoking on a kettle braai is really easy to do, especially if you are already comfortable cooking with indirect heat. Begin by filling a chimney starter about one-third full with briquettes. When they are fully lit, pour all of the charcoal on one side of the cooking grate (if desired, use a charcoal basket, which holds the coals close together so that they burn more slowly) and place a foil tray on the other side. Then, carefully add about 600 ml (2–3 cups) of water to the tray. The water is important because it helps to maintain a low cooking temperature. It also adds some moisture to the food, which in many cases will cook for hours and hours, so it could dry out otherwise. Allow 30 minutes to 1 hour for the coals to burn down to the correct temperature and the water to heat up. Next, drop damp wood chips or dry hardwood chunks directly onto the coals. Then place your food on top of the cooking grate over the water pan and cover your braai. Expect to add more coals every hour or so to maintain the heat.

Wood chips, even when they have been soaked in liquid, will smoke sooner than hardwood chunks, but they often burn out in a matter of minutes. Wood chunks tend to burn for an hour or more. I suggest using chunks and positioning them on the outer edge of a charcoal fire to prolong and extend smoking times even further.

You've got quite a lot of options in the wood chips category. Some of the most popular ones are hickory and mesquite. Mesquite has a strong aroma, so be careful about using too much of it for too long. In fact, be careful about using too much of any kind of wood. A common mistake is to keep adding wood throughout hours and hours of smoking. The aromas of the smoke can eventually overpower the food, so start with just a few handfuls, then stop. Next time, if you want a little more smokiness, add an additional handful or two.

In my opinion, hickory complements beef, lamb, and pork really well. Milder woods pair nicely with milder foods, for example, apple and pecan with chicken and fish. Don't worry about using the 'wrong' wood for any kind of food. It's almost impossible to make a mistake here. Some people latch on to a favourite kind of wood and use it to smoke almost anything. That's fine. The differences between the woods can be pretty subtle.

But please don't add soft, resinous wood, like pine, to your fire. It creates an acrid (and sometimes toxic) smoke. And never use any wood that has been treated with chemicals.

Q: IF SMOKING IS USUALLY DONE WITH LOW TEMPERATURES, HOW DO I GET MY KETTLE BRAAI TO DO THAT?

A: Many foods are smoked and simultaneously cooked in the temperature range of 130°–180°C (250°–350°F). You can maintain the correct level of heat by controlling the amount of charcoal and the airflow. This is why you begin the fire with a chimney filled only about one-third full with charcoal (about 30 briquettes). Adding 10–15 briquettes (or an equivalent amount of lump charcoal) every hour or so will help to maintain the temperature. So will opening and closing the vents on the lid. Opening the vents will help the fire burn faster and hotter. Closing them partially (not all the way, or you might put out the fire) will restrict the airflow and drop the temperature. Having a thermometer on the lid is very helpful here.

Q: CAN I SMOKE FOOD WITH A GAS BRAAI?

A: Yes, some gas braais come equipped with a metal smoker box that sits on top of a dedicated burner. Just turn on the burner and add as many wood chips as you like. You can control how quickly they smoke by turning the knob of the burner higher or lower. Some of the smoker boxes have a separate compartment for water, which will provide a steaming effect on the food, too.

Q: HOW DO I USE A WATER SMOKER?

A: A water smoker allows you to smoke meat at temperatures well below 150°C (300°F) for many hours. The Weber version is basically an upright bullet-shaped unit with three sections. The charcoal burns in the bottom section. For smoky aromas, add a few fist-sized chunks of hardwood to the coals right from the beginning. The meat will absorb the smoke best when it is uncooked.

The water sits in a pan in the middle section, preventing any fat from dripping onto the coals and, more importantly, keeping the temperature nice and low. The meat sits on one or two racks in the top section.

A water smoker has vents on both the bottom and top sections. Generally, it's a good idea to leave the top vent wide open so that smoke can escape. Use the bottom vents as your primary way of regulating the temperature. The less air you allow into the smoker, the lower the temperature will go.

Generally speaking, if the ring in the bottom section of the smoker is filled with lit charcoal, and the water pan is nearly filled, the temperature will stay in the range of 110°–130°C (225°–250°F) for 4–6 hours. This is an ideal range for braaiing food like pork ribs, turkeys, and large beef joints.

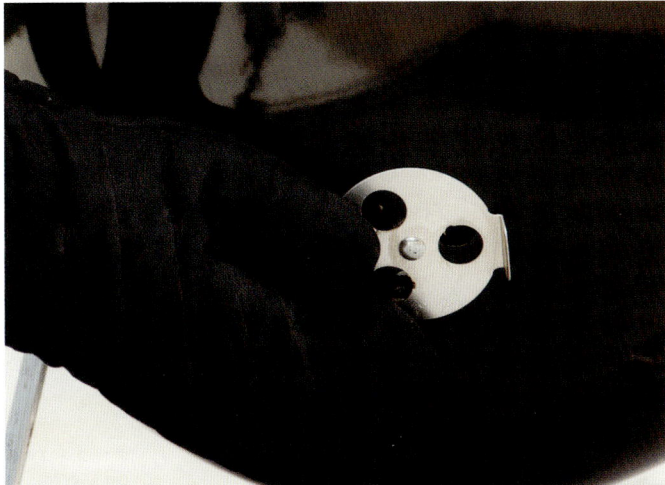

When you see that very little smoke is coming out of the top vent, add another chunk or two through the door on the side. Hardwood chunks burn slowly and evenly, so they are a better choice than wood chips in this situation. For cooking sessions that last longer than 6 hours, you will probably need to add more charcoal occasionally. The timing will depend on your type of charcoal and how fast it burns. If you are using charcoal made with unnatural fillers, you may want to light the briquettes in a chimney starter first; some people can taste off flavours in food cooked over unlit briquettes.

During long cooking times, also be sure to replenish the water pan every few hours with warm water. But keep the lid on the smoker as much as possible. That's critical for maintaining even heat.

MUST-HAVE TOOLS

Once you have a good braai that allows you to control the fire easily and cook your food over both direct and indirect heat, it's time to equip yourself with the right tools. I've broken down my recommendations into two groups. The first ten tools are essential for most tasks. The other ten will make many jobs a lot easier.

TONGS

Oh, the tongs. Definitely the hardest-working tool of all. You will need one pair to load raw food onto the braai and move it around. You will need another pair (clean tongs that haven't touched any raw meat, fish or poultry) to remove the cooked food. Dedicate a third pair for rearranging charcoal.

BRAAI BRUSH

Buy a solid, long-handled model with stainless steel bristles. Use it to clean off the grates before and after cooking, and you will eliminate many problems with food sticking to the grates. And your food won't taste like last night's dinner. Replace the brush when the bristles wear down to about one-half of their original length.

GRILL PAN

At first I didn't see the wisdom of a grill pan, but I came around on the issue when I saw (and tasted) how well a perforated grill pan can handle delicate fish fillets and small foods like chopped vegetables that might otherwise fall through the cooking grate. If you preheat a stainless steel grill pan properly, it will brown the food nicely and allow the smokiness from the fire to flavour the food.

CHIMNEY STARTER

Brilliantly simple, a chimney starter lets you start the coals faster and more evenly than you could with lighter fluid. And who needs all those chemicals in lighter fluid? Look for a chimney starter with a capacity of at least 5 litres of briquettes (roughly 80–100 pieces). Also, it should have two handles: a heatproof side handle for lifting the chimney and a hinged top handle to provide support when dumping hot coals onto the charcoal grate.

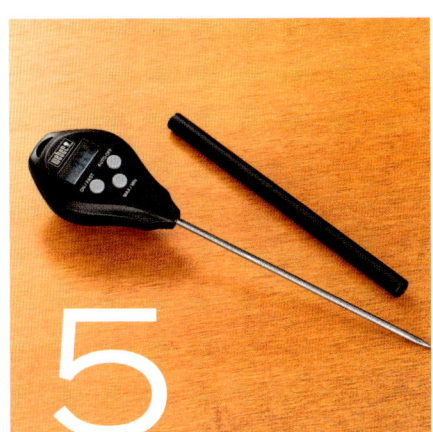

INSTANT-READ THERMOMETER

You only have to overcook a fine cut of meat once to learn the importance of a good digital thermometer. Small and relatively inexpensive, an instant-read thermometer is essential for quickly gauging the internal temperature of the meat. To get the most accurate read, insert it into the thickest part of the meat and avoid touching any bone, because the bone conducts heat.

ROASTING TRAY

I learned the value of a sturdy roasting tray when I was in culinary school, where there were dozens within reach in every kitchen. A shallow tray, like the one pictured here, is a great portable work surface for oiling and seasoning food, and there's nothing better to use as a landing pad for food coming off the braai.

BASTING BRUSH

In the past, basting brushes were made with wooden or plastic handles and synthetic or natural-boar bristles. Today you can find them made of stainless steel with silicone bristles that have beads at the tips to help load the brush with a sauce or marinade. While most old-style brushes had to be hand washed, this new high-tech style can go straight into the dishwasher. Nice.

BRAAI GLOVES

You'll need these to shield your hand and forearm when managing a charcoal fire or reaching towards the back of any hot braai. You will probably put them through the wash a lot, so invest in braai gloves (BBQ mitts) made from good-quality materials and workmanship. Silicone gloves are easy to care for because you can just wipe them off when they get dirty, but insulated cloth gloves will give better dexterity.

SPATULA

Look for a long-handled spatula designed with a bent (offset) neck so that the blade is set lower than the handle. This will make it easier to lift food off of the braai without hitting your knuckles. The blade itself should be at least 10 cm wide; you'll need a longer blade for turning whole fish.

SKEWERS

Bamboo skewers are simple and inexpensive, though they need to be soaked in water for at least 30 minutes prior to loading, in order to keep the wood from burning. If you don't want the hassle, use metal skewers, or freeze bamboo skewers in a bag after soaking them. The flat metal skewers and double-pronged ones are nice because they prevent the food from spinning when you turn the skewers.

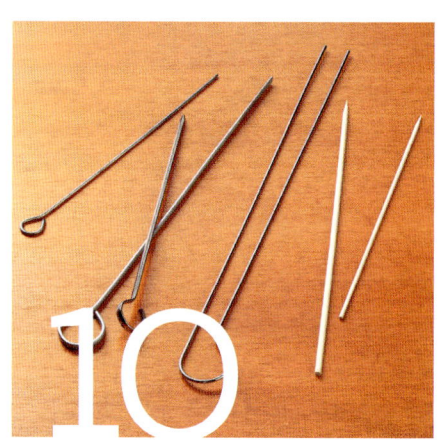

NICE-TO-HAVE TOOLS

TIMER

As the old saying goes, timing is everything. It's never truer than when you are trying to pull off a perfect meal at a braai. A rotary kitchen timer is adequate, but you can also opt for a more elaborate digital timer, preferably one that lets you track a couple of cooking times simultaneously.

WIRELESS MEAT THERMOMETER

While an instant-read thermometer is a must-have, a wireless thermometer is a cool little luxury. It's a high-tech gadget that monitors the temperature of meat using a wireless probe. You can walk away from the braai and a remote beeper will tell you when your food is ready.

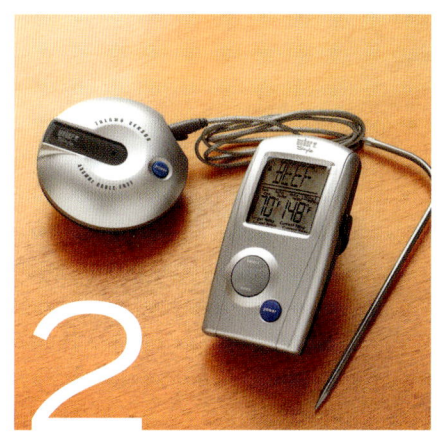

SMALL SHOVEL

Seeing this tool on the list might surprise you, but a small shovel is really helpful for pushing charcoal around. You can buy a shovel specifically for the task at a specialist retailer, or buy a ladies' shovel (one with no plastic parts) from a hardware store or garden shop.

ROTISSERIE

It's true that you can roast a chicken, turkey or pork loin on the braai without a rotisserie, but there is something wonderfully medieval about food spinning over a fire. Many people also argue that the rotisserie causes the meat to self-baste while cooking. I agree that food comes out juicier, so I am pro-rotisserie.

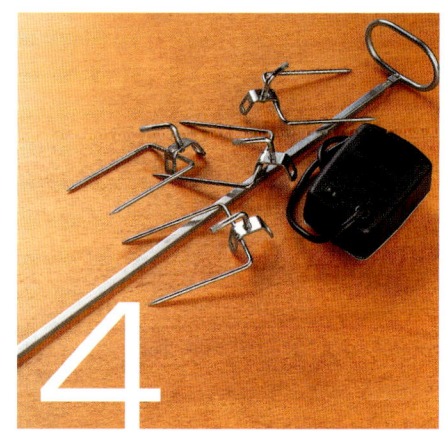

DISPOSABLE TRAYS

Available in large and small sizes, disposable foil trays offer many conveniences. Use them to move food to and from the braai, keep food warm on the cooking grate, soak wood chunks in them, or set them under the cooking grate to catch drippings and keep a charcoal braai clean.

CAST-IRON FRYING PAN

A big cast-iron frying pan allows you to make favourites in this book, like paella, gingerbread and a stunning pineapple upside-down cake. Once the pan gets hot on the braai, you can sauté, stew or pan-roast just about anything in it without ever worrying that the pan will discolour or deteriorate. It will last you forever.

RESEALABLE PLASTIC BAGS

Marinating foods in plastic bags allows you to force some of the marinade up and over the food, particularly when you set a bag snugly in a bowl, giving you better coverage and faster marinating times. Resealable bags also avoid dreaded spills in your refrigerator.

RIB RACK

This wire rack holds multiple slabs of ribs upright so that heat circulates around the ribs, cooking them evenly, and it encourages the pork fat to drip down and away from the ribs. Plus, it frees up real estate on the cooking grates for cooking other food at the same time.

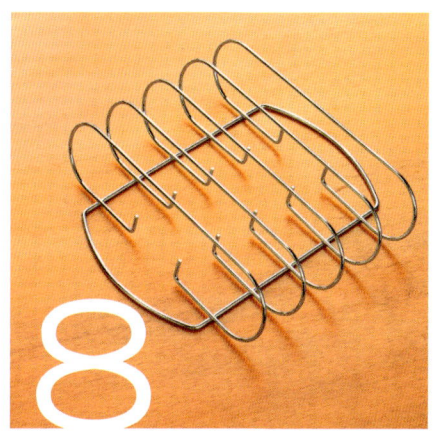

FISH BASKET

Many people resist braaiing fish, especially whole fish, for fear that it will stick and fall apart on the cooking grate. For them, there are hinged baskets that provide one degree of separation from the cooking grate, which makes turning simple. Using a fish basket sure beats the alternative of cooking fish inside the house and smelling it for days.

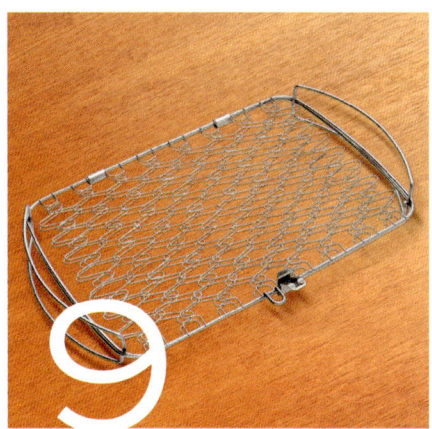

MICROPLANE GRATER

This is terrific for grating garlic, whole nutmeg and hard cheeses. It's even better used to zest citrus fruits. Microplane-type graters come in several shapes and sizes. I prefer the long, thin one, but choose what works best for you.

RED MEAT

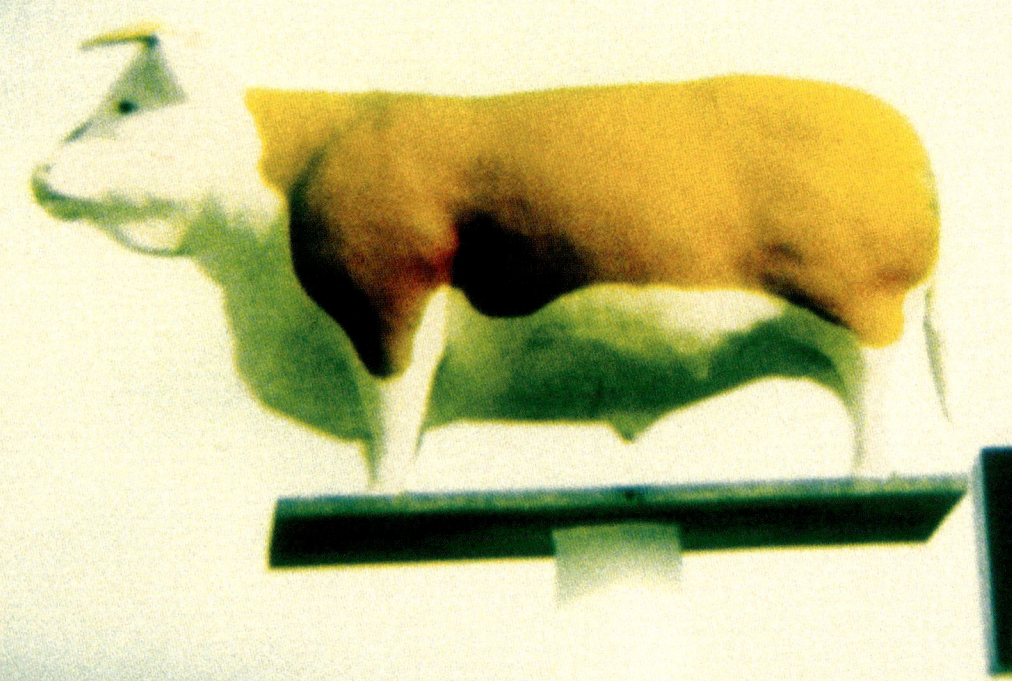

TECHNIQUES

34	How to braai **BURGERS**: Five things you need to know	64	How to braai **REALLY THICK STEAKS**
44	How to braai **STEAK**: Five things you need to know	66	How to prep **SKIRT STEAK**
45	How to butcher a **SIRLOIN**	70	How to stuff and roll **FLANK STEAK**
46	How to prep and braai **SIRLOIN STEAKS**	72	How to cube **TOP SIRLOIN**
49	How to check **STEAKS** for doneness	75	How to prep **VEAL CHOPS**
52	How to butcher a bone-in **RIB ROAST**	76	How to french a **RACK OF LAMB**
52	How to prep **RIB-EYE STEAKS**	84	How to braai **BEEF RIBS**
56	How to cook **PIADINI**	88	How to prep **BEEF FILLET**
58	How to cut bone-in steaks from a **RIB ROAST**	90	How to prep **RIB ROAST**
62	How to make **CROSS-HATCH MARKS**	92	How to smoke **BRISKET**

RECIPES

35	Classic **BURGER MELTS** on Rye
36	California **BURGERS** with Guacamole Mayonnaise
37	Cabernet **BURGERS** with Rosemary Focaccia
38	Brie and Shallot Parisian **BURGERS**
39	**KOFTA** in Pita Pockets with Cucumber and Tomato Salad
40	**LAMB BURGERS** with Tapenade and Goat's Cheese
41	**LAMB MEATBALLS** with Chopped Salad and Minted Yoghurt
42	Braaied **MEAT LOAF**
43	**HOT DOGS** with Pickled Onions
47	**SIRLOIN STEAKS** with Red-eye Barbecue Sauce
48	**STEAK SANDWICHES** with Braaied Onions and Creamy Horseradish Sauce
50	Panzanella **STEAK SALAD**
51	Sirloin **STEAK ESCALOPES**
53	**RIB-EYE STEAKS** with Espresso-Chilli Rub
55	**RIB-EYE STEAKS** with Pan-roasted Chilli Salsa
56	Steak and Gorgonzola **PIADINI**
59	Garlic-crusted **RIB-EYE STEAKS** with Braaied Tenderstem Broccoli
61	Tea-rubbed **FILLET STEAKS** with Buttery Mushrooms
63	**PORTERHOUSE STEAKS** with Red Wine-Shallot Butter
65	**BISTECCA ALLA FIORENTINA** and Barbecue-baked Beans alla Contadina
66	**SKIRT STEAKS** with Baby Potatoes and Feta
67	**CARNE ASADA** with Black Bean and Avocado Salsa
68	**BISTRO STEAKS** with Mustard Cream Sauce
69	Sesame-Ginger **FLANK STEAK** with Asparagus and Gomashio
71	**FLANK STEAK** with Roasted Pepper and Feta Stuffing
72	Argentine **BEEF SKEWERS** with Chimichurri Sauce
73	**BEEF KEBABS** with Finadene
74	**LAMB SOUVLAKI** with Cucumber-Yoghurt Sauce
75	Porcini-rubbed **VEAL CHOPS** with Herbed Mascarpone
77	**RACK OF LAMB** with Orange-Pomegranate Syrup
78	**LAMB CHOPS** with Indian Spices
79	**LAMB CHOPS** in Uzbek Marinade
81	**LAMB SHOULDER CHOPS** with Ratatouille Salad and Basil-Garlic Oil
83	**KOREAN BEEF** Barbecue
85	**BEEF RIBS** with Barbacoa Sauce
86	**LEG OF LAMB** with Moroccan Spices
87	Tropical **TRI-TIP ROAST** with Orange Barbecue Sauce
89	Herb-crusted **BEEF FILLET** with White Wine Cream Sauce
91	Wood-smoked Boneless **RIB ROAST** with Shiraz Sauce
93	**SMOKED BRISKET**

HOW TO BRAAI BURGERS
5 THINGS YOU NEED TO KNOW

1 WHAT MAKES THEM JUICY
Fat makes burgers juicy. That's a big reason why normal beef mince is better for burgers than lean beef mince. Typically, beef mince has about 20 percent fat, whereas lean beef mince is often down around 10 percent fat. The reality is that most of the minced beef sold in supermarkets comes from various parts of the animal, but that shouldn't stop you from asking the person behind the counter to prepare mince just for you, maybe mixing in some sirloin for extra flavour.

2 SEASONING WORKS
Minced beef alone makes a pretty dull-tasting hamburger, so make sure that the meat is combined with at least salt and pepper. Other ingredients, like Worcestershire sauce, Tabasco, or grated onions, will improve not only the taste but also the juiciness of your hamburgers.

3 SHAPING UP
The ideal thickness for a raw burger patty is about 1.5 cm. If it's any thinner, it's likely to overcook and dry out before a nice crust develops on the outside. If it's much thicker, the crust might turn black and unappetizing before the centre reaches the safe internal doneness level of medium.

4 LEVELLING OFF
Burgers tend to puff up in the centre as they cook, making the tops rounded and awkward for piling on the toppings. A good trick for avoiding this problem is to press a little indentation into the top of each raw patty with your thumb or the back of a spoon. Then, when the centre pushes up, the top of each burger will be relatively level.

5 FLIPPING ONLY ONCE
You should flip each burger once, and only when it's ready to flip. You'll know when by slipping the edge of a spatula underneath the burger and lifting it up very gently. If the meat sticks to the cooking grate, back off and try again a minute later. When you can lift the edge of the burger without sticking, it's ready to flip.

CLASSIC BURGER MELTS ON RYE

SERVES: 6
PREP TIME: 25 MINUTES

HEAT: DIRECT HIGH HEAT 230°–290°C (450°–550°F)
  AND DIRECT MEDIUM HEAT 180°–230°C (350°–450°F)
BRAAIING TIME: 11–13 MINUTES

    3 tablespoons canola oil or sunflower oil
    2 large onions, halved and thinly sliced
    ½ teaspoon sugar
    Coarse sea salt
    4 tablespoons unsalted butter, softened
    12 slices crusty rye bread, each about 1 cm thick
    900 g lean beef mince
    2 tablespoons Worcestershire sauce
    ½ teaspoon freshly ground black pepper
    375 ml grated Havarti or Emmental cheese
    Dijon or spicy brown mustard, optional

1. Warm the oil in a large frying pan over a medium heat. Add the onions, sprinkle with the sugar, and cook, covered, for 15–20 minutes, stirring occasionally, until the onions are tender and golden. Season to taste with salt, and remove from the heat.

2. Butter the bread on each side and set aside.

3. Prepare the braai for direct cooking over high heat. In a large bowl, gently mix the beef mince with the Worcestershire sauce, a pinch of salt and the pepper, incorporating the spices evenly. Shape into 6 equal-sized burgers, each about 1.5 cm thick. With your thumb or the back of a spoon, make a shallow indentation, about 2.5 cm wide, in the centre of each burger.

4. Brush the cooking grates clean. Cook the burgers over **direct high heat** for 8–10 minutes, keeping the lid closed as much as possible but turning once, until cooked to medium. Transfer the burgers to a work surface.

5. Lower the temperature of the braai to medium heat. Toast the bread slices over **direct medium heat** for about 1 minute, until toasted on one side only. Transfer the bread, toasted sides up, to a work surface.

6. Evenly divide the caramelized onions between 6 of the toasted bread slices and top each with a burger. Scatter over the cheese and top with the remaining bread slices, toasted sides down. Using a wide spatula, carefully place the burger melts back onto the cooking grate and cook over **direct medium heat** for about 1 minute, until the bread on the bottom is toasted, and then carefully turn the sandwiches and toast the other side. Serve the burger melts warm with mustard, if desired.

The sturdy texture of crusty rye bread holds up well under the weight of all the wonderfully messy ingredients in a burger melt.

HOW TO SPICE UP MAYONNAISE

1. Tame the sharp flavour and crunch of raw onion in your mayonnaise by grating the onion on the medium-sized holes of a grater. Then rinse the grated onion in a sieve for a sweet, mild taste.

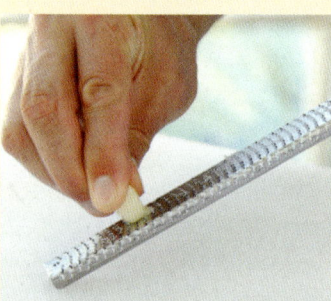

2. A microplane grater with tiny holes will quickly make a paste out of fresh garlic.

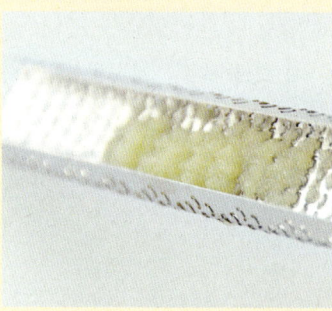

3. Swipe the paste off the back of the grater and into your mayonnaise.

CALIFORNIA BURGERS WITH GUACAMOLE MAYONNAISE

SERVES: 4
PREP TIME: 25 MINUTES

HEAT: DIRECT HIGH HEAT 230°–290°C (450°–550°F)
BRAAIING TIME: 18–20 MINUTES

GUACAMOLE MAYONNAISE
    2 tablespoons grated white onion
    1 ripe avocado, pitted and peeled
    2 tablespoons mayonnaise
    2 ripe tomatoes, cored, seeded, and chopped
    1 tablespoon finely chopped fresh coriander
    2 teaspoons fresh lime juice
    1 small garlic clove, grated
    Coarse sea salt

    2 jalapeño or serenade chillies
    700 g lean beef mince
    1½ teaspoons coarse sea salt
    1 teaspoon freshly ground black pepper
    4 hamburger rolls

1. Rinse the grated onion in a sieve under cold water and allow the excess water drain off. Mash the avocado and mayonnaise together in a bowl with a fork. Stir in the onion, tomatoes, coriander, lime juice, and garlic, then season generously with salt. Cover with clingfilm, pressing the film directly onto the surface, and set aside. (The mayonnaise can be prepared up to 8 hours ahead.)

2. Prepare the braai for direct cooking over high heat. Brush the cooking grates clean. Braai the chillies over **direct high heat** for about 10 minutes, keeping the lid closed as much as possible but turning occasionally, until the skin is blackened on all sides. Remove the chillies from the braai and allow to cool completely. Peel off and discard the blackened skin, and then remove and discard the stem, seeds and ribs. Chop the chillies into 1-cm dice.

3. In a large bowl, gently mix the minced beef, chillies, salt, and pepper, and shape into 4 equal-sized burgers, each about 1.5 cm thick. With your thumb or the back of a spoon, make a shallow indentation about 2.5 cm wide in the centre of each burger so that the centres are about 1 cm thick. This will help the burgers to cook evenly and prevent them from puffing up on the braai.

4. Braai the burgers over **direct high heat** for 8–10 minutes, keeping the lid closed as much as possible, turning once when the patties release easily from the grate without sticking, until cooked to medium. During the last minute of cooking time, toast the rolls, cut sides down, over direct heat. Top the burgers with the mayonnaise and serve warm.

CABERNET BURGERS WITH ROSEMARY FOCACCIA

SERVES: 4
PREP TIME: 25 MINUTES

HEAT: DIRECT HIGH HEAT 230°–290°C (450°–550°F)
AND DIRECT MEDIUM HEAT 180°–230°C (350° TO 450°F)
BRAAIING TIME: 10–14 MINUTES

GLAZE
500 ml Cabernet Sauvignon wine
1 tablespoon brown sugar

BUTTER
4 tablespoons unsalted butter, softened
1 tablespoon fresh rosemary leaves, finely chopped

BURGERS
700 g lean beef mince
4 tablespoons Cabernet glaze (above)
2 teaspoons coarse sea salt
½ teaspoon freshly ground black pepper

4 slices Cheddar cheese
8 slices ripe tomato, each about 1 cm thick
Extra-virgin olive oil
Coarse sea salt
4 focaccia squares, each about 11 cm, sliced in half horizontally, or 4 focaccia rolls, split
100 g rocket leaves
4 thick rashers cooked, crisp bacon

Thanks to a red wine reduction, the burger on the left has improved dramatically in flavour, moisture, and appearance.

1. Combine the wine and brown sugar in a heavy-based saucepan over medium heat and cook for 20–25 minutes until reduced to 125 ml. Set aside to cool.

2. In a small bowl, mix the butter and rosemary.

3. Prepare the braai for direct cooking over high heat. Combine the burger ingredients in a large bowl and shape into 4 equal-sized burgers, about 1.5 cm thick. With your thumb or the back of a spoon, make a shallow indentation about 2.5 cm wide in the centre of each burger.

4. Brush the cooking grates clean. Braai the burgers over **direct high heat** for 8–10 minutes, keeping the lid closed as much as possible, until cooked to medium. Brush with the glaze every 2 minutes and turn them once when the burgers release easily from the grate without sticking. During the last minute of cooking, place a slice of cheese on each burger to melt.

5. Reduce the temperature to medium heat. Brush the tomato slices with oil, season to taste with salt, and braai over **direct medium heat** for 2–4 minutes, turning once, until soft. Spread the cut sides of the focaccia with rosemary butter and place over **direct medium heat**, cut sides down, for about 1 minute, until lightly toasted. Assemble each burger with rocket, a burger, a rasher of bacon, and 2 slices of tomato. Serve warm.

BRIE AND SHALLOT PARISIAN BURGERS

SERVES: 4
PREP TIME: 30 MINUTES

HEAT: DIRECT HIGH HEAT 230°–290°C (450°–550°F)
BRAAIING TIME: 8–10 MINUTES

150 g shallots or small onions, thinly sliced
2 tablespoons extra-virgin olive oil

BURGERS
700 g lean beef mince
3 tablespoons dry bread crumbs
3 tablespoons beef or chicken stock
1 teaspoon coarse sea salt
½ teaspoon freshly ground black pepper

50 g Brie cheese
4 round crusty rolls, each about 10 cm in diameter
6 tablespoons wholegrain mustard
100 g rocket leaves, to serve

1. Fry the shallots in the oil over a low heat for about 20 minutes, stirring often, until they are browned but not scorched. Allow to cool to room temperature.

2. Prepare the braai for direct cooking over high heat. Mix the burger ingredients together in a large bowl, then shape into 4 equal-sized burgers, each about 1.5 cm thick. Make a hole in the centre of each burger for the cheese.

3. Trim away the rind of the Brie and bury about 15 g cheese into the hole in the centre of each burger, sealing it inside. Make sure there is about 1 cm of meat above and below the cheese so that it doesn't seep out.

4. Brush the cooking grates clean. Braai the burgers over **direct high heat** for 8–10 minutes, with the lid closed as much as possible, until cooked to medium, but turning once when the burgers release easily from the grate without sticking. During the last minute of cooking time, toast the rolls, cut sides down, over direct heat.

5. Assemble the burgers with the shallots, mustard and rocket. Serve warm.

HOW TO MAKE 'OUTSIDE IN' BURGERS

A fun way to turn a cheeseburger outside in is by placing a little knob of cheese in the centre of the burger and letting it soften slowly while the burger cooks.

1. Trim off any unwanted rind from the cheese.

2. Cut the pieces small enough so that the cheese won't seep out of the burger.

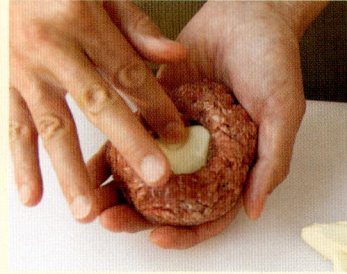

3. Place a piece of cheese in the centre of each burger.

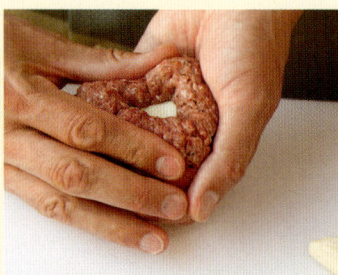

4. Seal each burger tightly to enclose the cheese completely.

KOFTA IN PITA POCKETS WITH CUCUMBER AND TOMATO SALAD

SERVES: 6

PREP TIME: 25 MINUTES

HEAT: DIRECT AND INDIRECT HIGH HEAT 230°–290°C (450°–550°F)

BRAAIING TIME: 8–10 MINUTES

DRESSING

    125 ml Greek-style yoghurt
    125 g sesame tahini
    4 tablespoons finely chopped fresh coriander or mint leaves, or a combination
    3 tablespoons fresh lemon juice
    2 tablespoons extra-virgin olive oil
    ½ teaspoon coarse sea salt

SALAD

    100 g English cucumber, chopped
    175 g cherry tomatoes, quartered
    1 red onion, finely chopped
    Coarse sea salt

KOFTA

    700 g lean beef mince
    125 ml finely chopped flat-leaf (Italian) parsley
    1 tablespoon very finely chopped garlic
    2 teaspoons ground coriander
    1½ teaspoons ground cumin
    1½ teaspoons coarse sea salt
    ½ teaspoon freshly ground black pepper
    ½ teaspoon ground allspice
    ¼ teaspoon ground cardamom
    ¼ teaspoon ground turmeric

    Extra-virgin olive oil
    3 wholewheat pitas

1. Combine the dressing ingredients in a small bowl. If the dressing is too thick, whisk in up to 3 tablespoons of water until your desired consistency is reached.

2. Combine the salad ingredients in another bowl, adding salt to taste.

3. Prepare the braai for direct and indirect cooking over a high heat. Combine the kofta ingredients in a bowl and shape into 6 equal-sized koftas, about 1.5 cm thick. With your thumb or the back of a spoon, make a shallow indentation about 2.5 cm wide in the centre of each kofta, then brush them with oil.

4. Sprinkle the pitas with water and wrap them in foil.

5. Brush the cooking grates clean. Braai the koftas over **direct high heat** for 8–10 minutes, keeping the lid closed as much as possible, but turning once when the patties release easily from the grate without sticking, until cooked to medium.

While they cook, warm the pita pockets over **indirect high heat** for 4–5 minutes, turning once.

6. Cut each pita in half. Scoop about 3 tablespoons of salad into each pita and spoon over some of the dressing. Place a kofta into each pita pocket and add a bit more dressing, if desired. Serve warm.

HOW TO SEASON KOFTA

1. The bold flavours of this dish rely on a variety of international ingredients.

2. Kofta refers to any kind of minced meat mixed with grains, vegetables, or spices.

3. Pressing a shallow indentation into each kofta prevents the meat from puffing up like a meatball during cooking.

As with any type of burger, the key to keeping this one flat instead of puffed up is to make a shallow indentation in the meat while it is raw. During the last minute of braaiing, scatter crumbled goat's cheese on top so that it oozes a little into the burger.

LAMB BURGERS WITH TAPENADE AND GOAT'S CHEESE

SERVES: 6
PREP TIME: 25 MINUTES

HEAT: DIRECT HIGH HEAT 230°–290°C (450°–550°F)
BRAAIING TIME: 8–10 MINUTES

TAPENADE
  1 medium garlic clove
  75 g pitted kalamata olives
  75 g pitted green olives
  2 tablespoons small capers, rinsed
  2 tablespoons extra-virgin olive oil
  ½ teaspoon Dijon mustard
  ½ teaspoon mixed herbs

  1 kg minced lamb
  ½ teaspoon mixed herbs
  ½ teaspoon coarse sea salt
  ½ teaspoon freshly ground black pepper
  150 g goat's cheese or feta, crumbled
  6 hamburger rolls
  3 ripe tomatoes, thinly sliced

1. Fit a food processor with the metal chopping blade. With the machine running, drop the garlic through the feed tube and chop very finely. Add the rest of the tapenade ingredients and pulse until coarsely chopped. (The tapenade can be made, and then covered and refrigerated for up to 1 week ahead. Bring to room temperature before serving.)

2. Prepare the braai for direct cooking over high heat. Using your hands, mix the lamb, herbs, salt and pepper together in a large bowl, then shape the meat into 6 equal-sized burgers, each about 10 cm across and 1.5 cm thick. With your thumb or the back of a spoon, make a shallow indentation about 1 inch wide in the centre of each burger.

3. Brush the cooking grates clean. Braai the burgers over **direct high heat** for 8–10 minutes, with the lid closed as much as possible but turning once, until cooked to medium. During the last minute of cooking, top each burger with the cheese to allow the cheese to soften, and toast the rolls.

4. Build the burgers with tomato slices and tapenade. Serve warm.

LAMB MEATBALLS WITH CHOPPED SALAD AND MINTED YOGHURT

SERVES: 6
PREP TIME: 30 MINUTES

HEAT: DIRECT MEDIUM-HIGH HEAT ABOUT 200°C (400°F)
BRAAIING TIME: 4–6 MINUTES
SPECIAL EQUIPMENT: METAL OR BAMBOO SKEWERS (IF BAMBOO, SOAK IN WATER FOR AT LEAST 30 MINUTES)

SALAD
- 4 tablespoons extra-virgin olive oil
- 2 tablespoons red wine vinegar
- 1 teaspoon finely grated lemon zest
- 2 teaspoons very finely chopped garlic
- 3 large ripe tomatoes, seeds removed and diced
- ½ English cucumber, diced
- ½ small red onion, finely diced
- 40 g feta cheese, crumbled
- 4 tablespoons flat-leaf (Italian) parsley
- ½ teaspoon coarse sea salt
- ¼ teaspoon freshly ground black pepper

MEATBALLS
- 700 g minced lamb
- 1 tablespoon very finely chopped garlic
- 2 teaspoons ground cumin
- 1 teaspoon coarse sea salt
- ½ teaspoon freshly ground black pepper
- Extra-virgin olive oil

SAUCE
- 375 ml Greek-style yoghurt
- 2 tablespoons fresh lemon juice
- 4 tablespoons coarsely chopped fresh mint leaves
- ½ teaspoon coarse sea salt

4–6 naan breads

1. Whisk the oil, vinegar, lemon zest and garlic together in a non-metallic bowl. Add the rest of the salad ingredients and gently toss with the dressing.

2. Using your hands, gently mix the meatball ingredients in a bowl. Do not overwork the mixture or the meatballs will be tough. Shape about 24 meatballs. Thread 4 meatballs onto each skewer. Lightly brush with oil.

3. Prepare the braai for direct cooking over medium-high heat.

4. In a small bowl mix the yoghurt and lemon juice. Fold in the mint and season with the salt.

5. Brush the cooking grates clean. Braai the meatballs over **direct medium-high heat** for 4–6 minutes, with the lid closed as much as possible, turning occasionally until they have browned but are still slightly pink in the centre. During the last 30 seconds of cooking time, heat the naan over direct heat.

6. Cut the naan in half, or into pieces large enough to hold 4 meatballs. Top with a generous spoonful of sauce and some salad.

Skewering these meatballs allows you to turn 4 of them at a time, rather than having to turn them individually. Skewers are ready to turn only when the meat releases from the cooking grate without any sticking.

HOW TO BRAAI MEAT LOAF

1. Fine breadcrumbs hold these meat loaves together without making them dense.

2. Check the internal temperature near the top because that part takes the longest to cook.

3. To remove each meat loaf in one whole piece, support both ends with spatulas.

BRAAIED MEAT LOAF

SERVES: 8–10
PREP TIME: 20 MINUTES

HEAT: INDIRECT MEDIUM-LOW HEAT ABOUT 150°C (300°F)
BRAAIING TIME: 50–60 MINUTES
SPECIAL EQUIPMENT: INSTANT-READ THERMOMETER

MEAT LOAF
    600 g lean beef mince
    600 g pork mince
    125 g fine breadcrumbs
    150 g onion, finely chopped
    1 large egg
    1 teaspoon Worcestershire sauce
    1 teaspoon garlic flakes
    1 teaspoon dried tarragon
    1 teaspoon coarse sea salt
    1 teaspoon freshly ground black pepper

SAUCE
    125 ml bottled barbecue sauce
    4 tablespoons tomato sauce

1. Using your hands, gently combine the meat loaf ingredients in a large bowl.

2. Divide the meat loaf mixture in half and form into 2 loaves, each about 10 cm wide and 15–18 cm long. Place the loaves on a baking tray. Prepare the braai for indirect cooking over medium-low heat.

3. Mix the sauce ingredients in a small bowl. Set aside half of the sauce to serve with the meat loaf. Top each meat loaf with 3 tablespoons of the remaining sauce and coat thoroughly.

4. Brush the cooking grates clean. Using a lifter, gently pick up each loaf from the baking tray and place directly on the cooking grate. Braai the meat loaves over **indirect medium-low heat** for 50–60 minutes, with the lid closed, until a thermometer inserted horizontally through the top of each loaf registers 68°C (155°F). Remove the loaves from the braai and rest for 10–15 minutes; the loaves will continue to cook, allowing them to reach the recommended 70°C (160°F) for minced beef and pork. Cut the loaves into 1 cm-thick slices and serve with the reserved sauce.

TO MAKE MEAT LOAF SANDWICHES
Cut the meat loaf into 1 cm-thick slices and slather both sides with some of the reserved sauce. Braai over **direct low heat** 120°–180°C (250°–350°F), with the lid closed as much as possible, for 4–6 minutes, turning once. Serve on sourdough bread. Also great with melted provolone cheese.

HOT DOGS WITH PICKLED ONIONS

SERVES: 8
PREP TIME: 15 MINUTES
MARINATING TIME: 2–3 HOURS

HEAT: DIRECT MEDIUM HEAT 180°–230°C (350°–450°F)
BRAAIING TIME: 5–7 MINUTES

PICKLED ONIONS
    1 small white onion
    1 small red onion
    125 ml cider vinegar
    125 ml white vinegar
    100 g sugar
    1 tablespoon coarse sea salt
    2 teaspoons celery seeds
    1 teaspoon red chilli flakes

    8 frankfurters or hot dog sausages
    8 hot dog rolls
    Mustard
    Tomato sauce

1. Trim off the ends of the onions. Cut each onion in half lengthways then, with a very sharp knife, cut the onions into paper-thin slices and place in a shallow, non-metallic dish. Combine the remaining onion ingredients in a bowl and whisk thoroughly until the sugar and salt have dissolved. Pour the vinegar mixture over the onions and stir to coat them evenly. Set aside at room temperature for about 3 hours, stirring occasionally. Drain the pickled onions and set aside.

2. Using a sharp knife, make a few shallow cuts in each sausage.

3. Prepare the braai for direct cooking over medium heat. Brush the cooking grates clean. Braai the sausages over **direct medium heat** for 5–7 minutes, turning occasionally but keeping the lid closed as much as possible, until lightly marked on the outside and hot all the way to the centre.

4. Place the sausages in the rolls. Squeeze your condiment of choice alongside and top with pickled onions. Serve warm.

HOW TO PICKLE ONIONS

1. Peel and halve the onions, and make sure the root and stem ends are completely removed.

2. Cut the onions into paper-thin slices, place them in a shallow glass dish, and pour the pickling liquid over them.

3. Stir to coat them evenly and set aside to marinate for about 3 hours.

HOW TO BRAAI STEAK

5 THINGS YOU NEED TO KNOW

1 SALTING EARLY PAYS OFF

You might have heard the warning that you shouldn't salt meat too far ahead of cooking because it can draw out moisture. It's true that salt draws moisture toward itself, but over the course of 20–30 minutes that's a good thing, because the salt begins to dissolve into that little bit of moisture. When the steak hits the hot cooking grate, the sugars and proteins in the moisture combine with the salt and other seasonings to create a delicious crust. Any moisture you might lose is well worth the flavour of that crust.

2 TAKING OFF THE CHILL SPEEDS UP COOKING

The goal of braaiing a steak is to brown and lightly char the surface while also cooking the interior to a perfectly juicy doneness, right? If the steak is too cold, the interior might require so much cooking time to reach that perfect doneness that the steak overcooks deep below the surface, turning grey and dry. Allow your steaks to stand at room temperature for about 20–30 minutes before braaiing. They will cook faster all the way to the centre and stay juicier.

3 SEARING EQUALS FLAVOUR

One good habit that separates professional chefs from many home cooks is that chefs spend more time searing their steaks. They understand that searing develops literally hundreds of flavours and aromas on the surface of steak, so they let their steaks sizzle over direct heat until the surfaces are dark, dark brown. Don't let anyone tell you that searing 'locks in the juices'. That's a myth. But searing sure does make steak tasty.

4 THICKER STEAKS SHOULD SLIDE OVER

Most steaks cook beautifully over direct high heat alone. The only time you might need to move them is if/when they cause flare-ups. However, some steaks are so thick that if you left them over direct heat alone, they would burn on the outside before they reached the internal doneness you like. If your steaks are thicker than about 2.5 cm, consider the sear-and-slide approach. After you have seared both sides nicely over direct high heat, slide the steaks to a part of the braai that is not so hot, perhaps over indirect heat, and finish cooking them safely there.

5 YOU CAN'T PUT MOISTURE BACK INSIDE A STEAK

As steaks cook over high heat, they lose moisture. Fat and juices are literally pushed out of the meat. That's the price we pay for making the steaks easier to digest. Perhaps the most important part of braaiing a steak is taking it off the heat before it has lost too much moisture. There is a short window of time, usually just a minute or two, when steaks go from medium rare to medium, or from medium to medium well. Catching that window requires vigilance. Don't walk away from a steak on the braai. And remember, it's always better to take it off when it's underdone and then return it to the braai to cook a bit more than it is to let a steak overcook.

HOW TO BUTCHER A SIRLOIN

1. Buying a whole sirloin is a great way to save money on steaks.

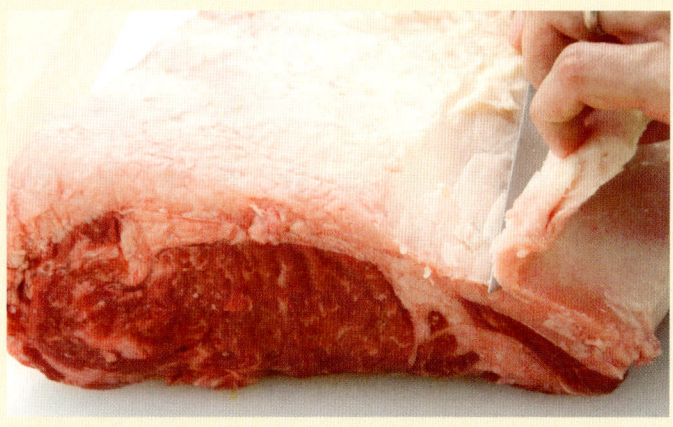

2. You'll need to trim away most of the thick 'fat cap' on the top side.

3. Next, remove the long section of scraggy meat and fat on the thinnest edge.

4. Cutting the sirloin yourself allows you to make the steaks just the right thickness.

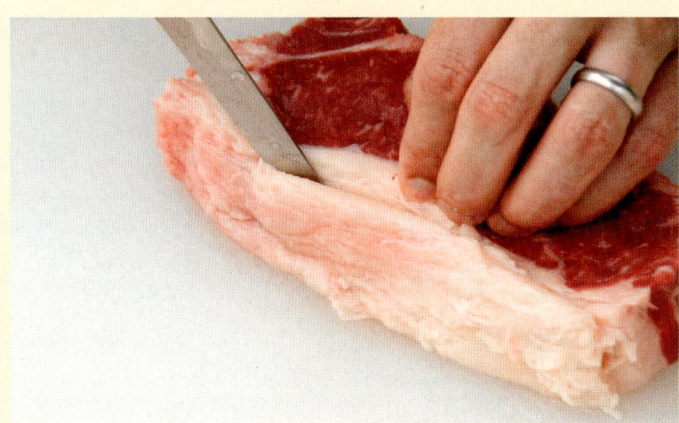

5. After cutting the steaks, go back and trim the fat around the outer edges to about 5 mm.

6. Braai some of the steaks now and freeze the remaining ones for another day. (For how to freeze steaks, see page 296.)

HOW TO PREP AND BRAAI SIRLOIN STEAKS

1. Lean sirloin steaks benefit from the rich flavour and slickness of extra-virgin olive oil.

2. Rub the oil evenly all over the steaks to prevent them from sticking to the cooking grate.

3. The oil also helps the seasonings to adhere to the meat.

4. Sometimes coarse sea salt and freshly ground pepper are all you need for a great-tasting steak.

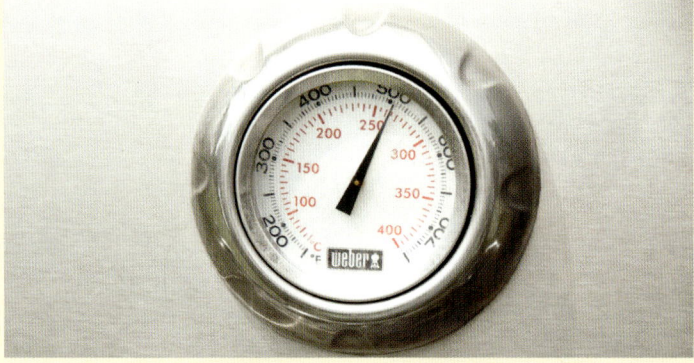

5. Bring the cooking temperature to 260°C (500°F). A hot cooking grate will sear the steaks quickly.

6. Once the cooking grates are smoking hot, they are easy to clean with a stainless steel-bristle brush.

7. Place each steak on the cooking grate over high heat as if it were the small hand of a clock pointing to 10 o'clock, then close the lid.

8. After a couple of minutes, lift each steak with tongs – not a fork! Piercing the steaks means losing the delicious juices.

9. Rotate the steaks so that they point to 2 o'clock, close the lid, and let them sear for another minute or two.

10. Flip each steak and check out those handsome crosshatch grill marks.

11. Putting crosshatches on the second side is optional. The key now is to finish the steaks, with the lid down, without overcooking them. An internal doneness of 52°C (125°F) will give you a medium-rare steak.

12. As the steaks rest for a few minutes after braaiing, the internal temperature will climb several degrees and the meat juices will redistribute evenly.

Occasionally the fat and juices dripping from a steak will cause flare-ups on the braai. Don't panic. Simply slide the steak to a cooler area of the grate. If your steak already has good charring on both sides, finish cooking it over indirect heat, with the lid closed. If you want more charring, slide the steak back over high heat once the flare-ups have died out.

SIRLOIN STEAKS WITH RED-EYE BARBECUE SAUCE

SERVES: 4
PREP TIME: 20 MINUTES

HEAT: DIRECT HIGH HEAT 230°–290°C (450°–550°F)
BRAAIING TIME: 6–8 MINUTES

RED-EYE BARBECUE SAUCE
    1 tablespoon unsalted butter
    2 teaspoons finely chopped shallot or small onion
    1 teaspoon finely chopped garlic
    125 ml tomato sauce
    4 tablespoons brewed dark-roast coffee or espresso
    1 tablespoon balsamic vinegar
    1 tablespoon brown sugar
    2 teaspoons chilli powder

    4 sirloin steaks, each 300–350 g and about 2.5 cm thick, trimmed of excess fat
    2 tablespoons extra-virgin olive oil
    ¾ teaspoon coarse sea salt
    ¾ teaspoon freshly ground black pepper

1. To make the sauce, melt the butter in a saucepan over medium heat. Add the shallot or onion and cook for about 3 minutes, stirring often, until it begins to brown. Add the garlic and cook for about 1 minute, until fragrant. Stir in the rest of the sauce ingredients and bring to a simmer. Reduce the heat to low and simmer for about 10 minutes, stirring often, until slightly reduced. Transfer to a bowl to cool.

2. Lightly brush the steaks on both sides with the oil and season evenly with salt and pepper. Allow the steaks to stand at room temperature for 20–30 minutes before braaiing. Prepare the braai for direct cooking over high heat.

3. Brush the cooking grates clean. Braai the steaks over **direct high heat**, keeping the lid closed as much as possible but turning once, until cooked to your desired doneness: 6–8 minutes for medium rare. Remove from the braai and leave the steaks to rest for 3–5 minutes. Serve the steaks warm with the sauce on the side.

Braaied red onions make a great addition to a steak sandwich, and here they benefit from soaking twice in a bold sweet-and-sour marinade: once before cooking and once afterwards.

STEAK SANDWICHES WITH BRAAIED ONIONS AND CREAMY HORSERADISH SAUCE

SERVES: 4
PREP TIME: 15 MINUTES
MARINATING TIME: 30 MINUTES

HEAT: DIRECT HIGH HEAT 230°–290°C (450°–550°F)
AND DIRECT MEDIUM HEAT 180°–230°C (350°–450°F)
BRAAIING TIME: 7–9 MINUTES

MARINADE
   500 ml red wine
   250 ml soy sauce
   4 tablespoons balsamic vinegar
   3 tablespoons dark brown (treacle) sugar
   1 tablespoon finely chopped garlic
   1 teaspoon freshly ground black pepper
   125 ml extra-virgin olive oil
   ½ teaspoon bicarbonate of soda

   4 sirloin steaks, each about 350 g and about 2.5 cm thick
   2 red onions, sliced into 5 mm rings

   125 ml sour cream
   4 tablespoons prepared horseradish
   1 teaspoon finely chopped fresh thyme
   Coarse sea salt
   Freshly ground black pepper

   4 panini rolls or mini-baguettes
   2 bunches watercress, trimmed and rinsed

1. Combine the marinade ingredients in a large bowl, whisking in the oil until blended. Divide the marinade, pouring 750 ml into a non-metallic ovenproof dish and leaving the rest in the bowl. Add the bicarbonate of soda to the marinade in the dish for a tenderizing effect (the mixture may fizz a little).

2. Put the steaks into the dish with the marinade and turn to completely coat the steaks. Allow to marinate at room temperature for 30 minutes, turning once.

3. Place the sliced onions in the bowl with the remaining marinade and gently stir to coat them evenly. Set aside and allow them to marinate alongside the steaks.

4. Mix the sour cream and horseradish in a bowl, then stir in the thyme, and season to taste with salt and pepper. Cover and refrigerate until ready to use.

5. Prepare the braai for direct cooking over high heat on one side of the grill and medium heat on the other. Brush the cooking grates clean. Remove the steaks from the dish, allowing most of the marinade to drip back into the dish. Discard the marinade. Braai the steaks over **direct high heat**, with the lid closed as much as possible but turning once, until cooked to your desired doneness: 6–8 minutes for medium rare. While the steaks are cooking, remove the onions from the marinade, retaining the marinade, and braai over **direct medium heat** for 6–8 minutes, turning once. Remove the onions from the braai and plunge back into the bowl of marinade. Toss to coat and allow the onions to soak up the marinade while the steaks rest for 3–5 minutes. Slice and toast the cut sides of the rolls over **direct medium heat** for about 1 minute.

6. To assemble the sandwiches, slice the steaks on the diagonal into thin strips. Pile the bottom of a roll with onions and layer with strips of steak. Top with horseradish sauce and watercress.

HOW TO CHECK STEAKS FOR DONENESS

1. Because steaks get firmer as they cook, one way to judge their doneness is by lightly squeezing the sides with tongs. It takes time to learn just how firm each type of steak will feel at each level of doneness, but this is how many restaurant chefs work, and it's a technique worth practising.

2. Another popular method is to press the surface of a steak with your fingertip. When the meat is no longer soft, but is not yet firm either, you know a steak has reached medium-rare doneness. See below for more hints on judging doneness by touch.

3. A more scientific approach is to use an instant-read thermometer. If you position the thermometer sensor right in the middle of the steak, you'll have a perfectly accurate reading of doneness.

4. Perhaps the most straightforward approach is to have a look at the colour of the meat inside the steak. On the underside of the steak (the side that will face the plate), cut a little slit down to the centre of the meat and peek inside. When it's cooked just the way you want it, turn the steak over and press the surface with your fingertip. Note how it feels so that next time you won't need to cut into your steak.

HOW TO CHECK DONENESS BY TOUCH

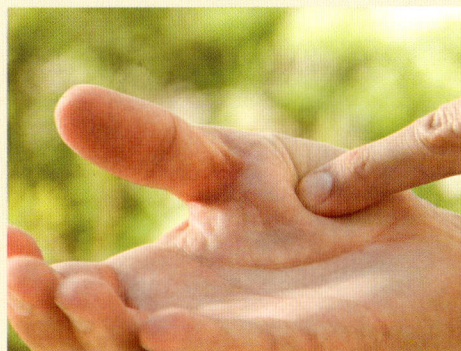

1. Most raw steaks are as soft as the base of your thumb when your hand is relaxed.

2. If you touch your index finger and thumb together, and then press the base of your thumb, that's how most steaks feel when they are rare.

3. If you touch your middle finger and thumb together, and then press the base of your thumb, that's how most steaks feel when they are medium rare.

PANZANELLA STEAK SALAD

SERVES: 4–6
PREP TIME: 20 MINUTES

HEAT: DIRECT AND INDIRECT HIGH HEAT 230°–290°C (450°–550°F)
BRAAIING TIME: 12–16 MINUTES
SPECIAL EQUIPMENT: BAMBOO SKEWERS, SOAKED IN WATER FOR AT LEAST 30 MINUTES

DRESSING
  3 tablespoons red wine vinegar
  1 teaspoon coarse sea salt
  1 teaspoon freshly ground black pepper
  2 teaspoons finely chopped garlic
  125 ml extra-virgin olive oil

  2 sirloin steaks, each about 300 g and 2.5 cm thick, trimmed of excess fat
  275 g dense, crusty bread, cut into 3.5 cm cubes
  6 tomatoes, cut in half lengthways, seeds removed
  1 onion, cut crossways into 1 cm-thick slices
  150 g oil-cured black olives, drained and pitted
  250 ml fresh basil leaves, torn into pieces

1. Combine the dressing ingredients in a small bowl, gradually whisking in the oil until emulsified.

2. Put the steaks in a shallow dish, pour over 3 tablespoons of the dressing, and turn to coat them evenly. Allow to stand at room temperature for 20–30 minutes before cooking. Set aside the remaining dressing.

3. Put the bread cubes into a large bowl, add 2 tablespoons of the dressing, and toss to coat them evenly. Thread the bread cubes onto skewers. Brush the cut sides of the tomatoes and the onion slices with 2 tablespoons of the dressing.

4. Prepare the braai for direct and indirect cooking over high heat.

5. Brush the cooking grates clean. Braai the tomatoes and onions over **direct high heat** and the bread skewers over **indirect high heat**, with the lid closed as much as possible, but turning as needed, until the tomatoes are lightly charred, the onions are browned, and the bread is toasted. The tomatoes will take 2–4 minutes and the onions and bread skewers will take 6–8 minutes. Remove the food from the braai as it is done.

6. Brush the cooking grates clean. Braai the steaks over **direct high heat**, with the lid closed as much as possible, but turning once, until cooked to your desired doneness: 6–8 minutes for medium rare. Remove from the braai and rest for 3–5 minutes.

7. Pull off and discard the tomato skins. Cut the onion, tomatoes, and steak into bite-sized chunks, and then place in a large serving bowl. Add the remaining dressing, olives, bread cubes and basil and gently mix. Serve immediately.

HOW TO PREP PANZANELLA STEAK SALAD

1. Toss big cubes of dense bread in salad dressing for flavour and even browning.

2. Skewer the bread cubes to make them easier to handle on the braai.

3. Firm but ripe tomatoes should maintain their shape even when you lightly char them.

4. Grilling the bread cubes over indirect heat allows you to brown them slowly, with little risk of burning.

SIRLOIN STEAK ESCALOPES

SERVES: 4
PREP TIME: 20 MINUTES

HEAT: DIRECT HIGH HEAT 230°–290°C (450°–550°F)
BRAAIING TIME: ABOUT 3 MINUTES

- 4 sirloin steaks, each 200–230 g and 1–1.5 cm thick, trimmed of all fat and silver skin
- Extra-virgin olive oil
- Coarse sea salt
- Freshly ground black pepper

DRESSING
- 4 tablespoons sour cream
- 4 tablespoons mayonnaise
- 2 tablespoons Dijon mustard
- ½ teaspoon Worcestershire sauce

- 1 large tomato, cut into 4 thick slices
- 4 thin slices red onion
- 50 g cream cheese, at room temperature

1. One at a time, place each steak between 2 sheets of clingfilm and pound to an even 5 mm thickness. Lightly brush the escalopes with oil and season them evenly with salt and pepper.

2. Combine the dressing ingredients in a small bowl, adding salt to taste.

3. Prepare the braai for direct cooking over high heat.

4. Lightly brush each tomato slice with oil and season to taste with salt and pepper. Brush the cooking grates clean. Braai the tomatoes over **direct high heat** for 2–3 minutes until slightly charred on one side. Transfer to a baking tray, cooked sides up.

5. Braai the escalopes over **direct high heat** for 1½–2 minutes with the lid open, turning when the first side is nicely marked. The second side will only take 10–15 seconds for medium-rare doneness (the escalopes will continue to cook as they rest).

6. Transfer the escalopes, with the first cooked sides facing up, to a serving platter or individual plates. Place a slice of tomato in the centre of each escalope.

7. Evenly divide the dressing over the tomatoes. Separate the slices of onion into rings and place a small mound on the tomatoes. Finish with a slice or spoonful of cream cheese and a grinding of pepper.

Three stages of a steak escalope. On the left, a sirloin steak as you would buy it. In the middle, a steak trimmed of all the fat around the edges, to make it easier to pound. On the right, an evenly pounded escalope ready for greasing, seasoning and braaiing.

HOW TO BUTCHER A BONE-IN RIB ROAST

Many chefs and carnivores will tell you that their favourite steak for braaiing is a rib-eye. The meat is magnificently tender and very flavourful, due in large part to the generous interior marbling of milky white fat. Sadly, many supermarket butchers cut rib-eyes too thin, so the steaks tend to overcook rather quickly, squandering some of their magnificence. One solution is to cut your own rib-eye steaks from a bone-in rib roast, also known as a prime rib.

   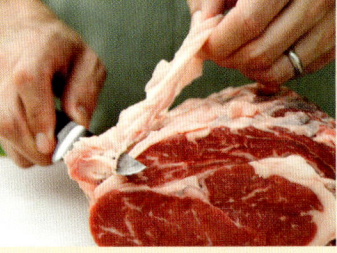

1. Use a long, sharp knife to cut right along the ribs, separating them from the meat.

2. Now cut along the bone at the base of the joint to separate the meat from the bones completely.

3. Don't throw away those ribs. Braai them! See page 85.

4. Trim off most of the surface fat from your boneless rib roast.

 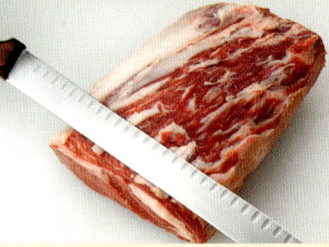  

5. At this point, you could braai the whole boneless roast in one piece for a big event (see page 91), or slice it into thick steaks and freeze those that you don't use right away. (For how to freeze steaks, see page 296.)

6. Use the blade of a carving knife to measure a consistent thickness for each steak.

7. Make a shallow slit at each point where you plan to slice.

8. Slice the steaks as evenly as possible. Avoid sawing back and forth, which tears the surface of the meat and gives the steaks a ragged appearance.

HOW TO PREP RIB-EYE STEAKS

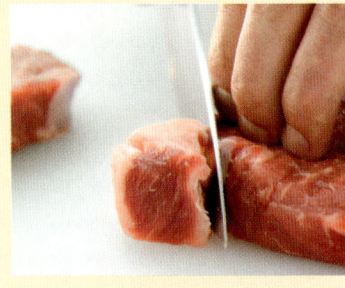   

1. As with any steak, trim off any sections along the edges that include more fat than meat.

2. A flavourful cut like rib-eye requires no marinade or elaborate sauce, but consider using a bold blend of dry seasonings as a complement to the meat's richness.

3. With so much marbling in the steak, just a light coating of oil is all you'll need to prevent sticking on the braai grid.

4. Allow your seasoned steaks to stand at room temperature for 20–30 minutes before braaiing to take the chill off. They will cook a little faster and stay juicier.

RIB-EYE STEAKS WITH ESPRESSO-CHILLI RUB

SERVES: 4
PREP TIME: 10 MINUTES

HEAT: DIRECT HIGH HEAT 230°–290°C (450°–550°F)
BRAAIING TIME: 6–8 MINUTES
SPECIAL EQUIPMENT: SPICE MILL

RUB
    2 teaspoons cumin seed, toasted
    2 tablespoons dark-roast coffee or espresso beans
    1 tablespoon chilli powder
    1 teaspoon sweet paprika
    1 teaspoon coarse sea salt
    1 teaspoon freshly ground black pepper

    4 rib-eye steaks, each about 200 g and 2.5 cm thick
    Extra-virgin olive oil

1. Grind the cumin seed and coffee beans together in a spice mill. Transfer to a small bowl, add the remaining rub ingredients, and stir to combine.

2. Lightly brush the steaks with oil and season evenly with the rub, pressing it into the meat. Cover and allow to stand at room temperature for 20–30 minutes before braaiing. Prepare the braai for direct cooking over high heat.

3. Brush the cooking grates clean. Braai the steaks over **direct high heat**, with the lid closed as much as possible, but turning once, until cooked to your desired doneness, 6–8 minutes for medium rare. (If flare-ups occur, move the steaks temporarily over indirect high heat.) Remove from the braai and allow to rest for 3–5 minutes. Serve warm.

HOW TO PREP ESPRESSO-CHILLI RUB

1. A coffee grinder works well for grinding spices. Clean it out later by whirling raw white rice in it to absorb the spice residue.

2. Grind your cumin and coffee to a coarse texture, similar to that of coarse sea salt.

HOW TO MAKE PAN-ROASTED CHILLI SALSA

1. The distinctive flavour of the salsa on the opposite page comes mostly from an ancho chilli, which is a dried poblano chilli. It is not terribly spicy, but it has a brilliant sweet heat, especially when it is toasted first.

2. Cut off and discard the stem of the chilli, then slice open the chilli so that you can lie it flat like a book.

3. A lot of the spiciness is in the seeds, so tap the chilli on a board or use a knife to remove them, if you like.

4. Use a fish slice to flatten the chilli in a hot, dry frying pan. This step brings out a lot of flavour. Next, soak the chilli in hot water for 20–30 minutes.

5. You can blacken and blister the tomatoes, onions, jalapeño chilli and garlic in the same pan. Don't be afraid to get them dark and caramelized.

6. Puréeing all the ingredients with some fresh lime juice, salt and origanum gives you an exciting salsa to serve with steaks. If the salsa seems a little too thick, thin it out with a touch of the water used to soak the ancho chilli.

RIB-EYE STEAKS WITH PAN-ROASTED CHILLI SALSA

SERVES: 4
PREP TIME: 20 MINUTES

HEAT: DIRECT HIGH HEAT 230°–290°C (450°–550°F)
BRAAIING TIME: 6–8 MINUTES
SPECIAL EQUIPMENT: 30 CM (12 INCH) CAST-IRON PAN

SALSA
- 1 medium dried ancho chilli
- 1 tablespoon extra-virgin olive oil
- 4 ripe tomatoes, quartered, stems and seeds removed
- 1 slice white onion, about 1.5 cm thick
- 1 medium jalapeño chilli, stem removed
- 1 large garlic clove (do not peel)
- 1 teaspoon fresh lime juice
- ½ teaspoon coarse sea salt
- ¼ teaspoon dried origanum

RUB
- 1 tablespoon coarse sea salt
- 2 teaspoons paprika
- 1 teaspoon onion flakes
- 1 teaspoon freshly ground black pepper

4 rib-eye steaks, each about 200 g and 2.5 cm thick
Extra-virgin olive oil

1. Bring 500 ml water to a simmer in a small saucepan. Preheat a 30-cm cast-iron or ovenproof frying pan over medium heat on your side burner or hob.

2. Remove and discard the stem from the ancho chilli, then open it like a book and discard the seeds. Flatten the chilli and place it in the hot, dry pan. Press down on the chilli with a fish slice to flatten it and dry fry until the aroma is obvious and you begin to see wisps of smoke. Transfer the chilli to the pan of hot water and soak for 20–30 minutes, until it is very soft. Reserve the water; you may need a little to thin out the salsa.

3. Meanwhile, add the oil, tomatoes, onion, jalapeño and garlic to the pan and fry over a medium heat for 10–15 minutes, turning occasionally, until the vegetables have blackened and blistered in spots. Remove the vegetables as they finish cooking (they may not be ready at the same time). Allow them to cool until you can handle the garlic, then squeeze the garlic out of its skin into a blender or food processor. Add the ancho chilli, tomatoes, onion, jalapeño, lime juice, salt and origanum and process to make a salsa. For a thinner consistency, add a little of the water used to soak the ancho chilli.

4. Combine the rub ingredients in a small bowl. Lightly brush both sides of the steaks with oil, season evenly with the rub, and allow to stand at room temperature for 20–30 minutes. Prepare the braai for direct cooking over high heat.

5. Brush the cooking grates clean. Braai the steaks over **direct high heat**, with the lid closed as much as possible, but turning once, until cooked to your desired doneness, 6–8 minutes for medium rare. (If flare-ups occur, move the steaks temporarily over indirect high heat). Remove from the braai and allow to rest for 3–5 minutes. Serve warm with the salsa.

HOW TO COOK PIADINI

1. Your dough should be at room temperature and you should have flour on both your board and your rolling pin.

2. Roll each piece of dough to a diameter of 20–25 cm and a thickness of about 8 mm. Stack the dough rounds between sheets of baking paper.

3. Braai the dough rounds over direct medium heat, with the lid closed, until they bubble on top and turn golden brown on the bottom. Then turn them over with a fish slice to toast the other side.

4. While the second side cooks, distribute the cheese on top so that it begins to melt. Rotate each dough round and move it around the grid as needed for even cooking.

STEAK AND GORGONZOLA PIADINI

SERVES: 4
PREP TIME: 30 MINUTES
RISING TIME: 1½–2 HOURS

HEAT: DIRECT HIGH HEAT 230°–290°C (450°–550°F)
AND DIRECT MEDIUM HEAT 180°–230°C (350°–450°F)
BRAAIING TIME: 14–18 MINUTES
SPECIAL EQUIPMENT: ELECTRIC STAND MIXER

DOUGH
　350 ml warm water (40°–90°C)
　1 sachet instant dry yeast
　½ teaspoon sugar
　625 g cake flour, plus extra for rolling the dough
　3 tablespoons extra-virgin olive oil
　2 teaspoons coarse sea salt

DRESSING
　2 tablespoons extra-virgin olive oil
　2 teaspoons balsamic vinegar
　½ teaspoon finely chopped garlic
　½ teaspoon Dijon mustard
　¼ teaspoon coarse sea salt
　pinch of freshly ground black pepper

　2 rib-eye steaks, each 200 g and about 2.5 cm thick
　Extra-virgin olive oil
　Coarse sea salt
　Freshly ground black pepper
　250 g Gorgonzola or other soft, mild blue cheese, broken into small pieces
　75 g baby rocket or spinach

1. Combine the water, yeast and sugar in the bowl of an electric stand mixer. Stir briefly and allow to stand for 5 minutes, or until the top surface has a thin, frothy layer (this indicates that the yeast is active). Add the flour, oil and salt. Fit the mixer with the dough hook and mix on low speed for about 1 minute or until the dough begins to come together. Increase the speed to medium and continue to mix for about 10 minutes until the dough is slightly sticky, smooth and elastic. Form the dough into a ball, place in a lightly oiled bowl, and turn it over to coat all sides. Tightly cover the bowl with clingfilm. Allow the dough to rise in a warm place for 1½–2 hours, until it has doubled in size.

2. Whisk the dressing ingredients in a small bowl.

3. Trim most of the exterior fat from the steaks. Allow to stand at room temperature for 20–30 minutes before braaiing. Prepare the braai for direct cooking over high heat.

4. Knock back the dough in the bowl. Transfer to a lightly floured surface and cut into 4 equal-sized pieces. Cut baking paper into 25-cm squares and lightly grease each sheet of

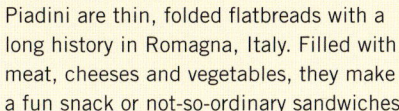

Piadini are thin, folded flatbreads with a long history in Romagna, Italy. Filled with meat, cheeses and vegetables, they make a fun snack or not-so-ordinary sandwiches.

paper on one side. Roll each piece of dough flat into rounds 20–25 cm in diameter. Place each dough round on a greased sheet of baking paper and lightly oil the top of each round. Stack the dough rounds between the sheets of baking paper and set aside on a baking tray.

5. Lightly brush both sides of the steaks with olive oil and season them evenly with salt and pepper. Brush the cooking grates clean. Braai the steaks over **direct high heat**, with the lid closed as much as possible, but turning once, until cooked to your desired doneness, 6–8 minutes for medium rare. (If flare-ups occur, move the steaks temporarily over indirect high heat). Remove the steaks from the braai, cover and keep warm.

6. Reduce the temperature of the braai to medium heat. Lay 2 dough rounds over **direct medium heat**, with the paper sides facing up. Grab one corner of the paper with tongs and peel it off. Cook the rounds for 2–3 minutes, rotating them occasionally for even cooking, until they are golden and marked on the underside.

7. Turn the flatbreads over and distribute a quarter of the cheese over each one, leaving a 1-cm border around the edges. Continue braaiing over **direct medium heat** for about 2 minutes, rotating them occasionally for even cooking, until the outsides are crisp and the cheese has melted. Transfer the flatbreads to a work surface, and repeat with the remaining flatbreads.

8. Place the rocket or spinach in a salad bowl, pour over the dressing and toss to combine.

9. Cut the steaks into thin slices, removing any pockets of fat, and distribute evenly over the flatbreads, then top with equal portions of the salad. Fold each piadini in half and eat it like a sandwich or, for easier eating or sharing, cut each piadini in half with a serrated knife after folding.

HOW TO CUT BONE-IN STEAKS FROM A RIB ROAST

You can tell a lot about the taste and tenderness of a cut of meat by where it comes from on the animal. The parts of the animal that get a lot of exercise, like the shoulder and the back end (the topside), develop more tough connective tissue than the parts of the animal that don't work so hard, like the sirloin and rib sections. From the sirloin, we get tender steaks like the porterhouse, the T-bone and, of course, sirloin steaks. The rib section, pictured below, is where you'll find incredibly tender and succulent rib steaks.

 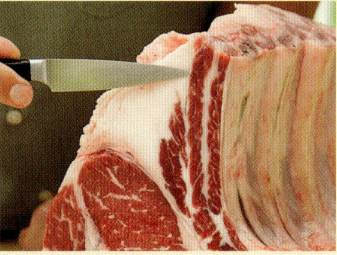  

1. Stand the rib joint on end so that you can clearly see the tips of the bones.

2. The advantage of braaiing rib-eye steaks with the bones attached is that the bones will add mouthwatering flavour to the steaks and help to keep the meat moist during cooking.

3. Using a very sharp knife, slice between the bones, trying not to saw back and forth too much. A hollow-ground knife will give the cleanest cut and best appearance.

4. What you have now is a big, brawny masterpiece called a bone-in rib-eye steak.

HOW TO MAKE GARLIC PASTE

Fresh garlic on a steak lights up all the endorphins in my brain. When time is short and I'm craving a full-throttled steak experience, I always turn to chopped garlic. The only problem is, I often cook my steak over very high heat, so that the bits and pieces of garlic sometimes burn, turning them bitter. I avoid this problem by making a garlic paste instead. The paste melts into the surface of the meat, and all the fat and juices collected there prevent it from burning.

1. Begin by thinly slicing the garlic cloves with a chef's knife.

2. Finely chop the garlic, keeping the knife tip on the board and moving the blade from side to side.

3. Add some coarse sea salt for flavour, crumbling it between your fingers if it is very coarse.

4. The salt will also hold the garlic together while you chop it very finely.

5. Now, drag the side of the knife over the garlic, putting extra pressure near the tip, to smash the garlic into a paste.

6. Keep swishing the knife back and forth until the garlic is so thin that it is almost transparent. Now it's ready to smear on your steaks.

GARLIC-CRUSTED RIB-EYE STEAKS WITH BRAAIED TENDERSTEM BROCCOLI

SERVES: 4
PREP TIME: 15 MINUTES

HEAT: DIRECT AND INDIRECT HIGH HEAT 230°–290°C (450°– 550°F)
BRAAIING TIME: 11–15 MINUTES

PASTE
- 4 large garlic cloves
- 1 tablespoon coarse sea salt
- 4 tablespoons finely chopped flat-leaf (Italian) parsley
- 4 tablespoons extra-virgin olive oil
- 2 teaspoons balsamic vinegar
- 1 teaspoon freshly ground black pepper

- 4 bone-in rib-eye steaks, each 300–350 g and about 2.5 cm thick, trimmed of excess fat
- 700 g tender-stem broccoli, with stalks no wider than 1 cm
- Extra-virgin olive oil
- Coarse sea salt

1. Finely chop the garlic on a chopping board, then sprinkle with the salt. Use the side of a knife to smash the garlic into a paste. Put the garlic paste into a small bowl and add the remaining paste ingredients.

2. Smear the paste evenly over both sides of each steak. Allow the steaks to stand at room temperature for 20–30 minutes before cooking.

3. Meanwhile, soak the broccoli in a bowl of water for 20–30 minutes so that it absorbs water. This will help the stems to steam a little on the braai.

4. Prepare the braai for direct and indirect cooking over high heat.

5. Drain the broccoli, lightly drizzle with some oil and season with ½ teaspoon salt. Toss to coat evenly with oil and salt.

6. Brush the cooking grates clean. Braai the steaks over **direct high heat**, with the lid closed as much as possible but turning once, until cooked to your desired doneness, 6–8 minutes for medium rare. (If flare-ups occur, move the steaks temporarily over indirect high heat.) Remove from the braai and allow to rest while you cook the broccoli.

7. Using tongs, lift the broccoli and allow any excess oil to drip back into the bowl. Braai the broccoli over **direct high heat** for 3–4 minutes, with the lid closed as much as possible but turning occasionally, until lightly charred. Finish cooking the broccoli over **indirect high heat** for 2–3 minutes. Serve warm with the steaks.

HOW TO MAKE TEA PASTE

1. Earl Grey tea leaves add a deep, unexpected fragrance to this spice rub.

2. To get the best peppery zing, grind whole black peppercorns in a spice mill with the other seasonings. As with other spices, whole peppercorns retain more aromatic flavour than ready-ground pepper.

3. Pulse all the seasonings into a coarse blend to release their flavours, then mix them in a bowl with oil to make a paste.

TEA-RUBBED FILLET STEAKS WITH BUTTERY MUSHROOMS

SERVES: 4
PREP TIME: 25 MINUTES

HEAT: DIRECT MEDIUM HEAT 180°–230°C (350°–450°F)
BRAAIING TIME: ABOUT 8 MINUTES
SPECIAL EQUIPMENT: SPICE MILL, 30-CM (12-INCH) CAST-IRON FRYING PAN

PASTE
 2 teaspoons (about 2 tea bags) Earl Grey tea leaves
 1 teaspoon whole black peppercorns
 1 teaspoon dried tarragon
 1 teaspoon coarse sea salt
 ½ teaspoon dried thyme
 3 tablespoons extra-virgin olive oil

4 fillet steaks, each 230–250 g and 2.5 cm thick

MUSHROOMS
 200 g button mushrooms
 2 tablespoons unsalted butter
 2 tablespoons extra-virgin olive oil
 4 large garlic cloves, thinly sliced
 ¼ teaspoon coarse sea salt
 pinch of freshly ground black pepper
 4 tablespoons roughly chopped flat-leaf (Italian) parsley
 1 teaspoon sherry or red wine vinegar

1. Whirl the tea leaves, peppercorns, tarragon, salt and thyme in a spice mill until finely ground. Pour the spice mix into a bowl, add the oil and stir to make a paste.

2. Brush all sides of each fillet with the paste, then allow to stand at room temperature for 20–30 minutes before cooking.

3. Before you cook the steaks, prepare the mushrooms and have all the other ingredients in place. Lie the mushrooms on their sides and cut off a 5 mm slice lengthways, then roll the mushrooms over so that the flat sides are on your chopping board and the mushrooms no longer roll around. Cut the mushrooms lengthways into 5 mm slices.

4. Prepare the braai for direct cooking over medium heat.

5. Brush the cooking grates clean. Braai the steaks over **direct medium heat**, with the lid closed as much as possible but turning once, until cooked to your desired doneness, about 8 minutes for medium rare. Remove from the braai and allow to rest while you sauté the mushrooms.

6. Melt the butter with the oil in a cast-iron frying pan over high heat on your braai's side burner or your hob. Add the mushrooms and spread them in a single layer so that most are touching the bottom of the pan. Cook the mushrooms without moving them for 2 minutes. Stir, then add the garlic, salt and pepper. Cook for a further 2–3 minutes, stirring 2 or 3 times, until the mushrooms are barely tender. Add the parsley and sherry vinegar and mix well. Season to taste with salt and pepper, if needed. Spoon the hot mushrooms over the steaks.

HOW TO BROWN MUSHROOMS

1. Cut off one round edge to make a flat, stable surface.

2. Then cut into 5-mm slices.

3. Melt the butter with a little oil, which helps to prevent the butter from burning.

4. Spread the mushrooms in a single layer and don't touch them for 2 minutes.

5. Add the salt towards the end of cooking because it draws moisture out of the mushrooms and hinders browning.

6. Adding a little sherry vinegar near the end of the cooking cuts the richness of the butter.

7. By resisting the urge to stir the mushrooms often, you will brown them better and create deeper flavours.

HOW TO MAKE FLAVOURED BUTTER

If you like to braai steaks – or any kind of meat, fish or poultry, for that matter – I think you should have at least one flavoured butter waiting for you at all times in the refrigerator or freezer. One of the surest ways to please your palate and delight your guests is to crown each braaiied steak with a slice of savoury butter blended with the flavours of your choice. The heat of the steak will melt the butter and send the flavours running to mingle with the meat juices for a luxurious sauce.

1. Start by mixing softened butter with fresh herbs and other seasonings, along with shallots that have been simmered in red wine.

2. Shape the butter into a little log on a piece of baking paper.

3. Wrap the log tightly in the baking paper and squeeze both ends to compact it.

4. Twist the ends of the baking paper in opposite directions to seal the log. Store the flavoured butter in the refrigerator.

5. When it's time to serve, trim off one end. Remember to remove the frozen butter from the freezer in enough time to thaw.

6. Cut as many rounds as you need and pull off the paper. Re-wrap any butter that is left over and return to the refrigerator or freezer.

HOW TO MAKE CROSS-HATCH MARKS

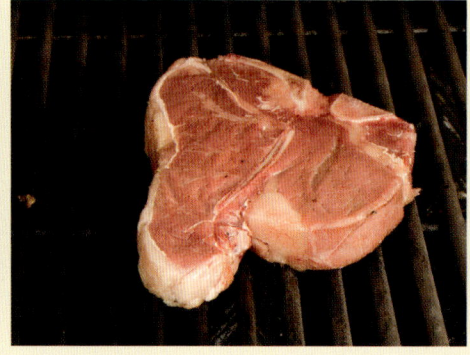

1. For a nice diamond pattern on your steaks, position them at a 45-degree angle to the bars of the cooking grate.

2. After searing for a couple of minutes, rotate your steaks 90 degrees.

3. Turn the steaks over and, if you like, mark the other side in the same way.

PORTERHOUSE STEAKS WITH RED WINE-SHALLOT BUTTER

SERVES: 4–6
PREP TIME: 15 MINUTES

HEAT: DIRECT HIGH HEAT 230°–290°C (450°–550°F)
BRAAIING TIME: 8–10 MINUTES

BUTTER
- 3 tablespoons hearty red wine
- 2 tablespoons very finely chopped shallot or small onion
- 125 g unsalted butter, softened
- 1 tablespoon finely chopped flat leaf (Italian) parsley
- 1 tablespoon finely chopped tarragon
- ½ teaspoon coarse sea salt
- ¼ teaspoon freshly ground black pepper

- 4 porterhouse steaks, each about 450 g and 3 cm thick
- 2 tablespoons extra-virgin olive oil
- 2 teaspoons coarse sea salt
- ½ teaspoon freshly ground black pepper

1. Bring the wine and shallot to a boil in a small, heavy-based saucepan over high heat. Boil for 3–5 minutes until the wine is reduced to a glaze and is absorbed mostly by the shallots. Transfer to a bowl and allow to cool completely.

2. Add the butter, parsley, tarragon, salt and pepper to the shallot-wine reduction and mix to combine. Scoop the mixture out of the bowl onto a sheet of baking paper or wax paper. Loosely shape the mixture into a log about 2.5 cm in diameter. Roll the butter log in the paper and twist the ends in opposite directions to form an even cylinder. Refrigerate until about 1 hour before serving. (The butter can be made up to 1 week ahead.)

3. Allow the steaks to stand at room temperature for 20–30 minutes before cooking. Prepare the braai for direct cooking over high heat.

4. Lightly brush the steaks with the oil and season evenly with the salt and pepper. Brush the cooking grates clean. Braai the steaks over **direct high heat**, with the lid closed as much as possible, but turning once, until cooked to your desired doneness, 8–10 minutes for medium rare. (If flare-ups occur, move the steaks temporarily over indirect high heat). Remove the steaks from the braai and allow to rest for 3–5 minutes. Serve the steaks hot with the butter smeared over the top.

HOW TO BRAAI REALLY THICK STEAKS

One of the noblest dishes in the pantheon of international grilled steaks is *Bistecca alla Fiorentina*, an enormous porterhouse steak cooked over and beside the hot coals until the outside is crisply charred and the interior is just rosy red and deliciously tender. The seasonings are pure and simple – nothing more than coarse salt, preferably sea salt, and freshly ground black pepper. The finishing touches are a squeeze of lemon juice and a drizzle of the best olive oil in the house.

1. Whereas most steaks do best when you don't fiddle with them on the grill, this one is so thick and monstrous that you will need to move it every few minutes.

2. Charcoal fires are inherently uneven, so don't be surprised if one part of the steak browns faster than another. Move the steak around to compensate for the unevenness.

3. This is a case where the charcoal is as much an ingredient in the recipe as the seasonings. The smokiness permeates the meat and delivers great primordial flavours.

BISTECCA ALLA FIORENTINA

SERVES: 4
PREP TIME: 5 MINUTES

HEAT: DIRECT AND INDIRECT MEDIUM HEAT 180°–230°C (350°–450°F)
BRAAIING TIME: 25–27 MINUTES

> 1 porterhouse steak, about 1.25 kg and 6 cm thick
> Coarse sea salt
> Freshly ground black pepper
> 2 lemons
> Extra-virgin olive oil

1. Allow the steak to rest at room temperature for 1 hour before cooking. During this time, you can prepare and cook the barbecue-baked beans, and then keep them warm.

2. Prepare the braai for direct and indirect cooking over a medium heat.

3. Liberally season the steak on both sides with salt and pepper. Rub the seasoning into the meat.

4. Braai the steak over **direct medium heat** for 10–12 minutes, rotating the steak 45 degrees about every 3 minutes to create a nice crust and turning once. Move the steak over **indirect medium heat** and continue to cook until the internal temperature reaches 52°C (125°F) for rare, about 15 minutes, rotating the steak as needed for even cooking. Allow the steak to rest for about 10 minutes before carving.

5. To carve the steak, cut the fillet side first as close to the bone as possible. Repeat the procedure for the sirloin side. Slice each piece crossways into 1-cm slices, keeping the slices intact. Transfer to a serving platter and reassemble the steak with the bone. Drizzle some extra-virgin olive oil over the slices and serve with fresh lemon and barbecue-baked beans.

BARBECUE-BAKED BEANS ALLA CONTADINA

PREP TIME: 10 MINUTES

HEAT: INDIRECT MEDIUM HEAT 180°–230°C (350°–450°F)
BRAAIING TIME: ABOUT 15 MINUTES

> 2 cans cannellini beans, rinsed
> 200 ml vegetable stock
> 4 tablespoons tomato sauce
> 1 tablespoon extra-virgin olive oil
> 1 teaspoon finely chopped fresh thyme
> ½ teaspoon coarse sea salt
> 1 teaspoon finely chopped garlic
> 4 teaspoons finely chopped flat-leaf parsley

1. Prepare the braai for indirect cooking over medium heat.

2. Place the beans in a 20-cm square ovenproof baking dish.

3. Combine the stock, tomato sauce, oil, thyme and salt in a small bowl, and pour over the beans. Lightly press the beans so that they are all immersed in the liquid. Bake the beans over **indirect medium heat** for about 15 minutes, with the lid closed, until they are bubbling and most of the liquid has reduced.

4. Blend the garlic with the parsley and scatter over the beans. Serve with the steak.

This dish hails from the culinary epicentre of Tuscany, so it is more than appropriate to serve it with another famed dish from that region: white beans simmered with stock, tomatoes and herbs.

HOW TO CARVE BISTECCA

1. The porterhouse is a large cut that includes a T-shaped bone, with meat from the sirloin on one side and the fillet on the other.

2. The traditional way to serve this is to remove all the meat from the bone in two big sections, then slice it.

3. Cut the sirloin crossways into nice thick slices.

4. Also cut the fillet section into thick slices, and then arrange all the slices back along the bone.

SKIRT STEAKS WITH BABY POTATOES AND FETA

SERVES: 4
PREP TIME: 15 MINUTES

HEAT: INDIRECT AND DIRECT HIGH HEAT 230°–290°C (450°–550°F)
BRAAIING TIME: 34–46 MINUTES
SPECIAL EQUIPMENT: PERFORATED GRILL PAN, LARGE DISPOSABLE FOIL TRAY

RUB
- 1 teaspoon coarse sea salt
- 1 teaspoon ground cumin
- ½ teaspoon garlic flakes
- ¼ teaspoon freshly ground black pepper

- 750 g small red-skinned potatoes (3.5 cm–5 cm diameter), or baby potatoes, cut into quarters
- 2 tablespoons extra-virgin olive oil
- ½ teaspoon coarse sea salt

- 2 skirt or flank steaks, about 350 g each, trimmed of excess fat
- 75 g crumbled feta cheese
- 2 tablespoons chopped fresh flat-leaf (Italian) parsley
- Coarse sea salt
- Freshly ground black pepper

1. Prepare the braai for indirect and direct cooking over high heat.

2. Combine the rub ingredients in a small bowl.

3. Combine the potatoes, oil and salt in a large bowl and stir to coat them evenly.

4. Preheat a grill pan over **indirect high heat** for about 10 minutes. Add the potatoes to the pan and cook them for 30–40 minutes, with the lid closed as much as possible but turning 2 or 3 times, until they are golden brown and tender.

5. After the potatoes have cooked for about 10 minutes, season the steaks evenly with the rub, pressing the spices into the meat. Allow the meat to stand at room temperature for 20–30 minutes before cooking.

6. When the potatoes are fully cooked, transfer them to a large disposable foil tray. Add the cheese and parsley and mix well, then season to taste with salt and pepper. To keep the potatoes warm, place the pan over indirect heat while the steaks cook.

7. Braai the steaks over **direct high heat**, with the lid closed as much as possible but turning once, until cooked to your desired doneness, 4–6 minutes for medium rare. Transfer the steaks to a chopping board and allow to rest for 3–5 minutes. Keep the potatoes warm on the braai. Cut the meat across the grain into thin slices. Serve warm with the potatoes.

HOW TO PREP SKIRT STEAK

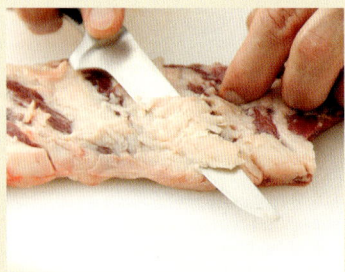
1. Using a sharp knife, trim away most of the fat that clings to both sides of the skirt steaks.

2. Thoroughly trimming the fat will help prevent flare-ups.

3. Cutting the steaks into lengths of about 30 cm will make them easier to handle on the braai.

4. Season the meat generously with the rub, patting it in with your fingertips so that it won't fall off during braaiing.

CARNE ASADA WITH BLACK BEAN AND AVOCADO SALSA

SERVES: 4–6
PREP TIME: 20 MINUTES

HEAT: DIRECT HIGH HEAT 230°–290°C (450°–550°F)
BRAAIING TIME: 4–6 MINUTES

SALSA

- 1 can (425 g) black beans, rinsed
- 1 ripe avocado, finely chopped
- 150 g onion, finely chopped, rinsed in a sieve
- 175 g ripe tomato, finely chopped
- 2 tablespoons roughly chopped fresh coriander
- 1 tablespoon fresh lime juice
- ½ teaspoon coarse sea salt
- ¼ teaspoon chilli powder
- ¼ teaspoon ground cumin
- pinch of freshly ground black pepper

RUB

- 1 teaspoon chilli powder
- 1 teaspoon coarse sea salt
- ½ teaspoon ground cumin
- ¼ teaspoon freshly ground black pepper

700 g skirt or flank steak, trimmed of excess fat
Extra-virgin olive oil

Raw onions can taste a little harsh in a salsa, but a good rinse will take the edge off.

1. Combine the salsa ingredients in a non-metallic bowl. Cover with clingfilm, pressing the film directly onto the surface of the onions, and set aside at room temperature for as long as 2 hours before serving.

2. Mix the rub ingredients together in a small bowl. Cut the steak into 30-cm lengths to make them easier to handle on the braai. Lightly coat both sides of the steaks with oil. Season evenly with the rub and allow to stand at room temperature for 20–30 minutes before braaiing. Prepare the braai for direct cooking over high heat.

3. Brush the cooking grates clean. Braai the steaks over **direct high heat**, with the lid closed as much as possible but turning once or twice, until cooked to your desired doneness, 4–6 minutes for medium rare. Remove the steaks from the braai and allow to rest for 3–5 minutes.

4. Cut the steaks across the grain into 1-cm slices. Serve warm with the salsa.

HOW TO PREP SHALLOTS

1. Trim off most of each root end.

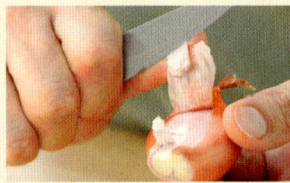
2. Peel off the papery skin.

3. Spread the shallots on foil and drizzle with oil.

4. Wrap the foil over the shallots to make a neat parcel.

HOW TO PREP RUMP FLAP STEAKS

1. Some rump flap, or feather, steaks, like the one on the right, have a tough streak running down the middle.

2. It's harder to see it after the steak is cooked.

3. To ensure that every slice is tender, cut away that tough streak before serving.

BISTRO STEAKS WITH MUSTARD CREAM SAUCE

SERVES: 4
PREP TIME: 15 MINUTES

HEAT: INDIRECT AND DIRECT MEDIUM HEAT 180°–230°C (350°–450°F)
BRAAIING TIME: ABOUT 1 HOUR

- 8 large shallots, about 375 g total
- Extra-virgin olive oil
- 1¾ teaspoons coarse sea salt
- 1 teaspoon dried thyme
- 1 teaspoon paprika
- ¾ teaspoon freshly ground black pepper
- 4 rump flap (feather) steaks, each 200 g and about 2.5 cm thick
- 125 ml sour cream
- 1 tablespoon Dijon mustard

1. Prepare the braai for indirect and direct cooking over medium heat.

2. Peel and trim the shallots, removing most of each root end. Cut the larger shallots in half lengthways or pull apart the distinct halves. Pile the shallots in the middle of a large square of heavyweight foil. Drizzle with 1 tablespoon of oil and season with ¼ teaspoon of the salt. Fold up the sides and seal to make a parcel. Braai over **indirect medium heat** for 20–30 minutes, with the lid closed as much as possible but turning once or twice, until a knife slides easily in and out of the shallots. Open the packet and continue to cook the shallots in the foil for 20–30 minutes more, turning them very gently once or twice, until nicely browned. Remove the parcel from the braai.

3. Mix the remaining 1½ teaspoons of salt with the thyme, paprika and pepper in a small bowl. Lightly coat the steaks on both sides with oil, then season evenly with the spices. Allow the steaks to stand at room temperature for 20–30 minutes before cooking.

4. Combine the sour cream and mustard in a small bowl.

5. Brush the cooking grates clean. Braai the steaks over **direct medium heat**, with the lid closed as much as possible but turning once, until cooked to your desired doneness, 8–10 minutes for medium rare. At the same time, reheat the parcel of shallots over **indirect medium heat**. Remove the steaks from the braai and allow to rest for 3–5 minutes before slicing. While the steaks rest, remove any charred outer layers from the shallots.

6. Cut each steak lengthways on either side of the gristle that runs down the middle. Thinly slice the steak against the grain and overlap the slices on serving dishes. Serve the steaks warm with the shallots and sauce.

SESAME-GINGER FLANK STEAK WITH ASPARAGUS AND GOMASHIO

SERVES: 4–6
PREP TIME: 25 MINUTES
MARINATING TIME: 3–4 HOURS

HEAT: DIRECT MEDIUM HEAT 180°–230°C (350°–450°F)
BRAAIING TIME: 12–16 MINUTES
SPECIAL EQUIPMENT: MORTAR AND PESTLE

MARINADE
  75 ml soy sauce
  2 tablespoons sugar
  3 tablespoons rice wine vinegar
  2 tablespoons toasted sesame oil
  1 tablespoon finely chopped garlic
  1½ tablespoons grated ginger
  1½ teaspoons sambal oelek or other fresh chilli paste
  150 g spring onions, white and light green parts, finely chopped
  4 tablespoons coarsely chopped fresh coriander

  1 skirt or flank steak, 700–900 g and about 2 cm thick

GOMASHIO
  4 tablespoons of sesame seeds
  1 teaspoon coarse sea salt

ASPARAGUS
  1 large bunch asparagus, about 500 g
  1 tablespoon extra-virgin olive oil
  ½ teaspoon coarse sea salt

  2 tablespoons finely chopped fresh coriander or flat-leaf (Italian) parsley

HOW TO MAKE GOMASHIO

1. Toast the sesame seeds just until they start to colour.
2. Grind coarsely with sea salt to make a delicious seasoning.

HOW TO SLICE FLANK STEAK

1. For the sake of tenderness, cut flank steak crossways, or against the grain.
2. Keep the slices no thicker than about 8 mm.

1. Whisk the soy sauce, sugar, vinegar, oil, garlic, ginger and chilli paste together in a small bowl. Add the spring onions and coriander. Place the steak in a glass or stainless-steel dish and pour in the marinade, turning the steak to coat both sides. Cover and refrigerate for 3–4 hours, turning the steak once or twice.

2. Toast the sesame seeds in a dry non-stick frying pan over low heat for 2–3 minutes, shaking and stirring until the seeds are golden brown, but before they begin to pop. Turn them onto a plate and allow to cool for 10 minutes. Add the sea salt and combine in a mortar and pestle. Lightly crush the seeds, so that some texture remains; do not make a fine powder. (Store the unused portion in a glass jar in the refrigerator for up to 2 months.)

3. Snap or cut off the dry, woody ends from the asparagus spears. Lightly coat them with the oil and season with the salt.

4. Prepare the braai for direct cooking over medium heat.

5. Remove the steak from the refrigerator and allow to stand at room temperature for 20–30 minutes before cooking. Brush the cooking grates clean. Braai the steak over **direct medium heat**, with the lid closed as much as possible but turning once, until cooked to your desired doneness, 8–10 minutes for medium rare. Transfer to a chopping board and allow to rest while you cook the asparagus.

6. Arrange the asparagus at right angles to the bars on the cooking grate. Braai over **direct medium heat** for 4–6 minutes with the lid closed as much as possible but rolling the spears a couple of times, until lightly charred and crisp-tender. Remove the spears and arrange them on one side of a large platter.

7. Thinly slice the steak on the bias and place it on the platter. Sprinkle over the gomashio and coriander. Serve warm.

HOW TO STUFF AND ROLL FLANK OR SKIRT STEAK

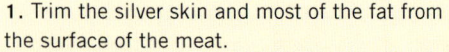

1. Trim the silver skin and most of the fat from the surface of the meat.

2. Holding your knife parallel to the board, make a shallow cut along the length of the steak.

3. Slice again, making the cut a little deeper.

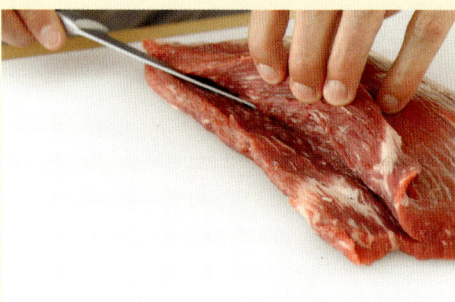

4. Keep making strokes with the tip of your knife as you open up the meat with your other hand.

5. Continue cutting until you come within about 1 cm of the opposite edge.

6. Now open up the steak like a book, laying it flat on the board.

7. Turn the steak over and carefully trim off the seam that sticks up.

8. Turn the steak back over so that the cut side is facing up.

9. With the grain of the meat running horizontally, spread the stuffing mixture to within 2 cm of the outer edges and a few centimetres from the top.

10. Roll up the meat from the bottom edge to the top.

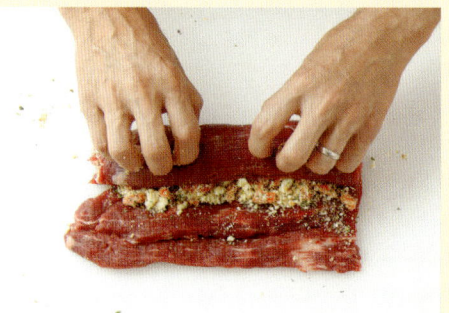

11. With no stuffing at the top of the meat, all the ingredients will stay nicely inside the roll.

12. Tie the roll every couple of centimetres with lengths of butcher's string.

FLANK STEAK WITH ROASTED PEPPER AND FETA STUFFING

SERVES: 6
PREP TIME: 40 MINUTES

HEAT: INDIRECT MEDIUM HEAT 180°–230°C (350°–450°F)
BRAAIING TIME: 20–30 MINUTES
SPECIAL EQUIPMENT: BUTCHER'S STRING

- 75 g feta cheese, drained and crumbled
- 50 g dried breadcrumbs
- 1 small red pepper, roasted, peeled, seeds removed and diced
- 1 large garlic clove
- 80 ml flat-leaf (Italian) parsley
- 1 tablespoon fresh thyme
- ½ teaspoon coarse sea salt
- ¼ teaspoon freshly ground black pepper

- 2 flank or skirt steaks, 700 g each
- 1 tablespoon extra-virgin olive oil
- Coarse sea salt
- Freshly ground black pepper

1. Combine the cheese, bread crumbs and diced pepper in a bowl. Finely chop the garlic and fresh herbs together and add to the bowl, then blend thoroughly with a fork. Season with the sea salt and black pepper.

2. Place the flank steak on a chopping board. Starting near one end of the steak, carefully insert a boning knife horizontally into one long edge (the edge parallel to the grain), splitting the steak evenly from top to bottom. Continue this cut until the entire steak can be opened up like a book (see directions at left). Repeat with the other flank steak.

3. Prepare your braai for indirect cooking over medium heat.

4. Evenly spread the stuffing mixture over the inside of the butterflied steaks to within 2.5 cm of the edges and a few centimetres from the top (you may not need all of it). Be careful not to overstuff or it will just fall out and make it harder to roll. Roll up the steaks around the filling, with the grain running the length of the roll. Tie the rolls every few centimetres with butcher's string. Brush the outside of the rolls with oil and lightly season with salt and pepper.

5. Brush the cooking grates clean. Braai over **indirect medium heat**, with the lid closed as much as possible but turning once, until cooked to your desired doneness, 20–30 minutes for medium rare. Transfer to a carving board, lightly cover with foil, and allow to rest for 10 minutes before slicing.

6. To serve, cut the rolls into 1–1.5-cm slices. Serve warm.

ARGENTINE BEEF SKEWERS WITH CHIMICHURRI SAUCE

SERVES: 4–6
PREP TIME: 20 MINUTES

HEAT: DIRECT HIGH HEAT 230°–290°C (450°–550°F)
BRAAIING TIME: 6–8 MINUTES
SPECIAL EQUIPMENT: BAMBOO SKEWERS, SOAKED IN WATER FOR AT LEAST 30 MINUTES

SAUCE
- 125 ml flat-leaf (Italian) parsley, leaves and tender stems
- 4 tablespoons basil leaves
- 4 tablespoons white onion, rinsed and finely chopped
- 4 tablespoons finely chopped carrot
- 1 garlic clove
- ½ teaspoon coarse sea salt
- 90 ml extra-virgin olive oil
- 2 tablespoons rice vinegar

RUB
- 1½ teaspoons coarse sea salt
- ½ teaspoon paprika
- ½ teaspoon ground coriander
- ½ teaspoon ground cumin
- ¼ teaspoon freshly ground black pepper

- 900 g sirloin or rump steak, 2.5–3 cm thick, cut into 2.5-cm cubes
- Extra-virgin olive oil
- 18 large cherry tomatoes

1. Finely chop the parsley, basil, onion, carrot, garlic and salt in a food processor or blender. With the machine running, add the oil and vinegar in a steady stream, using just enough oil to create a fairly thick sauce.

2. Mix the rub ingredients together in a small bowl.

3. Place the meat cubes in a large bowl. Lightly coat the meat with the oil and then season with the rub, stirring to coat the meat evenly. Allow the meat to stand at room temperature for 20–30 minutes before cooking. Prepare the braai for direct cooking over high heat.

4. Thread the meat and tomatoes alternately onto skewers. Brush the cooking grates clean. Braai the skewers over **direct high heat,** with the lid closed as much as possible but turning occasionally, until cooked to your desired doneness, 6–8 minutes for medium rare. Serve warm with the sauce on the side or drizzled over the top.

HOW TO CUBE SIRLOIN OR RUMP STEAK
When making kebabs, the goal is to create cubes of the same size and thickness so that they all cook at the same rate.

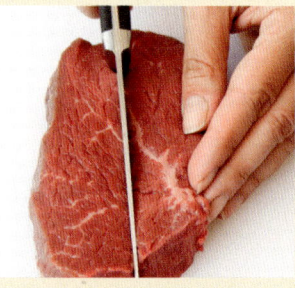

1. Start with a nice even piece of steak at least 2.5 cm thick.

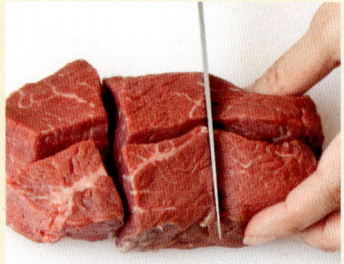

2. Cut it down the centre and crossways into 2.5-cm cubes.

3. Cubes give you plenty of opportunities to lightly char and flavour the surface of the meat.

4. Combine smaller cubes on a skewer of their own and cook them for less time.

The centre-cut section of a beef fillet is almost always the most expensive part. Save that to slice into steaks. To make skewers or kebabs, use the tail ends of the fillet and enjoy all the buttery texture for less cost. Some folded lemon slices complement the flavours in the *finadene*, a popular marinade and sauce from the tropical island of Guam, in the Pacific.

BEEF KEBABS WITH FINADENE

SERVES: 4–6
PREP TIME: 20 MINUTES
MARINATING TIME: 1–2 HOURS

HEAT: DIRECT HIGH HEAT 230°–290°C (450°–550°F)
BRAAIING TIME: 4–6 MINUTES
SPECIAL EQUIPMENT: BAMBOO SKEWERS, SOAKED IN WATER FOR AT LEAST 30 MINUTES

SAUCE
    125 ml soy sauce
    4 tablespoons of white onion, finely chopped
    3 tablespoons fresh lemon juice
    3 tablespoons water
    1 teaspoon finely chopped jalapeño chilli

    1.3 kg beef fillet
    4 tablespoons extra-virgin olive oil
    2 lemons, thinly sliced

1. Mix the sauce ingredients together in a bowl. In a separate small bowl, reserve 5 tablespoons of the sauce to spoon over the braaiied meat.

2. Trim any excess fat and sinew from the surface of the meat. Cut it crossways into steaks about 3 cm thick, then cut each steak into pieces 2.5–3 cm thick, cutting away and discarding any clumps of fat and sinew. Place the meat into a large, resealable plastic bag, pour in the remaining sauce and add the oil. Press the air out of the bag, seal tightly and turn the bag several times to incorporate the oil and evenly coat the meat. Refrigerate for 1–2 hours.

3. Thread the meat onto skewers, placing a folded slice of lemon between each piece so the meat cooks evenly. Allow the kebabs to stand at room temperature for 20–30 minutes before cooking. Prepare the braai for direct cooking over high heat.

4. Brush the cooking grates clean. Braai the skewers over **direct high heat**, with the lid closed as much as possible but turning 2 or 3 times, until the meat is cooked to your desired doneness, 4–6 minutes for medium rare. Serve warm with the reserved sauce spooned over the top.

HOW TO PREP CUCUMBER

1. Grate the unpeeled cucumber coarsely on the side of a box grater.

2. Arrange the grated cucumber in the middle of a sturdy piece of roller towel.

3. Squeeze gently to remove the water. Then mix the grated cucumber into the sauce.

LAMB SOUVLAKI WITH CUCUMBER-YOGHURT SAUCE

SERVES: 4
PREP TIME: 20 MINUTES
MARINATING TIME: 3–4 HOURS

HEAT: DIRECT HIGH HEAT 230°–290°C (450°–550°F)
BRAAIING TIME: 6–7 MINUTES
SPECIAL EQUIPMENT: BAMBOO SKEWERS, SOAKED IN WATER FOR AT LEAST 30 MINUTES

MARINADE
    125 ml extra-virgin olive oil
    1 tablespoon finely chopped garlic
    1 tablespoon finely chopped fresh origanum, or
        1 teaspoon crumbled dried origanum
    1 teaspoon coarse sea salt
    ¼ teaspoon freshly ground black pepper

    700 g deboned leg of lamb, trimmed of excess fat
        and cut into 4-cm chunks
    2 medium red or green peppers, cut into 2.5-cm squares
    24 large cherry tomatoes

SAUCE
    ½ English cucumber, coarsely grated
    250 ml Greek-style yoghurt
    2 tablespoons finely chopped red onion
    1 teaspoon finely grated lemon zest
    1 tablespoon fresh lemon juice
    ½ teaspoon finely chopped garlic
    Coarse sea salt
    Freshly ground black pepper

1. Whisk the marinade ingredients together in a small bowl. Thread the lamb chunks, pepper squares, and tomatoes alternately onto skewers. Place in a shallow dish, pour the marinade over the skewers, and turn to coat them evenly. Cover and refrigerate for 3–4 hours, turning occasionally. Allow to stand at room temperature for 20–30 minutes before cooking.

2. Squeeze the grated cucumber to remove as much liquid as possible. Transfer the cucumber to a small bowl and stir in the yoghurt, onion, lemon zest, lemon juice and garlic. Season to taste with salt and pepper. Cover and refrigerate until serving.

3. Prepare the braai for direct cooking over high heat. Brush the cooking grates clean. Remove the skewers from the dish and discard the marinade. Braai the skewers over **direct high heat**, with the lid closed as much as possible but turning occasionally, until the meat is cooked to your desired doneness, 6–7 minutes for medium rare. Serve warm with the sauce.

PORCINI-RUBBED VEAL CHOPS WITH HERBED MASCARPONE

SERVES: 4
PREP TIME: 15 MINUTES

HEAT: DIRECT MEDIUM HEAT 180°–290°C (350°–450°F)
BRAAIING TIME: ABOUT 6 MINUTES
SPECIAL EQUIPMENT: SPICE MILL

MASCARPONE
    75 ml mascarpone cheese
    1 teaspoon finely chopped fresh sage
    ¼ teaspoon coarse sea salt
    ¼ teaspoon freshly ground black pepper

    4 tablespoons dried porcini mushrooms
    2 teaspoons coarse sea salt
    1 teaspoon freshly ground black pepper

    4 veal rib chops, each about 250 g and 2.5 cm thick
    Extra-virgin olive oil

1. Combine the mascarpone ingredients in a small bowl. Cover and allow to stand at room temperature for 1 hour.

2. Using a spice mill, grind the mushrooms into a powder (this should yield about 2 tablespoons). Put the mushroom powder into a small bowl and mix with the salt and pepper. Pour some oil onto a baking tray and sprinkle the seasoning over the oil. Dredge the chops through the oil mixture to coat them evenly. Cover the chops and allow to stand at room temperature for 20–30 minutes before cooking. Prepare the braai for direct cooking over medium heat.

3. Brush the cooking grates clean. Braai the chops over **direct medium heat**, with the lid closed as much as possible but turning once, until cooked to your desired doneness, about 6 minutes for medium rare. Remove from the braai and allow to rest for 3–5 minutes. Serve the chops hot with the herbed mascarpone.

If your impression of veal comes mostly from overcrumbed and overcooked cutlets, you owe it to yourself to try this chop. Quickly grilling a lean, bone-in veal chop over a fragrant fire, Tuscan style, results in a succulent, tender taste experience.

HOW TO PREP VEAL CHOPS

1. Dried porcini mushrooms star in this veal chop recipe. Grind them finely in a spice mill or coffee grinder.

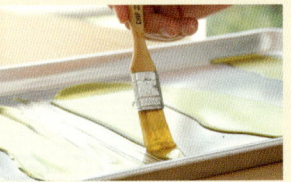

2. Pour some good olive oil onto a baking tray and sprinkle the finely ground mushrooms, salt and pepper over the oil.

3. Press the veal chops into the oil and seasonings.

4. Drag each chop back and forth on both sides to get an even coating.

HOW TO 'FRENCH' A RACK OF LAMB

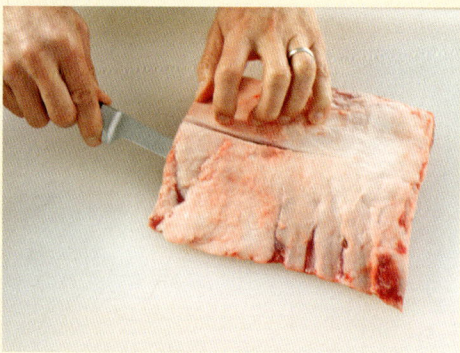 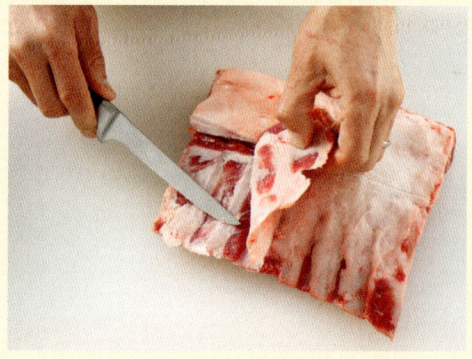

1. 'Frenching' means removing the fat from the bones that extend from a rack (or a single chop) and cleaning them thoroughly for a nice presentation.

2. Each rack of lamb has a 'fat cap' that runs on top of the rib bones and meat. Make a cut through the fat at the base of the bones.

3. Use the knife to help lift off the fat cap.

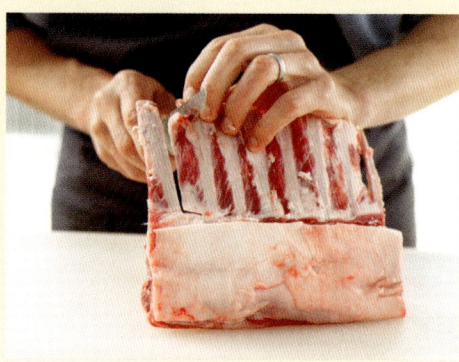  

4. Use your knife to cut out the rib meat between the bones and to scrape the bones clean.

5. Then trim off the fat clinging to the loin meat, to prevent flare-ups.

6. Ideally the meat will be pinkish red, not purple. A dark colour indicates an older animal.

HOW TO BRAAI RACK OF LAMB

Lamb chops are a buttery-soft luxury. You can certainly braai them individually, but they are likely to be juicier and more succulent if you cook whole racks first and then cut them into chops.

1. Prepare your braai by spreading the coals over one-half to three-quarters of the charcoal grate.

2. Braai the lamb as much as possible over direct heat.

3. If flare-ups occur, move the racks to the other side of the braai, over indirect heat.

4. Once the internal temperature reaches 52°C (125°F), remove the racks from the braai, cover them loosely with foil, and allow them to rest for about 5 minutes before cutting into chops.

RACK OF LAMB WITH ORANGE-POMEGRANATE SYRUP

SERVES: 4–6
PREP TIME: 40 MINUTES

HEAT: DIRECT MEDIUM HEAT 180°–230°C (350°–450°F)
BRAAIING TIME: 15–20 MINUTES

    2 lamb racks, 500–700 g each

PASTE
    2 tablespoons extra-virgin olive oil
    1 tablespoon finely chopped garlic
    1 tablespoon chilli powder
    2 teaspoons coarse sea salt
    1 teaspoon freshly ground black pepper

SYRUP
    125 ml fresh orange juice
    4 tablespoons pomegranate juice
    2 tablespoons honey
    1 tablespoon balsamic vinegar
    ½ teaspoon coarse sea salt

1. French the lamb racks as shown on the previous page.

2. Mix the paste ingredients in a small bowl. Spread the paste over the lamb racks and allow them to stand at room temperature for 20–30 minutes before cooking.

3. Combine the orange juice, pomegranate juice, honey and balsamic vinegar in a small saucepan over high heat and bring to a boil. Once boiling, reduce the heat to medium and simmer for 15–20 minutes until the liquid has reduced to about 3 tablespoons. Season the light syrup with the salt and allow to cool. (You can refrigerate the syrup for up to 3 days.)

4. Prepare the braai for direct cooking over medium heat. Brush the cooking grates clean. Braai the lamb, bone sides down first, over **direct medium heat**, with the lid closed as much as possible but turning once or twice and moving the racks over indirect heat if flare-ups occur, until cooked to your desired doneness, 15–20 minutes for medium rare. Remove from the braai when the internal temperature reaches 52°C (125°F). Allow the lamb to rest for 5 minutes before carving into chops (the internal temperature will rise during resting).

5. If necessary, warm the syrup over a low heat until it reaches your desired consistency. Serve the lamb warm with the syrup drizzled on top.

Of course you can buy pre-cut lamb rib chops, but cutting them yourself from a 'frenched' rack of lamb will probably save you some money and assure you that each chop is the same thickness. For a clear look at where the bones are, place the meaty side of each rack on a cutting board and then cut between each pair of ribs.

LAMB CHOPS WITH INDIAN SPICES

SERVES: 4
PREP TIME: 10 MINUTES
MARINATING TIME: 1–2 HOURS

HEAT: DIRECT HIGH HEAT 230°–290°C (450°–550°F)
BRAAIING TIME: 4–6 MINUTES

MARINADE
    4 tablespoons extra-virgin olive oil
    2 tablespoons fresh lime juice
    1 tablespoon finely chopped garlic
    1½ teaspoons coarse sea salt
    1 teaspoon ground coriander
    1 teaspoon ground cumin
    ½ teaspoon ground ginger
    ½ teaspoon freshly ground black pepper

16 rib lamb chops, each about 2 cm thick, trimmed of excess fat
Lime wedges to serve, optional.

1. Whisk the marinade ingredients together in a small bowl.

2. Arrange the chops on a large, rimmed plate. Spoon or brush the marinade over the chops, turning to coat them evenly. Cover with clingfilm and refrigerate for 1–2 hours.

3. Remove the chops from the refrigerator 20–30 minutes before cooking. Prepare the braai for direct cooking over high heat.

4. Brush the cooking grates clean. Braai the chops over **direct high heat**, with the lid closed as much as possible but turning once, until nicely marked on both sides and cooked to your desired doneness, 4–6 minutes for medium rare.

5. Remove the chops from the braai and allow to rest for 3–5 minutes. Serve warm with lime wedges, if desired, for squeezing over.

LAMB CHOPS IN UZBEK MARINADE

SERVES: 4
PREP TIME: 10 MINUTES
MARINATING TIME: 3–5 HOURS

HEAT: DIRECT HIGH HEAT 230°–290°C (450°–550°F)
BRAAIING TIME: ABOUT 8 MINUTES

MARINADE/SAUCE
  1 small onion, cut into chunks
  4 canned roma tomatoes
  125 ml extra-virgin olive oil
  4 large garlic cloves
  2 tablespoons red wine vinegar
  1 tablespoon sweet paprika
  1 tablespoon dried thyme
  1 tablespoon ground coriander
  2 teaspoons ground cumin
  2 teaspoons coarse sea salt
  ½ teaspoon ground cayenne pepper
  ½ teaspoon freshly ground black pepper

  8 lamb middle loin chops, each about 3 cm thick
  Extra-virgin olive oil

1. Process the marinade ingredients in a food processor for 1–2 minutes until very smooth.

2. Arrange the chops side by side in a shallow dish. Pour the marinade over the chops and turn to coat them on all sides. Cover with clingfilm and marinate in the refrigerator for 3–5 hours.

3. Remove the chops from the dish and wipe off most of the marinade. Discard the marinade. Lightly brush the chops with oil and allow to stand at room temperature for 20–30 minutes before cooking. Prepare the braai for direct cooking over a high heat.

4. Brush the cooking grates clean. Braai the chops over **direct high heat**, with the lid closed as much as possible but rotating and turning them once or twice for even cooking, until they are cooked to your desired doneness, about 8 minutes for medium rare. Each time you lift the chops off the grate to rotate them or turn them over, place them down on a clean area of the grate, and brush away the bits of marinade that will cling to the grate.

5. Remove the chops from the braai and allow to rest for 3–5 minutes. Serve warm.

After marinating lamb chops in a thick, coarse purée, wipe off most of the marinade before putting the chops on the braai. Otherwise, the coating will prevent the chops from searing nicely and developing a good char on the outside. Don't worry; the flavours of the marinade will have imbued the meat itself.

HOW TO MAKE BASIL-GARLIC OIL

1. Bring a saucepan of salted water to a boil. Add the basil leaves and blanch them (cook briefly) for 10 seconds.

2. Immediately remove the basil leaves with a slotted spoon and plunge them into a bowl of iced water to stop them cooking and retain the green colour.

3. Place the basil leaves on roller towels and pat them dry.

4. Combine the basil leaves, oil, and garlic in a food processor or blender.

5. Process until the basil is puréed, and then season the mixture with sea salt and crushed red chilli flakes.

6. Drizzle the basil-garlic oil over braaied meats. Save any remaining oil by straining out the solids and storing it in the refrigerator for up to a week.

HOW TO PREP LAMB SHOULDER (BRAAI) CHOPS

1. Lamb shoulder chops (braai chops) typically cost less than loin and rib chops, and their flavour is excellent.

2. First brush them with good olive oil and some bold seasonings, like dried herbes de Provence.

3. Their texture can be a little tough, so it's best to slow-cook them over indirect heat, which renders them tender.

HERBES DE PROVENCE

Herbes de Provence is an aromatic blend of dried herbs frequently used in the south of France. It typically includes thyme, marjoram, parsley, tarragon, lavender, celery seed, and bay leaf.

LAMB SHOULDER CHOPS WITH RATATOUILLE SALAD AND BASIL-GARLIC OIL

SERVES: 4
PREP TIME: 25 MINUTES

HEAT: DIRECT AND INDIRECT MEDIUM HEAT 180°–230°C (350°–450°F)
BRAAIING TIME: 51–58 MINUTES

OIL

    1 tablespoon plus ½ teaspoon sea salt
    250 ml fresh basil leaves
    200 ml extra-virgin olive oil
    1 medium garlic clove, peeled
    ¼ teaspoon crushed red chilli flakes

RATATOUILLE

    1 large red pepper
    1 medium brinjal, cut into 1-cm slices
    2 small courgettes, cut in half lengthways
    1 medium onion, cut crossways into 4 thick slices
    Extra-virgin olive oil
    4 ripe red tomatoes
    Coarse sea salt
    Freshly ground black pepper

    2 teaspoons dried herbes de Provence or mixed herbs
    4 lamb shoulder chops, 300–350 g each

1. Bring a small saucepan of water, with 1 tablespoon of the salt, to a boil over high heat. Add the basil leaves and blanch them for 10 seconds. Immediately remove the basil and plunge it into a bowl of ice water. Transfer to roller towels and pat away the excess water. Process the basil, oil, and garlic in a food processor or blender, until the basil is puréed. Season with the remaining ½ teaspoon salt and the red chilli flakes. Pour into a small jug and set aside.

2. Prepare the braai for direct and indirect cooking over a medium heat.

3. Remove the stem, ribs, and seeds from the pepper and cut into 4 pieces. Lightly brush the brinjal, courgette and onion with oil. Brush the cooking grates clean. Braai all the vegetables over **direct medium heat** for 6–8 minutes, turning occasionally, until the pepper is charred and blistered, the brinjal, courgette and onion are tender, and the tomato skins are seared and blistered. Transfer the vegetables to a platter as they are done, and season to taste with salt and pepper. Cut the vegetables into chunks and drizzle with 2 tablespoons of basil-garlic oil. Set aside.

4. Mix 2 teaspoons sea salt, ½ teaspoon pepper and the dried herbs together in a bowl. Lightly brush the lamb chops with oil and season with the spices.

5. Brush the cooking grates clean. Braai the chops over **indirect medium heat** for 45–50 minutes, with the lid closed as much as possible but turning once or twice, until the chops are fork tender.

6. Place equal portions of ratatouille on each of 4 dinner plates. Add a chop to each plate and garnish with another drizzle of basil-garlic oil on the plate around the lamb and vegetables.

HOW TO CUT SHORT RIBS

1. Short ribs are cut two different ways for Korean barbecue. You can buy 'flat rib' short ribs, as depicted at the bottom of this picture, or the more conventional short ribs, like the thicker pieces shown at the top of the picture.

2. To prepare the more conventional style of short ribs, begin by making a horizontal cut just over the bone of each rib.

3. Stop just before you cut all the way through the meat.

4. Continue to make horizontal cuts and butterfly the meat until it is about 1 cm thick.

5. Next, cut very shallow slits into the meat to tenderize it.

HOW TO BRAAI FLAT RIBS

1. Flat ribs are thin enough to require no cutting. Simply marinate them for a few hours in the refrigerator. When you lift them, allow any excess liquid drip back into the bowl before placing them on the braai.

2. Braai the ribs over direct hight heat, leaving the lid off so that you can keep an eye on them, and turn them over as they char.

KOREAN BEEF BARBECUE

SERVES: 4–6
PREP TIME: 10 MINUTES
MARINATING TIME: 2–4 HOURS

HEAT: DIRECT HIGH HEAT 230°–290°C (450°–550°F)
BRAAIING TIME: 3–5 MINUTES

MARINADE
  1 Asian pear or firm ripe pear, peeled, cored and
    roughly chopped
  3 spring onions, trimmed and roughly chopped
  6 large garlic cloves
  500 ml water
  175 ml soy sauce
  75 g sugar
  4 tablespoons rice vinegar

  12 beef flat ribs, about 2 kg total and 1.5 cm thick
  2 tablespoons toasted sesame seeds

1. Finely chop the pear, spring onions and garlic in a food processor. Add the remaining marinade ingredients and process until well combined.

2. Put the ribs in a large bowl and pour over the marinade. Mix well to coat the ribs evenly, then cover and refrigerate for 2–4 hours.

3. Prepare the braai for direct cooking over high heat.

4. Brush the cooking grates clean. One at time, lift the ribs and allow the liquid and solid bits to fall back into the bowl. Discard the marinade. Braai the ribs over **direct high heat** for 3–5 minutes with the lid open and turning occasionally, until they are nicely charred on both sides and cooked to a medium or medium-rare doneness. Remove the ribs from the braai and sprinkle with the sesame seeds.

Asian pears have crisp translucent flesh and make a sweet juice that is excellent for marinating beef. If you can't find them, use firm ripe pears instead.

RED MEAT

HOW TO BRAAI BEEF RIBS

1. Look for the meatiest beef ribs you can find and season them generously.

2. Line them up on their sides in a large disposable foil tray.

3. Add beef stock to create a moist cooking environment.

4. Cover the tray with foil, which will trap steam and help to tenderize the meat.

5. Seal the edges tightly so that the liquid does not evaporate.

6. The ribs should cook over indirect heat, with the lid closed, for the first hour.

7. It's important to maintain the cooking temperature at about 180°C (350°F).

8. At the start of the second hour, add more charcoal to maintain the heat.

9. Uncover the tray and turn the ribs over so that they cook evenly.

10. Wearing barbecue mitts or oven gloves, reseal the tray for the second hour of cooking.

11. Remove the ribs from the tray and brush them with the sauce.

12. Finish them over direct heat for a beautifully caramelized surface.

BEEF RIBS WITH BARBACOA SAUCE

SERVES: 2–4
PREP TIME: 45 MINUTES

HEAT: INDIRECT AND DIRECT MEDIUM HEAT 180°–230°C (350°–450°F)
BRAAIING TIME: ABOUT 2¼ HOURS
SPECIAL EQUIPMENT: LARGE DISPOSABLE FOIL TRAY, CAST-IRON FRYING PAN

RUB
    2 teaspoons garlic flakes
    1 teaspoon ground cinnamon
    1 teaspoon coarse sea salt
    1 teaspoon freshly ground black pepper

    ½ rack beef ribs (7 ribs), about 2–2.5 kg
    500 ml beef stock

SAUCE
    3 dried anchó chillies
    150 g finely chopped onion
    1 teaspoon dried origanum
    1 teaspoon ground cumin
    1 medium garlic clove, minced
    2 tablespoons cider vinegar
    1 tablespoon light brown sugar
    ¾ teaspoon coarse sea salt
    125 ml tomato sauce

1. In a small bowl combine the rub ingredients.

2. Prepare the braai for indirect and direct cooking over medium heat.

3. Cut the rack into individual ribs and arrange them on a sheet pan. Evenly coat each rib with the rub and then place them side by side in a large disposable foil tray, layering a few ribs if necessary. Add the beef stock to the tray and cover it tightly with heavyweight foil.

4. Place the tray over **indirect medium heat**, close the lid, and cook for 1 hour. After the first hour, using tongs and wearing insulated braai gloves mitts, carefully remove the foil cover and turn the ribs over. Put the foil cover back on the tray and continue to cook over **indirect medium heat** for another hour. If using a charcoal braai, to maintain the heat, add 6–8 unlit briquettes to each pile of lit charcoal about every hour.

5. While the ribs are cooking, make the sauce. Heat a cast-iron frying pan over medium-high heat. Add the chillies and cook for 3–5 minutes, occasionally pressing the chillies against the bottom of the pan, until they are lightly toasted, pliable and dark brick red in spots. The chillies may start to puff while in the pan. Allow the toasted chillies to cool until easy to handle, then split them open and remove and discard the stems, seeds and ribs. Transfer to a bowl, cover with 600 ml hot tap water and allow them to stand for about 20 minutes until they soften. Strain into a small bowl, reserving the chilli soaking liquid.

6. Combine the soaked chillies, onion, origanum, cumin and garlic in a blender or food processor. Add 125 ml of the reserved soaking liquid and blend to make a thick paste, adding more reserved liquid, if necessary. Combine the chilli paste, vinegar, brown sugar and salt in a saucepan over medium heat and bring to a boil, stirring often. Reduce the heat to medium-low and cook for about 5 minutes, until slightly thickened. Remove the pan from the heat and stir in the tomato sauce. Transfer to a bowl and allow the sauce to cool.

7. When the ribs are tender and the meat has visibly shrunk back from the bones, wearing insulated braai gloves, carefully remove the tray from the braai. Remove the ribs and place them on a baking tray. Discard the tray and the drippings. Liberally brush the ribs with the sauce and then braai the ribs over **direct medium heat** for 3–5 minutes. Brush the ribs again with more sauce, turn them over and braai for a further 3–5 minutes. Transfer the ribs to a platter and allow to rest for 5 minutes. Serve with the remaining sauce.

LEG OF LAMB WITH MOROCCAN SPICES

SERVES: 6–8
PREP TIME: 20 MINUTES
MARINATING TIME: 1 HOUR

HEAT: DIRECT HIGH HEAT 230°–290°C (450°–550°F)
BRAAIING TIME: 25–30 MINUTES

MARINADE
- 125 ml chopped onion
- 1 tablespoon grated lemon zest
- 4 tablespoons fresh lemon juice
- 3 tablespoons extra-virgin olive oil
- 2 garlic cloves
- 1½ teaspoons crushed chilli flakes
- 1 teaspoon ground coriander
- 1 teaspoon ground cumin
- 1 teaspoon paprika
- 1 teaspoon ground ginger
- 1 teaspoon coarse sea salt

1 deboned leg of lamb, about 1.25 kg, butterflied and trimmed of any excess fat and sinew

1. Combine the marinade ingredients in a food processor and pulse to make a smooth paste, scraping down the sides of the bowl as necessary. Place the lamb in a large, resealable plastic bag and pour in the marinade. Press the air out of the bag and seal tightly. Turn the bag to distribute the marinade and refrigerate for 1 hour. Allow the lamb to stand at room temperature for 20–30 minutes before cooking. Prepare the braai for direct and indirect cooking over high heat.

2. Remove the lamb from the bag, letting the marinade cling to the lamb. Discard the marinade in the bag. Brush the cooking grates clean. Braai the lamb over **direct high heat** for about 6 minutes, with the lid closed as much as possible but turning once, until nicely browned on both sides. Slide the lamb over **indirect high heat** and cook, with the lid closed, to your desired doneness, 15–20 minutes for medium rare. Remove the lamb from the braai and allow to rest for about 5 minutes before carving. Cut the lamb across the grain into thin diagonal slices and serve warm.

HOW TO BUTTERFLY A LEG OF LAMB

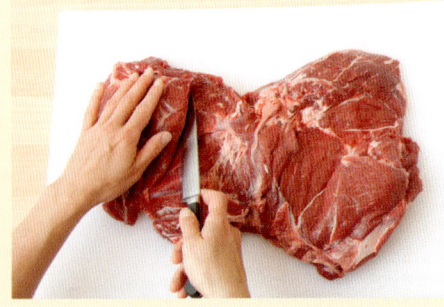  

1. A deboned leg of lamb is actually several muscles held together. The different muscles have various shapes and thicknesses.

2. In order to braai the whole leg evenly, you need to make the thickest parts thinner.

3. You do that by making angled cuts at the thickness you want and then spreading the meat open like a book.

TROPICAL TRI-TIP ROAST WITH ORANGE BARBECUE SAUCE

SERVES: 6

PREP TIME: 20 MINUTES

HEAT: DIRECT AND INDIRECT MEDIUM HEAT 180°–230°C (350°–450°F)

BRAAIING TIME: 23–30 MINUTES

PASTE
- 2 tablespoons extra-virgin olive oil
- 2 tablespoons finely chopped fresh ginger
- 2 tablespoons light brown sugar
- 2 teaspoons coarse sea salt
- 2 teaspoons finely chopped garlic
- 1 teaspoon chilli-garlic sauce (Sriracha or Sambal Olek)

- 1 top flap of rump (tri-tip roast) about 1 kg and 3 cm thick, excess fat and silver skin removed

SAUCE
- 250 ml thawed frozen orange juice concentrate
- 2 tablespoons packed light brown sugar
- 2 tablespoons cider vinegar
- 2 tablespoons soy sauce

1. Combine the paste ingredients in a bowl. Coat the meat evenly with the paste and allow to stand at room temperature for 20–30 minutes before cooking. Prepare the braai for direct and indirect cooking over medium heat.

2. Combine the sauce ingredients in a saucepan over medium heat and bubble for 10–15 minutes, whisking frequently, until thickened and reduced to about 175 ml. Set aside and reheat just before serving.

3. Brush the cooking grates clean. Braai the joint over **direct medium heat** for 8–10 minutes, turning once, until well marked on both sides. Move the meat over **indirect medium heat** and cook to your desired doneness (15–20 minutes for medium rare). Keep the lid closed as much as possible during cooking but turn the meat every 5 minutes or so. Remove the meat from the braai, cover with heavyweight foil and allow it to rest for 5–10 minutes. Cut the joint across the grain into thin slices. Serve warm with the sauce on the side.

It is the paste, which features fresh ginger, that gives this Hawaiian-style roast such great flavour. Before chopping the ginger, scrape off the skin with the back of a spoon. Take care not to overcook the joint; this is a very lean cut of meat and it is best served medium rare.

HOW TO PREP BEEF FILLET

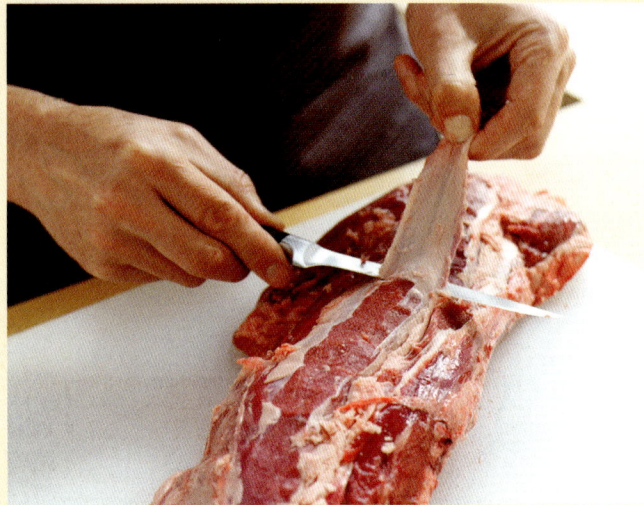

1. Slide a sharp knife just under any large clumps of fat, being careful not to cut into the meat. Remove the strips of silver skin, which are tough and chewy.

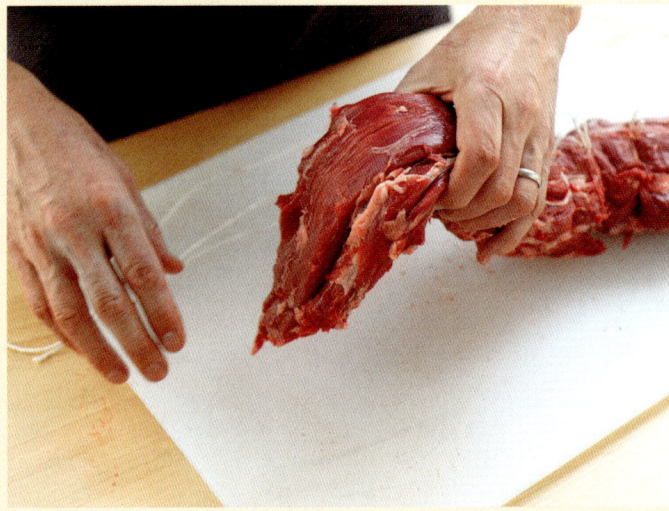

2. Tie the trimmed joint every couple of centimetres to make it even and compact. Because the tail is thinner than the rest of the joint, fold it underneath and tie it snugly for an even thickness end to end.

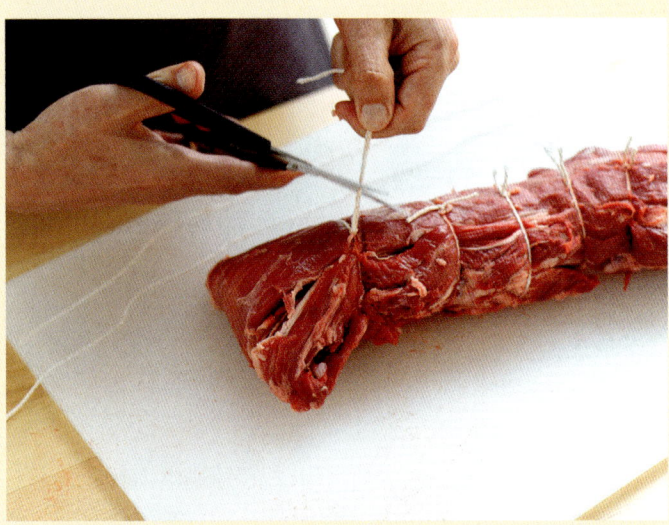

3. Cut off the loose ends of the string.

4. Rub oil all over the joint and season it with herbs and spices.

5. Braai the joint first over direct heat to brown it on all sides.

6. Finish cooking over indirect heat so that the exterior does not burn before the interior is cooked.

HERB-CRUSTED BEEF FILLET WITH WHITE WINE CREAM SAUCE

SERVES: 10–12
PREP TIME: 40 MINUTES

HEAT: DIRECT AND INDIRECT MEDIUM HEAT 180°–230°C (350°–450°F)
BRAAIING TIME: 35–45 MINUTES
SPECIAL EQUIPMENT: BUTCHER'S STRING

RUB
- 1½ tablespoons dried tarragon
- 2½ teaspoons coarse sea salt
- 2 teaspoons freshly ground black pepper
- 1½ teaspoons dried thyme
- 1 teaspoon dried sage

- 1 whole beef fillet, 3 kg, untrimmed
- Extra-virgin olive oil

SAUCE
- 125 ml finely chopped shallot
- 125 ml rice vinegar
- 1½ teaspoons dried tarragon
- ¼ teaspoon dried thyme
- 125 ml dry white wine
- 125 ml chicken stock
- 350 ml whipping cream
- 125 ml flat-leaf (Italian) parsley, finey chopped

Coarse sea salt

1. Mix the rub ingredients together in a small bowl.

2. Trim and discard the excess fat and silver skin from the fillet. Part of the thin 'tail' end of the fillet may separate as it is trimmed, but leave it connected to the main muscle as much as possible. Lie the fillet out flat and straight, with the smoothest side up, aligning the narrow pieces at the tail end. Neatly fold the tail end under itself to form an even thickness (one end may be larger). Tie the joint snugly with butcher's string at 5-cm intervals. Secure the folded end with two strings. Lightly coat the joint with oil, then season it all over with the rub.

3. Allow the prepared joint to stand at room temperature for 30–60 minutes before cooking. Prepare the braai for direct and indirect cooking over medium heat.

4. Combine the shallot, vinegar, tarragon and thyme in a large frying pan over high heat, and cook for 3–4 minutes, stirring often until the vinegar evaporates. Add the wine and stock and boil for 3–4 minutes until reduced to about 125 ml. Add the cream and continue boiling for a further 5–7 minutes until the surface is covered with large, shiny bubbles and the sauce is reduced to about 375 ml. Remove the pan from the heat, adjust the seasonings and set aside. Reheat and add the parsley just before serving.

5. Brush the cooking grates clean. Sear the joint over **direct medium heat** for about 15 minutes, turning a quarter turn once every 3–4 minutes. Slide the joint over **indirect medium heat** and cook, turning once, until it reaches your desired doneness, 20–30 minutes for medium rare. Keep the lid closed as much as possible during cooking. Remove the joint from the braai, loosely cover with foil and allow to rest for 10–15 minutes. The internal temperature will rise during this time.

6. Snip and remove all the string from the joint. Cut the meat crossways into slices 1–2.5 cm thick. Season to taste with salt. Serve warm with the sauce.

HOW TO PREP BONELESS RIB ROAST

1. For a special occasion, consider buying a rib roast a few days before you plan to serve it and dry-ageing it in your refrigerator. (For safety reasons, never do this for more than 4 days.) Patted dry and set on a rack over a roasting tray in the refrigerator, the meat will develop more concentrated flavours and a softer texture.

2. After you have seasoned the meat, allow it to stand at room temperature for 30–40 minutes so that the outer ring of the joint won't overcook before the centre reaches your ideal temperature on the braai.

HOW TO SMOKE A BONELESS RIB ROAST

1. Spread a layer or two of lit coals on one side of the charcoal grate. Position some wood chunks alongside the coals. On the opposite side, set up a water tray, which will absorb some heat and release it slowly.

2. Initially position the joint over the water tray with the thicker side of the meat toward the coals.

3. An instant-read thermometer takes all the guesswork out of doneness. For medium rare, remove the joint when it hits the 49°–52°C (120°–125°F) range. The internal temperature will climb as the meat rests.

The sweet, haunting aromas of smouldering wood are a distinctive part of this recipe. Bags of hardwood are readily available, but if you happen to have dried logs lying around, you can make your own chunks. Saw the logs into smaller sections and use a chisel and hammer to break off most of the bark, as it tends to add a bit of bitterness to the smoke. Then split the wood into fist-sized pieces. Unlike wood chips, larger chunks don't need to be soaked beforehand. Placed alongside the coals, they will burn slowly and permeate the meat with a taste of the great outdoors.

WOOD-SMOKED BONELESS RIB ROAST WITH SHIRAZ SAUCE

SERVES: 10
PREP TIME: 30 MINUTES

HEAT: INDIRECT MEDIUM HEAT 180°–190°C (350°–375°F)
BRAAIING TIME: ABOUT 1½ HOURS
SPECIAL EQUIPMENT: LARGE DISPOSABLE FOIL TRAY, INSTANT-READ THERMOMETER

- 1 boneless rib roast, about 2.5 kg, trimmed of excess surface fat
- Coarse sea salt
- Freshly ground black pepper
- 4 tablespoons Dijon mustard
- 80 ml coarsely chopped onion
- 3 garlic cloves, finely chopped
- 2 hardwood chunks (not soaked)

SAUCE

- 3 tablespoons cold unsalted butter
- 3 tablespoons finely chopped shallot or small onion
- 1 garlic clove, finely chopped
- 1 litre beef stock, preferably home-made
- 375 ml Shiraz wine
- 1 tablespoon soy sauce
- 1½ teaspoons tomato paste
- ¼ teaspoon dried thyme
- ½ bay leaf

1. Season the joint with sea salt and black pepper. Mix the mustard, onion and garlic together in a small bowl. Spread the mixture over the top of the joint and allow it to stand at room temperature for 30–40 minutes before cooking.

2. Prepare the braai for indirect cooking over medium heat (see instructions at left). Place 2 hardwood chunks alongside the coals. Brush the cooking grates clean. Position the joint with the thicker side facing the coals. Braai over **indirect medium heat** for about 1½ hours, with the lid closed as much as possible but rotating the joint 180 degrees halfway through the cooking time, until the internal temperature reaches 49°–52°C (120°–125°F) for medium rare. Keep the braai temperature between 180° and 190°C (350°–375°F).

3. Melt 1 tablespoon of the butter in a heavy-based saucepan over a medium heat (keep the remaining butter refrigerated). Add the shallot and cook for about 2 minutes until softened. Add the garlic and cook for about 1 minute until fragrant. Add the stock, wine, soy sauce, tomato paste, thyme and bay leaf. Bring to a boil over high heat and cook for about 30 minutes, uncovered, until reduced to about 500 ml. Season to taste with salt and pepper. Remove the bay leaf and keep the sauce warm.

4. Remove the joint from the braai, loosely cover with foil and rest for 20–30 minutes. The internal temperature will rise during this time. Carve the joint into 1-cm slices, reserving the juices. Just before serving, whisk the remaining cold butter into the sauce and stir in the carving juices. Serve warm with the sauce.

HOW TO SMOKE BRISKET

1. The first layer of flavour to apply is the sweet heat of a good spice rub and mustard. Next, cook the seasoned brisket on a smoker for 4–5 hours so that it absorbs a good amount of flavourful wood smoke. Place the brisket in a large disposable foil tray to catch the juices, with the layer of fat on top so that it bastes the meat below it.

2. When the internal temperature of the meat reaches 70°C (160°F), take it out of the foil roasting tray and wrap the brisket in two layers of heavyweight foil. This will trap some moisture and help to break down the tough fibres in the meat.

3. When the internal temperature reaches 88°–90.5°C (190°–195°F) in the thickest section, remove the brisket from the smoker and allow the precious meat juices to collect in the foil. The brisket will stay warm and continue to cook for an hour or two.

4. Carefully unwrap the foil, set the brisket aside, and bend the foil to funnel the juices into a serving bowl.

5. Slice a section of fat from the top side of the brisket so that you can see which way the grain of the meat runs. For the sake of tenderness, you want to slice against the grain.

6. Slice the brisket thinly with a sharp knife. That beautiful pink ring is a result of the wood smoke. Spoon the meat juices over the top and enjoy eating it.

SMOKED BRISKET

SERVES: 6
PREP TIME: 15 MINUTES
MARINATING TIME: 6–8 HOURS

HEAT: INDIRECT LOW HEAT 110°–130°C (225°–250°F)
SMOKING TIME: 6–8 HOURS, PLUS 1–2 HOURS RESTING TIME
SPECIAL EQUIPMENT: LARGE DISPOSABLE FOIL TRAY, INSTANT-READ THERMOMETER

RUB
- 4 teaspoons coarse sea salt
- 2 teaspoons chilli powder
- 2 teaspoons light brown sugar
- 2 teaspoons garlic flakes
- 2 teaspoons smoked paprika
- 1 teaspoon celery seed
- 1 teaspoon coarsely ground black pepper

- 1 brisket (flat cut), about 2.5 kg, untrimmed
- 4 tablespoons prepared American (yellow) mustard
- 6 hardwood chunks (not soaked)
- 500 ml favourite barbecue sauce

1. Mix the rub ingredients together in a small bowl.

2. Place the brisket, fat side up, on a large chopping board. Trim the layer of fat to a 1-cm thickness. Turn the brisket over and trim any hard fat or thin membrane covering the meat.

3. Season the brisket evenly with the mustard and then the rub. Cover and refrigerate for 6–8 hours.

4. Place the brisket, fat side up, in a large disposable foil tray.

5. Prepare your smoker, following manufacturer's instructions, for indirect cooking over low heat.

6. Place the tray with the brisket on the cooking grate. Smoke the brisket for 4–5 hours, starting with 2 chunks of hardwood, at 110°–130°C (225°–250°F), until the internal temperature of the meat reaches 70°–77°C (160°–170°F). Every hour or so, add another chunk of hardwood to the coals and, if necessary, add more coals to maintain the temperature of the smoker at 110°–130°C (225°–250°F).

7. When the internal temperature of the meat has reached 70°–77°C (160°–170°F), the collagen in the meat will have dissolved. At that point, remove the brisket and tray from the smoker (close the lid to maintain the heat). Baste the brisket with some of the juices and fat collected in the tray. Then wrap the joint in 2 large sheets of heavyweight foil. Discard the tray.

8. Return the brisket to the smoker and cook for 2–3 hours, without adding any more hardwood chunks, until the internal temperature of the brisket has reached 88°–90°C (190°–195°F) in the thickest section. The probe of the thermometer should slide in and out of the brisket with just a little resistance.

9. Remove the brisket from the smoker and allow to rest inside the foil at room temperature for 1–2 hours. It will stay hot and continue to tenderize.

10. Carefully unwrap the brisket, being careful not to lose any of the juices inside the foil. Move the brisket to a large chopping board and pour the juices into a small bowl.

11. If necessary, cut off a small chunk of brisket to identify the direction of the grain. Cut the brisket across the grain into 3-mm slices. Spoon or brush some of the juices over the slices. Serve warm with barbecue sauce on the side.

Brisket is the Mt. Everest of smoking. Not only is it huge, but it also poses challenges all along the way. If your first couple of attempts don't work out exactly as you had hoped, persevere. The rewards of mastering your own smoked brisket are unspeakably good. Among a cadre of outdoor cooks, you will have earned long-standing respect and admiration.

PORK

TECHNIQUES

96	How to braai **BRATWURST**
100	How to braai pork **CHOPS**: Five things you need to know
102	How to make pork **ESCALOPES**
102	How to braai pork **ESCALOPES**
105	How to braai pork **CHOPS** with Sofrito Barbecue Sauce
110	How to make rotisserie pork **LOIN**
112	How to braai bone-in pork **LOIN**
114	How to braai pork **SHOULDER**
116	How to make **PORCHETTA**
118	How to season a pork **JOINT**
118	How to braai a pork **JOINT**
120	How to braai pork **RIBS**: Five things you need to know
121	How to prep **BABY BACK RIBS**
121	How to set up a charcoal braai for **SMOKING**
122	How to braai **BABY BACK RIBS**
124	How to braai **STACKED RIBS**
126	How to prep **ST. LOUIS-STYLE RIBS**
126	How to use the '**TEXAS CRUTCH**'
128	How to cook **SPARERIBS** on a smoker

RECIPES

97	Cider-simmered **BRATWURST** with Apples and Onions
98	Pork **BURGERS** with Apple-Tarragon Slaw
99	Buttermilk Scones with Chilli Jam-glazed **HAM**
101	Cider-brined Pork **CHOPS** with Grilled Apples
103	Pork **ESCALOPES** with Romesco Sauce
104	**PORK**, Roasted Pepper and Cheddar Sandwiches
105	Pork **LOIN CHOPS** with Sofrito Barbecue Sauce
106	Pork **FILLETS** with Creamy Corn
107	Pork **FILLETS** with Smoked Paprika Rouille
108	Pork **MEDALLIONS** with Asian Black Bean Sauce
109	Pork **LOIN** with Cherry-Chipotle Glaze
111	Rotisserie Pork **LOIN** with Red Wine and Prune Sauce
113	Smoke-roasted Pork **LOIN** with Redcurrant Sauce
115	**PULLED PORK** Sandwiches
117	Porchetta-style Pork **SHOULDER**
119	Latino Pork **ROAST**
122	Slow Good **BABY BACK RIBS** with Soo-Wee Sauce
125	Stacked **BABY BACK RIBS**
127	Sweet Ginger and Soy-glazed **SPARERIBS**
129	Slow-smoked **SPARERIBS** with Sweet-and-sour Barbecue Sauce
130	Tamarind-glazed **COUNTRY-STYLE RIBS**
131	Chilli Verde **COUNTRY-STYLE RIBS**

HOW TO BRAAI BRATWURST

1. Before cooking, prick several small holes in each bratwurst to prevent them from bursting open.

2. For the first stage of braaiing, you will need a very hot fire on one side of the cooking grate.

3. Arrange the bratwurst in a single layer in a large foil tray with the cider or sparkling apple juice and sliced onions.

4. Simmer the bratwurst for about 20 minutes, turning them occasionally. If the liquid starts to boil, slide the tray over indirect heat.

5. Strain the onions and return them to the tray to caramelize with brown sugar.

6. Finish braaiing the bratwurst over direct heat to lightly char the surfaces.

CIDER-SIMMERED BRATWURST WITH APPLES AND ONIONS

SERVES: 5
PREP TIME: 15 MINUTES

HEAT: DIRECT HIGH HEAT 230°–290°C (450°–550°F)
AND DIRECT MEDIUM HEAT 180°–230°C (350°–450°F)
BRAAIING TIME: 6–8 MINUTES
SPECIAL EQUIPMENT: 2 LARGE DISPOSABLE FOIL TRAYS

MUSTARD
    2 tablespoons apple sauce
    2 tablespoons Dijon mustard
    2 tablespoons wholegrain mustard

    750 ml premium cider or sparkling apple juice
    2 onions, halved and cut into 5-mm slices
    5 fresh bratwurst, pierced several times
    1 tablespoon brown sugar
    5 hot dog rolls, halved lengthways
    2 Granny Smith apples, cored and thinly sliced

1. Mix the mustard ingredients together in a small bowl. Cover and allow to stand at room temperature until ready to serve.

2. Prepare the braai for direct and indirect cooking over high heat. Brush the cooking grates clean. Put the cider or apple juice, onions and bratwurst into a large disposable foil tray. Place the tray over **direct high heat** and bring the liquid to a simmer. Keep the braai lid closed as much as possible, but turn the bratwurst occasionally, until they are evenly coloured and have lost their raw look, about 20 minutes. If the liquid starts to boil, move the tray over indirect heat to prevent the bratwurst from splitting open.

3. Lower the temperature of the braai to medium heat. Transfer the bratwurst to another large foil tray. Strain the onions in a colander over the tray with the bratwurst (the liquid will keep the bratwurst warm while you cook the onions). Return the onions to the original tray and stir in the brown sugar. Cook the onions over **direct medium heat** for about 15 minutes, with the lid closed as much as possible but stirring occasionally, until they are golden brown. Move the onions over indirect heat to keep them warm.

4. Remove the bratwurst from the liquid and braai them over **direct medium heat** for 6–8 minutes, turning once or twice, until browned. During the last minute, place the rolls on the braai to toast.

5. Place the bratwurst in the rolls. Spread each with the mustard, and top with the glazed onions and a few apple slices. Serve hot.

One key to the juiciness of these burgers is mixing apple sauce into the minced pork. Another key is including green apples in the slaw. A box grater conveniently separates the moist flesh of a cored apple from its tough skin.

PORK BURGERS WITH APPLE-TARRAGON SLAW

SERVES: 4
PREP TIME: 20 MINUTES

HEAT: DIRECT MEDIUM HEAT 180°–230°C (350°–450°F)
BRAAIING TIME: 12–15 MINUTES

SLAW
    175 g thinly sliced green cabbage
    125 ml coarsely grated green apple
    125 ml coarsely grated carrot
    2 tablespoons finely chopped fresh tarragon
    2 tablespoons cider vinegar
    1 tablespoon sugar
    ½ teaspoon celery seed
    ¼ teaspoon coarse sea salt

BURGERS
    750 g pork mince
    80 ml apple sauce
    1½ teaspoons coarse sea salt
    1 teaspoon Tabasco, or to taste
    ½ teaspoon freshly ground black pepper

    4 hamburger rolls, split in half

1. Mix the slaw ingredients together in a large bowl. Cover and refrigerate until ready to assemble the burgers.

2. Gently mix the burger ingredients together in a large bowl. Shape into 4 equal-size burgers, each about 1.5 cm thick. With your thumb or the back of a spoon, make a shallow indentation about 2.5 cm wide in the centre of each burger. Prepare the braai for direct cooking over medium heat.

3. Brush the cooking grates clean. Braai the burgers over **direct medium heat** for 12–15 minutes with the lid closed as much as possible, but turning once when the burgers release easily from the grate without sticking, until cooked through. During the last minute of cooking time, toast the rolls, cut sides down, over **direct medium heat**. Place the burgers on the rolls and top with the slaw. Serve warm.

BUTTERMILK SCONES WITH CHILLI JAM–GLAZED HAM

SERVES: 6
PREP TIME: 20 MINUTES

HEAT: INDIRECT HIGH HEAT ABOUT 200°C (400°F)
AND DIRECT MEDIUM HEAT 180°–230°C (350°–450°F)
BRAAIING TIME: 16–21 MINUTES

SCONES
  550 g flour
  4 teaspoons baking powder
  1 teaspoon bicarbonate of soda
  1 teaspoon salt
  250 g cold Wooden Spoon white margarine
  350 ml cold buttermilk
  1 tablespoon unsalted butter, melted

  250 g chilli jam
  1 kg gammon or kassler steaks, about 1 cm thick

1. Prepare the braai for indirect cooking over high heat.

2. Combine the flour, baking powder, bicarbonate of soda and salt in a large bowl. Cut in the white margarine with your fingertips or a pastry blender until the mixture resembles coarse breadcrumbs. Add the buttermilk and stir just until the mixture sticks together. Turn the dough out onto a lightly floured surface and knead lightly for 20–30 seconds. Lightly dust your hands with flour and gently pat out the dough to a thickness of about 1.5 cm. Dip a 6-cm round biscuit cutter into flour and cut out 12 rounds of dough. Gather any scraps of dough and pat together, using a light touch so you don't overwork the dough. Place the scones close together on a greased baking tray. Brush the tops with melted butter.

3. Cook the tray of scones over **indirect high heat** for 12–15 minutes, until they are lightly browned. Keep the temperature as close to 200°C (400°F) as possible but check occasionally and move or rotate the tray as needed so that the base of the scones doesn't burn. Remove the scones from the braai and set aside to keep warm.

4. Prepare the braai for direct cooking over medium heat.

5. In a small saucepan over low heat, warm one-third of the chilli jam until it melts. Brush the cooking grates clean. Braai the gammon steaks over **direct medium heat** for 4–6 minutes, with the lid closed as much as possible, turning once and basting with the chilli jam before and after turning, until the gammon is nicely marked and crispy on the edges.

6. Cut the gammon into pieces about the same size as the scones. Split each scone horizontally. Serve the gammon warm in the scones with the remaining chilli jam on top.

HOW TO MAKE BUTTERMILK SCONES

1. Mix the dry ingredients in a medium bowl. Add cold white margarine and use a pastry blender or fork to 'cut it in' until the mixture resembles coarse crumbs with a few larger clumps.

2. Add buttermilk and stir just until the mixture comes together.

3. On a floured surface, pat the dough into a circle about 1.5 cm thick. Use a floured biscuit cutter to cut out rounds of dough.

HOW TO BRAAI PORK CHOPS
5 THINGS YOU NEED TO KNOW

1 NOT YOUR GRANDFATHER'S PORK
Today's pigs come to market younger and smaller than the pigs of yesteryear. They have had less time to develop much collagen and connective tissue – that is, the stuff that can make pork chewy. Therefore, pork chops are definitely tender enough for braaiing. That's the good news.

2 IT'S BRINE TIME
The bad news is that today's pigs are also much leaner than the pigs of yesteryear. In fact, pork chops are about as lean as chicken today, which means it doesn't take long for them to dry out on the braai. So it is always a good idea to brine pork chops first. Brining means soaking them in a flavourful salty liquid that the meat can absorb, giving them more moisture (and flavour) from the start.

3 CHOOSE YOUR CHOP WELL
Pork chops are cut from a pig's loin, which runs from the shoulder to the hip. The chops from the shoulder (blade chops and country-style ribs) are the most marbled and flavourful, but also the chewiest of the group. Chops from the hip (chump chops) are quite dry and tough, so I don't recommend those for braaiing. Chops from the mid-section of the loin (rib chops and loin chops) can be quite tender and juicy, if you braai them right.

4 EASY DOES IT
We don't serve pork chops charred on the outside and rare or medium rare in the middle, like steaks. We serve them with a relatively even doneness from top to bottom. This means a gentler heat on the braai so that the centres of the chops can reach the right degree of doneness well before the outsides are overdone.

5 THAT TOUCH OF PINK
There is really only one correct doneness level for pork chops. You'll know it when you see it and when you taste it. As the chop cooks, the colour of the meat inside will turn from reddish-pink to a very light pink. That's it. Stop there. If you cook pork chops any further than that, the meat will be grey and bland.

Good braaiing is all about layering flavours from the inside out. In this recipe, the pork chops benefit dramatically from a flavoursome brine that penetrates right to the centre of the meat, plus an apple-brandy glaze that coats the outside.

CIDER-BRINED PORK CHOPS WITH GRILLED APPLES

SERVES: 4
PREP TIME: 15 MINUTES
BRINING TIME: 1–1½ HOURS

HEAT: DIRECT MEDIUM HEAT 180°–230°C (350°–450°F)
BRAAIING TIME: ABOUT 12 MINUTES

BRINE
    350 ml premium cider or sparkling apple juice
    100 g coarse sea salt
    1 tablespoon dried rosemary
    1 tablespoon dried sage
    1½ teaspoons dried thyme
    ½ teaspoon whole black peppercorns

    4 centre-cut pork loin chops, each about 350 g and 3.5 cm thick, trimmed of excess fat
    Extra-virgin olive oil

GLAZE
    6 tablespoons apple jelly
    2 tablespoons unsalted butter
    2 tablespoons Calvados or brandy

    4 Granny Smith apples, each cut into 6 wedges and cores removed

1. Mix the brine ingredients together in a large bowl. Put the chops into a large, resealable plastic bag and pour in the brine. Press the air out of the bag and seal tightly. Place the bag in a bowl or a rimmed dish and refrigerate for 1–1½ hours, turning the bag every 30 minutes.

2. Remove the chops from the bag and discard the brine. Rinse the chops under cold water and pat dry with roller towels. Lightly brush the chops with oil and allow to stand at room temperature for 20–30 minutes before cooking. Prepare the braai for direct cooking over medium heat.

3. Warm the apple jelly and butter in a small saucepan over medium-low heat, stirring until the jelly melts. Remove from the heat and stir in the Calvados. If the glaze cools, reheat gently until fluid. Set aside half of the glaze to serve as a sauce with the grilled pork. Brush the remaining glaze over the apple slices and then the chops.

4. Brush the cooking grates clean. Cook the chops over **direct medium heat** for about 10 minutes, with the lid closed as much as possible but turning once, until they are slightly pink in the centre. Remove the chops from the braai and allow to rest for 3–5 minutes. While they rest, cook the apples over **direct medium heat** for about 2 minutes, turning once, until crisp-tender. Serve the chops and apples warm with the reserved glaze.

HOW TO PREP LEEKS

1. Remove the tough green tops from small, slender leeks and trim off just enough of the root end to get rid of the stringy parts.

2. Cut each leek in half lengthways to expose the many layers inside, making sure to leave some root end intact so that the layers remain attached.

3. Because leeks grow underground, you will often find dirt and sand trapped between the layers. Spread the layers open under running water to clean them before braaiing.

HOW TO MAKE PORK ESCALOPES

1. Begin with deboned pork loin chops at least 2.5 cm thick. Cut into the middle of the fat side to within about 1 cm of the other side, so that each chop opens up like a butterfly.

2. Flatten the meat with the palm of your hand and trim off any excess fat around the perimeter.

3. Lay each chop between 2 large sheets of clingfilm. Use the flat side of a meat tenderizer (or the base of a small, heavy frying pan) to flatten the meat to an even thickness of about 5 mm.

HOW TO BRAAI PORK ESCALOPES

1. While thick pork chops and steaks do best over medium heat, thinly pounded escalopes should be braaiied quickly over very high heat.

2. Cook the first side of each escalope with the lid closed until it has nice grill marks, usually about 3 minutes.

3. The second side should need no more than 1 minute to finish cooking.

PORK ESCALOPES WITH ROMESCO SAUCE

SERVES: 4
PREP TIME: 25 MINUTES

HEAT: DIRECT LOW HEAT 130°–180°C (250°–350°F) AND DIRECT HIGH HEAT 230°–290°C (450°–550°F)
BRAAIING TIME: 19–24 MINUTES

- 4 deboned pork loin chops, 170–200 g each and about 2.5 cm thick
- Extra-virgin olive oil
- Coarse sea salt
- Freshly ground black pepper
- 8 small leeks, no wider than 2.5 cm in diameter, optional

SAUCE
- 100 g roasted red pepper, roughly chopped
- 80 ml slivered almonds, toasted
- 1 tablespoon tomato purée
- 1 tablespoon extra-virgin olive oil
- 1 tablespoon fresh lemon juice
- 1 teaspoon roughly chopped garlic
- ½ teaspoon paprika
- ⅛ teaspoon ground cayenne pepper

- 1 tablespoon Italian (flat-leaf) parsley, finely chopped

1. Butterfly each chop from the fat side and trim them of excess fat. One at a time, place each chop between 2 sheets of clingfilm and pound to an even 5 mm thickness. Lightly brush or spray the escalopes with oil and season all sides with salt and pepper.

2. Remove the dark green tops from each leek, cutting about 5 cm above the point where the leaves begin to darken. Trim just enough of each root end to remove the stringy parts, but leaving enough so that the layers remain attached. Cut each leek in half lengthways and remove the tough outer leaves. Rinse the leeks under water, opening up the layers to remove any dirt, then pat dry. Lightly coat the leeks with oil and season to taste with salt and pepper.

3. Prepare the braai for direct cooking over low heat.

4. Brush the cooking grates clean. Braai the leeks over **direct low heat** for 15–20 minutes, with the lid closed as much as possible but turning the leeks every couple of minutes for even cooking, and moving them over indirect heat if they become too dark before they are tender, until softened and slightly charred on all sides.

5. Combine the sauce ingredients in a food processor or blender, pulsing until you get a semi-smooth consistency. Season to taste with salt.

6. Increase the temperature of the braai to high heat. Brush the cooking grates clean. Braai the escalopes over **direct high heat** for about 3 minutes on the first side, turning when the meat is nicely marked. The second side will need only a minute to finish cooking.

7. Transfer the escalopes, with the first grilled side facing up, to a serving platter or individual plates. Divide the sauce evenly and spoon over the meat. Arrange two leeks on top of each escalope. Garnish with some parsley over the top.

Once the rolls are assembled, you can reheat the meat and melt the cheese by wrapping each roll in baking paper or foil and braaiing them over direct medium heat, turning them occasionally.

PORK, ROASTED PEPPER AND CHEDDAR ROLLS

SERVES: 4
PREP TIME: 30 MINUTES
MARINATING TIME: 30 MINUTES

HEAT: DIRECT HIGH HEAT 230°–290°C (450°–550°F)
AND DIRECT MEDIUM HEAT 180°–230°C (350°–450°F)
BRAAIING TIME: 18–22 MINUTES

MARINADE
- 2 tablespoons fresh lemon juice
- 1 teaspoon dried origanum
- 1 teaspoon finely chopped fresh rosemary
- 1 teaspoon finely chopped garlic
- 1 teaspoon coarse sea salt
- ¼ teaspoon crushed red chilli flakes
- 80 ml extra-virgin olive oil

- 6 deboned pork loin chops, each 60–120 g and about 1–1.5 cm thick, trimmed of excess fat
- 2 red peppers
- 4 crusty rolls, split in half
- 4 slices Cheddar cheese
- 250 ml baby spinach leaves, rinsed and dried

1. Combine the lemon juice, origanum, rosemary, garlic, salt and chilli flakes in a small bowl, then whisk in the oil. Reserve 2 tablespoons of the marinade to use as a dressing.

2. Working with 1 chop at a time, place each chop between 2 sheets of clingfilm. Using a flat meat tenderizer, pound the steak until it is an even 5 mm thick. When all the chops are pounded, place them in a single layer in a large, resealable plastic bag and pour in the marinade. Press the air out of the bag and seal tightly. Turn the bag to distribute the marinade, place the bag on a plate, and allow to marinate at room temperature for 30 minutes. Prepare the braai for direct cooking over a high heat.

3. Brush the cooking grates clean. Braai the peppers over **direct high heat** for 10–12 minutes, with the lid closed as much as possible but turning every 3–5 minutes, until blackened and blistered all over. Place the peppers in a bowl, cover with clingfilm and allow to stand for 10–15 minutes. Remove the peppers from the bowl and peel away and discard the charred skins. Cut off the tops and remove the seeds. Cut lengthways into 1 cm-wide strips.

4. Remove the chops from the bag and discard the marinade. Sear the chops over **direct high heat** for about 4 minutes, with the lid closed as much as possible but turning once. During the last minute of cooking, toast the cut sides of the rolls over direct heat.

5. In a bowl, toss the spinach with the 2 tablespoons of reserved marinade. Build the rolls with 1–1½ pork chops, cut to fit the roll, a slice of cheese, strips of roasted pepper and baby spinach.

6. Lower the temperature of the braai to a medium heat. Completely wrap each roll in a 30 × 30 cm sheet of baking paper or foil, twisting the ends in opposite directions to enclose the filling. Braai over **direct medium heat** for 4–6 minutes until the cheese melts and the rolls are hot. Serve warm.

PORK LOIN CHOPS
WITH SOFRITO BARBECUE SAUCE

SERVES: 4
PREP TIME: 30 MINUTES

HEAT: DIRECT MEDIUM HEAT 180°–230°C (350°–450°F)
BRAAIING TIME: 7–9 MINUTES

SAUCE
- 250 g onion, cut into 5 mm dice
- 3 tablespoons extra-virgin olive oil
- 1 small bay leaf
- 1 tablespoon finely chopped garlic
- 1 tablespoon sherry vinegar
- 125 ml apple juice
- 1 can (425 g) chopped tomatoes
- 1 teaspoon paprika
- ½ teaspoon dried origanum
- ¼ teaspoon crushed red chilli flakes
- ¼ teaspoon coarse sea salt
- ¼ teaspoon freshly ground black pepper

RUB
- 1 teaspoon coarse sea salt
- ½ teaspoon paprika
- ½ teaspoon dried origanum
- ½ teaspoon freshly ground black pepper

- 4 bone-in pork loin chops, each 2–2.5 cm thick
- Extra-virgin olive oil

1. Combine the onion, oil and bay leaf in a frying pan over a medium heat. When the onion starts to sizzle, adjust the heat to medium-low and cook for about 30 minutes, stirring frequently and adding the garlic after 15 minutes, until the onions are evenly browned and caramelized. Add the vinegar and cook until it has almost evaporated. Then add the apple juice and simmer until the liquid in the pan has reduced by half. Add the rest of the sauce ingredients and continue to simmer gently for about 5 minutes.

2. Remove the bay leaf. Transfer the sauce to a food processor or blender and purée until smooth. Reserve 125 ml of the sauce for basting and keep the rest to serve with the chops.

3. Combine the rub ingredients in a small bowl. Lightly coat the chops with oil and season with the rub. Allow the chops to stand at room temperature for 20–30 minutes before cooking. Prepare the braai for direct cooking over high heat.

4. Brush the cooking grates clean. Braai the chops over **direct medium heat** for 4–5 minutes, with the lid closed as much as possible but turning once, until they are nicely marked on each side. Then brush both sides with the reserved sauce and continue braaiing for 3–4 minutes, turning once or twice, until the sauce cooks into the meat a bit and the centres are barely pink. Remove the chops from the braai and allow to rest for 2–3 minutes. Serve warm with the reserved sauce.

HOW TO BRAAI PORK CHOPS WITH SOFRITO BARBECUE SAUCE

1. In Spain and throughout much of Latin America, it is common to begin sauces with a *sofrito*, which is slowly browned onions and garlic followed by tomatoes.

2. When combined with apple juice and spices, this *sofrito* becomes a barbecue sauce. Use it for brushing onto the chops and as a dipping sauce.

3. Mark the pork chops well on both sides before brushing on the sauce. Then let the flavours of the sauce cook into the meat.

To remove the tough silver skin from the surface, slip the tip of a narrow, sharp knife under a piece of silver skin. Then grab the loosened end and stretch it taut. Slide the knife just over the pinkish meat below, angling it upwards to avoid cutting into the meat. The goal is to 'clean' the fillets without losing any more meat than necessary.

PORK FILLETS WITH CREAMY CORN

SERVES: 4–6
PREP TIME: 25 MINUTES
MARINATING TIME: 1–3 HOURS

HEAT: DIRECT MEDIUM HEAT 180°–230°C (350°–450°F)
BRAAIING TIME: 25–30 MINUTES

PASTE
    3 large garlic cloves
    4 tablespoons origanum leaves and tender stems
    1 teaspoon coarse sea salt
    4 tablespoons extra-virgin olive oil
    2 tablespoons cider vinegar
    ½ teaspoon freshly ground black pepper

2 pork fillets, about 500 g each
5 fresh sweetcorn cobs, husked
Extra-virgin olive oil
125 ml finely chopped red onion
3 spring onions, thinly sliced crossways
250 ml cream
¼ teaspoon coarse sea salt
pinch of freshly ground black pepper
1 tablespoon finely chopped fresh origanum
Tabasco or other hot sauce, optional

1. Roughly chop the garlic, then sprinkle over the origanum and salt and continue to chop until finely chopped. Periodically use the side of your knife blade to press the garlic onto the cutting board to create a paste. Transfer the garlic paste to a bowl and mix in the oil, vinegar and black pepper.

2. Trim the pork fillets of any surface fat and silver skin. Brush the paste all over the surface of the meat. Cover and refrigerate for 1–3 hours. Allow the meat to stand at room temperature for 20–30 minutes before cooking. Prepare the braai for direct cooking over medium heat.

3. Lightly brush the sweetcorn with oil. Brush the cooking grates clean. Braai the corn over **direct medium heat** for about 10 minutes, with the lid closed as much as possible but turning occasionally, until browned in spots and barely tender. Using a sharp knife, cut the corn kernels off the cobs.

4. Warm 2 tablespoons of olive oil in a frying pan over medium heat. Add the onion and the spring onions and cook for 3–4 minutes, stirring occasionally. Add the corn kernels, cream, salt and pepper and mix well. Reduce the heat to low and simmer for 5–7 minutes, until about half of the cream has evaporated. Add the origanum and a dash of Tabasco, if desired. Set aside.

5. Braai the pork over **direct medium heat** for 15–20 minutes, with the lid closed as much as possible but turning every 5 minutes, until the outsides are evenly seared and the centres are barely pink. The internal temperature of the fillets should be 65°C (150°F) when fully cooked.

6. Remove the pork from the braai and allow to rest for 3–5 minutes before slicing. Meanwhile, warm the corn mixture over medium heat. Cut each fillet crossways into slices about 1 cm thick. Arrange the slices on a platter or individual plates. Serve warm with the creamy corn.

PORK FILLETS WITH SMOKED PAPRIKA ROUILLE

SERVES: 6
PREP TIME: 15 MINUTES

HEAT: DIRECT MEDIUM HEAT 180°–230°C (350°–450°F)
BRAAIING TIME: 27–35 MINUTES

ROUILLE
  2 medium red peppers
  2–3 small garlic cloves
  ¾ teaspoon coarse sea salt
  100 g dried breadcrumbs
  3 tablespoons fresh lemon juice
  ¾ teaspoon smoked paprika
  150 ml extra-virgin olive oil

  2 pork fillets, about 500 g each
  Extra-virgin olive oil
  ½ teaspoon coarse sea salt
  ¼ teaspoon freshly ground black pepper

A *rouille* is a rust-coloured garlicky paste that it is traditionally added to bouillabaisse (fish stew), but if you thin out a *rouille* with a bit more extra-virgin olive oil, it also makes a very nice sauce. The key to a smooth texture is adding the oil very slowly while the paste whirls in a food processor or blender. Some food processors have a handy little hole in the feed tube that prevents too much oil from pouring into the emulsion all at once.

1. Prepare the braai for direct cooking over medium heat. Brush the cooking grates clean. Braai the peppers over **direct medium heat** for 12–15 minutes, with the lid closed as much as possible but turning every 3–5 minutes, until blackened and blistered all over. Place the peppers in a bowl, cover with clingfilm and allow to stand for 10–15 minutes. Remove the peppers from the bowl and peel away and discard the charred skins, tops and seeds.

2. Finely chop the garlic in a blender or food processor, then add the roasted peppers, salt and breadcrumbs. Add the lemon juice and paprika and, with the motor running, slowly add the oil. Blend until very smooth and orangey-red in color. If the rouille is too thick, add about 1 tablespoon of water. Season to taste with more salt, if needed.

3. Trim the fillets of any surface fat and silver skin. Lightly brush the fillets with oil and season evenly with the salt and pepper. Allow the meat to stand at room temperature for 20–30 minutes before cooking.

4. Braai the fillets over **direct medium heat** for 15–20 minutes, with the lid closed as much as possible, but turning every 5 minutes, until the outsides are evenly seared and the centres are barely pink. The internal temperature of the fillets should be 65°C (150°F) when fully cooked.

5. Remove the pork from the braai and allow it to rest for 3–5 minutes. Cut each fillet crossways into thin slices. Serve warm, or at room temperature, with the rouille.

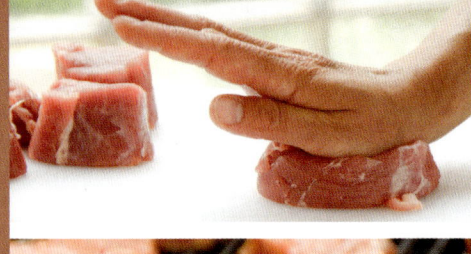

Cut each pork fillet crossways into pieces about 3.5 cm thick. Use the heel of your hand to flatten each piece into a medallion about 2.5 cm thick. For juicy results, marinate the medallions for at least 1 hour, and then grill them gently over medium heat until barely pink in the centre.

PORK MEDALLIONS WITH ASIAN BLACK BEAN SAUCE

SERVES: 4
PREP TIME: 25 MINUTES
MARINATING TIME: 1 HOUR

HEAT: DIRECT MEDIUM HEAT 180°–230°C (350°–450°F)
BRAAIING TIME: 4–5 MINUTES

MARINADE
    ½ teaspoon grated orange zest
    4 tablespoons fresh orange juice
    4 tablespoons Chinese rice wine or dry sherry
    2 tablespoons soy sauce
    1 tablespoon hoisin sauce
    1 tablespoon finely chopped fresh ginger
    1 tablespoon toasted sesame oil
    ¼ teaspoon crushed red chilli flakes

    2 pork fillets, about 500 g each, trimmed of silver skin

SAUCE
    2 tablespoons Chinese fermented black beans
    125 ml chicken stock
    2 tablespoons Chinese rice wine or dry sherry
    1 tablespoon soy sauce
    1 teaspoon sugar
    1½ teaspoons cornflour
    1 tablespoon peanut oil or canola oil
    2 teaspoons peeled and finely chopped fresh ginger
    1 garlic clove, finely chopped
    2 tablespoons fresh orange juice

1. Whisk the marinade ingredients together in a bowl.

2. Cut off the thin, tapered end from each fillet and reserve for another use, or marinate and braai along with the medallions. Cut each fillet crossways into 6 equal pieces, each about 3.5 cm thick. One at a time, place the pork slices on a work surface and, using the heel of your hand, flatten into a round medallion about 2.5 cm thick. Place the medallions in a large, resealable plastic bag and pour in the marinade. Press the air out of the bag and seal tightly. Turn the bag several times to distribute the marinade and refrigerate for at least 1 hour, turning the bag occasionally.

3. Soak the fermented black beans for 10–20 minutes in a small bowl filled with warm water, then drain well. Coarsely chop the beans and set aside. In a medium bowl whisk together the stock, rice wine, soy sauce and sugar until the sugar dissolves. Sprinkle in the cornflour and stir to dissolve. Set aside.

4. Warm the oil in a small saucepan over medium-high heat. Add the ginger and garlic and stir for about 20 seconds, until softened. Stir in the beans, then the stock mixture and bring to a full boil, stirring constantly, until the sauce is slightly thickened. Remove from the heat and stir in the orange juice.

5. Prepare the braai for direct cooking over medium heat. Brush the cooking grates clean. Remove the pork from the bag and discard the marinade. Cook the medallions over **direct medium heat** for 4–5 minutes, with the lid closed as much as possible but turning once, until the outsides are evenly seared and the centres are barely pink. Remove from the braai and allow to rest for 2–3 minutes. Serve hot with the black bean sauce.

PORK LOIN WITH CHERRY-CHIPOTLE GLAZE

SERVES: 4–6
PREP TIME: 25 MINUTES
BRINING TIME: 1–2 HOURS

HEAT: DIRECT AND INDIRECT HIGH HEAT 230°–290°C (450°–550°F)
BRAAIING TIME: 33–42 MINUTES
SPECIAL EQUIPMENT: LARGE DISPOSABLE FOIL TRAY

   1 litre Dr. Pepper (do not use the diet version)
   100 g coarse sea salt
   1.5–2 kg deboned pork loin

GLAZE
   275 g black cherry preserve
   125 ml Dr. Pepper
   125 ml water
   1–2 tablespoons chipotle in adobo, finely chopped
   4 teaspoons Dijon mustard

   Canola oil or sunflower oil

1. Pour the Dr Pepper into a large bowl and slowly add the salt (the mixture will foam up quite a bit so use a bowl large enough to prevent overflowing). Stir for 1–2 minutes, until the salt dissolves completely. Place a large, disposable plastic bag inside a large bowl and carefully pour the brine into the bag.

2. Trim excess fat and silver skin from the pork. Submerge the pork in the brine, seal the bag and refrigerate for 1–2 hours.

3. Combine the glaze ingredients in a small bowl.

4. Remove the pork from the bag and discard the brine. Pat dry with roller towel. Lightly coat the pork with oil and allow to stand at room temperature for 20–30 minutes before cooking. Prepare the braai for direct and indirect cooking over high heat.

5. Brush the cooking grates clean. Sear the pork over **direct high heat** for 8–12 minutes, with the lid closed as much as possible but turning once, until the surface is well marked but not burned.

6. Place a large foil roasting tray over **indirect high heat** and pour the glaze into the tray. Transfer the pork to the tray and turn to coat with the glaze. Braai the pork over **indirect high heat** for 25–30 minutes with the lid closed as much as possible but turning in the glaze every 8–10 minutes, until the meat is barely pink in the centre and the internal temperature reaches 63°–65°C (145°–150°F). If the glaze gets too thick or starts to scorch, add a little water or Dr Pepper to the roasting tray. Transfer the pork to a chopping board and allow it to rest for about 5 minutes. Cut the pork crossways into 1 cm-thick slices and serve with the remaining pan juices on the side.

If it's not treated right, pork loin can dry out all too quickly on the braai. The surest way to prevent this is to brine it first in a sweet and savoury solution, swelling the meat with moisture and flavour. Next, brown the roast over direct heat and finish cooking it over indirect heat, glazing it periodically.

HOW TO MAKE ROTISSERIE PORK LOIN

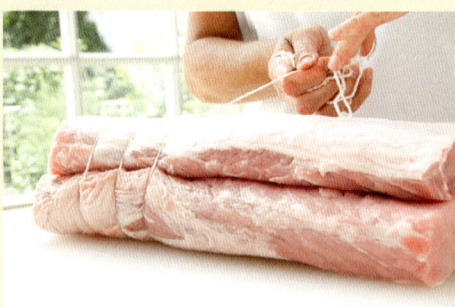

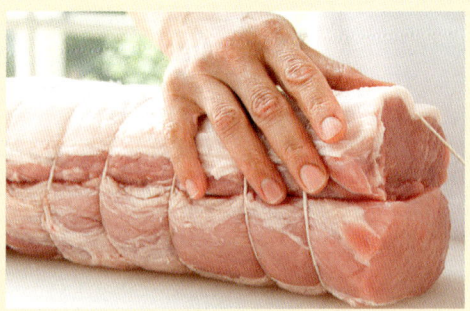

1. Large, thick pieces of meat will almost always be juicier after cooking than small narrow ones will, so improve your chances of wonderfully moist results by tying two sections of pork loin together.

2. Place one roast on top of the other, with the fat sides on the outside, and tie them together crossways with individual lengths of butcher's string separated by 2 cm or so.

3. Cut 2 very long pieces of string, each about 1 m. Tie one end of each piece to a crossways piece at one end of the roast. Weave the long pieces of string lengthways in and out of the crossways pieces and all the way around the length of the roast.

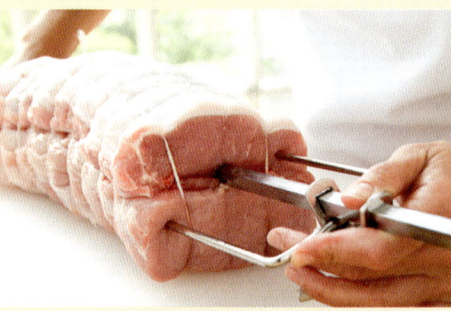

4. Tie off each lengthways piece of string at the knot where it began, on the first crossways piece. The string will hold the meat in place as it shrinks a little on the rotisserie.

5. Slide the centre rod (spit) of the rotisserie between the sections of pork loin, making sure to push the fork prongs well inside the meat.

6. Allow the meat to rest at room temperature for 1 hour before cooking. Brush the meat with oil and season it evenly with salt and pepper before putting the rotisserie into position.

7. Natural juices will baste the meat inside and out as the roast turns slowly on the rotisserie. Place a large foil roasting tray underneath the meat to prevent grease from falling into the braai.

8. Check the internal temperature at the centre of the meat. When it reaches 63°–65°C (145°–150°F), turn off the rotisserie and, wearing insulated braai mitts or oven gloves, remove it from the braai. While the meat rests at room temperature, it will continue to cook.

ROTISSERIE PORK LOIN WITH RED WINE AND PRUNE SAUCE

SERVES: 12–14
PREP TIME: 45 MINUTES

HEAT: INDIRECT HEAT ABOUT 200°C (400°F)
GRILLING TIME: 1–1¼ HOURS
SPECIAL EQUIPMENT: BUTCHER'S STRING, ROTISSERIE, LARGE DISPOSABLE FOIL ROASTING TRAY

SAUCE
- 2 tablespoons extra-virgin olive oil
- 375 g onions, finely chopped
- ½ teaspoon coarse sea salt
- 750 ml red wine
- 125 g pitted prunes, finely chopped
- 150 g raisins
- 1 tablespoon finely grated orange zest
- 175 ml fresh orange juice
- pinch of ground cloves
- Coarse sea salt
- Freshly ground black pepper

- 2 deboned pork loins, about 1.5 kg each
- 2 tablespoons extra-virgin olive oil
- 1½ teaspoons coarse sea salt
- 1 teaspoon freshly ground black pepper

1. Warm the oil in a medium saucepan over medium heat. Add the onions and salt and cook for about 15 minutes, stirring often, until the onions are quite soft. Increase the heat to high, add the wine and boil for about 8 minutes, until reduced by half. Stir in the prunes, raisins and orange zest, reduce the heat to medium and cook for 5–10 minutes, stirring occasionally, until the fruit is tender. Add the orange juice and ground cloves and season to taste with salt and pepper. Keep warm.

2. Trim the pork loins to match in size and then place one on top of the other, making sure the sides with the layers of fat are facing outwards. This fatty layer will help protect the meat while it cooks. Tie the two loins together to make one large cylindrical joint. Allow the meat to stand at room temperature for 1 hour before cooking. Brush the joint with the oil and season with the salt and pepper.

3. Prepare the braai for rotisserie cooking over indirect heat. If your gas braai has one, turn on the infrared burner to **low** and set the outer burner control knobs to **low heat**. The temperature of the braai should be around 200°C (400°F). You may need to adjust the outer burners to medium heat.

4. Carefully slide one pronged fork onto the spit, with the tines facing inwards, about 25 cm from the end of the spit. Secure the fork but do not tighten at this time. Slide the spit through the centre of the joint and gently push the roast onto the fork tines so that they are deep inside the roast. Add the other pronged fork to the spit with the tines facing inwards and slide down until they are firmly imbedded in the joint. Secure the fork, but do not completely tighten at this time. Wearing braai mitts or oven gloves, place the pointed end of the spit into the rotisserie motor. If necessary, adjust the joint so that it is centred on the spit and tighten the forks into place. Place the foil roasting tray beneath the joint to catch any grease. Turn on the motor to begin the rotisserie.

5. Cook the joint for 1–1¼ hours until the internal temperature reaches 63°–65°C (145°–150°F). To check the temperature, turn off the rotisserie motor and insert a thermometer down the centre of one of the loins. Wearing braai mitts or oven gloves, carefully remove the spit from the braai. Gently loosen the forks and slide the joint off of the spit. Transfer the pork to a chopping board, loosely cover with foil and allow to rest for 15–30 minutes (the meat will continue to cook during this time).

6. Slice the joint and serve with the sauce.

HOW TO BRAAI BONE-IN PORK LOIN

1. A moderately hot fire of about 180°C (350°F) is just right for roasting a bone-in pork loin. Begin with a chimney starter filled about two-thirds full with charcoal briquettes. Let the coals burn down until they are completely covered with ash and then dump them onto the charcoal grate.

2. Spread the briquettes in a single layer over one side of the charcoal grate and place a hardwood log beside them. The wood will smoulder and smoke, filling the pork with enticing outdoorsy aromas.

3. Cook the joint on the cooler side of the braai opposite the bed of charcoal, with the bone side facing down and the thick meaty side towards the coals. If the wood catches fire, use a spray bottle filled with water to douse the flames.

4. After cooking with the lid on for 45 minutes, rotate the joint 180 degrees so that the tips of the bones face the coals. As the meat finishes cooking, the temperature of the braai should fall to about 150°C (300°F).

5. Remove the joint when the internal temperature of the meat reaches 63°–65°C (145°–150°F). Loosely cover the joint with foil and let it rest for 15 minutes, so the juices will stay in the meat when you slice it.

6. The easiest way to carve the joint is to turn it over so that the bone side is facing up. Then you can see exactly where the bones are and slice right between them.

When you buy a bone-in pork loin, make sure the butcher has removed the chine bone (backbone), which runs along the top of all the rib bones. Otherwise it will be nearly impossible to slice between the ribs and serve individual chops. Also, don't be afraid to season the meat generously before cooking. This is a thick roast that can handle plenty of salt and pepper.

SMOKE-ROASTED PORK LOIN WITH REDCURRANT SAUCE

SERVES: 8
PREP TIME: 20 MINUTES

HEAT: INDIRECT MEDIUM HEAT 150°–180°C (300°–350°F)
BRAAIING TIME: 1½–2 HOURS

   3.5–4 kg bone-in pork loin
   3 tablespoons extra-virgin olive oil
   2 teaspoons coarse sea salt
   1 teaspoon freshly ground black pepper

   1 hardwood log, about 45 cm long and 10 cm in diameter

SAUCE
   200 ml redcurrant preserve
   125 ml tomato purée
   125 ml apple juice
   2 tablespoons cider vinegar
   1 tablespoon soy sauce
   1 tablespoon whisky
   ½ teaspoon crushed chilli flakes

1. Lightly coat the pork with the oil and season with the salt and black pepper. Allow the pork to stand at room temperature for 30 minutes while you prepare the braai.

2. Starting with about two-thirds of a chimney of lit coals, arrange them over one-third of the charcoal grate. Place the hardwood log alongside the outer edge of the coals, but not directly on top of them. The log should slowly start to smoulder but should not catch fire. If it does catch fire, use a spray bottle filled with water to douse the flames. Put the cooking grate in place and position the pork, bone side down and with the meaty section facing the fire, over **indirect medium heat** (about 180°C or 350°F). Cook for 45 minutes, with the lid closed.

3. After about 45 minutes, to maintain the heat, add another 8–10 lit briquettes to the coals and rotate the meat 180 degrees so that the bone section is facing the heat. Continue to cook over **indirect medium heat** for 45–75 minutes with the lid closed, until the internal temperature reaches 63°–65°C (145°–150°F). The fire should slowly lose heat and finish cooking the joint at about 150°C (300°F).

4. Combine the sauce ingredients in a medium saucepan over medium heat. Let the sauce come to a simmer and cook, stirring occasionally, until the preserve has melted and the sauce is well combined. Remove from the heat.

5. Transfer the roast to a chopping board, loosely cover with foil and allow to rest 15–30 minutes. To carve the meat, slice between each bone. Serve warm with the sauce.

HOW TO BRAAI PORK SHOULDER

1. A water smoker can maintain temperatures between 110°C (225°F) and 130°C (250°F) for several hours, which is just what you need to break down the connective tissue in pork shoulder joints.

2. Fill the water pan in the middle section of the smoker. It will absorb some of the charcoal's heat and release it slowly with some humidity.

3. After 8–10 hours of cooking, the meat will be so tender that you can slide the bone out cleanly.

4. Ideally you will need both a fish slice and a pair of tongs to lift the pork shoulders without the meat falling apart.

5. Shred the meat, using your fingers or two forks. Discard any clumps of fat, but hold onto the crispy bits of 'bark' that have developed on the outside of the meat.

6. The pinkish colour of the meat is a good sign that smoke has penetrated the surface and filled the pork with an authentic smoky braai flavour.

PULLED PORK SANDWICHES

SERVES: 10–12
PREP TIME: 25 MINUTES

HEAT: INDIRECT LOW HEAT 110°–130°C (225°–250°F)
BRAAIING TIME: 8–10 HOURS

RUB
    2 tablespoons chilli powder
    2 tablespoons coarse sea salt
    4 teaspoons garlic flakes
    2 teaspoons freshly ground black pepper
    1 teaspoon dry mustard

    2 bone-in pork shoulder joints, 2.5–3 kg each
    3 large handfuls hickory wood chips, soaked in water for at least 30 minutes

SAUCE
    250 ml tomato purée
    175 ml apple cider vinegar
    4 tablespoons lightly packed light brown sugar
    1½ teaspoons Worcestershire sauce
    1 teaspoon Tabasco, or to taste
    1 teaspoon coarse sea salt
    ½ teaspoon dry mustard
    ¼ teaspoon freshly ground black pepper

    12 hamburger rolls, split in half

1. Prepare your smoker, following manufacturer's instructions, for indirect cooking over low heat.

2. Combine the rub ingredients in a small bowl. Season the pork shoulders with the rub, pressing the spices all over the meat.

3. Smoke the pork over **indirect low heat**, with the lid closed, adding a handful of drained wood chips to the coals every hour for the first 3 hours, until the internal temperature of the meat reaches 88°C (190°F). At this point the bone should easily slip out of the meat, and the meat should be falling apart in some areas. The total cooking time will be 8–10 hours. Maintain the heat of the smoker at 110°–130°C (225°–250°F).

4. Whisk the sauce ingredients together in a heavy-based saucepan. Bring to a simmer over medium heat and cook for about 5 minutes, stirring occasionally. Taste and adjust the seasonings, if necessary. It should be spicy and tangy.

5. Transfer the pork joints to a roasting tray and tightly cover with foil. Allow the pork to rest for 30 minutes.

6. Pull the warm meat apart with your fingers, or use two forks to shred the meat. Discard any large pieces of fat or sinew. Put the pork into a large bowl and moisten with as much sauce as you like (you may not need all of the sauce). Pile the pork onto hamburger rolls. Serve warm with coleslaw, if desired.

HOW TO MAKE PORCHETTA

1. Trim off the relatively thin pieces of meat at the ends of the pork shoulder roast. Also trim the thick sections of the joint to create a fairly even thickness from end to end.

2. Ideally you will have 250–300 g of trimmed meat and fat to mix with delicious herbs, spices, garlic and olive oil. This will be the porchetta filling.

3. Pulse the ingredients in a food processor 20–25 times until they have the look and texture of sausage meat. Then spread the filling over the interior of the joint.

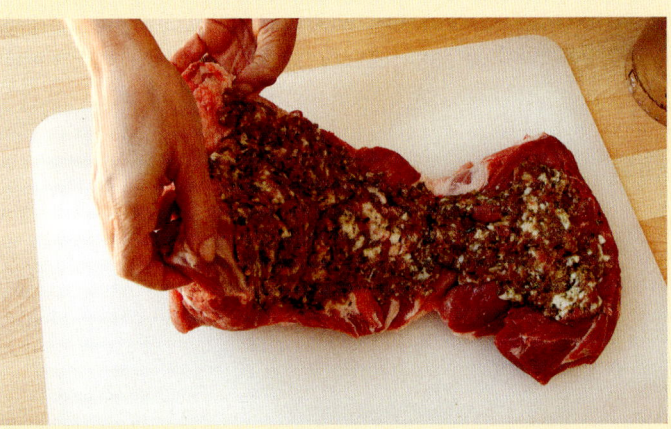

4. Leave a border around the edges of the joint so that the filling does not spill out when you roll the meat. Press the filling into any grooves in the meat.

5. Now roll up the meat from one short end to the other, creating an evenly shaped and compact cylinder.

6. Use several long pieces of butcher's string to tie the joint both crossways and lengthways. Allow the joint to stand at room temperature for 20–30 minutes before cooking.

PORCHETTA-STYLE PORK SHOULDER

SERVES: 6–8
PREP TIME: 30 MINUTES

HEAT: INDIRECT MEDIUM HEAT 180°–200°C (350°–400°F)
BRAAIING TIME: 2–2½ HOURS
SPECIAL EQUIPMENT: BUTCHER'S STRING

FILLING
- 125 ml extra-virgin olive oil
- 3 sprigs rosemary leaves
- 16 large sage leaves
- 1 tablespoon finely grated lemon zest
- 1 tablespoon finely chopped garlic
- 1 teaspoon coarse sea salt
- ½ teaspoon whole fennel seed
- ½ teaspoon crushed red chilli flakes

- 1 deboned pork shoulder joint, about 2.5 kg, butterflied, ends trimmed to produce 250–300 g meat and fat
- 1 tablespoon extra-virgin olive oil
- ½ teaspoon coarse sea salt
- ½ teaspoon freshly ground black pepper

1. Process the filling ingredients in a food processor until they form a smooth purée. Add the trimmed meat and fat and pulse for 20–25 pulses, until it resembles sausage meat.

2. Place the joint, skin side down, on a work surface. Evenly distribute the filling over the pork, leaving a border around the edges of the joint. Roll up the meat and tie with butcher's string in 5 or 6 places. Rub the outside of the joint with the oil, salt and pepper, then allow to stand at room temperature for 20–30 minutes before cooking. Prepare the braai for indirect cooking over medium heat.

3. Brush the cooking grates clean. Braai the joint over **indirect medium heat** for 2–2½ hours, with the lid closed, until the internal temperature reaches 82°–85°C (180°–185°F).

4. Transfer the joint to a chopping board, loosely cover with heavyweight foil, and allow to rest for 20–30 minutes. Remove the string and carve the meat into thin slices. Serve warm.

In and around Rome, Italy, porchetta *is a bacchanalian dish that involves stuffing a whole pig with wild fennel, garlic and spices, and then cooking it on a rotisserie spit. Assuming that you may not be inclined to tackle such a huge project, here's a simpler version that calls for a pork shoulder filled with the authentic flavours.*

HOW TO SEASON A PORK JOINT

1. Finely grate some cloves of garlic.

2. Make shallow cross-hatch slashes about 5 cm apart through the fat but do not cut into the flesh.

3. Smear the garlic-and-herb paste all over the joint, pressing it into the slashes and crevices.

4. Cover the joint and refrigerate for between 12 and 24 hours.

HOW TO BRAAI A PORK JOINT

1. Cook a bone-in pork shoulder over indirect low heat (about 130°C/300°F) so that its collagen and fat will melt and make the meat succulent before the outside burns. This requires starting the fire with a charcoal chimney starter filled about halfway and adding 8–10 briquettes every hour or so.

2. When the meat's internal temperature reaches 85°–88°C (185°–190°F), remove the joint from the braai, wrap it tightly in foil and allow the meat to rest and the juices to redistribute for a full hour.

3. Cut the joint into 1 cm-thick slices or tear it into bite-sized chucks. Serve the roasted pork with a bold garlic-citrus sauce called mojo (pronounced 'mo-ho').

LATINO PORK ROAST

SERVES: 6–8
PREP TIME: 30 MINUTES
MARINATING TIME: 12–24 HOURS

HEAT: INDIRECT LOW HEAT ABOUT 130°C (250°F)
BRAAIING TIME: 5–7 HOURS, PLUS 1 HOUR RESTING TIME

PASTE
- 5 large garlic cloves, finely grated
- 3 tablespoons extra-virgin olive oil
- 3 tablespoons apple cider vinegar
- 2 tablespoons dried origanum
- 1 tablespoon plus 2 teaspoons coarse sea salt
- 1 tablespoon freshly ground black pepper

- 3–3.5 kg bone-in pork shoulder joint, with an outer layer of fat
- 4 handfuls hickory wood chips, soaked in water for at least 30 minutes

MOJO SAUCE
- Finely grated zest of 1 orange
- 250 ml fresh orange juice
- 125 ml fresh grapefruit juice
- 80 ml finely chopped onion
- 2 tablespoons white grape vinegar
- 1 small serrano chilli, finely chopped
- 1 garlic clove, finely chopped
- 1 teaspoon sugar
- Coarse sea salt

- 3 tablespoons finely chopped fresh coriander

1. Combine the paste ingredients in a small bowl.

2. Score the fat on the joint in a cross-hatch pattern, about 5 cm apart, cutting through the fat just to the flesh. Rub the paste all over the joint, then place it in a bowl, cover and refrigerate for between 12 and 24 hours. Allow the joint to stand at room temperature for 1 hour before cooking.

3. Prepare the braai for indirect cooking over low heat. Brush the cooking grates clean. Drain 1 handful of the wood chips and scatter them over the coals or in the smoker box of a gas braai, following the manufacturer's instructions. Braai the pork, fat side down, over **indirect low heat** for 5–7 hours, with the lid closed as much as possible, turning once after about 3 hours and adding a handful of drained wood chips each hour until they are used up, until the meat is so tender that it gives no resistance when pierced with a meat fork and the internal temperature registers 85°–88°C (185°–190°F). Transfer the joint to a platter and loosely cover with heavyweight foil, then allow to rest for about 1 hour.

4. Combine the mojo ingredients, including salt to taste, in a small serving bowl, stirring to dissolve the sugar and salt. Cover and set aside. Just before serving, stir in the coriander.

5. Cut the joint into 1 cm-thick slices (it may fall apart into chunks and not carve neatly, but that's okay). Serve warm with the mojo sauce.

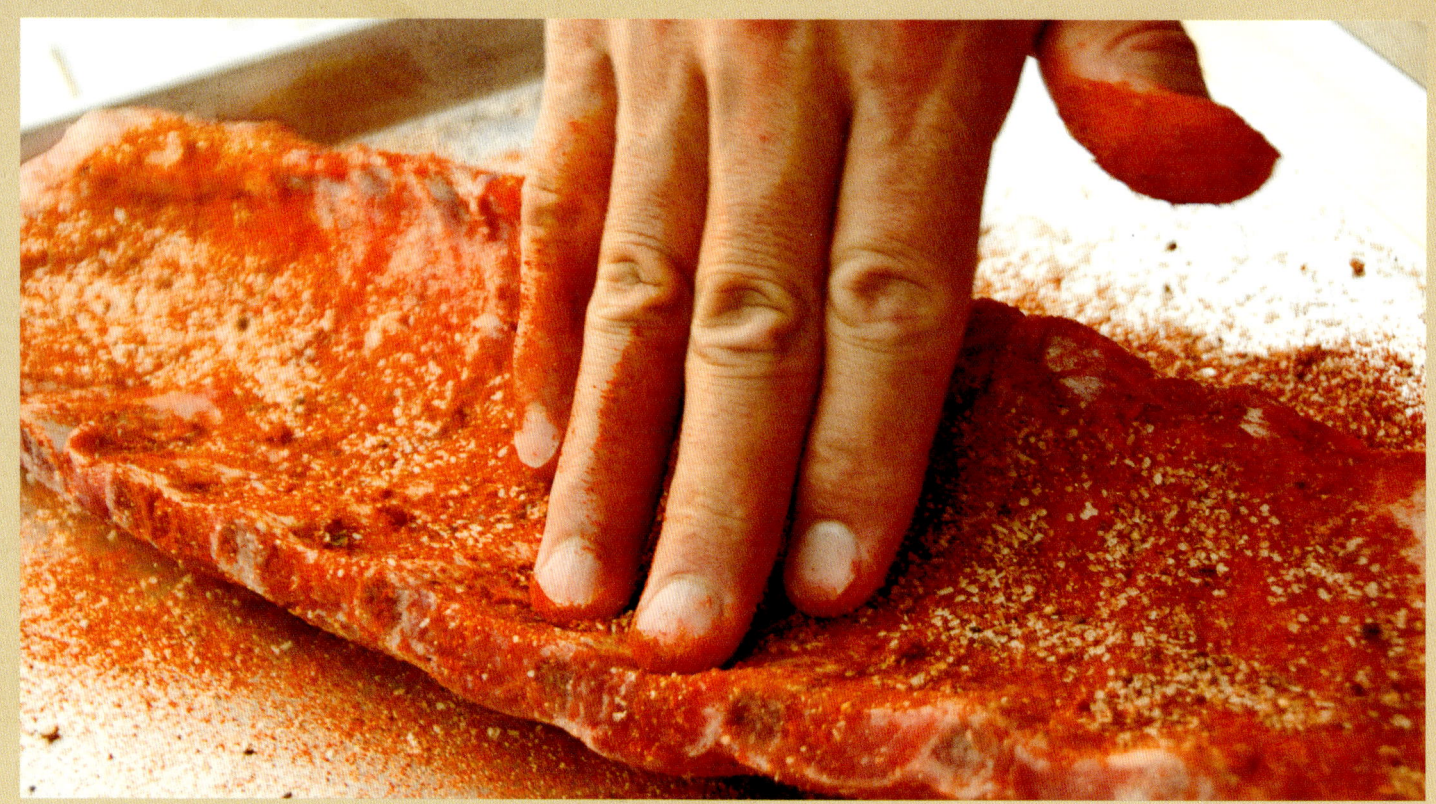

HOW TO BRAAI PORK RIBS
5 THINGS YOU NEED TO KNOW

1 STRIKE THE BALANCE
A perfectly braaiied rack of ribs achieves a seamless harmony of effects. The slightly crisp texture of a handsome, glossy surface gives way to morsels of luscious meat with a fragrant wood-smoke flavour. At each step of cooking, your goal is to balance the spices, sauce and smoke with the inherently beautiful flavour of slow-roasted pork, never letting one effect outdo the others.

2 USE WHAT YOU HAVE
You can make satisfying, tasty ribs on a gas or charcoal braai, or a smoker. Each one is capable of slowly tenderizing the rib meat and scenting it with wood smoke, although with a braai, you will need a smoker box attachment.

3 WATCH THAT HEAT
The key to tender ribs is maintaining a low cooking temperature for several hours. Spikes and valleys of heat will tend to tighten and dry out the meat, but consistently low temperatures will produce soft and succulent meat.

4 ALL IN GOOD TIME
It's one thing to wait the required 3–4 hours for baby back ribs or 5–6 hours for spareribs, but that's not the only timing issue. You must not sauce any ribs too early, especially if you are using a sweet sauce, as the sugars will burn and threaten your precious ribs. Sauce them during the final 30 minutes of cooking, or just before you wrap them in foil.

5 WRAP 'EM UP
Wrapping ribs in foil during the final stages of cooking holds in some moisture and helps to tenderize the meat. This is a little trick that some braai professionals dismiss as the 'Texas crutch', but you know what? It works!

HOW TO PREP BABY BACK RIBS

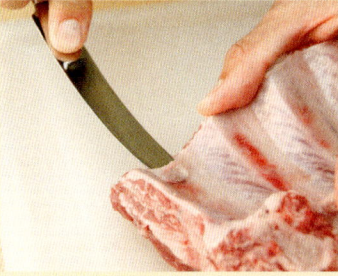 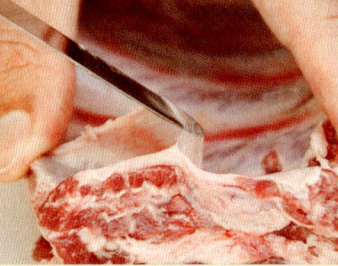 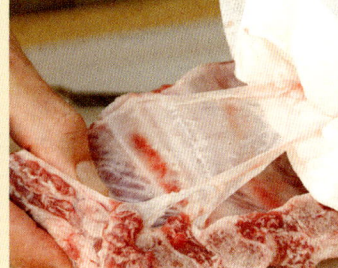 

1. At one end of the rack, slide a flat-bladed knife under the membrane and over a bone.

2. Lift and loosen the membrane until it tears.

3. Grip the edge of the membrane with roller towel and pull it off.

4. The membrane may come off in one whole piece, or you may need to remove it in smaller pieces.

5. Season the ribs mostly on the meaty side, pressing the spices into the meat so that they don't fall off.

6. Stand the ribs in a rib rack to double the number of ribs you can cook in a limited cooking space.

HOW TO SET UP A CHARCOAL BRAAI FOR SMOKING

1. If you are using wood chips, soak them first in water for at least 30 minutes so that they smoulder and smoke slowly rather than flare up.

2. Dump the charcoal on one side of the charcoal grate. A charcoal basket holds the coals together in a compact bunch and slows down the burning. Tap the edge of the basket with tongs every hour or so to knock the ashes through the basket holes.

3. Place a large foil tray on the other side of the charcoal grate and fill it at least halfway with water to create a little steam inside the braai. The ribs will cook on the cooking grate directly above the water tray.

4. Drain some wood chips and lie them right on the coals. Replenish them after the first hour of cooking, ideally when you replenish the coals, too.

HOW TO BRAAI BABY BACK RIBS

1. To protect the meat, begin with the bone side of the ribs facing the coals.

2. After the first hour of cooking, baste the ribs with a vinegar baste.

3. Periodically swap the positions of the ribs in the rib rack for even cooking.

4. Towards the end of cooking, face the meaty sides of the ribs towards the coals to brown and crisp the surface.

5. The meat should be so tender that it tears when you bend a rack backwards.

6. Lightly brush each rack of ribs with some sauce as it comes off the braai.

7. Wrap each rack individually in heavyweight foil.

8. The ribs will stay warm and continue to cook a bit for at least 30 minutes.

SLOW GOOD BABY BACK RIBS WITH SOO-WEE SAUCE

SERVES: 4–6
PREP TIME: 20 MINUTES

HEAT: INDIRECT LOW HEAT 130°–150°C (250°–300°F)
BRAAIING TIME: 3–4 HOURS
SPECIAL EQUIPMENT: RIB RACK

RUB
  2 tablespoons coarse sea salt
  2 tablespoons paprika
  4 teaspoons garlic flakes
  4 teaspoons chilli powder
  2 teaspoons dry mustard
  2 teaspoons freshly ground black pepper

  4 racks baby back ribs, 1–1.25 kg each

SAUCE
  250 ml apple juice
  137 ml tomato purée
  3 tablespoons apple cider vinegar
  1 tablespoon soy sauce
  2 teaspoons molasses or treacle syrup
  ½ teaspoon chilli powder
  ½ teaspoon garlic flakes
  ½ teaspoon dry mustard
  ¼ teaspoon coarse sea salt
  ¼ teaspoon freshly ground black pepper

BASTE
  175 ml red wine vinegar
  175 ml water
  2 tablespoons soy sauce

  4 handfuls hickory wood chips, soaked in water for at least 30 minutes

1. Prepare a charcoal braai for indirect cooking over low heat (see page 121).

2. Mix the rub ingredients together in small bowl.

3. Using a flat-bladed knife, slide the tip under the membrane covering the back of each rack of ribs. Lift and loosen the membrane until it breaks, and then grip a corner of it with roller towel and pull it off. Season the ribs all over with the rub, putting more of it on the meaty sides than the bone sides. Arrange the ribs in a rib rack, all facing the same direction. Allow the ribs to stand at room temperature for between 30 minutes and 1 hour before cooking.

4. When the fire has burned down to about 180°C (350°F), drain 2 handfuls of hickory wood chips and place them on top of the coals. The damp wood will lower the temperature a bit. Put the cooking grate in place. Place the ribs in the rack over **indirect low heat** (positioned over the foil tray) as far from the coals as possible, with the bone sides facing towards the coals. Close the lid. Close the top vent about halfway. Allow the ribs to cook and smoke for 1 hour. During this time, maintain the temperature at 130°–150°C (250°–300°F) by opening and closing the top vent. Meanwhile, make the sauce and the baste.

5. Mix the sauce ingredients together in a small saucepan over a medium heat. Simmer for about 5 minutes, then remove the saucepan from the heat. Taste and add more salt and pepper, if desired.

6. Mix the baste ingredients together in a small bowl.

7. After the first hour of cooking the ribs, add 8–10 unlit briquettes and the remaining 2 handfuls of wood chips (drained) to the lit coals. Move the ribs from the rack and spread them out on 2 roasting trays. Brush them generously on both sides with some of the baste. Leaving the lid off for a few minutes while you brush the ribs will help the new briquettes to light. Return the ribs to the rack, all facing the same direction, now with the bone sides facing away from the coals.

8. Close the lid and cook for another hour. During this time, maintain the temperature at 130°–150°C (250°–300°F) by opening and closing the top vent.

9. After 2 hours of cooking, add 8–10 unlit briquettes to the fire. Move the ribs from the rack and spread them out on 2 roasting trays. Brush them generously on both sides with some of the baste, leaving the lid off for a few minutes while you brush the ribs to help the new briquettes to light. Return the ribs to the rack, all facing in the same direction, but this time turned over so that the ends that were facing down are now face up. Also position any ribs that appear to be cooking faster than others towards the back of the rib rack, further away from the coals. This time the bone sides should face the coals.

10. Close the lid and allow the ribs to cook for a third hour. During this time, maintain the temperature at 130°–150°C (250°–300°F) by opening and closing the top vent.

11. After 3 hours of cooking, check to see if any rack is ready to come off the braai. They are done when the meat has shrunk back from most of the bones by 5 mm or more. When you lift a rack by picking up one end with tongs, the rack should bend in the middle and the meat should tear easily. If the meat does not tear easily, continue to cook the ribs. The total cooking time could be anywhere from 3–4 hours. Not all racks will cook in the same amount of time. Lightly brush the ribs with some sauce. Transfer the racks to a clean roasting tray and brush the ribs on both sides with some of the sauce. Wrap each rack individually in heavyweight foil and allow to rest for about 30 minutes. Serve the warm ribs with the remaining sauce on the side.

HOW TO BRAAI STACKED RIBS

1. One space-saving solution, whether you are cooking with charcoal or gas, is to stack the racks of ribs on top of each other in the middle of the braai.

2. Cook the ribs for about 45 minutes, with the lid closed and low heat radiating from both sides of the braai.

3. Then undo the stack of ribs on the cooking grate.

4. Baste the ribs on both sides with some of the reserved marinade.

5. Stack them again, swapping the positions of the ribs by moving the top rack to the bottom, the bottom rack to the middle, and the middle rack to the top.

6. Continue to cook the ribs, basting and swapping positions of the racks occasionally, until the meat has shrunk back at least 5 mm from the ends of the bones.

STACKED BABY BACK RIBS

SERVES: 6–8
PREP TIME: 20 MINUTES
MARINATING TIME: 30 MINUTES

HEAT: INDIRECT AND DIRECT LOW HEAT 150°–170°C (300°–325°F)
BRAAIING TIME: 2¾–3¼ HOURS

MARINADE
- 250 ml sweet chili sauce
- 250 ml water
- Grated zest of 3 limes
- 80 ml fresh lime juice
- 4 large garlic cloves
- 4 tablespoons soy sauce
- 3 tablespoons roughly chopped fresh ginger

- 3 racks baby back ribs, 1–1.25 kg each
- 1 tablespoon coarse sea salt

1. Combine the marinade ingredients in a blender or food processor and process for about 1 minute to purée the ingredients. Set aside 250 ml of the marinade to use as a basting sauce.

2. Remove the thin membrane from the back of each rack of ribs (see page 121). Season the ribs on the meaty sides with salt. Brush the remaining marinade over all the ribs. Allow the ribs to stand at room temperature for 30 minutes before cooking. Prepare the braai for indirect cooking over a low heat.

3. Brush the cooking grates clean. Stack the ribs on top of each other, with the bone sides facing down, and braai over *indirect low heat* for 45 minutes, with the lid closed.

4. Undo the stack of ribs and brush the meaty sides with some of the reserved marinade. Stack the ribs, with the bone sides facing down, moving the top rack to the bottom, the bottom rack to the middle, and the middle rack to the top. Cook over *indirect low heat* for another 45 minutes, with the lid closed.

5. Undo the stack of ribs on the braai again. Brush the meaty sides with some of the reserved marinade. Stack the ribs, with the bone sides facing down, moving the top rack to the bottom, the bottom rack to the middle, and the middle rack to the top. Cook over *indirect low heat* for 1–1½ hours, with the lid closed. During this third round of cooking, move the relative positions of the ribs occasionally so the racks that are browning a little faster cook in the middle of the stack and those that are not as brown cook at the top. As you move the ribs, brush the meaty sides with the reserved marinade.

6. Undo the stack of ribs and place them side by side, bone sides facing down, over *direct low heat* for 10–15 minutes, turning occasionally to prevent burning. Brush with some of the reserved marinade and continue cooking until the meat is very tender and has shrunk back from the ends of the bones.

7. Transfer the racks to a roasting tray, cover with foil and allow to rest for 15 minutes before cutting into individual ribs. Serve warm.

HOW TO PREP ST. LOUIS–STYLE SPARERIBS

1. There is a tough flap of meat, called the skirt, hanging from the bone side of a full rack of spareribs. The first step for converting 'regular' spareribs to the St. Louis-style cut is to remove that flap.

2. The next step is to cut off the long strip of cartilaginous meat, called the brisket, which runs along the bottom of the rack.

3. Then trim off any meat dangling from either end of each rack. The goal is to make a handsome rectangular rack of ribs.

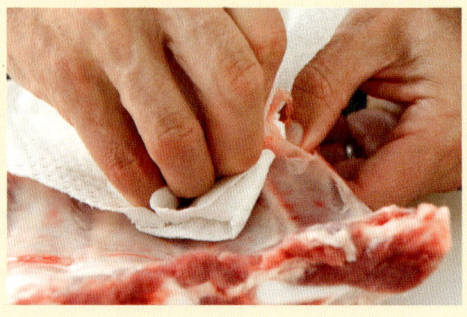

4. Use a flat-bladed knife to get under the membrane and lift it so that you can grab an edge with roller towel. Then peel off the membrane.

5. The rack on top is a St. Louis-style cut. It is about the same length as the rack of baby back ribs, shown at the bottom, but the St. Louis-style cut is wider and meatier. It's also tougher, so it requires longer cooking.

6. You can bump up the flavour and give the ribs a crispy surface by marinating them in a sweet-and-savoury marinade for a few hours before cooking.

HOW TO USE THE 'TEXAS CRUTCH'

1. In the world of competition barbecuing in the USA, the 'Texas crutch' refers to the technique of wrapping ribs in heavyweight foil during the final stages of cooking, often with some liquid trapped inside.

2. The theory is that the humidity inside the foil moistens and tenderizes the meat. Some purists shun this approach – hence the mocking sobriquet. It's unclear why the technique is associated with Texas.

3. Home cooks can also use this technique, with great success, by finishing their ribs in foil on the smoker or by wrapping their ribs in foil and allowing them to rest after they have been removed from the smoker.

SWEET GINGER AND SOY-GLAZED SPARERIBS

SERVES: 6
PREP TIME: 30 MINUTES
MARINATING TIME: 3 HOURS

HEAT: INDIRECT LOW HEAT ABOUT 150°C (300°F)
BRAAIING TIME: 4–5 HOURS

MARINADE
    100 g brown sugar
    125 ml soy sauce
    137 ml tomato purée
    125 ml dry sherry
    2 tablespoons finely chopped fresh ginger
    1½ teaspoons finely chopped garlic

2 racks pork spareribs, about 2 kg each

1. Combine the marinade ingredients in a large bowl.

2. Prepare the racks of spareribs as detailed at left. Put the spareribs, meaty side up, on a chopping board. Follow the line of fat that separates the meaty ribs from the much tougher tips at the base of each rack, and cut off the tips. Turn each rack over. Cut off the flap of meat attached in the centre of each rack. Also cut off the flap of meat that hangs below the shorter end of the ribs. (The flaps and tips can be grilled separately, but they will not be as tender as the ribs.) Remove the thin membrane from the back of each rack of ribs.

3. Place the ribs in one layer on a large roasting tray. Pour the marinade over the ribs and turn to coat them evenly. Cover and refrigerate for 3 hours, turning occasionally. Remove the ribs from the tray and reserve the marinade. Allow the ribs to stand at room temperature for 30 minutes before braaiing. Prepare the braai for indirect cooking over low heat.

4. Brush the cooking grates clean. Braai the ribs over **indirect low heat** for 2 hours, with the lid closed. Remove the ribs from the braai and brush them on both sides with the reserved marinade. Wrap the ribs in foil, return them to the braai and continue to cook for 2–3 hours, until the meat has shrunk back by about 1 cm from the ends of the rib bones and the meat is tender enough to tear with your fingers.

5. Transfer the ribs (still wrapped in foil) to a large roasting tray and allow to rest for 30 minutes. Serve warm.

HOW TO COOK SPARERIBS IN A SMOKER

1. Fill the ring in the bottom section of the smoker with fully lit charcoal. Briquettes will burn much longer than lump charcoal, so they are a good choice for meats like pork spareribs, which require long, slow smoking.

2. Toss a few chunks of hardwood on the coals right at the start. Don't bother soaking the chunks first. They won't absorb much water, and they are large enough to smoke for quite a while. Put the middle section in place and immediately fill the water pan three-quarters of the way with water. The water pan gets hot fast, so don't wait to fill the pan or water will splatter all over!

3. The vent on the lid should be open right from the start, as it allows much of the smoke to escape. Otherwise, the meat could be overpowered. Also, the vent keeps the air flowing so the coals stay lit.

4. Regulate the temperature in the smoker by adjusting the bottom vents. If the temperature begins to fall, open the bottom vents a bit more to allow more airflow. If the temperature begins to rise, close the bottom vents to restrict airflow.

5. After the first few chunks of hardwood have burned out, open the side door and drop one or two more onto the burning coals. Work quickly when the door is open so that you don't allow too much air into the smoker and create havoc with the cooking temperatures.

6. If necessary, for really long cooking times, you can add a few more handfuls of briquettes to the coals.

SLOW-SMOKED SPARERIBS WITH SWEET-AND-SOUR BARBECUE SAUCE

SERVES: 8
PREP TIME: 30 MINUTES

HEAT: INDIRECT LOW HEAT 110°–130°C (225°–250°F)
BRAAIING TIME: 5–6 HOURS

RUB
- 3 tablespoons coarse sea salt
- 2 tablespoons chilli powder
- 2 tablespoons light brown sugar
- 2 tablespoons garlic flakes
- 2 tablespoons paprika
- 4 teaspoons dried thyme
- 4 teaspoons ground cumin
- 4 teaspoons celery seed
- 2 teaspoons freshly ground black pepper

- 4 racks St. Louis-style spareribs (see page 126)

BASTE
- 250 ml apple juice
- 125 ml apple cider vinegar
- 2 tablespoons Worcestershire sauce

- 5 fist-sized chunks of hardwood (not soaked)

SAUCE
- 500 ml tomato purée
- 250 ml cup apple juice
- 150 ml apple cider vinegar
- 2 tablespoons Worcestershire sauce
- 2 tablespoons honey
- 2 tablespoons reserved rub

1. Prepare your smoker, following the manufacturer's instructions, for indirect cooking over low heat.

2. Mix the rub ingredients together in a medium bowl. Set aside 2 tablespoons for the sauce.

3. See the top of page 126, steps 1–4, for how to prep the St. Louis-style ribs. Season the ribs all over with the rub, putting more of it on the meaty sides than the bone sides.

4. Mix the baste ingredients together in a small bowl.

5. Smoke the spareribs, adding 2 hardwood chunks at the start of cooking and 1 chunk each hour after that, until the chunks are gone. Cook until the meat has shrunk back from the bones at least 1 cm in several places and the meat tears easily when you lift each rack, brushing the ribs on both sides with the baste every 2 hours. The total cooking time could be anywhere between 5 and 6 hours. Not all racks will cook in the same amount of time. Maintain the temperature of the smoker at between 110° and 130°C (225°–250°F) by opening and closing the vents.

6. Mix the sauce ingredients together in a saucepan over a medium heat and cook for about 5 minutes. Remove the saucepan from the heat.

7. When the meat has shrunk back at least 1 cm in several places, lightly brush the ribs on both sides with sauce.

8. Cook the ribs for a further 30–60 minutes. Remove them from the smoker and, if desired, lightly brush the ribs on both sides with sauce again. Then cut the racks into individual ribs. Serve warm with the remaining sauce on the side.

Tamarind pods (top) provide a pulp that is responsible for an addictive sour flavour in many Southeast Asian dishes. Finding the pods can be a challenge, but Asian food shops and many supermarkets carry tamarind paste (bottom). The paste needs to be diluted in a liquid before using in a marinade or glaze.

TAMARIND-GLAZED COUNTRY-STYLE RIBS

SERVES: 6
PREP TIME: 10 MINUTES
MARINATING TIME: 20–30 MINUTES

HEAT: INDIRECT MEDIUM HEAT 180°–230°C (350°–400°F)
BRAAIING TIME: 45–50 MINUTES

MARINADE
- 150 g tamarind paste
- 80 ml soy sauce
- 80 ml light brown sugar
- 4 tablespoons water
- ½ teaspoon freshly ground black pepper
- ½ teaspoon garlic flakes
- ¼ teaspoon ground cayenne pepper

12 belly pork ribs, 1.5–1.75 kg total weight

1. Whisk the marinade ingredients together in a bowl. Set aside 4 tablespoons for brushing on the ribs during cooking.

2. Liberally brush the ribs with the marinade. Allow the ribs to marinate at room temperature for 20–30 minutes before braaiing. Prepare the braai for indirect cooking over medium heat.

3. Brush the cooking grates clean. Braai the ribs over **indirect medium heat** for 20 minutes, with the lid closed. Turn the ribs over, brush with the reserved marinade and continue to cook for another 25–30 minutes.

4. Remove the ribs from the braai, tightly wrap with foil and allow them to rest for 30 minutes. Serve warm.

CHILLI VERDE COUNTRY-STYLE RIBS

SERVES: 6–8
PREP TIME: 30 MINUTES

HEAT: DIRECT MEDIUM HEAT 180°–230°C (350°–450°F)
BRAAIING TIME: 30 MINUTES
SPECIAL EQUIPMENT: LARGE DISPOSABLE FOIL TRAY

- 1.5 kg boneless belly pork ribs, 2–3 cm thick, trimmed of fat
- 1 medium white onion, cut into 1 cm slices
- 2 jalapeño chillies
- Canola or sunflower oil

RUB
- 1 tablespoon ground cumin
- 1 tablespoon packed brown sugar
- 2 teaspoons coarse sea salt
- 1 teaspoon chilli powder
- 1 teaspoon ground coriander
- 1 teaspoon dried origanum

SAUCE
- 1 can (425 g) diced green chillies with juice
- 1 can (425 g) diced tomatoes with juice
- 400 ml chicken stock
- 1 tablespoon finely chopped garlic
- 1 teaspoon ground cumin
- 1 teaspoon dried origanum

- 12 corn or flour tortillas (18–20 cm)
- 250 ml sour cream
- 1 ripe avocado, peeled and diced
- 100 g Cheddar cheese, grated
- 80 ml fresh coriander, finely chopped
- 2 limes, cut into wedges

1. Lightly brush the ribs, onion slices and jalapeño chillies with oil.

2. Mix the rub ingredients together in a small bowl. Generously coat the ribs on both sides with the rub. Allow the ribs to stand at room temperature for 20–30 minutes before cooking. Prepare the braai for direct cooking over medium heat.

3. Brush the cooking grates clean. Braai the ribs, onion slices, and chillies over **direct medium heat** for 10–12 minutes, with the lid closed as much as possible but turning once, until the meat is well browned but still a little pink and the onions and chillies are lightly charred and softened.

4. Remove the meat and vegetables from the braai and allow to cool for a few minutes. Cut the pork into 1.5 cm cubes and set aside. Roughly chop the onions. Remove and discard the skins, seeds and stems from the chillies and finely chop them.

5. Combine the sauce ingredients in a large disposable foil tray. Place the tray over **direct medium heat** and bring the sauce to a simmer. Add the meat and vegetables to the sauce and simmer for 15–20 minutes, with the lid closed, until the pork is tender when tested with a fork (if the liquid is cooking too fast, move the tray to indirect medium heat). Carefully slide the foil tray onto a baking sheet and remove it from the braai.

6. Braai the tortillas in a single layer over **direct medium heat** for about 1 minute, turning once (just long enough to warm and soften them). Stack the warmed tortillas and wrap them in a clean dish cloth.

7. Spoon the pork and a generous amount of sauce into warm bowls. Top with sour cream, avocado, grated cheese and coriander. Serve with warm tortillas and lime wedges.

Looking more like pork chops than ribs, belly ribs are cut from the upper shoulder. You can buy them with or without bones. Either way, the meat is a little tough, but simmering slowly in a spicy chilli verde (green chilli) sauce makes it tender.

POULTRY

TECHNIQUES

134	How to braai **CHICKEN INVOLTINI**
136	How to braai **CHICKEN ESCALOPES**
140	How to prep **DUCK BREASTS**
143	How to make **CHICKEN SKEWERS**
144	How to prep **CHICKEN BREASTS**
146	How to braai **CHICKEN WINGS**
147	How to braai **CHICKEN DRUMETTES**
148	How to prep **WHOLE CHICKEN LEGS**
150	How to roast **DUCK LEGS**
151	How to braai **CHICKEN PIECES**
152	How to cedar-plank **BONE-IN CHICKEN THIGHS**
154	How to braai **BONELESS CHICKEN THIGHS**
158	How to split **POUSSINS**
160	How to smoke **BEER CAN CHICKEN**
162	How to cook **ROTISSERIE CHICKEN**
164	How to **ROAST CHICKEN**
166	How to braai **BUTTERFLIED CHICKEN**
168	How to braai bacon-wrapped **TURKEY BREAST**
170	How to cook **TURKEY**: Five things you need to know
171	How to prep **TURKEY** the day before
171	How to smoke **TURKEY**
172	How to carve **TURKEY**
174	How to smoke **TURKEY BURGERS** on planks

RECIPES

135	**CHICKEN INVOLTINI** with Prosciutto and Basil
137	**CHICKEN ESCALOPES** with Tomato and Olive Relish
138	Lemon-Origanum **CHICKEN BREASTS**
139	Tandoori **CHICKEN BREASTS** with Mango-Mint Chutney
141	**DUCK BREASTS** with Port Wine and Plum Sauce
142	**DUCK BREAST TACOS** with Sour Orange and Onion Salsa
143	Jerk **CHICKEN SKEWERS** with Honey-Lime Cream
145	Tunisian **CHICKEN** with Parsley Pesto
146	Honey-Garlic **CHICKEN WINGS**
147	Hickory **DRUMETTES** with Bourbon-Molasses Glaze
149	Provençal Marinated **CHICKEN LEGS**
150	Slow-roasted **DUCK LEGS** with Hoisin-Orange Glaze
151	Triple-play **BARBECUED CHICKEN**
153	Cedar-planked **CHICKEN THIGHS** with Soy-Ginger Glaze
154	Layered Mexican **CHICKEN SALAD**
155	Persian **CHICKEN KEBABS**
157	Chicken and Vegetable **QUESADILLAS** with Guacamole
158	**POUSSINS** marinated in Bourbon, Honey and Soy
159	Huli-Huli **CHICKEN**
161	Smoked **BEER CAN CHICKEN**
163	**ROTISSERIE** Buttermilk Chicken with Apricot Glaze
165	Orange-Tarragon **ROASTED CHICKEN**
167	Nutmeg **CHICKEN** under a Cast-iron Pan
169	Bacon-wrapped **TURKEY BREAST** with Herb Stuffing
172	Hickory-smoked **TURKEY** with Bourbon Gravy
174	Cedar-planked **TURKEY BURGERS**
175	**TURKEY BURGERS** with Salsa Slaw

HOW TO BRAAI CHICKEN INVOLTINI

1. The brilliance of involtini, an Italian dish of stuffed and rolled meat, is that it allows you to fill fairly bland pieces of meat, such as chicken breasts, with gorgeous flavours like fresh basil, prosciutto and provolone cheese.

2. First flatten the chicken breasts, smooth side down, between layers of clingfilm. Then season each one with sea salt, garlic flakes and freshly ground black pepper.

3. Place a slice of prosciutto on each piece of chicken, followed by one or two slices of cheese and some basil leaves.

4. Roll up the chicken lengthways, keeping it as compact as you can.

5. Tie each piece of chicken with 2 pieces of butcher's string. Then lightly brush the surface with olive oil.

6. Braai over direct medium heat for about 12 minutes, turning every few minutes until the chicken is fully cooked and the cheese has begun to melt.

CHICKEN INVOLTINI WITH PROSCIUTTO AND BASIL

SERVES: 4
PREP TIME: 20 MINUTES

HEAT: DIRECT MEDIUM HEAT 180°–230°C (350°–450°F)
BRAAIING TIME: ABOUT 12 MINUTES
SPECIAL EQUIPMENT: BUTCHER'S STRING

- 4 boneless, skinless chicken breasts, about 200 g each, with the fillets removed
- 1 teaspoon coarse sea salt
- 1 teaspoon garlic flakes
- ½ teaspoon freshly ground black pepper
- 4 very thin slices prosciutto or parma-style ham
- 4 thin slices provolone cheese, halved
- 8 large basil leaves, plus more for garnish
- Extra-virgin olive oil
- 450 ml good-quality tomato salsa or purée

1. Prepare the braai for direct cooking over medium heat.

2. For each piece of chicken, use about 30 cm of clingfilm. Place the chicken, smooth side down, to one side of the plastic, about 5 cm from the edge. Fold the remaining clingfilm over the chicken leaving 1–2 cm from the folded edge. This will allow the chicken to spread out as it gets thinner. Starting from the thick side, gently pound the chicken with the flat side of a tenderizer or the bottom of a small, heavy pan, moving to different areas with every stroke until it is about 5 mm thick and double in size. Do not pound too hard or the chicken might break apart.

3. Season each piece of chicken on both sides with the salt, garlic flakes and pepper. Arrange the chicken with the smooth side down on a work surface.

4. Place a slice of prosciutto on each piece of chicken. Top with a slice of the provolone and some basil leaves. Carefully roll up the chicken, keeping it snug as you work. Tie 2 pieces of butcher's string around each piece of chicken to keep it together. Trim the loose ends of string. Lightly brush each rolled piece of chicken with oil.

5. Brush the cooking grates clean. Braai the chicken over **direct medium heat** for about 12 minutes, with the lid closed as much as possible but turning a quarter turn every 3 minutes until golden on all sides. Remove from the braai and allow to rest for 3–5 minutes. Meanwhile, warm the tomato salsa or purée in a small saucepan over medium-high heat.

6. Remove the string from the chicken breasts. Cut each breast into two or three slices, and serve warm on a pool of tomato salsa or purée. Garnish with torn pieces of basil.

HOW TO BRAAI CHICKEN ESCALOPES

1. On the underside of some store-bought chicken breasts is a thin strip of meat called the fillet (or tenderloin). To pound the chicken breasts thinly for this recipe, remove each fillet first and save it for another use.

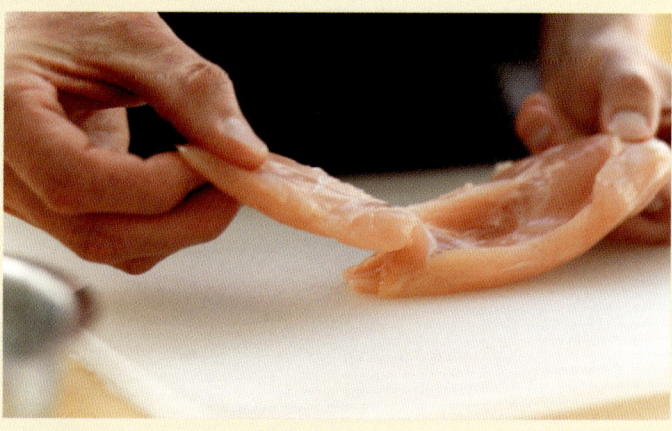

2. Holding each breast steady with one hand, use your other hand to grab the fillet near the thick end of each breast and pull it off.

3. Place each chicken breast, smooth side down, between 2 pieces of clingfilm and pound it to a thickness of about 5 mm.

4. For an even thickness, aim the back of a small, heavy frying pan at the centre of each breast and push the pan towards the thinner edges as you make contact.

5. Braai each chicken breast over a direct high heat, mostly on the first side. When the edge of the second side is turning opaque, it's time to turn the breast.

6. Check the doneness by firmness. The chicken should yield just a little to pressure. It should not be too soft or firm.

CHICKEN ESCALOPES WITH TOMATO AND OLIVE RELISH

SERVES: 4
PREP TIME: 30 MINUTES

HEAT: DIRECT HIGH HEAT 230°–290°C (450°–550°F)
BRAAIING TIME: 4–5 MINUTES

RUB

    1 tablespoon ground fennel seed
    1½ teaspoons coarse sea salt
    ½ teaspoon garlic flakes
    ½ teaspoon freshly ground black pepper

    4 boneless, skinless chicken breasts, about 170 g each
    Extra-virgin olive oil

RELISH

    200 ml deseeded and diced tomato
    160 ml chopped celery, with some light green leaves
    125 ml kalamata olives, rinsed, pitted and diced
    125 ml green olives, rinsed, pitted and diced
    2 tablespoons extra-virgin olive oil
    2 teaspoons finely chopped fresh thyme
      or ½ teaspoon dried thyme leaves
    Coarse sea salt

    1 lemon

1. Combine the rub ingredients in a smal bowl.

2. Remove the fillets from the underside of each chicken breast (save these for another use). One at a time, place each breast, smooth side down, between 2 sheets of clingfilm and pound to an even 5-mm thickness. Lightly brush the chicken with oil and season on both sides with the rub.

3. Prepare the braai for direct cooking over high heat.

4. Combine the relish ingredients, including salt to taste, in a large bowl.

5. Brush the cooking grates clean. Braai the chicken, smooth side down, over **direct high heat** for 3–4 minutes, with the lid closed as much as possible, until no longer pink. Turn over and braai just long enough to sear the surface, about 1 minute. Transfer the chicken, with the first grilled sides facing up, to a serving platter or individual plates. Spoon some relish over each breast and squeeze fresh lemon juice on top just before serving.

LEMON-ORIGANUM CHICKEN BREASTS

SERVES: 6
PREP TIME: 15 MINUTES
MARINATING TIME: 1–2 HOURS

HEAT: DIRECT MEDIUM HEAT 180°–230°C (350°–450°F)
BRAAIING TIME: 8–12 MINUTES

MARINADE
    90 ml extra-virgin olive oil
    Finely grated zest and juice of 2 lemons
    1 tablespoon dried origanum
    1 tablespoon finely chopped garlic
    2 teaspoons paprika
    1½ teaspoons coarse sea salt
    ½ teaspoon freshly ground black pepper

    6 boneless, skinless chicken breasts, about 170 g each

1. Whisk the marinade ingredients together in a bowl.

2. Place the breasts on a large, rimmed plate. Spoon or brush the marinade over the breasts, turning to coat them evenly. Cover with clingfilm and refrigerate for 1–2 hours.

3. Prepare the braai for direct cooking over medium heat.

4. Brush the cooking grates clean. Braai the chicken, smooth side down, over **direct medium heat** for 8–12 minutes, with the lid closed as much as possible but turning once or twice, until the meat is firm to the touch and opaque all the way to the centre. Serve warm.

HOW TO ZEST LEMON

1. A Microplane grater can quickly remove the outermost skin, or rind, of a lemon.

2. The oil-rich zest (rind) holds a wealth of flavour, but avoid the bitter, white pith.

HOW TO SQUEEZE A LEMON

1. Cut off each end of the lemon to expose a small amount of fruit. Then cut the lemon in half.

2. This makes the lemon much easier to squeeze.

TANDOORI CHICKEN BREASTS WITH MANGO-MINT CHUTNEY

SERVES: 4
PREP TIME: 20 MINUTES
MARINATING TIME: 2 HOURS

HEAT: DIRECT MEDIUM HEAT 180°–230°C (350°–450°F)
BRAAIING TIME: 10–14 MINUTES

MARINADE
- 250 ml plain yoghurt
- 3 tablespoons fresh lemon juice
- 1 tablespoon finely chopped garlic
- 1 tablespoon finely chopped fresh ginger
- 2 teaspoons garam masala
- 2 teaspoons coarse sea salt
- 1 teaspoon sweet paprika

4 boneless, skinless chicken breasts, about 170 g each

CHUTNEY
- 2 firm ripe mangoes, flesh cut off the stone
- ½ tablespoon canola or sunflower oil
- 2 tablespoons finely chopped fresh mint
- 2 tablespoons cider vinegar
- ½ teaspoon sugar
- ¼ teaspoon coarse sea salt
- ¼ teaspoon freshly ground black pepper

Canola or sunflower oil

1. Blend the marinade ingredients together in a food processor to a uniform consistency, adding 1–2 tablespoons of water, if needed. Place the chicken in a large, resealable plastic bag and pour in the marinade. Press the air out of the bag and seal it tightly. Turn the bag several times to distribute the marinade and refrigerate for 2 hours, turning occasionally.

2. Prepare the braai for direct cooking over medium heat.

3. Lightly brush the mango sides with the oil. Brush the cooking grates clean. Braai the mango over **direct medium heat** for about 2 minutes, flat sides down and without turning, with the lid closed as much as possible, until they brown. Remove the mango from the braai and cut cross-hatch marks in the flesh down to the skin, then scoop out the little pieces. Combine the mango with the remaining chutney ingredients in a small bowl.

4. Remove the chicken from the bag and discard the marinade. Wipe off most of the marinade clinging to the chicken and then brush the chicken with oil. Braai over **direct medium heat** for 8–12 minutes, with the lid closed as much as possible but turning once, until the meat is firm to the touch and no longer pink in the centre. Serve warm with the chutney.

HOW TO CUT A MANGO

1. Inside each mango is a flat stone that runs from side to side.

2. To cut around the stone, rotate the mango so the stone runs parallel to the blade of your knife.

3. Cut each mango lengthways along each side of the stone.

HOW TO MAKE PLUM SAUCE

1. For the sauce, grill halved red plums until they are soft and sweet.

2. Simmer the grilled plums with port, sugar and finely chopped shallots or onion. Strain the sauce through a sieve, pressing the solids to extract as much flavour as possible.

HOW TO PREP DUCK BREASTS

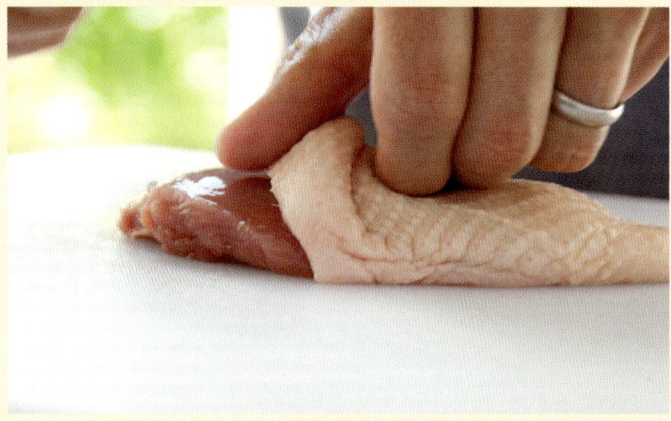

1. The skin of a duck breast is very fatty. To avoid flare-ups on the braai, one good option is to remove the skin first.

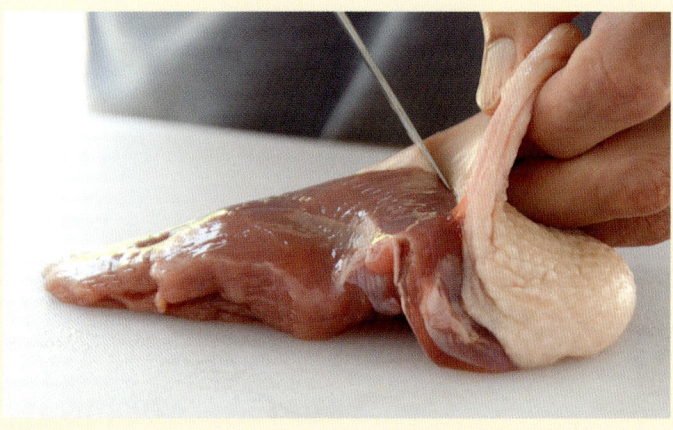

2. Lift the edge of the skin and use the sharp tip of a paring knife to separate the skin from the flesh as you pull back the skin.

3. The secret ingredient used in both the rub and the sauce is smoked sea salt. Look for it in speciality food shops.

4. The salt in the rub not only adds flavour, it also breaks down some muscle fibres, making the duck meat more tender.

DUCK BREASTS WITH PORT WINE AND PLUM SAUCE

SERVES: 4
PREP TIME: 30 MINUTES

HEAT: DIRECT MEDIUM HEAT 180°–230°C (350°–450°F)
BRAAIING TIME: ABOUT 12 MINUTES

SAUCE

    500 g red plums, halved and stoned
    1 tablespoon extra-virgin olive oil
    125 ml port-style wine
    3 tablespoons sugar
    1 shallot or small onion, thinly sliced
    Smoked sea salt
    Freshly ground black pepper

RUB

    1 tablespoon smoked sea salt
    1 tablespoon coarse sea salt
    1 tablespoon brown sugar

    4 duck breasts, 150 g each, skin removed
    1 tablespoon extra-virgin olive oil

1. Prepare the braai for direct cooking over medium heat. Brush the cooking grates clean.

2. Lightly brush the plums with the oil. Braai the plums over **direct medium heat** for about 4 minutes, with the lid closed as much as possible but turning once, until they have light grill marks and are starting to soften. Remove them from the braai and place in a medium saucepan with the port, sugar and shallot. Bring the mixture to a boil, then reduce the heat to medium, cover and simmer for about 10 minutes, stirring occasionally. After the sauce has cooked, use a wooden spoon to gently crush the plums into the sauce. Strain the sauce through a coarse sieve into a bowl, pushing as much plum pulp as possible through the sieve. Discard the remaining plum skin and pulp. Season to taste with smoked salt and pepper. Warm the sauce just before serving.

3. Combine the rub ingredients in a small bowl. Place the duck breasts into a large, resealable plastic bag and add the rub. Seal the bag and toss to coat thoroughly with the rub. Allow to stand at room temperature for 10 minutes, then remove the duck from the bag, pat dry with roller towels and brush with oil.

4. Brush the cooking grates clean. Braai the duck over **direct medium heat** for about 8 minutes for medium rare, with the lid closed as much as possible but turning once, until cooked to your desired doneness. Allow to rest for 5 minutes, then slice crossways into 5-mm thick slices. Serve warm with the sauce.

For a different take on tacos, try salt-cured duck breasts with thinly sliced savoy cabbage and cooked red onions.

DUCK BREAST TACOS WITH SOUR ORANGE AND ONION SALSA

SERVES: 4–6
PREP TIME: 30 MINUTES

HEAT: DIRECT MEDIUM HEAT 180°–230°C (350°–450°F)
BRAAIING TIME: ABOUT 9 MINUTES

- 4 boneless duck breasts, 150 g each
- 2 tablespoons coarse sea salt
- 2 tablespoons sugar

SALSA
- 300 g red onion, thinly sliced
- 125 ml fresh orange juice
- 4 tablespoons fresh lime juice
- 4 tablespoons finely chopped fresh chilli
- 1 tablespoon sugar
- ¼ teaspoon coarse sea salt
- 4 tablespoons chopped fresh coriander

Extra-virgin olive oil

- 16 corn tortillas (18 cm diameter)
- 1 ripe avocado, peeled and sliced
- 125 g radishes, thinly sliced
- 100 g savoy (Chinese) cabbage, thinly sliced

1. Using a small, sharp knife, remove and discard the thick layer of fat and skin from the duck breasts (see page 140).

2. Mix the salt and sugar together in a large bowl, then add the duck breasts and turn to coat them. Allow the breasts to stand at room temperature for 20–30 minutes before cooking, turning them over once or twice.

3. Combine the onion, orange and lime juices, chilli, sugar and salt in a large frying pan and cook over medium-high heat for 15–18 minutes, stirring occasionally to avoid any burning, until most of the liquid has evaporated. Remove the pan from the heat and stir in the coriander.

4. Prepare the braai for direct cooking over medium heat.

5. Pat the duck breasts dry and generously coat them on both sides with oil.

6. Brush the cooking grates clean. Braai the breasts over **direct medium heat** for about 8 minutes, with the lid closed as much as possible but turning once, until lightly browned on each side and still rosy pink in the centre. Transfer to a chopping board and, while the duck rests, braai the tortillas.

7. Brush the cooking grates clean. Braai the tortillas over **direct medium heat** for about 10 seconds on each side. Stack the hot tortillas and wrap them in a clean dishtowel to keep them hot.

8. Thinly slice the duck and serve with the warm tortillas, salsa, avocado, radish and cabbage.

JERK CHICKEN SKEWERS WITH HONEY-LIME CREAM

SERVES: 4–6
PREP TIME: 30 MINUTES
MARINATING TIME: 2–3 HOURS

HEAT: DIRECT HIGH HEAT 230°–290°C (450°–550°F)
BRAAIING TIME: 6–8 MINUTES
SPECIAL EQUIPMENT: RUBBER OR PLASTIC GLOVES; 8–12 BAMBOO SKEWERS, SOAKED IN WATER FOR AT LEAST 30 MINUTES

PASTE
- 1 habanero or Scotch bonnet chilli
- 250 ml fresh coriander leaves and tender stems
- 125 ml extra-virgin olive oil
- 4 spring onions, white and light green parts, roughly chopped
- 6 garlic cloves
- 2 tablespoons finely chopped fresh ginger
- 2 tablespoons sugar
- 1 tablespoon fresh lime juice
- 1 tablespoon ground allspice
- 2 teaspoons coarse sea salt
- 1 teaspoon freshly ground black pepper

6 boneless, skinless chicken breasts, 150 g each

SAUCE
- 125 ml sour cream
- ½ teaspoon finely grated lime zest
- 1 tablespoon fresh lime juice
- 1 tablespoon extra-virgin olive oil
- 2 teaspoons honey
- ¼ teaspoon coarse sea salt
- pinch of freshly ground black pepper

1. To avoid burning your skin, wear rubber or plastic gloves when you handle the chilli. After handling the chilli, do not touch your face or any other part of your body, as that might cause a burning sensation. Remove and discard the stem of the chilli, then cut away and discard the hot whitish veins and seeds. Put the chilli flesh into the bowl of a food processor. Add the remaining paste ingredients and process until smooth.

2. Trim the chicken of any fat and remove the fillets. Cut the chicken lengthways into even strips 1–1.5 cm thick.

3. Place the chicken strips and fillets into a large, resealable plastic bag and spoon in the paste. Work the paste into the chicken, then press the air out of the bag and seal tightly. Place in the refrigerator and allow to marinate for 2–3 hours.

4. Whisk the sauce ingredients together in a small bowl. Cover with clingfilm and refrigerate. Allow the sauce to stand at room temperature for about 30 minutes before serving. Prepare the braai for direct cooking over high heat.

5. Wearing rubber or plastic gloves, thread the chicken strips onto the skewers, being sure to keep each skewer well within the flesh of the chicken. If you don't use gloves, wash your hands thoroughly after this step.

6. Brush the cooking grates clean. Braai the skewers over **direct high heat** for 6–8 minutes, with the lid closed as much as possible but turning once or twice, until the meat is firm and the juices run clear. Serve warm with the sauce.

HOW TO MAKE CHICKEN SKEWERS

1. Wearing rubber or plastic gloves, remove and discard the incredibly fiery seeds and whitish veins in habanero chillies.

2. Marinate the chicken pieces in the puréed chilli paste and thread them onto skewers. Make sure the skewer runs through the centre of the chicken pieces.

3. Continue threading the chicken pieces onto the skewers until only the tip and base of each skewer is visible.

HOW TO PREP CHICKEN BREASTS

1. For a sauce of puréed parsley with olive oil, nuts and garlic, you can use all but the toughest stalks of parsley. Hold the stalks in one hand and use the other to shave off the leaves and tender stems.

2. This Tunisian-inspired spice paste will be particularly aromatic if you toast the spices first in a dry frying pan over medium heat.

3. Crush the toasted spices with a mortar and pestle, or use a clean coffee grinder (or spice grinder) to grind them to a powder.

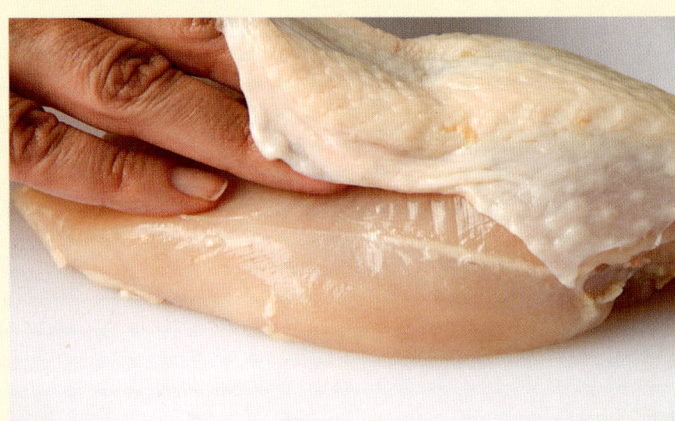

4. To get the spices right into the meat, very gently work your fingertips under the skin at the thin end of the breast, lifting the skin, but leaving it attached at the other end.

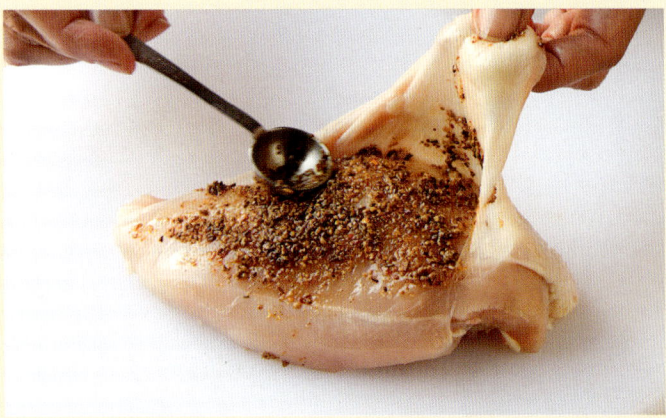

5. Spread the spice paste all over the exposed meat.

6. Pull the skin back into place and spread a bit more of the spice paste on top of the skin.

TUNISIAN CHICKEN WITH PARSLEY PESTO

SERVES: 4
PREP TIME: 20 MINUTES

HEAT: DIRECT AND INDIRECT MEDIUM HEAT 180°–230°C (350°–450°F)
BRAAIING TIME: 23–35 MINUTES
SPECIAL EQUIPMENT: MORTAR AND PESTLE OR COFFEE (OR SPICE) GRINDER

SAUCE
- 375 ml flat-leaf (Italian) parsley, leaves and tender stems
- 4 tablespoons whole unsalted almonds
- 1 garlic clove
- 125 ml extra-virgin olive oil
- 2 teaspoons Dijon mustard
- 1 teaspoon honey
- ¼ teaspoon coarse sea salt

PASTE
- 4 teaspoons coriander seed
- 2 teaspoons caraway seed
- 2 teaspoons cumin seed
- 2 teaspoons crushed red chilli flakes
- 2 tablespoons extra-virgin olive oil
- 1 teaspoon coarse sea salt

4 chicken breasts (with bone and skin), 300 g each

1. Pulse the parsley, almonds and garlic together in the bowl of a food processor until finely chopped. With the motor running, slowing add the oil to create an emulsion. Stir in the mustard, honey and salt. Emulsify the sauce again just before serving.

2. Toast the seeds and chilli flakes in a frying pan over medium heat for 2–3 minutes, until fragrant, then put into a mortar and pestle or coffee grinder and grind to a powder. Transfer to a bowl, add the oil and salt, and stir to make a paste.

3. Using your fingertips, carefully lift the skin from the chicken breasts, leaving the skin closest to the breastbone attached. Rub 1 teaspoon of the paste under the skin of each chicken breast, then pull the skin back in place and rub the remaining paste evenly over all the pieces of chicken. Place the chicken on a plate and cover with clingfilm. Allow the chicken to stand at room temperature for 20–30 minutes before grilling. Prepare the braai for direct and indirect cooking over medium heat.

4. Brush the cooking grates clean. Braai the chicken, skin side down, over **direct medium heat** for 3–5 minutes, until the skin is browned. Turn the chicken over and continue to cook over **indirect medium heat** for 20–30 minutes, with the lid closed, until the meat is opaque all the way to the bone. Transfer the chicken to a platter and allow to rest for 5–10 minutes. Serve warm with the sauce.

HOW TO BRAAI CHICKEN WINGS

1. You don't have to use skewers to braai chicken wings. You'll get great results without them, but skewers are helpful for spreading the wings flat, as if they were 'in flight'.

2. Flatter wings have more contact with the cooking surface, which means crispier skins and more flavour.

3. Brushing the wings with a honey-garlic glaze just before serving helps add flavour, too.

HONEY-GARLIC CHICKEN WINGS

SERVES: 4–6 AS AN APPETIZER
PREP TIME: 20 MINUTES
MARINATING TIME: UP TO 4 HOURS

HEAT: DIRECT AND INDIRECT MEDIUM HEAT 180°–230°C (350°–450°F)
BRAAIING TIME: 19–25 MINUTES
SPECIAL EQUIPMENT: 12 BAMBOO SKEWERS, SOAKED IN WATER FOR AT LEAST 30 MINUTES

MARINADE
    3 tablespoons fresh lemon juice
    1 tablespoon finely chopped garlic
    1 teaspoon coarse sea salt
    ½ teaspoon freshly ground black pepper

    1 kg chicken wings
    3 tablespoons fresh lemon juice
    125 ml runny honey
    1 tablespoon Tabasco or other hot sauce, or to taste

1. Combine the lemon juice, the garlic, salt and pepper for the marinade in a large bowl. Add the wings and toss to coat them evenly, then cover and refrigerate for up to 4 hours.

2. Combine the lemon juice, honey and Tabasco in a small bowl.

3. Prepare the braai for direct and indirect cooking over a medium heat.

4. Thread each wing onto a bamboo skewer, being sure to skewer each portion of the wing all the way up into the cartilage in the wingtip and then spreading it out as if it were 'in flight'.

5. Brush the cooking grates clean. Braai the wings over **direct medium heat** for 4–5 minutes, with the lid closed as much as possible, but turning once. Move the wings over **indirect medium heat** and cook for 15–20 minutes, basting with the honey mixture once or twice during the last 10 minutes of cooking time, until the meat is no longer pink at the bone. Keep the lid closed as much as possible during braaiing. Remove the wings from the braai, brush once more with the glaze and serve warm.

HICKORY DRUMETTES WITH BOURBON-MOLASSES GLAZE

SERVES: 6–8 AS AN APPETIZER
PREP TIME: 20 MINUTES

HEAT: INDIRECT MEDIUM HEAT 180°–230°C (350°–450°F)
BRAAIING TIME: 20–30 MINUTES

RUB
- 1 tablespoon smoked paprika
- 2 teaspoons dry mustard
- 1 teaspoon coarse sea salt
- ½ teaspoon garlic flakes
- ½ teaspoon onion flakes
- ¼ teaspoon chilli powder

20 chicken wing drumettes, about 1.5 kg

GLAZE
- 2 tablespoons soy sauce
- 2 tablespoons bourbon (Jack Daniels) or brandy
- 1 tablespoon molasses
- 1 tablespoon unsalted butter

2 handfuls hickory wood chips, soaked in water for at least 30 minutes

1. Mix the rub ingredients together in a small bowl. Add the drumettes and toss to coat them evenly.

2. Prepare the braai for indirect cooking over medium heat.

3. Bring the glaze ingredients to a boil in a small, heavy-based saucepan over high heat and cook just until the butter melts. Transfer to a small bowl and allow the glaze to cool.

4. Drain and scatter the soaked wood chips over lit charcoal or put them into the smoker box of a gas braai, following the manufacturer's instructions. Brush the cooking grates clean. Braai the drumettes over **indirect medium heat** for 20–30 minutes, with the lid closed as much as possible but turning and basting with the glaze once or twice during the last 20 minutes of cooking, until the meat is no longer pink at the bone. Serve warm.

HOW TO BRAAI CHICKEN DRUMETTES

1. Each chicken wing has three parts: a wingtip (left), a two-bone mid-section (centre), and an upper wing (right).

2. The upper wing is called the 'drumette' because it looks like a little drumstick.

3. Braai drumettes over indirect heat to break down some of the chewiness of the meat, and give them some good hickory smoke and a sweet boozy glaze.

HOW TO PREP WHOLE CHICKEN LEGS

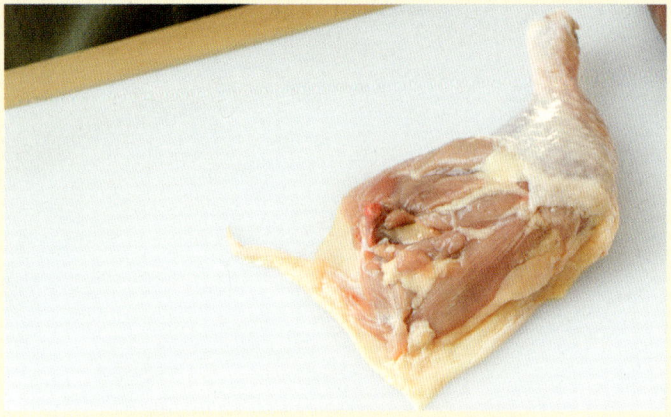

1. Turn each chicken leg skin-side down and trim off the excess skin. The fat under the excess skin tends to melt into the fire and can pose a threat of flare-ups.

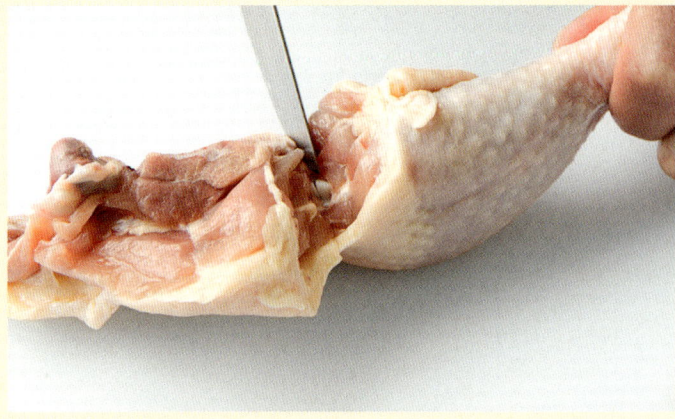

2. The meat nearest the joint of a chicken leg will take the longest to cook, so cut an opening between the drumstick and thigh to expose that innermost meat and speed up its cooking time.

3. Making some slashes on the outside of the leg will allow the marinade to penetrate faster and deeper.

4. The Provençal flavours in this recipe come from a blend of dried herbs that usually includes thyme, marjoram, parsley, tarragon, lavender, celery seed and bay leaf. It is sold as herbes de Provence.

5. Place the chicken in a large, resealable plastic bag and pour over the marinade. Press the air out of the bag, seal it tightly and turn it several times, making sure all the chicken pieces are evenly coated.

6. When you are dealing with raw chicken and a messy marinade, it's always a good idea to avoid spills by putting the bag in a bowl before refrigerating it.

PROVENÇAL MARINATED CHICKEN LEGS

SERVES: 6
PREP TIME: 15 MINUTES
MARINATING TIME: 4–8 HOURS

HEAT: INDIRECT MEDIUM HEAT 180°–230°C (350°–450°F)
BRAAIING TIME: 50–60 MINUTES

MARINADE
  250 ml dry white wine
  5 tablespoons extra-virgin olive oil
  3 tablespoons whole-grain mustard
  3 tablespoons white wine vinegar
  2 tablespoons herbes de Provence
  3 garlic cloves, finely chopped
  2 teaspoons coarse sea salt
  ½ teaspoon crushed red chilli flakes

6 whole chicken legs, 300 g each

1. Whisk the marinade ingredients together in a bowl.

2. Using a sharp knife, cut a few deep slashes into the meaty parts of each chicken leg. Place the legs in a large, resealable plastic bag and pour in the marinade. Press the air out of the bag and seal tightly. Turn the bag to distribute the marinade. Refrigerate for 4–8 hours, turning occasionally.

3. Prepare the braai for indirect cooking over medium heat.

4. Remove the chicken from the bag, letting the herbs cling to the chicken. Discard the marinade. Brush the cooking grates clean. Braai the chicken over **indirect medium heat** for 50–60 minutes, with the lid closed as much as possible but turning once, until the juices run clear and the internal temperature reaches 77°C (170°F) in the thickest part of the thigh (not touching the bone). To crisp the skin, braai the chicken over **direct medium heat** for the last 5 minutes of cooking time, turning once. Remove from the braai and cut into thighs and drumsticks.

■ ■ ■

Boneless chicken pieces do well braaied quickly over direct heat, but bone-in pieces take longer and direct heat alone would burn them, so use indirect heat (or both direct and indirect) for bone-in pieces.

■ ■ ■

HOW TO ROAST DUCK LEGS

1. Duck legs have so much fat under their skins that they are prone to flare-ups if you braai them over direct heat, but the 'ring of fire' gives you ample room in the centre of the cooking grate to smoke-roast them safely over indirect heat.

2. While the charcoal burns down to the right temperature and the hardwood chunks begin smoking, trim any fat hanging from the edges of the duck legs.

3. Cook the duck legs, skin side up, until dark brown and crispy. Brush on the orange-hoisin glaze near the end of the cooking time so that it does not burn.

SLOW-ROASTED DUCK LEGS WITH HOISIN-ORANGE GLAZE

SERVES: 4
PREP TIME: 10 MINUTES

HEAT: INDIRECT MEDIUM HEAT 170°C (325°F)
BRAAIING TIME: ABOUT 1 HOUR

GLAZE
    4 tablespoons orange marmalade
    4 tablespoons fresh orange juice
    4 tablespoons mirin (rice wine)
    2 tablespoons hoisin sauce
    ½ teaspoon crushed red chilli flakes

RUB
    2 teaspoons coarse sea salt
    ¾ teaspoon freshly ground black pepper
    ¾ teaspoon Chinese five-spice powder

    8 whole duck legs, 200 g each, trimmed of excess fat
    5 hardwood chunks (not soaked)

1. Prepare the braai for indirect cooking over medium heat using the ring-of-fire configuration (see top photo).

2. Combine the glaze ingredients in a small saucepan over medium-high heat. Bring to a simmer to melt the marmalade, then remove from the heat.

3. Combine the rub ingredients in a small bowl, then season the duck evenly with the rub.

4. Add the hardwood chunks directly onto burning coals. As soon as the wood starts to smoke, cook the duck, skin side up, over **indirect medium heat** for about 1 hour, with the lid closed as much as possible but turning and basting with the glaze during the last 15–20 minutes of cooking time, until the duck is evenly browned and crisp and is fully cooked. Serve warm.

HOW TO BRAAI CHICKEN PIECES

1. Season the chicken thighs and drumsticks with the spices.

2. After browning the chicken over direct heat, move it to indirect heat to smoke and finish cooking.

3. A couple of handfuls of damp wood chips should provide smoke for 20–30 minutes.

4. Spices, smoke and, finally, a light coating of barbecue sauce. That's a triple play of flavour.

TRIPLE-PLAY BARBECUED CHICKEN

SERVES: 4
PREP TIME: 30 MINUTES

HEAT: DIRECT AND INDIRECT MEDIUM HEAT 180°–230°C (350°–450°F)
BRAAI TIME: 43–45 MINUTES

SAUCE
- 2 tablespoons extra-virgin olive oil
- 1 medium onion, finely chopped
- 2 teaspoons finely chopped garlic
- 250 ml tomato purée
- 125 ml lemon-lime carbonated beverage (not diet)
- 4 tablespoons fresh lemon juice
- 4 tablespoons light brown sugar
- 2 tablespoons wholegrain mustard

RUB
- 2 teaspoons smoked paprika
- 2 teaspoons coarse sea salt
- Finely grated zest of 1 lemon
- ½ teaspoon garlic flakes
- ½ teaspoon freshly ground black pepper

- 4 chicken thighs and 4 chicken drumsticks
- 2 handfuls hickory wood chips, soaked in water for 30 minutes

1. Heat the oil in a saucepan and cook the oil, onion and garlic for about 10 minutes, stirring often, until golden. Add the rest of the sauce ingredients and stir to combine. Bring the sauce to a simmer, reduce the heat to low and cook for 10–15 minutes, stirring often, until slightly thickened.

2. Mix the rub ingredients together in a small bowl. Sprinkle the rub evenly over the chicken pieces and allow to stand at room temperature for 20–30 minutes before braaiing. Prepare the braai for direct and indirect cooking over a medium heat.

3. Brush the cooking grates clean. Braai the chicken, skin side down, over **direct medium heat** for 8–10 minutes, with the lid closed as much as possible but turning occasionally, until golden brown. Move the chicken pieces over **indirect medium heat**. Drain the wood chips and scatter them over the lit charcoal or put into the smoker box of a gas braai, following the manufacturer's instructions. Continue to braai the chicken, with the lid closed, for about 20 minutes, then brush both sides with a thin layer of the sauce and cook for a further 15 minutes, turning occasionally and brushing with the sauce, until the juices run clear and the meat is no longer pink at the bone. Serve warm or at room temperature with the remaining sauce on the side.

HOW TO CEDAR-PLANK BONE-IN CHICKEN THIGHS

1. Soak the cedar plank in beer or water for at least 1 hour.

2. Weigh the plank down with something heavy so it doesn't float.

3. Place the soaked plank over direct medium heat and close the lid to start the plank smoking.

4. When the plank starts smoking, turn it over and arrange the marinated chicken thighs on top.

5. Finish cooking the chicken thighs with the plank over indirect heat, basting them occasionally with the reserved marinade. If you leave the plank over direct heat for too long, it could ignite.

6. To check for doneness, pull one of the thickest thighs from the braai and cut into the underside. If the colour of the meat near the bone is still pink, put it back on the plank until it is fully cooked.

7. Using 2 pairs of tongs, carefully remove both the plank and the chicken thighs to a heatproof surface.

8. Before serving, glaze the chicken thighs one more time.

CEDAR-PLANKED CHICKEN THIGHS WITH SOY-GINGER GLAZE

SERVES: 4–6
PREP TIME: 30 MINUTES

HEAT: DIRECT AND INDIRECT MEDIUM HEAT 180°–230°C (350°–450°F)
BRAAIING TIME: 40–50 MINUTES
SPECIAL EQUIPMENT: 1 UNTREATED CEDAR PLANK, 30–45 CM LONG AND 1–1.5 CM THICK, SOAKED IN BEER OR WATER FOR AT LEAST 1 HOUR

GLAZE
    200 ml soy sauce
    125 ml balsamic vinegar
    125 ml light brown sugar
    1 tablespoon finely chopped garlic
    1 tablespoon finely chopped fresh ginger
    1 teaspoon crushed red chilli flakes
    4 tablespoons toasted sesame oil

10 chicken thighs on the bone, 150 g each, skin removed

1. Combine the soy sauce, vinegar and sugar in a small, non-reactive saucepan over medium-low heat and simmer for about 20 minutes, until reduced by half. Remove the saucepan from the heat and add the garlic, ginger and chilli flakes. Cool slightly and then whisk in the oil. Reserve 125 ml of the glaze for basting the chicken.

2. Put the thighs in a large bowl, pour over the rest of the glaze, and toss to coat. Refrigerate until you are ready to braai.

3. Prepare the braai for both direct and indirect cooking over medium heat. Place the soaked plank over **direct medium heat** and close the lid. After 5–10 minutes, when the plank begins to smoke and char, turn it over.

4. Remove the thighs from the bowl and discard the glaze. Arrange the thighs on the smoking plank and cook over **direct medium heat**, with the lid closed, for 5–10 minutes. Move the plank over **indirect medium heat** and continue cooking for 35–40 minutes, with the lid closed as much as possible but basting occasionally with the reserved glaze during the last 10–15 minutes of cooking time, until the juices run clear. Remove the plank and thighs from the braai and baste with the glaze once more before serving.

LAYERED MEXICAN CHICKEN SALAD

SERVES: 4–6
PREP TIME: 35 MINUTES
MARINATING TIME: 30–60 MINUTES

HEAT: DIRECT MEDIUM HEAT 180°–230°C (350°–450°F)
BRAAIING TIME: 16–20 MINUTES

MARINADE
- 4 tablespoons extra-virgin olive oil
- 2 tablespoons fresh lime juice
- 1 teaspoon dried thyme
- 1 teaspoon dried marjoram
- ½ teaspoon coarse sea salt
- ¼ teaspoon freshly ground black pepper

6 boneless, skinless chicken thighs, about 100 g each

DRESSING
- 1 large mild to medium-hot chilli
- 125 ml sour cream
- 125 ml fresh coriander leaves and tender stems
- 1 tablespoon fresh lime juice
- 1 tablespoon extra-virgin olive oil
- 1 large garlic clove
- ½ teaspoon ground cumin
- ½ teaspoon coarse sea salt
- ¼ teaspoon freshly ground black pepper

SALAD
- 250 g cos lettuce, thinly sliced or shredded
- 175 g tortilla chips, lightly crushed
- 175 g ripe tomato, diced
- 2 avocados, diced
- 1 can (425 g) pinto or black beans, rinsed

1. Whisk the marinade ingredients together in a medium bowl. Add the chicken thighs, turning several times to coat them evenly, then cover and refrigerate for 30–60 minutes.

2. Prepare the braai for direct cooking over medium heat. Brush the cooking grates clean. Braai the chilli over **direct medium heat** for 8–10 minutes, with the lid closed as much as possible, but turning occasionally, until the skin is blackened and blistered. Transfer the chilli to a small bowl, cover with clingfilm and leave to steam for about 10 minutes. Gently peel the skin from the chilli and remove the seeds. Put the chilli in a blender with the remaining dressing ingredients and process until smooth. Refrigerate until ready to serve.

3. Arrange a bed of lettuce on a large platter and then add the chips, tomato, avocado and beans in separate sections on top.

4. Braai the chicken over **direct medium heat** for 8–10 minutes, with the lid closed as much as possible but turning once or twice, until the meat is firm and the juices run clear. Transfer the chicken to a chopping board and cut into 1 cm-wide strips. Place the chicken on a separate section of the platter. Serve the dressing alongside.

HOW TO BRAAI BONELESS CHICKEN THIGHS

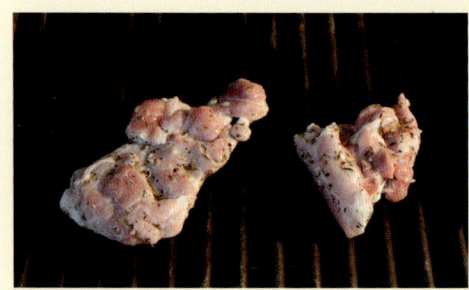

1. Place the chicken thighs, smooth side down first, over direct heat and resist the urge to turn them for at least 4 minutes. Otherwise, you might tear the meat.

2. However, if the meat is bunched on top of itself, unfold it so that it lies as flat as possible on the grate for better charred flavour.

3. You can check the doneness by bending back a thigh and opening up the meat. If there is no trace of pink, it's done.

KEEPING FROZEN SKEWERS ON HAND

To avoid having to soak bamboo skewers each time you need them, soak a big batch once for an hour or so, then drain them and freeze them in a plastic bag. When it's time to braai, take out as many skewers as you need.

Ingredients like chicken pieces will stay juicier for longer if they are touching (but not crammed) onto the skewers.

PERSIAN CHICKEN KEBABS

SERVES: 4–6
PREP TIME: 15 MINUTES
MARINATING TIME: 30 MINUTES

HEAT: DIRECT MEDIUM HEAT 180°–230°C (350°–450°F)
BRAAIING TIME: 8–10 MINUTES
SPECIAL EQUIPMENT: BAMBOO SKEWERS, SOAKED IN WATER FOR AT LEAST 30 MINUTES

MARINADE
  1 large onion, coarsely chopped
  125 ml fresh lemon juice
  2 tablespoons dried origanum
  2 teaspoons sweet paprika
  2 teaspoons finely chopped garlic
  250 ml extra-virgin olive oil

  10 boneless, skinless chicken thighs, about 100 g each, cut into 4-cm pieces

1. Purée the onion, lemon juice, origanum, paprika and garlic together in a food processor or blender. With the motor running, slowly add the oil.

2. Place the chicken pieces in a large, resealable plastic bag and pour in the marinade. Press the air out of the bag and seal tightly. Turn the bag to distribute the marinade and allow the chicken to marinate at room temperature for 30 minutes.

3. Prepare the braai for direct cooking over medium heat.

4. Remove the chicken from the marinade and thread onto skewers so that the pieces are touching, but not crammed together. Discard the marinade.

5. Brush the cooking grates clean. Braai the kebabs over **direct medium heat** for 8–10 minutes, with the lid closed as much as possible but turning once, until the meat is fully cooked but not dry. Serve warm.

HOW TO BRAAI QUESADILLAS

1. Most great quesadillas involve guacamole, and that means avocado. To stone an avocado, cut lengthways around the stone and then twist the halves in opposite directions.

2. Tap the exposed stone with the heel of your knife. It will pull out easily from the avocado.

3. You can chop the avocado right in the skin by cross-hatching it and then scooping the pieces into a bowl with a spoon. Next, mash the avocado with lime juice, garlic and salt.

4. Load up one side of each tortilla with grilled chicken, vegetables, and some grated cheese, but don't add so much that the filling might spill out the sides.

5. Fold the other half of the tortilla over the top and firmly press down on it. At this point, you can set the quesadillas aside for a couple of hours before cooking them.

6. Braai the quesadillas over direct medium heat until toasted on each side. This is one of the few times when it is best to leave the braai lid open, so that you can keep an eye on the quesadillas and prevent them from burning.

CHICKEN AND VEGETABLE QUESADILLAS WITH GUACAMOLE

SERVES: 4–6
PREP TIME: 30 MINUTES

HEAT: DIRECT MEDIUM HEAT 180°–230°C (350°–450°F)
BRAAIING TIME: 10–13 MINUTES

RUB
- 1 teaspoon chilli powder
- 1 teaspoon coarse sea salt
- ½ teaspoon dried origanum
- ¼ teaspoon garlic flakes
- ¼ teaspoon onion flakes
- ¼ teaspoon freshly ground black pepper

- 4 boneless, skinless chicken thighs, about 100 g each
- 2 large courgettes, trimmed and halved lengthways
- 2 sweetcorn mealie cobs
- Extra-virgin olive oil
- 2 teaspoons chopped fresh origanum
- 1 teaspoon finely chopped garlic
- 1 tablespoon fresh lime juice
- Coarse sea salt
- Freshly ground black pepper

GUACAMOLE
- 2 medium avocados, diced
- 2 teaspoons fresh lime juice
- 1 teaspoon finely chopped garlic
- ¼ teaspoon coarse sea salt

- 10 flour tortillas (25 cm diameter)
- 400 g grated Cheddar cheese

1. Prepare the braai for direct cooking over medium heat.

2. Combine the rub ingredients in a small bowl. Lightly brush the chicken, courgettes and sweetcorn cobs with oil. Season the chicken with the rub.

3. Brush the cooking grates clean. Braai the chicken and vegetables over **direct medium heat**, with the lid closed as much as possible but turning the chicken once and the vegetables occasionally, until the meat is firm and the juices run clear, the courgette is barely tender, and the sweetcorn is golden brown in spots. The chicken will take 8–10 minutes and the vegetables will take 6–8 minutes. Remove the chicken and vegetables from the braai as they are cooked and allow to cool.

4. Cut the chicken and courgette into 5-mm chunks. Cut the kernels from the cobs. In a large bowl combine the courgette and corn with the origanum, garlic and lime juice, and season to taste with salt and pepper. Add the chopped chicken to the vegetable mixture and stir to combine.

5. Mash together the guacamole ingredients in a small bowl.

6. Place the tortillas in a single layer on a work surface. Evenly divide the chicken and vegetable mixture, and then the cheese, over half of each tortilla. Fold the empty half of each tortilla over the filling, creating a half circle, and press down firmly.

7. Braai the quesadillas over **direct medium heat**, with the lid open, for 2–3 minutes, turning once. Transfer the cooked quesadillas to a chopping board and cut into wedges. Serve warm with the guacamole.

HOW TO SPLIT POUSSINS

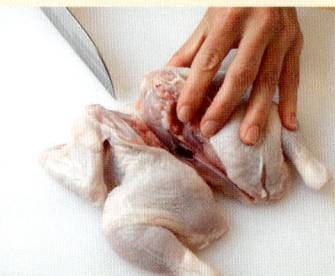

1. Use poultry shears to cut along both sides of the backbone, then discard it.

2. Cut through the centre of the breast.

3. The breastbone will stay attached to one of the halves.

4. Poussins cut into halves will absorb marinades more easily and cook faster than whole ones.

POUSSINS MARINATED IN BOURBON, HONEY AND SOY

SERVES: 4
PREP TIME: 30 MINUTES
MARINATING TIME: 4–8 HOURS

HEAT: INDIRECT MEDIUM HEAT 180°–230°C (350°–450°F)
BRAAIING TIME: 20–25 MINUTES

MARINADE
  350 ml soy sauce
  175 ml bourbon (Jack Daniels) or brandy
  6 garlic cloves, finely chopped
  2 tablespoons honey
  1½ tablespoons grated fresh ginger

  4 poussins, 400–500 g each
  Extra-virgin olive oil
  ½ teaspoon freshly ground black pepper

1. Combine the marinade ingredients in a bowl.

2. Remove and discard any giblets from the poussins. Using poultry shears, cut along both sides of each backbone and discard it, then cut through the centre of each breast.

3. Place the poussins side by side in a shallow, non-metallic dish and pour over the marinade. Turn the poussins to coat them evenly, then cover and refrigerate for 4–8 hours. (Do not marinate overnight or the ginger will cause the meat to break down and become mushy.)

4. Remove the poussins from the dish and reserve the marinade. Lightly brush the poussins with oil and season with the pepper. Allow them to stand at room temperature for 20–30 minutes before cooking. Prepare the braai for indirect cooking over medium heat.

5. Pour the reserved marinade into a small saucepan and bring to a boil over high heat for about 30 seconds. Set aside to use as a basting sauce.

6. Brush the cooking grates clean. Braai the poussins, skin side up, over **indirect medium heat** for 20–25 minutes, with the lid closed but basting the poussins with the sauce a couple of times during the last 10 minutes of cooking, until the skin is golden brown and the internal temperature in the thickest part of the thigh reaches 77°C (170°F). Remove the poussins from the braai and serve warm.

HULI-HULI CHICKEN

SERVES: 4–6
PREP TIME: 15 MINUTES
MARINATING TIME: ABOUT 4 HOURS

HEAT: INDIRECT MEDIUM HEAT 180°–230°C (350°–450°F)
BRAAIING TIME: 45–60 MINUTES

MARINADE
- 250 ml pineapple juice
- 125 ml soy sauce
- 4 tablespoons tomato purée
- 2 tablespoons finely chopped fresh ginger
- 2 teaspoons finely chopped garlic

- 2 whole chickens, 1.2–1.6 kg each
- 4 handfuls mesquite wood chips, soaked in water for at least 30 minutes

1. Whisk the marinade ingredients together in a bowl.

2. Place a chicken, breast side down, on a chopping board. Using poultry shears, cut along each side of the backbone and discard it. Open the chicken like a book, and cut the chicken in half lengthways along one side of the breastbone. Pull off and discard any lumps of fat. Remove and discard the wingtips. Repeat the process with the other chicken. Place the chicken halves in a very large, resealable plastic bag and pour in the marinade. Press the air out of the bag and seal it tightly. Turn the bag several times to coat the chicken evenly with the marinade. Place the bag in a bowl and refrigerate for about 4 hours, turning the bag occasionally.

3. Remove the chicken from the bag and discard the marinade.

4. Prepare the braai for indirect cooking over medium heat.

5. Drain half of the wood chips and toss them onto burning coals or into the smoker box of a gas braai, following the manufacturer's instructions. Begin cooking the chicken when the wood starts to smoke.

6. Brush the cooking grates clean. Braai the chicken, skin side up first, over **indirect medium heat**, for 45–60 minutes, with the lid closed as much as possible but turning the chicken every 15 minutes, until the juices run clear and the internal temperature reaches 77°C (170°F) in the thickest part of the thigh (not touching the bone). Drain the rest of the wood chips and add them after the first 15 minutes of cooking.

7. Remove the chicken from the braai and allow it to rest for about 10 minutes before serving.

'Huli-huli' is a Hawaiian term meaning 'turn-turn', which is what you need to do here to prevent the sweet marinade from burning. Turn the chicken halves carefully, using a spatula and tongs, so that they hold together. And don't forget the wood smoke; it is as important as any other ingredient in the recipe.

HOW TO SMOKE BEER CAN CHICKEN

1. Coating a chicken in salt and refrigerating it for a couple hours draws out some moisture and strengthens the chicken flavours. Don't worry; the chicken will not be salty. The next step is to rinse off the salt.

2. After you have rinsed and seasoned the chicken, open a beer can and pour half the beer into a cold mug. With a can opener, make 2 more holes in the top of the can to allow steam to escape.

3. Fold the wingtips behind the back of the chicken to shield the tips from the heat.

4. Working on a solid surface, slide the chicken over the beer can as far as it will go.

5. Set up the braai with a pan of water in the centre and coals on either side. Add a couple of handfuls of damp wood chips to each pile of coals.

6. When the wood starts to smoke, place the chicken in the centre of the cooking grate. Position the chicken legs towards the front so that they balance the chicken on the can, like a tripod.

7. When the chicken is fully cooked (77°C/170°F in the thickest part of the thigh), grab the back with tongs and slide a spatula under the can to lift it. Be careful; the beer will be very hot. Allow the chicken to rest and cool for about 10 minutes before sliding it off the can.

SMOKED BEER CAN CHICKEN

SERVES: 4
PREP TIME: 10 MINUTES
SALT-CURING TIME: 1½–2 HOURS

HEAT: INDIRECT MEDIUM HEAT 180°–230°C (350°–450°F)
BRAAIING TIME: 1–1¼ HOURS

    1 whole chicken, about 1.5–2 kg
    4 tablespoons coarse sea salt

RUB
    2 teaspoons onion flakes
    2 teaspoons garlic flakes
    1 teaspoon chilli powder
    ½ teaspoon freshly ground black pepper

    1 can beer, at room temperature
    4 handfuls hickory wood chips, soaked in water for
       at least 30 minutes

1. If necessary, remove and discard the neck, giblets and any excess fat from the chicken. Sprinkle salt over the entire surface and inside the cavity of the chicken, covering it all, like a light blanket of snow. Wrap the chicken well in clingfilm and refrigerate for 1½–2 hours.

2. Combine the rub ingredients in a small bowl.

3. Rinse the chicken inside and out with cold water and gently pat it dry with roller towels. Season it all over with the rub. Fold the wingtips behind the chicken's back. Allow the chicken to stand at room temperature for 20–30 minutes before cooking. Prepare the braai for indirect cooking over medium heat.

4. Open the beer can and pour out about half the beer. Using a can opener, make 2 more holes in the top of the can. Place the beer can on a solid surface and carefully ease the chicken cavity over the beer can.

5. Drain the wood chips and add them directly to the burning coals or to the smoker box of a gas braai, following the manufacturer's instructions. When the wood chips begin to smoke, transfer the bird-on-a-can to the braai, balancing the bird on its two legs and the can, like a tripod. Cook over **indirect medium heat** for 1–1¼ hours, with the lid closed, until the juices run clear and the internal temperature registers 77°C (170°F) in the thickest part of the thigh (not touching the bone). Carefully remove the chicken and can from the braai (take care; the contents of the beer can will be very hot). Allow the chicken to rest for about 10 minutes before lifting it from the beer can and cutting into serving pieces. Serve warm.

HOW TO COOK ROTISSERIE CHICKEN

1. To truss the chicken, remove the wingtips and slide a 1-metre length of string under the legs and back.

2. Lift both ends of the string, cross it between the legs, then run one end under one drumstick.

3. Run the other end of the string under the other drumstick and pull both ends to draw the drumsticks together.

4. Bring the string along both sides of the chicken so that it holds the legs and wings against the body.

5. Tie a knot in the ends between the neck and top of the breast. If necessary, push the breast down a little to expose more of the neck.

6. Marinate the trussed chicken in a large bag with the buttermilk mixture for 2–4 hours in the refrigerator.

7. Position one set of fork prongs on the far end of the centre rod (spit) and slide the spit into the opening between the neck and the knotted string, through the chicken and out the other side, just underneath the drumsticks. Slide the other set of fork prongs onto the spit and drive the prongs into the back of the chicken. Make sure the chicken is centred on the spit before tightening the fork prongs into place.

8. Position the chicken over a drip tray of water. Turn on the motor and cook the chicken over indirect heat, adjusting the burners to maintain a cooking temperature of about 200°C (400°F). During the last 30 minutes of cooking, brush the chicken a few times with the glaze, but keep the lid closed as much as possible. For a crispy skin, turn on the infrared burner at the back of the braai during the final minutes of cooking.

ROTISSERIE BUTTERMILK CHICKEN WITH APRICOT GLAZE

SERVES: 4
PREP TIME: 25 MINUTES
MARINATING TIME: 2–4 HOURS

HEAT: INDIRECT MEDIUM HEAT ABOUT 200°C (400°F)
BRAAIING TIME: 1–1¼ HOURS
SPECIAL EQUIPMENT: BUTCHER'S STRING, ROTISSERIE, LARGE DISPOSABLE FOIL TRAY, INSTANT-READ THERMOMETER

MARINADE
   500 ml buttermilk
   4 tablespoons fresh rosemary leaves, roughly chopped
   4 large garlic cloves, finely chopped
   2 tablespoons coarse sea salt
   1 teaspoon freshly ground black pepper

   1 whole chicken, 1.5–2 kg

GLAZE
   250 ml apricot juice
   3 tablespoons maple syrup
   1 tablespoon Dijon mustard
   1 tablespoon white wine vinegar

1. Combine the marinade ingredients in a large bowl.

2. Truss the chicken with butcher's string (see opposite page). Place the chicken in a very large, resealable plastic bag and pour in the marinade. Press the air out of the bag and seal it tightly. Turn the bag several times to coat the chicken evenly and place in a large bowl, starting with the breast side facing down. Marinate in the refrigerator for 2–4 hours, turning the bag once or twice. Allow the chicken to stand at room temperature for about 30 minutes before cooking. Prepare the braai for indirect cooking at 200°C (400°F), with the outside burners on medium to high and the middle burners turned off.

3. Whisk the glaze ingredients together in a small saucepan over a medium-high heat. Bring to a boil, reduce the heat and gently simmer for about 5 minutes until you have about 250 ml remaining. Reserve half of the glaze to use as a sauce.

4. Remove the chicken from the bag. Wipe off most of the marinade and discard the rest. Following the manufacturer's instructions, secure the chicken in the centre of a rotisserie spit, put the spit in place and turn on the motor. Place a large disposable foil tray under the chicken to catch drippings and pour about 250 ml warm water into the tray. Cook the chicken over **indirect medium heat** for 1–1¼ hours, keeping the lid closed, but brushing the chicken with the glaze a few times during the last 30 minutes of cooking, until the internal temperature reaches 77°C (170°F) in the thickest part of the thigh (not touching the bone).

5. When the chicken is fully cooked, turn off the rotisserie motor. Wearing insulated gloves, carefully remove the spit from the braai. Tilt the chicken upright over the foil tray so that any liquid that has accumulated in the body cavity pours into the tray. Slide the chicken from the spit onto a chopping board and allow it rest for about 10 minutes before carving into serving pieces. Serve warm with the reserved sauce.

HOW TO ROAST CHICKEN

Most chickens in supermarkets today have been bred primarily for their appearance. Large-scale farmers select their breeds for plump breast meat and yellow skins, and raise the chickens in cramped cages, feeding them cheap diets that promote quick growth but contribute very little to flavour. One way around the blandness problem is to buy organic free-range chickens instead. They might cost you more, but they do taste better. Another way around the blandness problem is to roast supermarket chickens with plenty of butter, fresh herbs and seasonings under the skin.

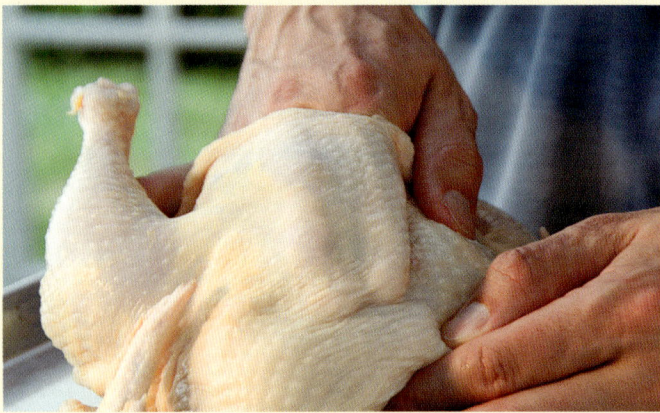

1. Starting at the bottom of the breast, work your fingertips gently under the skin and over the meat. Try not to tear the skin.

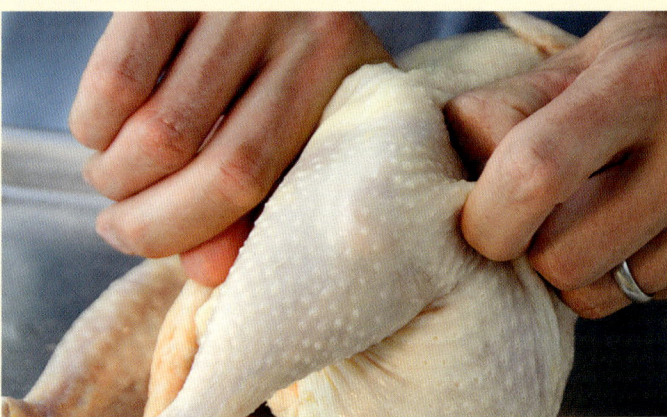

2. Use just one finger to reach down each drumstick and along the thigh meat.

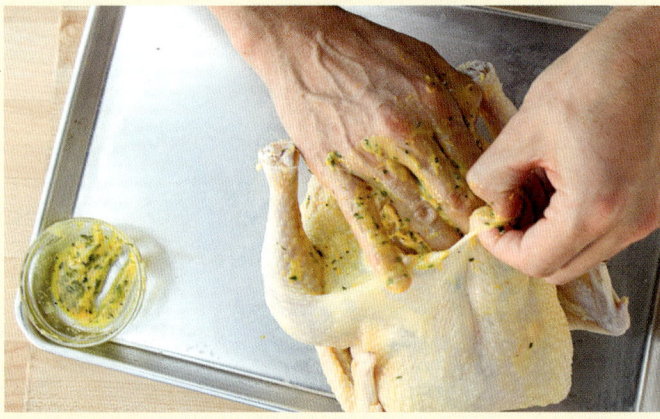

3. Smear the flavoured butter over the breast meat and cover as much of the thigh meat as possible without tearing the skin. Use the remaining flavoured butter to coat the outside of the chicken evenly.

4. Wrap a piece of butcher's string under and around the drumsticks, cross it in the centre, and pull the ends to draw the drumsticks together.

5. Cross the string above the drumsticks and tie a knot. This will hold the chicken in a compact shape and help the meat cook more evenly.

6. Roast the chicken in a disposable foil tray to catch the melted butter and drippings. Baste the chicken occasionally with what's in the tray and rotate the tray as necessary for even browning.

ORANGE-TARRAGON ROASTED CHICKEN

SERVES: 4
PREP TIME: 15 MINUTES

HEAT: INDIRECT MEDIUM HEAT 180°–230°C (350°–450°F)
BRAAIING TIME: 1–1¼ HOURS
SPECIAL EQUIPMENT: LARGE DISPOSABLE FOIL TRAY, BUTCHER'S STRING

BUTTER
    4 tablespoons unsalted butter, softened
    1 tablespoon finely chopped fresh tarragon
    2 teaspoons finely grated orange zest
    ½ teaspoon coarse sea salt
    ¼ teaspoon freshly ground black pepper

    1 whole chicken, 1.5–2 kg
    1 teaspoon coarse sea salt
    ½ teaspoon freshly ground black pepper

1. Using the back of a fork, mix and mash the butter ingredients in a small bowl.

2. Remove and discard the neck, giblets and any excess fat from the chicken. Loosen the chicken skin gently with your fingertips and spread the butter under the skin onto the breast meat and as far as you can reach on the drumsticks and thighs.

3. Season the chicken inside and out with the salt and pepper. Truss the chicken legs with butcher's string. Place the chicken, breast side up, in a large disposable foil tray. Allow the chicken to stand at room temperature for 20–30 minutes before cooking. Prepare the braai for indirect cooking over medium heat.

4. Brush the cooking grates clean. Cook the chicken over **indirect medium heat** for 1–1¼ hours, with the lid closed but rotating the pan as needed for even browning and occasionally basting the chicken with the melted butter collected in the bottom of the tray, until the juices run clear and the internal temperature in the thickest part of the thigh reaches 77°C (170°F). When fully cooked, transfer the chicken to a platter and loosely cover with heavyweight foil. Allow to rest for about 10 minutes, then remove the string and carve the chicken. Serve warm.

HOW TO BRAAI BUTTERFLIED CHICKEN

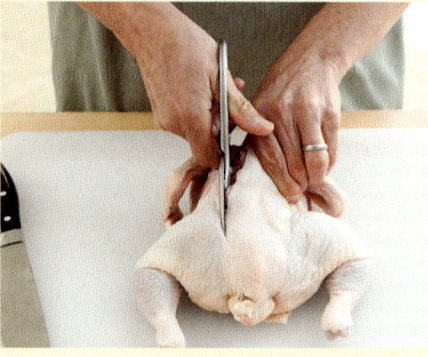
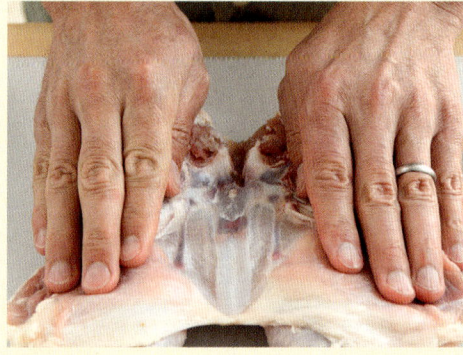

1. Pull out and discard the loose clumps of fat that are typically just inside the chicken. Otherwise they might drip into the braai and cause flare-ups.

2. Turn the chicken over so that the back is facing up and the neck end is closest to you. Use poultry shears to cut along both sides of the backbone, and then discard it.

3. Open the chicken like a butterfly spreading its wings, and press down to flatten it.

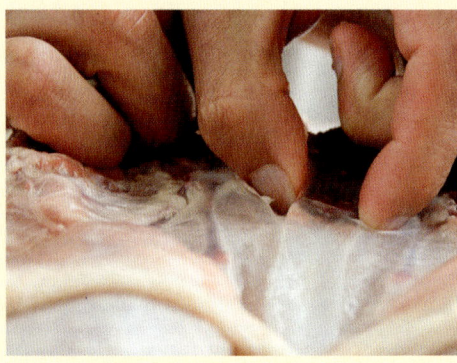
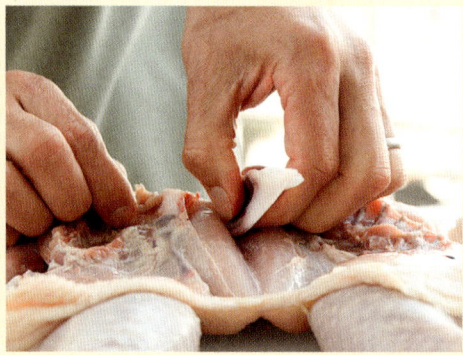
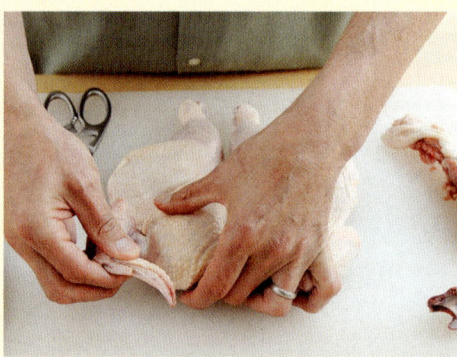

4. Run your fingertips along both sides of the breastbone to expose it.

5. Dig your fingers down along the breastbone until it comes loose from the meat. Then pull it out and discard it.

6. Fold the wing tips behind the chicken's back to prevent them from burning.

7. Now you have overcome one of the key challenges of cooking a whole chicken: an uneven shape. By butterflying (spatchcocking) the bird, you have created a relatively even shape and thickness.

8. Braai the chicken, bone side down first, with a heavy weight on top. Use a medium-low heat to gently cook the meat.

9. After about 25 minutes, carefully turn the chicken over with a spatula and put the weight back on top. With the skin side down, flare-ups are more likely. If necessary, turn off the middle burners or move the chicken to finish cooking over indirect heat.

NUTMEG CHICKEN UNDER A CAST-IRON PAN

SERVES: 4
PREP TIME: 30 MINUTES
MARINATING TIME: 2 HOURS

HEAT: DIRECT MEDIUM-LOW HEAT ABOUT 180°C (350°F)
BRAAIING TIME: ABOUT 40–60 MINUTES
SPECIAL EQUIPMENT: CAST-IRON PAN OR SHALLOW ROASTING TRAY AND 2 FOIL-WRAPPED BRICKS, INSTANT-READ THERMOMETER

MARINADE
    4 tablespoons extra-virgin olive oil
    2 tablespoons finely chopped fresh rosemary
    1 tablespoon finely chopped fresh garlic
    1 tablespoon freshly grated nutmeg
    1 tablespoon coarse sea salt
    1 tablespoon sugar
    1 teaspoon freshly ground black pepper

    1 whole chicken, 1.5–2 kg

1. Combine the marinade ingredients in a large shallow platter or roasting tray.

2. Place the chicken, breast side down, on a chopping board. Using sturdy kitchen shears or a very sharp knife, cut from the neck to the tail end, along either side of the backbone, to remove it. Take special care if you are using a knife; you'll be cutting through small bones and will have to use some force.

3. Once the backbone is out, you'll be able to see the interior of the chicken. Make a small slit in the cartilage at the bottom end of the breastbone. Then, placing both hands on the rib cage, crack the chicken open like a book. Run your fingers along either side of the cartilage between the breasts to loosen it from the flesh. Grab the bone and pull up on it to remove it along with the attached cartilage. The chicken should now lie flat.

4. Place the chicken on a platter or roasting tray and turn it a few times to coat it evenly with the marinade. Cover with clingfilm and refrigerate for about 2 hours.

5. Prepare the braai for direct cooking over a medium-low heat.

6. Brush the cooking grates clean. Place the chicken, bone side down over **direct medium-low heat**, and put a heavy cast-iron frying pan (or a roasting tray weighted down with 2 foil-wrapped bricks) directly on top of the chicken. Braai for 20–30 minutes with the lid closed. Remove the weight and turn the chicken over. Replace the weight, close the lid and braai for a further 20–30 minutes until the juices run clear and an instant-read thermometer inserted into the thigh (not touching the bone) registers 77°C (170°F). Remove the chicken from the braai and allow to rest for 3–5 minutes. Serve warm.

HOW TO BRAAI BACON-WRAPPED TURKEY BREAST

1. With the smooth side facing the board, open up the breast and cut down the centre (but not all the way through) to make the breast as flat and even as possible.

2. Place the butterflied turkey breast between 2 large sheets of clingfilm and pound it to a thickness of about 2 cm.

3. Spread the stuffing evenly over the turkey breast, but leave a margin all around the perimeter. Don't overstuff the breast.

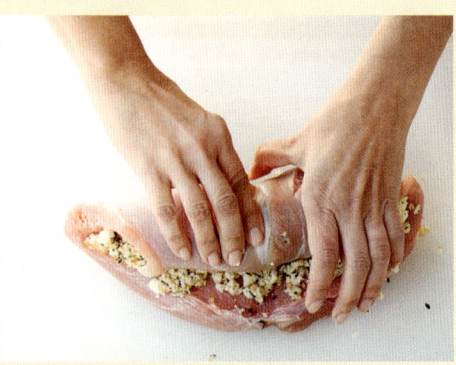

4. Roll up the breast lengthways to create a cylinder. If any excess stuffing falls out, discard it.

5. Arrange the bacon slices on a work surface in 6 tightly spaced parallel rows, overlapping the ends of 2 slices to make each row.

6. Place the rolled turkey breast in the centre of the bacon and then crisscross the bacon around the turkey.

7. Tie the turkey crossways with butcher's string at 2.5-cm intervals.

8. Thread a long piece of string lengthways, in and out of the crossways pieces, and tie the ends together to create a uniform roast and to secure the bacon.

9. Place a large disposable foil tray under the cooking grate to catch the bacon fat. Cook the roast, using indirect heat, until the internal temperature of the meat and stuffing reaches 74°C (165°F), turning to ensure even cooking.

BACON-WRAPPED TURKEY BREAST WITH HERB STUFFING

SERVES: 4–6
PREP TIME: 30 MINUTES

HEAT: INDIRECT HIGH HEAT 230°–290°C (450°–550°F)
BRAAIING TIME: 1–1¼ HOURS
SPECIAL EQUIPMENT: BUTCHER'S STRING, LARGE FOIL TRAY, INSTANT-READ THERMOMETER

STUFFING
- 375 ml fresh breadcrumbs
- 4 tablespoons chicken stock
- 1 tablespoon finely chopped garlic
- 2 teaspoons finely chopped fresh rosemary
- 2 teaspoons finely chopped fresh origanum
- 1 teaspoon finely grated lemon zest
- ½ teaspoon coarse sea salt
- ½ teaspoon freshly ground black pepper

- 450 g streaky bacon
- 1 boneless, skinless turkey breast, about 1 kg, butterflied

1. Combine the stuffing ingredients in a bowl. The stuffing should be moist, mounding nicely on a spoon, but should not be sopping wet. Add more stock if needed.

2. Carefully place a large disposable foil tray underneath the cooking grate to catch the bacon fat. Prepare the braai for indirect cooking over high heat.

3. Place the butterflied turkey breast on a work surface between 2 sheets of clingfilm and pound to an even thickness. Spread the stuffing evenly over the turkey breast and then roll up the breast lengthways to create a cylinder. Arrange the bacon slices on a work surface in 6 tightly spaced parallel rows, overlapping the ends of 2 slices to make each row. Place the rolled turkey breast in the centre of the bacon and crisscross the bacon around the turkey. Tie the turkey with butcher's string to create a uniform roast and to secure the bacon.

4. Brush the cooking grates clean. Centre the turkey over the drip pan and braai over *indirect high heat* for 1–1¼ hours, with the lid closed as much as possible but turning occasionally to ensure the bacon gets crispy on all sides, until the internal temperature reaches 74°C (165°F). Transfer the meat to a carving board and allow to rest for 10 minutes (the internal temperature will rise during this time). Remove the string and carve the turkey breast into 2 cm-thick slices.

HOW TO BRAAI TURKEY

5 THINGS YOU NEED TO KNOW

Every December, millions of cooks tighten up with stress at the thought of how to cook a golden, succulent turkey for Christmas. Let me tell you; it's not that difficult. Focus on a handful of critical elements.

1 BRINING A DAY AHEAD

Because turkey meat is so lean and bland, some kind of brining is important. In the following recipe I call for a dry brine, which just means coating the turkey with sea salt the day before cooking. Overnight, in the refrigerator, the salt will draw out some moisture, which will mix with the salt, and then the meat will reabsorb much of that flavourful moisture.

2 MAINTAINING AN EVEN COOKING TEMPERATURE

An even temperature of 180°–200°C (350°–400°F) is key here. That's easy enough to achieve on a gas braai, assuming there is plenty of gas in the cylinder. It's a bit more challenging with a charcoal braai. Before cooking your first turkey over charcoal, make sure you have had some experience maintaining a live fire over the course of several hours.

3 SHIELDING THE BREAST MEAT

Because the breast meat cooks faster than the leg meat, you should protect the breast and slow down its rate of cooking. I do that by facing the breast down inside a stock-and-vegetable-filled pan for the first hour of cooking.

4 CATCHING THE PERFECT DONENESS

In a very short period of time, a turkey can turn from moist and fabulous to dry and stringy, so it's imperative to use an instant-read thermometer and remove the turkey from the braai when the internal temperature in the thickest part of the thigh reaches 77°C (170°F).

5 GETTING ENOUGH REST

Finally, don't omit the resting step after the turkey comes off the braai. This allows the turkey to finish cooking and the juices to redistribute.

HOW TO PREP TURKEY THE DAY BEFORE

1. Generously season the turkey, inside and out, with coarse sea salt and freshly ground black pepper.

2. Refrigerate the seasoned turkey on a roasting tray, uncovered, for 12 hours. It's okay if the skin looks dry and tight at the end.

HOW TO SMOKE TURKEY

1. Remove the turkey from the refrigerator and allow it to sit at room temperature for 1 hour. Brush the legs, breast and wings with butter.

2. Place one large disposable foil tray inside another and add the vegetables, herbs and 500 ml chicken stock.

3. Arrange the charcoal in a semi-circle on one side of the charcoal grate. A drip tray filled with warm water will help to maintain the temperature of the fire.

4. Place the turkey, breast side down, inside the foil tray and over the vegetables.

5. Add wood chips to the charcoal and set the tray over the water pan, with the turkey legs facing the hottest side of the braai.

6. Keep the cooking temperature in the range of 180°–200°C (350°–400°F), adding more charcoal as needed.

7. After cooking for 1 hour, flip over the turkey so that the breast side is facing up.

8. Continue cooking and smoking the turkey, occasionally adding damp wood chips.

9. After about 1½ hours, cover any parts of the turkey that are getting too dark with foil.

HOW TO CARVE TURKEY

1. Remove each half of the turkey breast by cutting lengthways along either side of the breastbone.

2. Pull the first half of the breast away from the breastbone, using a sharp knife to carefully release the meat from the rib cage.

3. It is much easier to carve the turkey breast crossways into slices once it has been removed than it is to carve the breast while it is still attached to the body.

HICKORY-SMOKED TURKEY WITH BOURBON GRAVY

SERVES: 8–12
PREP TIME: 20 MINUTES
DRY BRINING TIME: 12 HOURS

HEAT: INDIRECT MEDIUM HEAT 180°–200°C (350°–400°F)
BRAAIING TIME: ABOUT 2½ HOURS
SPECIAL EQUIPMENT: 3 LARGE DISPOSABLE FOIL ROASTING TRAYS, INSTANT-READ THERMOMETER

- 1 turkey, about 5 kg
- 2 tablespoons coarse sea salt
- 2 teaspoons freshly ground black pepper
- 3 tablespoons unsalted butter, softened

AROMATICS
- 1 large onion, chopped
- 1 large carrot, chopped
- 2–3 sticks celery, chopped
- 1 teaspoon dried rosemary
- 1 teaspoon dried thyme
- 1 teaspoon dried sage

- 500 ml chicken stock, plus extra for gravy
- 4 handfuls hickory wood chips, soaked in water for at least 30 minutes

GRAVY
- 125 ml flour
- 3 tablespoons bourbon (Jack Daniels) or brandy
- ½ teaspoon coarse sea salt
- ¼ teaspoon freshly ground black pepper

1. The day before cooking, prepare the turkey. Remove the giblets and set aside for another use. Rinse the turkey with cold water and shake off the excess, but do not pat dry. Combine the salt and pepper in a small bowl and rub it all over the turkey, inside and out. Place the turkey in a large foil roasting tray and refrigerate, uncovered, for 12 hours.

2. Remove the turkey from the refrigerator. The skin may look dry, but that's okay. Do not rinse the turkey. Allow the turkey to stand at room temperature for 1 hour. Brush the legs, breast and wings with the butter.

3. Place one disposable foil roasting tray inside the other and combine the aromatics in the top tray. (Do not use a high-quality metal roasting tray, as the smoke may discolour it.) Add 500 ml chicken stock. Place the turkey, breast side down, inside the foil trays, on top of the aromatics.

4. Drain and add 2 handfuls of wood chips directly onto burning coals or to the smoker box of a gas braai, following the manufacturer's instructions. Cook the turkey over **indirect medium heat** for 1 hour, with the lid closed, keeping the temperature between 180° and 200°C (350°–400°F).

5. After cooking for 1 hour, wearing oven gloves or barbecue mitts and using a pair of tongs, flip the turkey over so that the breast side is facing up. For charcoal braaiing, add 12–15 unlit briquettes to the coals to maintain the heat of the braai. Add the remaining 2 handfuls of wood chips. Continue cooking and smoking the turkey for 1½ hours, until it is golden brown and a thermometer inserted in the thickest part of the thigh (not touching the bone) reaches 77°C (170°F). After the turkey has been on the braai for 1½ hours, check to see whether the wingtips or ends of the drumsticks are getting too dark. If so, wrap them with foil.

6. Carefully remove the turkey and both roasting pans from the braai. Transfer the turkey to a carving board and allow to rest for 20–30 minutes. Save the juices and vegetables to make the gravy.

7. Strain the pan juices into a fat separator, pressing the vegetables firmly with a wooden spoon to extract as much liquid as possible. Discard the vegetables left in the strainer. Allow the pan juices to stand for about 2 minutes, until the fat rises to the surface. Pour the pan juices into a 1-litre measuring jug and add more hot chicken stock, if needed, to make 750 ml. Measure the turkey fat; you should have 125 ml. Add melted butter, if needed.

8. Warm the fat in a heavy-based saucepan over a medium heat. Whisk in the flour and allow to bubble for about 2 minutes, until golden brown. Whisk in the stock mixture and the bourbon or brandy. Gently heat until lightly thickened, stirring often. Season with salt and pepper.

9. Carve the turkey and serve with the gravy.

CEDAR-PLANKED TURKEY BURGERS

SERVES: 6
PREP TIME: 20 MINUTES

HEAT: DIRECT MEDIUM HEAT 180–230°C (350°–450°F)
BRAAIING TIME: 20–30 MINUTES
SPECIAL EQUIPMENT: 2 UNTREATED CEDAR OR MAPLE PLANKS, EACH 30–45 CM LONG AND 1–1.5 CM THICK, SOAKED IN BEER OR WATER FOR AT LEAST 1 HOUR

SAUCE
   125 ml tomato purée
   75 ml Worcestershire sauce
   3 tablespoons soy sauce
   1 tablespoon apple cider vinegar
   1 tablespoon brown sugar
   1½ teaspoons dry mustard
   1½ teaspoons ground cumin
   1 teaspoon Tabasco or other hot sauce, or to taste

   1 kg minced turkey thigh meat
   4 tablespoons finely chopped shallot
   4 tablespoons rolled oats (Jungle Oats)
   1 teaspoon coarse sea salt
   ½ teaspoon freshly ground black pepper

   6 hamburger rolls
   18 sweet pickle slices
   18 red onion slices

1. Combine the sauce ingredients in a bowl. Set aside about 125 ml of the sauce to serve with the burgers.

2. Mix the turkey mince with the shallot, oats, salt and pepper and form into 6 burgers, each about 2 cm thick. With your thumb or the back of a spoon, make a shallow indentation about 2.5 cm wide in the centre of each burger so that the centres are about 1 cm thick.

3. Prepare the braai for direct cooking over medium heat.

4. Brush the cooking grates clean. Drain the planks and heat them over **direct medium heat** for 5–10 minutes with the lid closed, until they begin to char and lightly smoke. Turn the planks over and place 3 burgers on each plank. Braai the burgers over **direct medium heat** for 15–20 minutes, with the lid closed as much as possible, but turning and basting with the sauce once after 10 minutes.

5. During the last minute of cooking time, lightly toast the cut sides of the rolls over **direct medium heat**. Serve the burgers on rolls with pickles, onions and the reserved sauce, if desired.

HOW TO SMOKE TURKEY BURGERS ON PLANKS

1. Cook the burgers for about 10 minutes on the planks, then begin basting them with sauce and turn them over.

2. Cook for 5–10 minutes, basting occasionally, until there's no red left in the centre and the internal temperature registers 74°C (165°F).

3. You will find that burgers made with dark thigh meat are juicer than burgers made with light breast meat.

HOW TO REMOVE CORN KERNELS

1. Cut the stem end off an ear of corn (mealie cob) to create a flat surface.

2. Stand the cob, stem side down, in a bowl. Slice off the kernels from top to bottom so that they fall into the bowl.

HOW TO SHRED CABBAGE

1. Halve a head of cabbage lengthways and cut out the tough, triangular core of each half.

2. Place each half flat on a chopping board and slice (shred) it as thinly as you can.

TURKEY BURGERS WITH SALSA SLAW

SERVES: 4
PREP TIME: 20 MINUTES

HEAT: DIRECT MEDIUM HEAT 180°–230°C (350°–450°F)
BRAAIING TIME: 8–10 MINUTES

SLAW
- 150 g finely shredded savoy cabbage
- 250 ml fresh tomato salsa (see page 291), drained
- 4 tablespoons finely chopped fresh coriander
- 3 tablespoons sour cream

BURGERS
- 700 g minced turkey thigh meat
- 80 ml fresh corn kernels
- 4 tablespoons finely chopped pickled jalapeño chilli, or to taste
- 1 tablespoon chilli powder
- 2 teaspoons finely chopped garlic
- 1½ teaspoons coarse sea salt
- 1 teaspoon ground cumin

- 4 wholegrain hamburger rolls

1. Mix the slaw ingredients in a bowl. Cover and refrigerate. Stir and then drain well just before serving.

2. Prepare the braai for direct cooking over medium heat.

3. Gently mix the burger ingredients together in a bowl. Shape into 4 burgers, each about 2 cm thick. With your thumb or the back of a spoon, make a shallow indentation about 2.5 cm wide in the centre of each patty so that the centres are about 1 cm thick. This will help the burgers cook evenly and prevent them from puffing up on the braai.

4. Brush the cooking grates clean. Braai the burgers over **direct medium heat** for 8–10 minutes, with the lid closed as much as possible but turning once, until fully cooked yet still juicy. During the last minute of cooking time, lightly toast the cut sides of the rolls over **direct medium heat**. Top the burgers with slaw and serve on the toasted rolls.

SEAFOOD

TECHNIQUES

184	How to braai **PRAWN POPS**
188	How to make **PAELLA**
192	How to char-grill **OYSTERS**
194	How to prep and braai **CRAYFISH TAILS**
196	How to prep and braai **CRABS**
200	How to braai **FISH**: Five things you need to know
201	How to braai **SALMON**
203	How to braai **SALMON** on a plank
204	How to bone **SALMON** steaks
214	How to braai **FISH FILLETS** in banana leaves
216	How to fillet **LINE FISH**
219	How to prep **WHOLE FISH**
220	How to braai **TROUT** in a basket
224	How to prep **SQUID**
226	How to braai **CALAMARI** under bricks

RECIPES

178	**SCALLOPS** with Roasted Tomato Sauce
179	Prosciutto-wrapped **SCALLOPS** with Lentil Salad
180	Cedar-planked **SCALLOPS** with Grilled Corn Salad
181	Thai **PRAWNS** with Watermelon Salsa
182	**PRAWN ROLLS** with Rémoulade
183	Orange-Fennel **PRAWNS** Over Watercress
185	Vietnamese **PRAWN POPS** with Peanut Sauce
187	Juicy **PRAWNS** with Roasted Chilli and Avocado Sauce
189	**PAELLA**
190	Coconut-Curry **MUSSELS**
191	Cajun-style **CLAMBAKE**
193	Char-grilled **OYSTERS**
195	**CRAYFISH (ROCK LOBSTER)** Rolls
197	**WHOLE CRABS** with White Wine-Garlic Butter
198	**CRAB** and Avocado Quesadillas
199	**SEAFOOD** Zuppa
201	**SALMON** with Nectarine Salsa
202	**SALMON** with Red Curry-Coconut Sauce
203	Cedar-planked **SALMON** with Hazelnut Sauce
205	**SALMON** with Fennel and Olive Salad
206	**FISH WRAPS** with Chipotle-Lime Slaw
207	**HAKE** with Bombay Tomato Sauce
209	**DORADO** with Corn and Mushroom Salsa
210	Braaied **TUNA** Poke
211	Smoked **TUNA SALAD** with Grilled Mango
212	Grilled **HAKE** in a Caribbean Citrus Marinade
213	**SWORDFISH** Escabèche
215	Ginger and Miso **LINE FISH** in Banana Leaves
217	**LINE FISH** in Coconut Broth
218	**MEXICAN GRILL-PAN FISH**
219	Whole **LINE FISH** in Moroccan Marinade
221	Sake-marinated **TROUT**
223	Cedar-planked **TROUT** with Rocket, Fennel and Orange
225	Thai **SQUID (CALAMARI)**
227	Brickyard **CALAMARI SALAD**

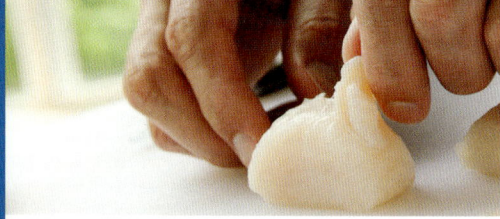

Before braaiing, remove any tough little side muscles still attached to the scallops (top photo). After braaiing, the interior of the scallops should be barely opaque, like the one in the centre of the bottom photo. The scallop on the left is a little underdone and the scallop on the right is overdone.

SCALLOPS WITH ROASTED TOMATO SAUCE

SERVES: 4
PREP TIME: 25 MINUTES
MARINATING TIME: 10–15 MINUTES

HEAT: DIRECT MEDIUM HEAT 180°–230°C (350°–450°F)
BRAAIING TIME: 14–16 MINUTES

SAUCE
    500 g ripe red tomatoes
    3 spring onions, tops and root ends trimmed
    1 teaspoon finely grated lemon zest
    2 tablespoons fresh lemon juice
    1 tablespoon sugar
    1 teaspoon yellow mustard seed
    1 teaspoon fennel seed
    ½ teaspoon coarse sea salt

    12 jumbo sea scallops, about 50 g each

MARINADE
    1 tablespoon unsalted butter, melted
    1 tablespoon extra-virgin olive oil
    1 teaspoon finely grated lemon zest
    1 tablespoon fresh lemon juice
    ½ teaspoon coarse sea salt
    ¼ teaspoon freshly ground black pepper

    1 tablespoon finely chopped fresh basil or flat-leaf parsley

1. Prepare the braai for direct cooking over medium heat. Brush the cooking grates clean.

2. Braai the tomatoes and spring onions over **direct medium heat**, with the lid closed as much as possible but turning as needed, until the tomato skins blister and brown and the spring onions are lightly browned. The tomatoes will take about 10 minutes and the spring onions will take 4–5 minutes. Transfer the vegetables to a chopping board. Carefully pull off and discard the tomato skins and trim and discard the stem ends. Chop the tomatoes into 5-mm pieces and transfer them, with their juices, to a large frying pan. Thinly slice the spring onions, including the tops, and add to the tomatoes with the rest of the sauce ingredients. Simmer the sauce over medium heat for 5–6 minutes, stirring occasionally, until the flavours blend. Keep warm. (The sauce can be made a day ahead and reheated.)

3. Remove the small, tough side muscle that might be left on each scallop. Combine the marinade ingredients in a small bowl. Toss the scallops in the marinade and allow to stand at room temperature for 10–15 minutes.

4. Brush the cooking grates clean. Lift the scallops from the bowl and place them slightly apart on the cooking grate. Discard the marinade. Braai over **direct medium heat** for 4–6 minutes, with the lid closed as much as possible but turning once, until lightly browned and just opaque in the centre (check one by cutting it open).

5. Add the basil to the tomato sauce. Divide the sauce evenly onto 4 warmed plates and top with hot scallops.

PROSCIUTTO-WRAPPED SCALLOPS WITH LENTIL SALAD

SERVES: 4
PREP TIME: 25 MINUTES
MARINATING TIME: 1 HOUR

HEAT: DIRECT MEDIUM HEAT 180°–230°C (350°–450°F)
BRAAIING TIME: 4–6 MINUTES

12 jumbo sea scallops, about 50 g each
6 thin slices prosciutto, cut in half lengthways

MARINADE
3 tablespoons finely chopped shallot or small onion
3 tablespoons fresh lemon juice
2 tablespoons extra-virgin olive oil
1½ tablespoons Dijon mustard
¾ teaspoon dried tarragon
¼ teaspoon freshly ground black pepper

LENTILS
6 thin slices prosciutto, finely chopped
2 tablespoons extra-virgin olive oil
250 ml finely chopped button mushrooms
80 ml finely chopped shallot or small onion
½ teaspoon dried tarragon
200 g green or brown lentils
750 ml chicken stock
1 teaspoon finely grated lemon zest
4 tablespoons fresh flat-leaf (Italian) parsley, finely chopped
Coarse sea salt
Freshly ground black pepper

1. Remove the small, tough side muscle that may be left on each scallop.

2. Wrap one slice of prosciutto around each scallop and secure with a cocktail stick.

3. Mix the marinade ingredients together in a shallow, non-metallic dish. Gently turn the scallops in the marinade and then lay them flat in the dish. Cover with clingfilm and refrigerate for 1 hour. Meanwhile prepare the lentils.

4. Combine the chopped prosciutto, oil, mushrooms, shallot, and tarragon in a large saucepan over medium-high heat. Stir often for 5–7 minutes until the vegetables are limp and slightly browned.

5. Sort through the lentils and discard any debris. Rinse and drain the lentils and add them to the saucepan along with the stock. Bring to a boil, reduce the heat, cover and simmer until the lentils are tender, 40–55 minutes. Stir in the lemon zest and parsley. Season to taste with salt and pepper. Keep warm.

6. Prepare the braai for direct cooking over medium heat. Brush the cooking grates clean. Braai the scallops, unwrapped sides down, over **direct medium heat** for 4–6 minutes, with the lid closed as much as possible but turning once, until the scallops are lightly browned and opaque in the centre. Remove from the braai and serve warm with the lentils.

HOW TO PREP SCALLOPS

1. Cut each prosciutto slice to fit the scallops.

2. Wrap a strip of prosciutto around each scallop and secure it with a cocktail stick.

3. Braai the scallops for 2–3 minutes, until they can easily lift off the grate without sticking.

4. Turn the scallops over and finish cooking. Cook so that the flat sides lie on the hot grate.

CEDAR-PLANKED SCALLOPS WITH GRILLED CORN SALAD

SERVES: 4–6
PREP TIME: 25 MINUTES

HEAT: DIRECT MEDIUM HEAT 180°–230°C (350°–450°F)
BRAAIING TIME: 23–32 MINUTES
SPECIAL EQUIPMENT: 1 UNTREATED CEDAR PLANK, ABOUT 30 CM LONG AND 1–2 CM THICK, SOAKED IN WATER FOR AT LEAST 1 HOUR

MARINADE
    75 ml extra-virgin olive oil
    75 ml fresh lime juice
    1 tablespoon honey
    1 teaspoon coarse sea salt

    20 large sea scallops, each about 3 cm in diameter

SALAD
    ½ small red onion, cut into 3 wedges
    3 ears fresh sweetcorn
    1 red pepper
    Extra-virgin olive oil
    Coarse sea salt
    Freshly ground black pepper
    ½ teaspoon ground cumin
    1 teaspoon Tabasco or other hot sauce, or to taste

1. Whisk the marinade ingredients together in a bowl. Transfer 3 tablespoons of the marinade to a large bowl to use for dressing the salad. Set the 2 bowls aside.

2. Remove the small, tough side muscle that may be left on each scallop. Refrigerate the scallops until ready to braai.

3. Prepare the braai for direct cooking over a medium heat. Lightly brush or spray the onion, corn and pepper with oil and season evenly with salt and pepper. Brush the cooking grates clean. Braai the vegetables over **direct medium heat**, with the lid closed as much as possible but turning the vegetables as needed, until the onion has softened and started to collapse, the corn kernels are mostly brown, with some beginning to char, and the pepper is blackened and blistered all over. The onion will take about 4 minutes, the corn will take 6–8 minutes and the pepper, 10–12 minutes. Place the pepper in a bowl, cover with clingfilm and allow to cool.

4. When the vegetables are cool enough to handle, cut the onion into a small dice, cut the kernels off the cobs and remove and discard the charred skin, stem, ribs and seeds from the pepper. Cut the pepper into a medium dice, saving the juice. Combine the onion, corn, pepper with juice, cumin and hot sauce in the large bowl with the reserved marinade.

5. Place the soaked plank over **direct medium heat** and close the lid. After 5–10 minutes, when the plank begins to smoke and char, turn the plank over. Put the scallops in the bowl with the marinade and toss to coat. Place the scallops in a single layer on the plank. Close the braai lid and cook for 8–10 minutes until they are slightly firm on the surface and opaque in the centre. Serve the scallops warm with the salad.

HOW TO CUT ONION WEDGES

1. The layers of the onion wedges will hold together on the braai if you leave part of the root end attached.

2. After you have cut your wedges, peel off the papery skin.

CHECKING DONENESS

When smoked scallops are done, they will feel slightly firm on top and look lightly coloured all over by the smoke.

THAI PRAWNS WITH WATERMELON SALSA

SERVES: 4
PREP TIME: 25 MINUTES
MARINATING TIME: 30 MINUTES

HEAT: DIRECT HIGH HEAT 230°–290°C (450°–550°F)
BRAAIING TIME: 3–5 MINUTES
SPECIAL EQUIPMENT: 8 BAMBOO SKEWERS, SOAKED IN WATER FOR AT LEAST 30 MINUTES

SALSA
- 2 tablespoons finely chopped shallot or small onion
- 2 teaspoons rice vinegar
- 1 teaspoon sugar
- 1–2 tablespoons finely chopped jalapeño chilli
- 325 g watermelon, seeds removed and cut into 1-cm cubes
- 1 8-cm section English cucumber, halved lengthways, seeds removed and thinly sliced into half-moons
- 1 teaspoon finely chopped fresh mint
- ¼ teaspoon coarse sea salt

MARINADE
- 125 ml fresh coriander leaves and tender stems
- 4 tablespoons fresh mint leaves
- 3 garlic cloves
- 2 tablespoons coarsely chopped fresh ginger
- 2 tablespoons rice vinegar
- 2 tablespoons vegetable oil
- 2 teaspoons sugar
- 1 teaspoon Thai red curry paste
- ¼ teaspoon coarse sea salt

500 g king prawns, peeled and deveined but with the tails left on

1. Mix the shallot, vinegar, sugar and jalapeño in a large bowl. Add the watermelon, cucumber, mint and salt and toss gently to combine. Allow the salsa to stand at room temperature for 30–60 minutes to fully incorporate the flavours.

2. Combine the marinade ingredients in a food processor. Process to create a coarse purée, occasionally scraping down the sides of the bowl to incorporate the ingredients evenly.

3. Transfer the marinade to a medium bowl. Add the prawns and toss to coat them evenly. Cover the bowl and refrigerate for 30 minutes, turning the prawns after 15 minutes. Prepare the braai for direct cooking over a high heat.

4. Remove the prawns from the bowl and discard the marinade. Thread the prawns onto skewers. Brush the cooking grates clean. Braai the skewers over **direct high heat** for 3–5 minutes, with the lid closed as much as possible but turning once, until the prawns are firm to the touch, lightly charred and just turning opaque in the centre. Serve the prawns warm or at room temperature with the salsa.

Fresh and frozen prawns can range from very small (less than 2.5 cm long) to 33 cm for Black Tiger prawns. The terms 'standard', 'medium', 'large', 'king' and 'jumbo' are used inconsistently, with the very smallest prawns called 'shrimp'. To add to the confusion, large and jumbo-sized warm-water prawns (freshwater or seawater) can both be sold as 'kings'. Supermarkets and fishmongers generally sell prawns by weight and you have to make a choice based on sight. Choose the size most suitable for your recipe, raw or cooked. Prawns the size of the two largest examples above are the best choice for braaiing, because they are easy to peel and they don't dry out as quickly as smaller prawns would.

PRAWN ROLLS WITH RÉMOULADE

SERVES: 6
PREP TIME: 20 MINUTES

HEAT: DIRECT HIGH HEAT 230°–290°C (450°–550°F)
BRAAIING TIME: 3-5 MINUTES
SPECIAL EQUIPMENT: PERFORATED GRILL PAN

RÉMOULADE
- 125 ml mayonnaise
- 2 tablespoons Dijon mustard
- 2 tablespoons sweet pickle relish
- 1 tablespoon prepared horseradish
- 2 teaspoons finely chopped fresh tarragon
- 1 teaspoon finely chopped garlic
- ½ teaspoon Tabasco or other hot sauce, or to taste
- ½ teaspoon sweet paprika
- ½ teaspoon coarse sea salt
- ¼ teaspoon freshly ground black pepper

- 1 kg king prawns, peeled and deveined, tails removed
- 2 tablespoons extra-virgin olive oil
- 1 tablespoon Cajun seasoning
- 6 crispy rolls, split horizontally
- Iceberg lettuce, chopped
- 18 slices ripe tomato

Rémoulade is a mayonnaise-based spread flavoured with mustard and other condiments. Among mustards, Creole is one of the spiciest, thanks to its horseradish and vinegar-marinated brown mustard seeds.

1. Combine the rémoulade ingredients in a small bowl. Cover and refrigerate until serving.

2. Prepare the braai for direct cooking over high heat. Preheat the grill pan for about 10 minutes.

3. Toss the prawns with the oil and then coat with the Cajun seasoning. Spread the prawns on the grill pan and cook over **direct high heat** for 2–4 minutes, with the lid closed as much as possible but turning once, until firm to the touch and just turning opaque in the centre. Remove from the braai and keep warm.

4. Braai the rolls, cut sides down, over **direct high heat** for 30–60 seconds, until lightly toasted. Spread the rémoulade on the rolls and add lettuce, tomatoes and prawns. Serve warm.

ORANGE-FENNEL PRAWNS OVER WATERCRESS

SERVES: 4
PREP TIME: 25 MINUTES
MARINATING TIME: 1 HOUR

HEAT: DIRECT HIGH HEAT 230°–290°C (450°–550°F)
BRAAIING TIME: 2–4 MINUTES
SPECIAL EQUIPMENT: PERFORATED GRILL PAN

MARINADE
- Grated zest of 2 oranges
- 125 ml fresh orange juice
- 75 ml extra-virgin olive oil
- 2 tablespoons fresh lime juice
- 1 tablespoon finely chopped garlic
- 1 teaspoon ground fennel
- 1 teaspoon coarse sea salt
- ½ teaspoon ground cayenne pepper

700 g king prawns, peeled and deveined, tails left on
100 g watercress leaves and tender stems

1. Mix the marinade ingredients together in a bowl. Set aside 125 ml of the marinade to use as a dressing for the salad.

2. Place the prawns in a large, resealable plastic bag and pour in the marinade. Press the air out of the bag and seal tightly. Turn the bag several times to distribute the marinade, lie the bag flat on a plate and refrigerate for 1 hour.

3. Prepare the braai for direct cooking over high heat. Preheat the grill pan for about 10 minutes.

4. Drain the prawns in a sieve. Spread the prawns in a single layer on the grill pan and cook over **direct high heat** for 2–4 minutes, with the lid closed as much as possible but shaking the pan once or twice and turning the prawns over for even cooking, until they are slightly firm on the surface and completely opaque in the centres. Remove the pan from the braai and rest it on a baking tray. Transfer the prawns to a large bowl to stop the cooking.

5. Add the watercress to the prawns in the large bowl. Spoon the reserved dressing over the watercress and prawns (you may not need all of it). Toss gently to coat all the ingredients evenly. Serve right away.

HOW TO PEEL AND DEVEIN PRAWNS

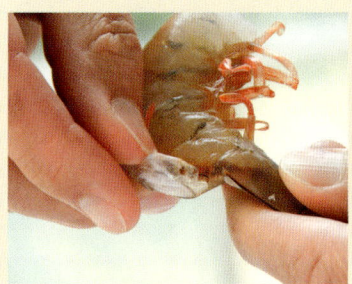

1. Grab the shell just above the tail and break it loose.

2. Peel off the shell along with all the little legs.

3. With a sharp paring knife, make a shallow slit along the back of each prawn.

4. Carefully lift any black vein out of the slit and discard it.

HOW TO BRAAI PRAWN POPS

1. By using two spoons moving in opposite directions, you can make little oval-shaped mixtures called quenelles.

2. Move the top spoon over and behind the prawn mixture while moving the bottom spoon under and in front.

3. Continue to move the spoons over the surface of the mixture a few times to smooth it out and shape it.

4. Slide a short bamboo skewer through the centre of each quenelle, and turn the prawn mixture on an oiled baking tray to coat it with oil.

5. Braai the pops over high heat, with the bare ends of the skewers shielded by a folded sheet of heavyweight foil.

6. Cook the pops for long enough on the first side so that you can roll them over without any sticking, rather than picking them up with tongs and squeezing them.

VIETNAMESE PRAWN POPS WITH PEANUT SAUCE

SERVES: 4–6
PREP TIME: 30 MINUTES
CHILLING TIME: 30–60 MINUTES

HEAT: DIRECT HIGH HEAT 230°–290°C (450°–550°F)
BRAAIING TIME: 4–6 MINUTES
SPECIAL EQUIPMENT: BAMBOO SKEWERS, SOAKED IN WATER FOR AT LEAST 30 MINUTES

SAUCE
- 250 ml unsweetened coconut milk, stirred
- 125 g peanut butter, stirred
- 1 teaspoon finely grated lime zest
- 3 tablespoons fresh lime juice
- 1 tablespoon soy sauce
- 1 tablespoon brown sugar
- 1 teaspoon hot chilli sauce, such as Sriracha
- ½ teaspoon grated fresh ginger

PRAWN POPS
- 500 g pork mince
- 375 g prawns, peeled and deveined
- 125 ml coarsely chopped fresh basil
- 4 tablespoons fine bread crumbs
- 2 large garlic cloves
- 1 tablespoon soy sauce
- ½ teaspoon freshly ground black pepper

- 4 tablespoons sunflower or canola oil

1. Combine the sauce ingredients in a heavy-based saucepan over a medium heat. Cook (but do not simmer), for 2–3 minutes, whisking constantly, just until the sauce is smooth and slightly thickened (the sauce will thicken further as it cools). Remove from the heat.

2. Put the prawn pop ingredients into a food processor or blender and process until a chunky paste is formed. Pour the sunflower oil onto a baking tray and brush it evenly all over the surface. Using 2 spoons, shape the mixture into small ovals or quenelles, placing them on the oiled tray as you make them. Turn them, making sure they are well coated with oil. Refrigerate the quenelles for 30–60 minutes to firm up the texture.

3. Prepare the braai for direct cooking over high heat.

4. Place one quenelle on the end of each skewer. Brush the cooking grates clean. Braai the prawn pops over **direct high heat** for 4–6 minutes, with the lid closed as much as possible but turning once or twice, until they are opaque throughout (cut one open with a sharp knife to test for doneness). Arrange the prawn pops on a serving platter. Serve warm with the dipping sauce.

HOW TO MAKE ROASTED CHILLI AND AVOCADO SAUCE

1. Braai mildly spicy Jalapeño or Anaheim chillies over direct medium heat until the skins are blackened and blistered.

2. Discard the chilli stems, skins and seeds. Then combine the roasted chillies in a food processor with sour cream, mayonnaise, fresh dill, garlic, salt and pepper.

3. Give the sauce a good whizz, stopping occasionally to scrape down the sides of the bowl.

4. If the sauce seems a little thick, add a touch of water to thin it out. The sauce will keep well in the refrigerator for a couple of days.

HOW TO PREP THE PRAWNS

1. Choose prawns that are the same size so that you can nestle them together with no empty spaces between them.

2. Begin by skewering one prawn through both the head and tail ends. Skewer the next prawn through the head end only, with the tail end pointing in the opposite direction. Skewer the remaining prawns just like the second one, with all their tails facing the same way.

3. The prawns should fit closely together on the skewers, without spaces in between. This means they will stay juicy on the braai a little bit longer.

JUICY PRAWNS WITH ROASTED CHILLI AND AVOCADO SAUCE

SERVES: 4–6
PREP TIME: 20 MINUTES

HEAT: DIRECT MEDIUM HEAT 180°–230°C (350°–450°F) AND DIRECT HIGH HEAT 230°–290°C (450°–550°F)
BRAAIING TIME: 10–16 MINUTES
SPECIAL EQUIPMENT: 8–10 FLAT-SIDED OR ROUND BAMBOO SKEWERS, SOAKED IN WATER FOR AT LEAST 30 MINUTES

SAUCE
- 3 jalapeño or Anaheim chillies, each about 15 cm long
- 1 medium avocado
- 4 tablespoons sour cream
- 4 tablespoons mayonnaise
- 2 tablespoons roughly chopped fresh dill
- 1 large garlic clove
- ½ teaspoon coarse sea salt
- ¼ teaspoon freshly ground black pepper

RUB
- 1 teaspoon garlic flakes
- 1 teaspoon paprika
- ¾ teaspoon coarse sea salt
- ½ teaspoon ground cumin
- ¼ teaspoon freshly ground black pepper

1 kg king prawns, peeled and deveined, tails left on
Extra-virgin olive oil

1. Prepare the braai for direct cooking over medium heat. Brush the cooking grates clean. Braai the chillies over **direct medium heat** for 8–12 minutes, with the lid closed as much as possible but turning occasionally, until they are blackened and blistered in spots all over. Put the chillies into a bowl, cover with clingfilm and allow to steam for 10 minutes. When cool enough to handle, remove and discard the stem ends, skins and seeds. Drop the chillies into a food processor or blender and add the remaining sauce ingredients. Process to create a smooth dipping sauce. If the sauce seems too thick, add a little water. Spoon the sauce into a serving bowl.

2. Combine the rub ingredients in a small bowl.

3. Place 5–7 prawns on a work surface and arrange them so that the prawn on one end lies one way and all the others lie in the same direction (see photo at left). Choose prawns that are the same size so that you can fit them together with no empty spaces between them. This will help to keep the prawns from spinning and prevent them from drying out on the braai. Pick up and skewer each prawn through the middle, pushing the prawns together on each skewer. Repeat the process with the remaining prawns and skewers. Lightly brush the prawns with oil and then season them evenly with the rub.

4. Increase the temperature of the braai to high heat. Brush the cooking grates clean. Braai the prawns over **direct high heat** for 2–4 minutes, with the lid closed as much as possible but turning once, until slightly firm on the surface and opaque in the centre. Remove the prawns from the braai and serve warm with the dipping sauce.

The 'fresh' prawns glistening on a bed of shaved ice at the market were almost certainly frozen previously, usually on the boat. Then they were thawed at the market. In fact, prawns will be closer to 'fresh' if you buy them frozen and thaw them yourself just before cooking.

HOW TO MAKE PAELLA

Paella is a rice dish that is traditionally cooked outdoors in a wide, shallow pan of the same name. Spreading the rice out in such a wide pan helps it to absorb the aromas of burning wood or charcoal. A big cast-iron frying pan substitutes well for the traditional paella pan, but there is no substitute for paella's quintessential spice: saffron.

1. Heat the stock with prawn shells, white wine, bay leaves, smoked paprika, salt, red chilli flakes and saffron.

2. Braai the prawns over direct high heat, but cook them only about halfway. They will finish cooking in the rice.

3. Cook the prosciutto in the pan until it releases its fat and begins to crisp.

4. Cook the onions, peppers and garlic with the prosciutto to create an aromatic base that is full of flavours.

5. Add a medium- or round-grain rice, such as Arborio, not a long-grain rice.

6. Stir to cook the rice lightly and to coat all the grains in the pan juices.

7. Add the hot, strained stock and close the lid of the braai so that the liquid gently simmers and the wood smoke does not escape.

8. At some point you may need to rotate the pan or move it to another part of the braai to even out the cooking.

9. The rice is done when it has absorbed most of the stock and the texture is tender but not mushy.

PAELLA

SERVES: 6–8
PREP TIME: 40 MINUTES
SOAKING TIME FOR WILD MUSSELS: 30–60 MINUTES
(SEE NOTE ON PAGE 190)

HEAT: DIRECT HIGH HEAT 230°–290°C (450°–550°F)
AND DIRECT MEDIUM HEAT 180°–230°C (350°–450°F)
BRAAIING TIME: 35–37 MINUTES
SPECIAL EQUIPMENT: 30-CM CAST-IRON FRYING PAN

250 g king prawns, tails left on, shells reserved for stock
2 teaspoons extra-virgin olive oil
Coarse sea salt
Freshly ground black pepper

STOCK
Shells from peeled prawns
1 litre chicken stock
175 ml dry white wine
2 bay leaves
1½ teaspoons smoked paprika
1 teaspoon coarse sea salt
½ teaspoon crushed red chilli flakes
¼ teaspoon crushed saffron threads

12 black mussels, scrubbed and beards removed
3 tablespoons extra-virgin olive oil
100 g prosciutto, cut into 5-mm dice
125 ml finely chopped red onion
200 ml finely chopped red pepper
1 tablespoon finely chopped garlic
400 g medium-grain rice, such as Arborio
250 ml frozen baby peas

1. Peel and devein the prawns, reserving the shells to make the stock. Toss the prawns with the oil in a large bowl and season evenly with salt and pepper. Cover and refrigerate until ready to braai.

2. Bring the prawn shells and the stock ingredients to a simmer in a saucepan over high heat. Strain, discarding the shells and bay leaves, and reserve the stock. (The stock can be made up to 2 hours ahead.)

3. Check each mussel and discard those with broken shells, any that don't close up when you lightly tap on their shells, and any others that feel unusually heavy because of sand trapped inside.

4. Prepare the braai for direct cooking over high heat on one side and medium heat on the other side. Brush the cooking grates clean. Braai the prawns over **direct high heat** for about 2 minutes, turning once, until cooked halfway (the prawns will finish cooking in the stock). Remove from the braai and set aside to cool.

5. Place a 30-cm cast-iron frying pan on the cooking grate over **direct high heat.** Heat the oil in the pan. Add the prosciutto and cook for about 3 minutes, stirring occasionally, until it begins to crisp. Add the onion, red pepper and garlic and cook, stirring occasionally and rotating the pan for even cooking, for about 5 minutes, until the onion is translucent. Slide the pan away from the fire.

6. Place the pan over **direct medium heat**, stir in the rice and cook for about 2 minutes, until well coated with the pan juices. Stir in the prawn stock and the frozen peas. Close the braai lid and let the rice cook at a brisk simmer for about 15 minutes until the rice is al dente. Tuck the prawns into the rice. Add the mussels, hinged sides down. Cook, with the braai lid closed, for 8–10 minutes, until the mussels open. (Remove and discard any unopened mussels.)

7. Remove the pan from the heat, cover with foil and allow the paella to stand for 5 minutes. Serve hot, straight from the pan.

WILD MUSSELS VERSUS FARM-RAISED MUSSELS

Check each mussel and discard those with broken shells, any that don't close up when you lightly tap on their shells, and any others that feel unusually heavy because of sand trapped inside. Soak the mussels in cold, salted water for 30–60 minutes and then drain. The soaking is to remove sand, but that's only an issue with wild mussels (pictured at left) that grow in sandy places. If you use farm-raised mussels (pictured at right), you can omit the soaking step.

COCONUT-CURRY MUSSELS

SERVES: 4
PREP TIME: 15 MINUTES
SOAKING TIME FOR WILD MUSSELS: 30–60 MINUTES

HEAT: DIRECT MEDIUM HEAT 180°–230°C (350°–450°F)
BRAAIING TIME: 17–22 MINUTES
SPECIAL EQUIPMENT: LARGE DISPOSABLE FOIL TRAY

SAUCE

    1 can (425 ml) coconut milk, light or regular
    1 tablespoon Thai green curry paste
    1 tablespoon fresh lime juice
    2 teaspoons light brown sugar
    2 teaspoons fish sauce
    2 tablespoons peanut oil
    1 tablespoon finely chopped fresh ginger
    1 tablespoon finely chopped garlic

    1 kg black mussels, scrubbed and beards removed
    4 tablespoons fresh coriander leaves, finely chopped

Crusty bread to serve (optional)

1. Prepare the braai for direct and indirect cooking over medium heat.

2. Whisk the coconut milk, curry paste, lime juice, brown sugar and fish sauce together in a bowl.

3. Combine the peanut oil, ginger and garlic in a large disposable foil tray. Place the tray over **direct medium heat**, close the braai lid and let the aromatics cook for about 1 minute. Add the coconut milk mixture to the tray and gently stir to combine. Cook for 5–6 minutes to bring the sauce to a boil.

4. Add the mussels to the sauce. Cover the foil tray with a baking tray (to trap the steam and cook the mussels), close the braai lid, and cook for 8–10 minutes. Check the mussels to see if they are open. If not, continue to cook 3–5 minutes more. Wearing braai mitts or oven gloves, carefully remove the baking tray from the foil tray and carefully remove the foil tray from the braai. Remove and discard any unopened mussels. Sprinkle the coriander on top. Serve the mussels and sauce in bowls, with crusty bread, if desired.

CAJUN-STYLE CLAMBAKE

SERVES: 4
PREP TIME: 45 MINUTES

HEAT: DIRECT MEDIUM HEAT 180°–230°C (350°–450°F)
BRAAIING TIME: 20–25 MINUTES

    125 g unsalted butter, melted
    75 ml fresh lemon juice
    1 tablespoon finely chopped garlic
    1 tablespoon Cajun seasoning
    2 teaspoons chopped fresh thyme leaves
    4 medium potatoes, halved and cut into thick slices
    375 g large prawns, peeled and deveined, tails left on
    1 kg clams, rinsed and scrubbed
    350 g andouille or chorizo sausage, thinly sliced
    2 cobs fresh sweetcorn, each cut into 4 pieces

1. Combine the butter, lemon juice, garlic, seasoning and thyme in a small bowl.

2. Prepare the braai for direct cooking over medium heat.

3. Cut 8 sheets of heavyweight foil, each about 30 × 50 cm. Line a 20 × 20-cm cake tin with 2 sheets of foil, arranged at right angles. Layer the bottom of the foil-lined pan with the sliced potatoes (this will help insulate the shellfish and keep them from overcooking). Top the potatoes with the prawns, clams, sausage and sweetcorn pieces. Drizzle each parcel evenly with the butter mixture. Close the parcel by bringing the ends of the two inner sheets together, folding them on top of the filling and then bringing the ends of the two outer sheets together, folding them down. Repeat this procedure with the remaining parcels.

4. Cook the parcels over **direct medium heat** for 20–25 minutes with the lid closed, until the clams have opened, the prawns have turned opaque and the potatoes are cooked. To check for doneness, using tongs, gently unfold one of the parcels and carefully remove a potato, being careful not to puncture the bottom of the foil. Using a knife, gently pierce the potato to ensure doneness. When everything is cooked, remove the parcels from the braai. Carefully open each parcel to let the steam escape and then pour the contents into warm bowls and serve immediately.

HOW TO PREP FOR A CLAMBAKE

1. Rinse and scrub the clams under cold water and soak in ice-cold water mixed with salt (1 teaspoon per 250 ml water) for a few hours to remove sand and grit from inside the shells.

2. You can peel and devein the prawns ahead of time, but keep them cold until ready to cook.

3. Arrange the sliced potatoes on the bottom of the tray so that they protect the other ingredients from the heat.

4. Be generous with the lemon butter mixture.

5. Fold up the ends of the foil tightly to prevent any liquid from escaping.

6. Remove each parcel from the tin and cook it directly on the braai so that all the ingredients steam and simmer inside.

HOW TO CHAR-GRILL OYSTERS

1. For char-grilling or braaiing, choose oysters with deep rounded shells that will retain all the juices.

2. Holding each oyster in a towel with the flat side up, push the tip of an oyster knife into the small opening at the hinge of the shell.

3. Twist the knife and wiggle it back and forth to pop open the shell.

4. Drag the knife along the seam between the top and bottom shells.

5. Use the side of the knife to cut the oyster meat loose from the top shell.

6. Slide the knife under the oyster meat to release it from the bottom.

7. As you finish shucking each oyster, lie it flat on a baking tray, keeping as much liquid as possible in the shells.

8. The grilling goes quickly, so have all your sauces and serving platters ready.

9. Spoon the sauces into the raw oysters, but don't overfill the shells.

10. A very hot charcoal fire is crucial for cooking oysters in just a few minutes.

11. As soon as the juices start to bubble, remove the oysters from the braai.

12. The meat of the oyster should be warm but not cooked all the way through.

CHAR-GRILLED OYSTERS

SERVES: 4–6
PREP TIME: 30 MINUTES

HEAT: DIRECT HIGH HEAT 230°–290°C (450°–550°F)
BRAAIING TIME: 2–4 MINUTES
SPECIAL EQUIPMENT: OYSTER KNIFE

- 24 large, fresh oysters
- Lemon wedges
- Tabasco or other hot sauce
- Cocktail sauce

1. Grip each oyster, flat side up, in a folded kitchen towel. Find the small opening between the shells near the hinge and pry it open with an oyster knife. Try not to spill the delicious juices, known as the 'oyster liqueur', in the bottom shell. Cut the oyster meat loose from the top shell and then loosen the oyster from the bottom shell by running the oyster knife carefully underneath the body. Discard the flatter top shell, keeping the oyster and its juices in the deeper bottom shell.

2. Prepare the braai for direct cooking over high heat.

3. Spoon some of your favourite dipping sauce on top of each oyster (recipes follow).

4. Brush the cooking grates clean. Braai the oysters, shell sides down, over **direct high heat** for 2–4 minutes, with the lid closed as much as possible, until the oyster juices start to bubble and the edges curl. Using tongs, carefully remove the oysters from the braai. Serve with lemon wedges, a few drops of Tabasco, cocktail sauce and your favourite dipping sauce.

GARLIC-THYME BUTTER
MAKES: ENOUGH FOR 24 OYSTERS

- 4 tablespoons unsalted butter, divided
- 1 tablespoon very finely chopped garlic
- 2 teaspoons sherry vinegar
- 4 tablespoons white wine
- 2 teaspoons finely chopped fresh thyme
- ¼ teaspoon coarse sea salt

1. Melt 1 tablespoon of the butter in a small pan over a medium heat. Add the garlic and sauté for about 2 minutes, until it starts to brown. Add the vinegar and wine and simmer for a further 2 minutes until the sauce reduces by half. Remove from the heat, whisk in the remaining butter and stir in the thyme and salt.

GRAPEFRUIT-BASIL AÏOLI
MAKES: ENOUGH FOR 24 OYSTERS

- 4 tablespoons mayonnaise
- 1 tablespoon chopped fresh basil
- 1½ teaspoons finely grated grapefruit zest
- 2 teaspoons fresh grapefruit juice
- 1 teaspoon very finely chopped garlic
- ¼ teaspoon coarse sea salt

1. Combine the ingredients in a small bowl and mix thoroughly.

ASIAN BUTTER SAUCE
MAKES: ENOUGH FOR 24 OYSTERS

- 1 tablespoon sesame oil
- 2 teaspoons very finely chopped fresh ginger
- 2 tablespoons oyster sauce
- 1 teaspoon soy sauce
- ¼ teaspoon Dijon mustard
- 4 tablespoons unsalted butter, cut into small chunks

1. Combine the oil and ginger in a small pan over medium heat, and heat until the oil begins to foam. Remove from the heat; stir in the oyster sauce, soy sauce and mustard. Whisk in the butter a few chunks at a time until incorporated.

GORGONZOLA-TOMATO SAUCE
MAKES: ENOUGH FOR 24 OYSTERS

- 1 tablespoon unsalted butter
- 1 tablespoon very finely chopped shallot
- 1 teaspoon very finely chopped garlic
- 125 ml tomato juice or tomato cocktail
- 2 teaspoons prepared horseradish
- ½ teaspoon coarse sea salt
- 4 tablespoons crumbled Gorgonzola cheese

1. Melt the butter in a small saucepan over medium heat. Add the shallot and garlic and sauté for about 2 minutes. Add the tomato juice, horseradish and salt. Bring to a simmer and then remove from the heat. Add the sauce to the oysters, then sprinkle the cheese on top and braai.

HOW TO PREP AND BRAAI CRAYFISH TAILS

1. Mature lobster (crayfish) tails vary in size throughout the world. Shown here, left to right, are New Zealand (175–250 g); Maine, USA (150–175 g); Western Australia (250–300 g); and South Africa (135–150 g). Adjust cooking times according to size.

2. Use kitchen scissors to cut through the centre of the shell on the underside of each tail.

3. Turn each tail over and cut through the harder back shell all the way to the fins.

4. Use a sharp, heavy knife to cut each tail in half lengthways, passing through the openings you have already made.

5. Braai the tails, meat side down, until the surface of the meat turns opaque.

6. Then turn the tails over onto their shells and brush with garlic butter while the meat turns opaque all the way to the centre.

CRAYFISH (ROCK LOBSTER) ROLLS

SERVES: 4
PREP TIME: 25 MINUTES

HEAT: DIRECT MEDIUM HEAT 180°–230°C (350°–450°F)
BRAAIING TIME: 6–7 MINUTES

- 3 large garlic cloves, lightly crushed
- 90 g salted butter
- 4 crayfish (rock lobster) tails
- Coarse sea salt
- 4 tablespoons mayonnaise
- 125 ml finely diced ripe tomato
- 2 tablespoons finely chopped spring onion
- 2 teaspoons fresh lemon juice
- Tabasco or other hot sauce
- 2 teaspoons chopped fresh chervil or tarragon
- 4 hot dog rolls, split in half
- Cos lettuce, shredded

1. Warm the garlic and butter in a small saucepan over medium-low heat until the butter melts. Set aside about 2 tablespoons for brushing on the buns.

2. Prepare the braai for direct cooking over medium heat. Carefully cut the crayfish tails in half lengthways. Season the crayfish meat with a little salt and brush some garlic butter over the surface of each one. Brush the cooking grates clean. Braai the tails, meat side down, over **direct medium heat** for 2–3 minutes with the lid open, until the meat is opaque. Turn the tails over, brush with more garlic butter and braai for a further 3 minutes until the meat is slightly firm. Set aside to cool.

3. Combine the mayonnaise, tomato, spring onion and lemon juice in a large bowl. Season to taste with salt and hot sauce. Remove the crayfish meat from the shells and cut into 1-cm pieces. Add the crayfish meat to the mayonnaise mixture. For best flavour, chill for at least 1 hour. Mix in the chopped chervil or tarragon just before serving.

4. Using a serrated knife, trim some of the crust from the sides of the rolls. Brush the remaining garlic butter on the cut sides (outside only) of the rolls and toast over **direct medium heat** for about 1 minute, turning once, until golden brown on both sides.

5. Place some shredded Cos lettuce on the bottom of each roll and top with the crayfish mixture.

HOW TO PREP AND BRAAI WHOLE CRABS

1. Place each crab flat on its back. Use a cleaver and mallet to cut right down the centre and all the way through.

2. Cut off the dangling tail flap attached to the underside of one half.

3. Also cut off the tail flap dangling on the other half.

4. Find the parts of the mouth that protrude from the front of each half and cut those off.

5. Turn each half over and pull off the top shell.

6. Remove the feathery gills, known as 'dead man's fingers'.

7. Rinse out the brownish viscera in a bowl of cold water.

8. The half on the left is cleaned. The one on the right is not.

9. Cut through the shell between each leg with the cleaver or a sharp knife.

10. You should have five legs from each half crab.

11. Use a clean hammer or a nutcracker to crack the shells prior to grilling.

12. Grill the crab legs over direct high heat for a couple of minutes on each side to absorb the charcoal aromas.

13. Move the crab legs to a frying pan with butter, garlic, wine, lemon juice and chillies.

14. Turn and coat the crab legs in the buttery mixture as they finish cooking.

WHOLE CRABS WITH WHITE WINE-GARLIC BUTTER

SERVES: 2 AS A MAIN COURSE OR 4 APPETIZERS
PREP TIME: 30 MINUTES

HEAT: DIRECT HIGH HEAT 230°–290°C (450°–550°F)
BRAAIING TIME: 9–11 MINUTES
SPECIAL EQUIPMENT: 30-CM CAST-IRON FRYING PAN

2 large whole crabs
125 g unsalted butter, cut into 8 equal pieces
2 tablespoons finely chopped garlic
Finely grated zest and juice of 1 lemon
½ teaspoon crushed red chilli flakes
½ teaspoon coarse sea salt
¼ teaspoon freshly ground black pepper
150 ml dry white wine
1 baguette, torn into bite-sized pieces

1. Prepare the braai for direct cooking over high heat.

2. To kill a live crab, place it on its back and hold it down with a large cleaver. Use a hammer to tap the top edge of the cleaver and cut the crab in half lengthways all the way through. Remove and discard the dangling tail flaps and mouth parts. Turn the crab over. Pull off and discard the top shell. Remove and discard the gills. Rinse each half of the crab under cold running water and use your finger to scoop out and discard the dark viscera. Slice each half into 5 pieces by cutting between each leg and through the body. Using the hammer again (or a nutcracker or crab cracker), crack each section of each leg to make eating easier after the crabs are cooked.

3. Combine the butter, garlic, lemon zest and juice, chilli flakes, salt and pepper in a large cast-iron frying pan. Mix well.

4. Place the pan over **direct high heat** and cook for 2–3 minutes, keeping the lid open, until the butter melts and the garlic turns golden. Add the wine and cook until it comes to the boil. Remove the pan from the braai and place it on a heat-proof surface.

5. Braai the crab pieces over **direct high heat** for about 4 minutes, keeping the lid open and turning once, then move them to the pan. Return the pan over **direct high heat** and gently turn the crab pieces with tongs to coat them with the sauce. Cook for 2–3 minutes, until the liquid boils and the crab is fully cooked. Serve warm, with pieces of bread to dip into the liquid remaining in the pan.

CRAB AND AVOCADO QUESADILLAS

SERVES: 4–6
PREP TIME: 20 MINUTES

HEAT: DIRECT MEDIUM HEAT 180°–230°C (350°–450°F)
BRAAIING TIME: 2–4 MINUTES

- 500 g fresh crabmeat
- 80 ml finely chopped fresh basil
- Finely grated zest of 2 lemons
- Juice of 2 lemons
- 1 tablespoon finely chopped jalapeño chilli
- ½ teaspoon coarse sea salt
- ¼ teaspoon freshly ground black pepper
- 125 ml sour cream
- 6 flour tortillas
- 2 ripe avocados, deseeded, peeled and cubed
- 175 g tomatoes, finely chopped
- 200 g Cheddar cheese, grated
- Extra-virgin olive oil

The difference in quality between fresh and canned crabmeat is striking. While crabmeat hand-picked from freshly caught, seasonal crabs is sweet and luscious, what you often find in cans is pasteurized and metallic in flavour. Even the crabmeat from previously frozen crabs can't compete with the truly fresh stuff. For this recipe, the variety of crab is less important than freshness. However, don't bother spending high prices on 'jumbo' crab (the big unbroken pieces of meat). Broken pieces of crabmeat, or even crayfish, will work just as well.

1. Combine the crabmeat, basil, half of the lemon zest, the lemon juice, jalapeño, salt and pepper in a bowl and mix well.

2. Combine the sour cream with the remaining half of the lemon zest in a separate bowl. Set aside.

3. Prepare the braai for direct cooking over medium heat.

4. Lay the tortillas in a single layer on a work surface. Evenly divide the crabmeat mixture, avocados, tomatoes and cheese over half of each tortilla. Fold the other half of each tortilla over the filling, creating a half circle, and press down firmly. Lightly brush the tortillas with oil. Brush the cooking grates clean. Braai the quesadillas over **direct medium heat** for 2–4 minutes, with the lid closed as much as possible but carefully turning once, until the cheese melts and the tortillas are well marked. Cut each quesadilla into wedges. Serve with the sour cream mixture.

SEAFOOD ZUPPA

SERVES: 4
PREP TIME: 30 MINUTES

HEAT: DIRECT MEDIUM HEAT 180°–230°C (350°–450°F) AND DIRECT HIGH HEAT 230°–290°C (450°–550°F)
BRAAIING TIME: 17–19 MINUTES
SPECIAL EQUIPMENT: PERFORATED GRILL PAN

ZUPPA
  2 small fennel bulbs
  1 lemon, ends trimmed, cut in half
  2 red peppers, cut into flat pieces
  4–5 shallots, about 200 g, peeled
  Extra-virgin olive oil
  500 ml vegetable stock
  ½ teaspoon paprika
  pinch of crushed red chilli flakes
  pinch of saffron threads
  Coarse sea salt
  Freshly ground black pepper

  4 large or jumbo scallops, 40–50 g each
  8 jumbo or king prawns, peeled and deveined
  1 line fish fillet, about 250 g, skinned and cut into 4 pieces
  1 swordfish fillet, about 250 g, skinned and cut into 4 pieces

  4 thick slices bread
  4 tablespoons finely chopped flat-leaf (Italian) parsley

1. Prepare the braai for direct cooking over medium heat.

2. Preheat the grill pan over **direct medium heat** for about 10 minutes. While the pan preheats, prepare the vegetables. Cut off the thick stalks above the fennel bulbs and save them for another use. Cut each fennel bulb into quarters and remove the thick triangular-shaped core. Slice the fennel vertically into 5 mm-thick slivers. Place the fennel, lemon halves, peppers and shallots in a bowl, add 4 tablespoons oil, and toss to coat the vegetables evenly. Place the vegetables on the grill pan and cook over **direct medium heat** for about 10 minutes, with the lid closed as much as possible but turning as needed, until the vegetables are tender.

3. Place the vegetables in a large bowl, cover with foil and steam for 10 minutes. Remove and discard any charred skin from the shallots. Coarsely chop the shallots and the red peppers.

Combine the fennel, peppers, shallots and the juice of one grilled lemon half in a blender and purée until smooth. Add the vegetable stock and purée again (the blender will be very full). Pour the *zuppa* through a strainer into a saucepan and discard any bits left in the strainer. Season with the paprika, chilli flakes and saffron. Keep warm over low heat. Add additional grilled lemon juice, salt and pepper to taste.

4. Increase the temperature of the braai to high heat. Remove the small, tough side muscle that might be left on each scallop. Lightly coat the shellfish and fish fillets with oil and season with salt and pepper. Brush the cooking grates clean. Braai the seafood over **direct high heat**, with the lid closed as much as possible but turning the pieces once, until the prawns are lightly charred on the outside and just turning opaque in the centre, the scallops are slightly firm on the surface and opaque in the centre, and the fish fillets are just beginning to separate into layers and the colour is opaque at the centre. The prawns will take 3–5 minutes, the scallops will take 4–6 minutes and the fish fillets will take 6–8 minutes.

5. Toast the bread over direct heat for about 1 minute, turning once. Evenly divide the shellfish and fish among individual bowls. Ladle the *zuppa* into each bowl. Garnish with parsley and serve with the bread.

HOW TO BRAAI FISH
5 THINGS YOU NEED TO KNOW

1 PRACTICE MAKES PERFECT
Many braaiers consider fish their biggest challenge. They remember the times when fish stuck to the grate and fell to pieces when they tried to take it off the braai. To greatly improve your chances of success, learn to braai firm fish first, especially the ones that are a bit oily, including snoek, yellowtail, swordfish, tuna and salmon.

2 DON'T OVERDO IT
Fish and seafood don't have the muscle structure and firmness that many four-legged creatures have. Therefore marinades work more quickly to break down the structure of fish. So, to prevent mushy textures, limit marinating times to just a few hours. And, above all, don't overcook fish portions and fillets.

3 FEED THE FIRE
Don't be afraid of high heat. It creates a bit of a crust on the surface of fish, and the crust helps the fish release from the cooking grate. The thinner the fillets or portions you have, the higher the heat should be.

4 NO FLIP-FLOPPING
Every time you turn fish on the braai, you create a new possibility for sticking, so turn it only once.

5 QUICK FINISH
Braai the first side for longer than the second side. This ensures a nicely developed crust on the first side. Plus, if you are braaiing with the lid closed (as you should), the second side will begin to cook while the first side is on the grate. So the second side will not need as long on the grate.

SALMON WITH NECTARINE SALSA

SERVES: 4
PREP TIME: 20 MINUTES

HEAT: DIRECT HIGH HEAT 230°–290°C (450°–550°F)
BRAAIING TIME: 8–11 MINUTES

SALSA
- 3–4 nectarines, about 500g, cut into 1-cm dice
- 125 ml finely diced red pepper
- 4 tablespoons finely diced red onion
- 4 tablespoons finely chopped fresh chervil or flat-leaf parsley
- 1 jalapeño chilli, seeded and finely diced
- 2 tablespoons finely chopped fresh mint
- 1 tablespoon honey
- 1 tablespoon fresh lime juice
- ¼ teaspoon dried red chilli flakes
- ¼ teaspoon coarse sea salt

- 4 salmon portions (with skin), 175–200 g each and about 2.5 cm thick
- ½ teaspoon coarse sea salt
- ¼ teaspoon crushed red chilli flakes
- 2 tablespoons fresh lime juice
- 1 tablespoon extra-virgin olive oil

1. Combine the salsa ingredients in a non-metallic bowl. Cover and refrigerate until ready to serve.

2. Prepare the braai for direct cooking over high heat.

3. Season the salmon portions on both sides with the salt and chilli flakes and then drizzle with the lime juice and oil. Brush the cooking grates clean. Braai the salmon, flesh side down, over **direct high heat** for 6–8 minutes, with the lid closed as much as possible, until you can lift the portions off the grate with tongs without sticking. Turn the portions over and cook for a further 2–3 minutes for medium rare, or longer for well done. Slide a fish slice or spatula between the skin and the flesh, and transfer the salmon to serving plates. Serve warm with the salsa.

HOW TO BRAAI SALMON PORTIONS

1. Start by placing generously oiled portions flesh side down on a clean, hot grate.

2. Braai them over high heat and roll them over when the flesh side releases easily.

3. When the salmon is done, wiggle a fish slice into the seam between the flesh and skin.

4. Slide the flesh off the skin and pat yourself on the back. Serving the skin is optional.

The sauce for this recipe features some classic Thai ingredients, including coconut milk and red curry paste. The cream that rises to the top of chilled coconut milk contains a good amount of oil, so use it to fry the curry paste, releasing its spicy flavours, before adding the rest of the coconut milk and the other sauce ingredients.

SALMON WITH RED CURRY-COCONUT SAUCE

SERVES: 4–6
PREP TIME: 25 MINUTES

HEAT: DIRECT HIGH HEAT 230°–290°C (450°–550°F)
BRAAIING TIME: 3–6 MINUTES
SPECIAL EQUIPMENT: 12 BAMBOO SKEWERS, SOAKED IN WATER FOR AT LEAST 30 MINUTES

300 ml chilled coconut milk
3½ tablespoons Thai red curry paste
1 tablespoon fish sauce
1 tablespoon soy sauce
1½ teaspoons light brown sugar
1 salmon side, about 1 kg, skin removed
2 tablespoons canola or sunflower oil
2 tablespoons finely chopped spring onions

1. Scoop 4 tablespoons of the coconut cream from the top of the chilled coconut milk and transfer it to a small saucepan. Place over medium heat and bring to a boil. Add 2 tablespoons of the curry paste and cook for 3–5 minutes, stirring constantly, until very fragrant. Stir the remaining coconut milk to achieve a smooth consistency, and then slowly incorporate it into the curry paste mixture. Add the fish sauce, soy sauce and sugar and return the mixture to the boil, stirring constantly. Reduce the the heat to maintain a steady simmer and cook for 5–10 minutes, stirring frequently, until thickened to a thin sauce consistency. Set aside.

2. Prepare the braai for direct cooking over high heat.

3. Remove any remaining pin bones from the salmon. Cut the salmon into 1.5 cm-thick slices. Thread them on to skewers.

4. Combine the remaining 1½ tablespoons curry paste with the oil in a small bowl and generously brush the salmon with the mixture. Brush the cooking grates clean. Braai the skewers over **direct high heat** for 2–4 minutes, with the lid closed as much as possible, until you can lift them off the cooking grate with tongs without sticking. Turn the skewers over and cook them for a further 1–2 minutes for medium, or longer for more well done. Reheat the sauce and spoon it onto a serving dish, or divide evenly among individual plates. Top with the salmon and scatter the spring onions over the top. Serve warm.

CEDAR-PLANKED SALMON WITH HAZELNUT SAUCE

SERVES: 4
PREP TIME: 20 MINUTES

HEAT: DIRECT MEDIUM HEAT 180°–230°C (350°–450°F)
BRAAIING TIME: 20–30 MINUTES
SPECIAL EQUIPMENT: 1 UNTREATED CEDAR PLANK, 30–40 CM LONG AND 1–1.5 CM THICK, SOAKED IN SALTED WATER FOR AT LEAST 1 HOUR

SAUCE
  2 slices firm white bread, crusts removed
  2 garlic cloves
  125 ml hazelnuts, lightly toasted and skinned
  3 tablespoons fresh lemon juice
  125 ml extra-virgin olive oil
  4 tablespoons fresh flat-leaf (Italian) parsley leaves
  Coarse sea salt
  Freshly ground black pepper

  1 side of salmon (skin on), about 1 kg
  125 ml brown sugar

1. Soak the bread briefly in water, squeeze dry, and set aside. Combine the garlic and hazelnuts in a food processor and process until the nuts are finely ground. Add the bread and lemon juice and process until smooth. With the motor running, add the oil in a slow, steady stream. Add the parsley, ½ teaspoon salt and ¼ teaspoon pepper and pulse quickly. Season to taste with additional salt, pepper and lemon juice, if desired. Cover with clingfilm and chill until required.

2. Prepare the braai for direct cooking over a medium heat. Remove any remaining pin bones from the salmon. Cut the salmon crossways to make 4 servings, but do not cut through the skin. Generously season with salt and pepper.

3. Place the soaked plank over **direct medium heat** and close the lid. After 5–10 minutes, when the plank begins to smoke and char, turn the plank over and then place the salmon on the plank. Carefully sprinkle the brown sugar over the entire surface of the salmon. Close the lid and let the salmon cook for 15–20 minutes until lightly browned on the surface for medium rare, or longer for more well done. The cooking time will vary according to the thickness of the salmon. Serve warm with the sauce on the side.

HOW TO BRAAI SALMON ON A PLANK

Braaiing salmon on a cedar plank prevents the fish from sticking to the cooking grate and imbues it with delicious smoky flavours.

1. Run your fingertips over the salmon to feel for any bones. Using needle-nose pliers, grab the ends of any tiny pin bones and pull them out.

2. Cut the raw fish into individual portions, right down to the skin but not through it, to make it easier to serve later.

3. Lay the salmon on a lightly charred, smouldering plank and sprinkle brown sugar over the top.

4. The sugar will melt and caramelize on the surface while the cedar smoke permeates the flesh.

HOW TO PREP FENNEL

1. Cut off the thick stalks above the bulb, leave the root end attached to hold the bulb together, then cut the bulb in half through the root end.

2. Chop some of the flavourful fronds to season the salad.

3. Simmer the fennel halves in salted water until just tender. Immediately plunge the fennel into an ice bath to stop the cooking.

4. Trim off the root end and thinly slice the fennel.

HOW TO DEBONE SALMON STEAKS

1. Find any pin bones and remove them with needle-nose pliers.

2. Trim off any thin, dangling flaps of flesh.

3. Starting at the top of the steak, cut alongside the bone.

4. Continue to cut all along the bone and rib sections.

5. Cut along the other side of the bones, too.

6. The goal is to isolate the bones only, without cutting away too much of the flesh.

7. Cut the bones free near the top, leaving just a bit of bone to hold the flesh together.

8. Bring the sides together and secure the ends with a shortened bamboo skewer.

SALMON WITH FENNEL AND OLIVE SALAD

SERVES: 4
PREP TIME: 30 MINUTES

HEAT: DIRECT HIGH HEAT 230°–290°C (450°–550°F)
BRAAIING TIME: 8–11 MINUTES
SPECIAL EQUIPMENT: 8 BAMBOO SKEWERS, SOAKED IN WATER FOR AT LEAST 30 MINUTES

SALAD
- 1 fennel bulb
- 125 ml green olives with pimentos, quartered
- 3 spring onions, white and light green parts, finely chopped
- 2 tablespoons chopped fennel fronds
- 1 tablespoon extra-virgin olive oil
- ½ teaspoon finely grated lemon zest

- 4 salmon steaks or portions, each 175–200 g and 2–3 cm thick
- 2 tablespoons extra-virgin olive oil
- ½ teaspoon coarse sea salt
- ¼ teaspoon freshly ground black pepper

1. If the fennel stalks have the fronds attached, trim off the fronds and chop enough to make 2 tablespoons; set aside. Cut off the thick stalks above the bulb and save the stalks for another use. Leave the root end attached to hold the bulb together. Cut the fennel bulb in half. Fill a small saucepan with water. Lightly salt the water and bring to a boil over medium-high heat. Reduce the heat to medium and gently simmer the fennel bulb for 3 minutes. Remove from the water and plunge into iced water to rapidly cool it. Remove the bulb from the water, trim off the root end and thinly slice.

2. Combine the salad ingredients in a bowl. Toss to coat and set aside to let the flavours marinate while you braai the salmon.

3. Prepare the braai for direct cooking over high heat.

4. Prepare the salmon steaks as detailed at left. Brush the salmon with the oil and season with the salt and pepper. Brush the cooking grates clean. Braai the salmon over **direct high heat** for 6–8 minutes, with the lid closed as much as possible, until you can lift the steaks off the grate with tongs without sticking. Turn the steaks over and cook for a further 2–3 minutes for medium, or longer for more well done. If using portions, to easily remove the skin, just slip a fish slice or spatula between the skin and the flesh, and lift the salmon flesh from the braai. Transfer the salmon to plates and top with the salad.

A potent ingredient in any griller's pantry, chipotles are dried and smoked jalapeño chillies. They are often found packed in adobo, which is a tomato-based sauce with vinegar, onions, garlic and spices. To freeze leftover chipotles, spoon one chilli, with a little sauce, into each hole of an icecube tray. After they have frozen, pop them out of the tray, tightly wrap them in clingfilm, and place them in a resealable freezer bag.

FISH WRAPS WITH CHIPOTLE-LIME SLAW

SERVES: 6
PREP TIME: 20 MINUTES

HEAT: DIRECT HIGH HEAT 230°–290°C (450°–550°F)
BRAAIING TIME: 7–8 MINUTES

RUB
  ½ teaspoon chilli powder
  ½ teaspoon ground cumin
  ½ teaspoon coarse sea salt
  ¼ teaspoon ground cayenne pepper
  ¼ teaspoon ground cinnamon

4 fresh hake or salmon portions or 2 of each (with skin), about 175–200g each and 2–3 cm thick
Canola or sunflower oil

SLAW
  275 g very thinly sliced green cabbage
  4 tablespoons coarsely chopped fresh coriander
  4 tablespoons mayonnaise
  2 tablespoons fresh lime juice
  2 teaspoons sugar
  1 teaspoon chipotle chilli in adobo, finely chopped
  ½ teaspoon coarse sea salt

6 flour tortillas

1. Mix the rub ingredients together in a small bowl. Lightly brush the fillets with oil and then apply the rub evenly. Cover and set aside in the refrigerator.

2. Combine the slaw ingredients in a bowl and toss to coat. Set aside until ready to assemble the wraps.

3. Prepare the braai for direct cooking over high heat. Brush the cooking grates clean. Braai the portions over **direct high heat** for about 4 minutes, with the lid closed as much as possible, until you can lift them off the cooking grate with a fish slice without sticking. Turn the portions over and cook them for a further 2–3 minutes until they are opaque in the centre. Transfer them to a plate. Warm the tortillas over **direct high heat** for 30–60 seconds, turning once.

4. To assemble the wraps, break a portion into large chunks and arrange on one half of a warm tortilla, then top with some of the slaw. Roll the tortilla to enclose the fillings, fold in the sides, and continue rolling to the end. Cut the wrap in half. Serve warm or at room temperature.

Hake has a mild flavour, but the flesh is quite lean, so it dries out quickly if it's overcooked. The key is to remove the fish from the braai before it begins to flake apart. Check each portion with a paring knife to make sure the flesh is no longer translucent at the centre.

HAKE WITH BOMBAY TOMATO SAUCE

SERVES: 4
PREP TIME: 30 MINUTES

HEAT: DIRECT MEDIUM HEAT 180°–230°C (350°–450°F)
AND DIRECT HIGH HEAT 230°–290°C (450°–550°F)
BRAAIING TIME: 19–23 MINUTES
SPECIAL EQUIPMENT: 30-CM CAST-IRON FRYING PAN

SAUCE

    3 tablespoons peanut oil or canola oil
    1 onion, halved and thinly sliced
    1 tablespoon finely chopped garlic
    2 teaspoons finely grated fresh ginger
    1 teaspoon ground coriander
    1 teaspoon paprika
    ½ teaspoon turmeric
    ½ teaspoon coarse sea salt
    ¼ teaspoon ground cayenne pepper
    2 cans peeled, chopped tomatoes with juice
    175 ml unsweetened coconut milk, stirred

    4 tablespoons peanut oil or canola oil
    1 teaspoon finely grated fresh ginger
    1 teaspoon coarse sea salt
    ½ teaspoon freshly ground black pepper
    ¼ teaspoon turmeric
    4 fresh hake portions, 175–200 g each and 2–3 cm thick
    2 tablespoons torn fresh basil leaves, optional

1. Prepare the braai for direct cooking over medium heat on one side and high heat on the other side. Brush the cooking grates clean. Warm the oil in a 30-cm cast-iron frying pan over **direct medium heat**. Add the onion and cook for about 5 minutes, stirring often, until it softens and begins to brown. Add the garlic, ginger, coriander, paprika, turmeric, salt and cayenne. Mix well and cook for 2–3 minutes, stirring often to avoid burning. Add the tomatoes and coconut milk. Taste and adjust the seasoning, if needed. Allow the sauce to simmer for 5 minutes or so while you prepare the hake.

2. Mix the oil, ginger, salt, pepper and turmeric in a small bowl. Generously brush the hake on both sides with the oil mixture.

3. Braai the portions over **direct high heat** for 4–5 minutes, with the lid closed and without turning, until they release easily from the cooking grate. Lift the portions, one at a time, with a fish slice and turn them over into the pan with the sauce, so the cooked side is facing up. Arrange the portions in the sauce, close the lid, and allow them to cook over **direct medium heat** for 3–5 minutes, until they just begin to flake when you prod them gently with the tip of a knife.

4. Remove the frying pan from the braai. Scatter the basil on top of the portions and serve warm.

HOW TO PREP HAKE PORTIONS

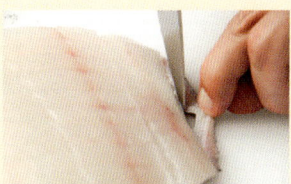 

1. The first step is to skin the fish. Along one end of a portion, cut a slit all the way through the skin large enough to get your finger though it.

2. Holding the skin steady with your finger in the slit, angle the blade of a large, sharp knife inside the seam between the flesh and skin.

3. Cut away from you and over the top of the skin, always with the knife angled slightly downwards.

4. Braai the portions on one side only until they release easily from the grate.

5. Move the portions, cooked sides facing up, to the pan with the warm tomato sauce.

6. The sauce helps to keep the hake portions moist as they finish cooking.

HOW TO SKIN DORADO PORTIONS

  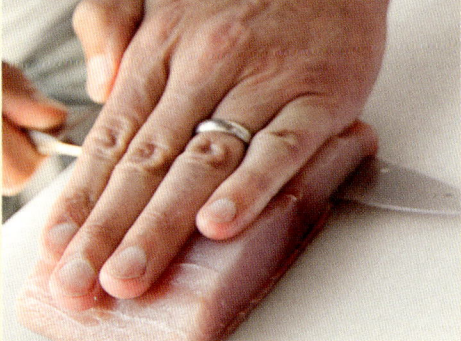

1. Angle the blade of a large, sharp knife into the seam between the flesh and skin on one end of a portion.

2. Hold the fish steady with your other hand and slide the knife cleanly over the skin.

3. For safety's sake, in case the knife slips, cut away from your body, and tilt the blade downwards so that you don't cut into the flesh.

HOW TO MAKE CORN AND MUSHROOM SALSA

1. The cooking goes quickly, so have all your ingredients chopped and measured beforehand. Chefs refer to this as their *mise en place*.

2. Cook the corn in a smoking-hot pan, stirring occasionally to prevent the kernels from popping right out of the pan.

3. The goal is to caramelize the natural sugars in the corn, turning the kernels golden brown and super sweet.

4. Cook the mushrooms in the same hot pan. The less you stir them, the browner and more delicious they will be.

5. Cook the cucumber, black beans and garlic just until the garlic begins to brown, too.

6. Combine all the vegetables in the pan, adjust the seasonings and cook just long enough to merge the flavours.

HOW TO CHECK FOR DONENESS

 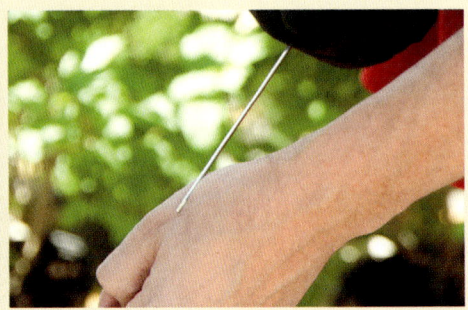

When you insert the end of a metal skewer into the centre of a piece of fish and then quickly and carefully touch the end of the skewer to the outside of the base of your thumb, it should feel warm. If it feels less than warm, the fish is undercooked. If it feels hot, the fish is overcooked.

DORADO WITH CORN AND MUSHROOM SALSA

SERVES: 4
PREP TIME: 25 MINUTES
MARINATING TIME: UP TO 1 HOUR

HEAT: DIRECT HIGH HEAT 230°–290°C (450°–550°F)
BRAAIING TIME: 13–15 MINUTES
SPECIAL EQUIPMENT: 30-CM CAST-IRON FRYING PAN

RUB
- 1 teaspoon chilli powder
- 1 teaspoon garlic flakes
- 1 teaspoon paprika
- 1 teaspoon coarse sea salt
- ½ teaspoon ground coriander
- ½ teaspoon ground cumin
- ½ teaspoon freshly ground black pepper

- 4 skinless dorado portions, each about 200 g and 2 cm thick
- 4 tablespoons extra-virgin olive oil

SALSA
- Kernels cut from 2 cobs fresh sweetcorn
- 1–2 portabello mushrooms, stems removed and caps diced
- ½ cucumber, peeled, seeded and finely chopped
- 3 tablespoons extra-virgin olive oil
- 125 ml canned black beans, drained
- 2 teaspoons finely chopped garlic
- 2 tablespoons fresh coriander, roughly chopped
- 2 teaspoons fresh lime juice
- ½ teaspoon coarse sea salt
- ¼ teaspoon freshly ground black pepper
- Tabasco or other hot sauce, to taste

1. Mix the rub ingredients together in a small bowl. Generously coat the dorado portions on both sides with the oil. Season evenly with the rub. Cover and refrigerate for up to 1 hour.

2. Assemble all the salsa ingredients so that everything is ready for quick cooking.

3. Prepare the braai for direct cooking over high heat.

4. To make the salsa, warm 1 tablespoon of the oil in the frying pan over **direct high heat**. When it is smoking hot, add the corn and spread the kernels in an even layer. Cook for about 2 minutes, stirring 2 or 3 times, until most of the kernels are golden brown and crisp-tender, then transfer to a bowl. Add another tablespoon of oil to the pan, and when the oil begins to smoke, add the mushrooms and spread them out in a single layer. Cook without touching them for 30 seconds, then give them a stir and cook for about 3 minutes, until the mushrooms are browned and tender. Add the mushrooms to the bowl with the corn. Add another tablespoon of oil to the pan and immediately add the cucumber, black beans and garlic. Mix well and cook for about 30 seconds until the garlic begins to brown. Add the corn kernels and the mushrooms from the bowl, as well as the remaining salsa ingredients and heat for about 1 minute. Taste and adjust the seasonings, if necessary. Pour the salsa into the bowl and set it aside to cool while you cook the fish.

5. If cooking over charcoal, you'll probably need to add more briquettes to the fire so that it is hot enough to cook the fish properly. Braai the dorado portions over **direct high heat** for 6–8 minutes, with the lid closed as much as possible but turning once, until the fish is fully cooked but still moist.

6. Serve the fish portions warm with the salsa on the side.

Recipe from the chefs at Weber Grill® Restaurant

SEAFOOD

Poke is a popular Hawaiian dish of finely chopped raw fish tossed with edible seaweed, seeds or nuts and a dressing. In this recipe, the flavour and texture of the fish benefit from a quick sear on the braai. If you use dried seaweed, be sure to rehydrate it in water for about 15 minutes.

BRAAIED TUNA POKE

SERVES: 4 AS AN APPETIZER
PREP TIME: 15 MINUTES

HEAT: DIRECT HIGH HEAT 230°–290°C (450°–550°F)
BRAAIING TIME: ABOUT 2 MINUTES

- 2 tablespoons dried Japanese arame or other thin edible seaweed, finely chopped
- 4 tablespoons finely chopped onion
- 4 tablespoons spring onion, white and light green parts, thinly sliced
- 2 tablespoons soy sauce
- 1 tablespoon dark sesame oil
- 1 teaspoon grated fresh ginger
- ½ teaspoon finely chopped serrano chilli

- 2 sushi-grade tuna portions, each about 175–200 g and 2–3 cm thick
- Canola or sunflower oil
- Coarse sea salt
- Freshly ground black pepper
- 2 tablespoons toasted sesame seed
- 1 lemon, cut into wedges, optional

1. If using dried seaweed, place the seaweed in a small bowl, add enough water to cover, and set aside to soften for 15 minutes. Drain and coarsely chop before using.

2. Prepare the braai for direct cooking over high heat.

3. Mix the onion, spring onion, soy sauce, sesame oil, ginger and chilli in a bowl. Add the seaweed.

4. Brush the tuna with oil and lightly season with salt and pepper, patting the seasoning into the fish. Brush the cooking grates clean. Braai the tuna over **direct high heat**, for about 2 minutes, with the braai lid open and turning once, just until seared on both sides but still rare inside.

5. Transfer the tuna to a chopping board and cut into 1–1.5 cm cubes. Add to the bowl containing the onion mixture and toss to combine. Divide equally into individual bowls. Sprinkle with the sesame seeds. Serve warm with lemon wedges, if desired.

SMOKED TUNA SALAD WITH GRILLED MANGO

SERVES: 4–6
PREP TIME: 30 MINUTES

HEAT: DIRECT MEDIUM HEAT 180°–230°C (350°–450°F)
BRAAIING TIME: ABOUT 10–12 MINUTES
SPECIAL EQUIPMENT: 2 HANDFULS APPLE OR CHERRY WOOD CHIPS, SOAKED IN WATER FOR AT LEAST 30 MINUTES

DRESSING
- 80 ml runny honey
- 3 tablespoons Dijon mustard
- 2 tablespoons rice wine vinegar
- 2 tablespoons mayonnaise
- ½ teaspoon coarse sea salt
- ¼ teaspoon chilli powder
- 2 firm but ripe mangoes
- Canola or sunflower oil
- 300 g sugar snap peas
- ¼ teaspoon coarse sea salt

- 2 tuna portions, each about 450 g and 2.5 cm thick
- 150 g mixed baby greens, rinsed and crisped
- 125 g roasted and salted cashews
- Freshly ground black pepper

1. Whisk the dressing ingredients in a small bowl until thoroughly combined. Set aside 5 tablespoons of the dressing for the tuna.

2. Slice the sides from the mangoes, cutting along either side of the stone. Carefully, and without cutting through the skin, slice 3–4 short lines along the inside of the flesh. Using the point of the knife, cut 3–4 lines in the opposite direction of the first set of cuts to create mango cubes. Brush the mango halves with oil.

3. Place the sugar snap peas just off-centre on a 30 × 30-cm sheet of foil and season them with the salt. Fold the foil over the snap peas and seal to create a parcel.

4. Prepare the braai for direct cooking over medium heat. Drain the wood chips and scatter them on the burning charcoal or put them into the smoker box of a gas braai, according to the manufacturer's instructions. Close the braai lid.

5. Liberally brush the tuna portions with the reserved dressing. When smoke begins to pour out of the vents, braai the tuna portions over **direct medium heat** for about 6–8 minutes, with the lid closed as much as possible but turning once, until the tuna is pink but still juicy. Remove the tuna from the braai and gently break it into small pieces.

6. Place the mangos and the foil parcel over **direct medium heat** and cook for about 4 minutes, with the lid closed as much as possible but turning once. Remove from the braai. Open the parcel to let the steam escape so that the peas do not overcook. When the mangoes are cool enough to handle, hold each mango slice in both hands and press up on the skin side to expose the cubes, then slice them off the skin.

7. Divide the salad greens between serving plates. Top with grilled mango, sugar snap peas, flaked tuna and cashews. Drizzle with dressing and finish with a grinding of pepper.

HOW TO SMOKE TUNA IN CEDAR PAPERS

1. If you can get them, cedar papers are perfect for smoking fish. Start by submerging the cedar papers and some string in water for 10 minutes.

2. Cut the tuna into strips that will fit inside the papers. Lay a strip of tuna on each paper, parallel to the grain of the wood. Brush the tuna with the dressing.

3. Roll the paper around the tuna strips and secure the parcel with a piece of well-soaked string.

4. Braai the tuna parcels for a few minutes on each side to produce some smoke while the fish cooks.

A key rule for braaiing seafood is that freshness and firmness always matter more than a particular type of fish. Don't go to the store thinking, for example, that only kingklip or hake will work for this recipe. If your preferred fish is not fresh that day, choose whatever else is firm and fresh. Other options are swordfish, scallops, prawns and sea bass.

GRILLED HAKE IN A CARIBBEAN CITRUS MARINADE

SERVES: 6
PREP TIME: 15 MINUTES
MARINATING TIME: 3 HOURS

HEAT: DIRECT HIGH HEAT 230°–290°C (450°–550°F)
BRAAIING TIME: 8–10 MINUTES (FILLETS) OR 4–6 MINUTES (SHELLFISH)

MARINADE
- 2 teaspoons grated orange zest
- 125 ml fresh orange juice
- 1 teaspoon grated lime zest
- 4 tablespoons fresh lime juice
- 4 tablespoons extra-virgin olive oil
- 4 tablespoons chilli powder
- 1½ tablespoons finely chopped garlic
- 1½ teaspoons ground coriander
- 1 teaspoon finely chopped jalapeño chilli
- ¾ teaspoon ground allspice
- ¾ teaspoon freshly ground black pepper
- ¼ teaspoon ground cayenne pepper

6 fish portions with skin (such as hake, kingklip or sea bass), each 150–175 g and about 2.5 cm thick, or 700 g prawns or scallops
Extra-virgin olive oil
Coarse sea salt

1. Combine the marinade ingredients in a non-metallic bowl. Reserve 5 tablespoons of the marinade to serve with the grilled fish.

2. Place the fish portions or shellfish side by side in a 20 x 20-cm glass or other non-metallic ovenproof dish. Pour the remaining marinade over the fish portions or shellfish and turn to coat them. Cover and refrigerate both the fish and the reserved marinade for 3 hours.

3. Prepare the braai for direct cooking over high heat.

4. Remove the fish or shellfish from the dish and discard the marinade. Lightly brush with oil and season with some salt.

5. Brush the cooking grates clean. Braai the fish, skin side up, over **direct high heat** for 8–10 minutes, with the lid closed as much as possible but turning once after 6–7 minutes when they release easily from the cooking grate, until just opaque in the centre. If using prawns or scallops, braai over **direct high heat** for 4–6 minutes, turning once. Serve the fish or shellfish with the reserved marinade spooned over.

SWORDFISH ESCABÈCHE

SERVES: 4
PREP TIME: 30 MINUTES
MARINATING TIME: UP TO 2 HOURS

HEAT: DIRECT MEDIUM HEAT 180°–230°C (350°–450°F)
BRAAIING TIME: 14–18 MINUTES

MARINADE
- 125 ml extra-virgin olive oil
- 3 tablespoons sherry vinegar
- 1 tablespoon finely chopped garlic
- 1 teaspoon dried origanum
- ¾ teaspoon coarse sea salt
- ½ teaspoon crushed red chilli flakes
- ¼ teaspoon freshly ground black pepper

- 8 button mushrooms
- 2 ripe tomatoes, cored and halved lengthways
- 1 large serenade or jalapeño chilli
- 200 g yellow patty pans, halved lengthways
- 4 swordfish steaks, 250–300g each and 2.5 cm thick

ESCABÈCHE
- 250 ml chicken stock
- 1 tablespoon sherry vinegar
- ¼ teaspoon dried origanum
- pinch of freshly ground black pepper

1. Whisk the marinade ingredients together in a bowl. Transfer 4 tablespoons of the marinade to another bowl. Add the vegetables to the second bowl and mix to coat them evenly.

2. Place the swordfish steaks flat on a plate large enough to fit them in a single layer. Spoon the remaining marinade over the steaks, turning them over to coat them evenly. Cover with clingfilm and refrigerate for up to 2 hours.

3. Prepare the braai for direct cooking over medium heat. Brush the cooking grates clean. Braai the vegetables over **direct medium heat** for 6–8 minutes, with the lid closed as much as possible but turning occasionally, until the vegetables are lightly marked and tender. Remove the vegetables from the braai.

4. Place the braaied chilli in a bowl and cover with clingfilm. When cool enough to handle, remove and discard the stem, seeds and skin. Roughly chop all the vegetables.

5. In a frying pan over medium-high heat, combine the escabèche ingredients and bring the liquid to a boil. Add the chopped vegetables and spread them out in the pan. Cook for 3–5 minutes until the vegetables are tender. Remove the pan from the heat, cover and keep warm.

6. Lift the swordfish steaks off the plate and let the excess marinade drip onto the plate. Discard the marinade. Brush the cooking grates clean. Braai the steaks over **direct medium heat** for 8–10 minutes, with the lid closed as much as possible but turning once, until the centre is opaque but the flesh is still juicy. Serve the swordfish warm with the vegetable mixture.

HOW TO MAKE SWORDFISH ESCABÈCHE

1. Swordfish steaks work well, as would any firm-fleshed fish. Remove the tough outer skin before marinating and braaiing the swordfish.

2. Grilling the tomatoes and chilli (and the patty pans and mushrooms, too) adds depth and complexity to the final dish.

3. Escabèche is a preparation involving fish with hot vinegar-based liquid poured over the top. Grilled vegetables enliven the savoury liquid.

HOW TO BRAAI FISH FILLETS IN BANANA LEAVES

As you get closer to the equator, you will find that many people in the tropics use banana leaves to wrap and steam fish, rice and vegetables. These inexpensive leaves, which are available frozen in most Asian stores and markets, trap moisture and add a subtle tea-like fragrance to food. Thaw them in the refrigerator for a few hours or pour boiling water over them to make them pliable quickly.

1. Cut the banana leaves into rectangles large enough to wrap around each fish fillet. Leave the sturdy fibrous vein along one edge intact, as it holds the leaves together.

2. Wipe both sides with a damp cloth to clean the leaves, moving in the same direction as the grain so you don't split them open.

3. Fold one side of the leaf over the marinated fish, and then overlap the first side with the opposite side.

4. Fold down the top and bottom sides so that they overlap in the middle. If the leaf splits, use a second leaf to double-wrap the fish.

5. Thread a toothpick in and out of the overlapping leaves but not into the fish itself.

6. Brush each parcel generously with water to prevent drying out. Place the parcels on a baking tray and cover with damp dishcloths until ready to braai.

7. Allow the charcoal to burn down to medium heat.

8. Braai the parcels with the toothpicks on the top most of the time so that the wood does not burn.

9. When the fish is fully cooked, you can carefully unwrap the banana leaves and use them as serving plates.

GINGER AND MISO LINE FISH IN BANANA LEAVES

SERVES: 6
PREP TIME: 20 MINUTES
MARINATING TIME: 2 HOURS

HEAT: DIRECT MEDIUM HEAT 180°–230°C (350°–450°F)
BRAAIING TIME: 8–10 MINUTES

MARINADE
    75 ml white miso paste
    4 tablespoons unsweetened coconut milk, stirred
    2 teaspoons finely chopped garlic
    2 teaspoons sugar
    1 teaspoon finely grated fresh ginger

    6 skinless line fish fillets, 150–175 g each and about 1 cm thick
    6 banana leaves, each about 30 × 30 cm
    6 spring onions, white and light green parts, thinly sliced
    1½ teaspoons low-sodium soy sauce
    About 1 kg steamed rice, optional

1. Whisk the marinade ingredients into a smooth paste in a small bowl. Smear the paste all over the fillets. Cover with clingfilm and refrigerate for 2 hours.

2. Rinse the banana leaves under cool running water or carefully wipe them clean with a soft, damp cloth.

3. Prepare the braai for direct cooking over medium heat.

4. Remove the excess marinade from the fillets, discard the marinade. Place each fillet in the centre of a banana leaf and top with some spring onions. Fold the leaf over to completely enclose the fillet and make a parcel. Secure with a toothpick, being careful not to pierce the fish. Brush each parcel on both sides with water.

5. Brush the cooking grates clean. Braai the parcels over **direct medium heat** for 8–10 minutes, with the lid closed as much as possible but turning once, until the leaves are blackened in some parts. (If the leaves begin to burn through, move the parcels over *indirect medium heat*.) Remove one of the parcels from the braai to check the fish for doneness. If it is opaque all the way through, the fish is done. If not, return to the braai for a few more minutes.

6. Carefully open each parcel, remove any pin bones from the fillets, drizzle each with ¼ teaspoon of soy sauce, or more to taste, and serve with steamed rice, if desired.

HOW TO FILLET WHOLE LINE FISH

1. Scale the fish, remove the head, and make a shallow cut all along one side of the backbone.

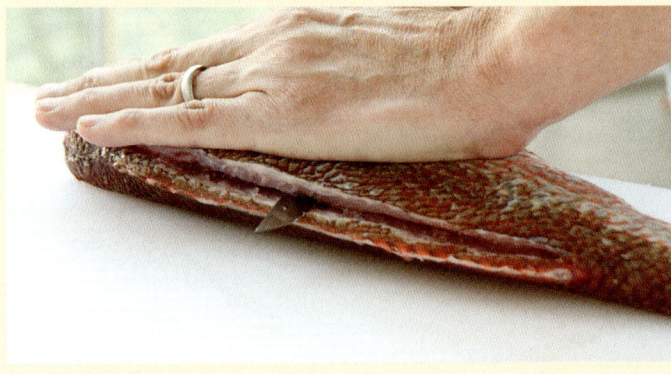

2. Run the knife under the top fillet and over the fish bones.

3. Use your other hand to steady the fish as you slide the knife towards the tail. Remove the top fillet.

4. Turn the fish over and make a second shallow cut, this time on the other side of the backbone.

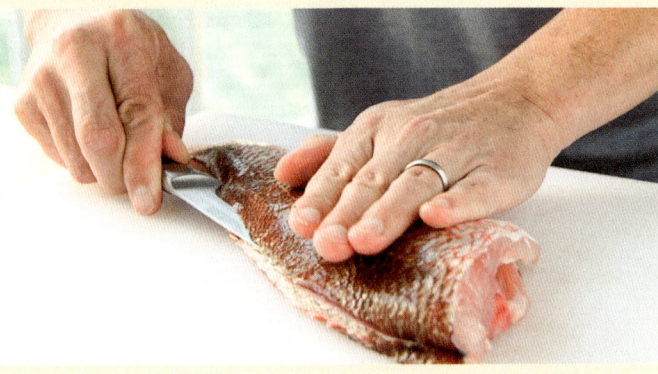

5. Use the tip of the knife to make deeper and deeper cuts along the tops of the bones.

6. Use your other hand to pull the fillet gently upwards so that you can see where to cut.

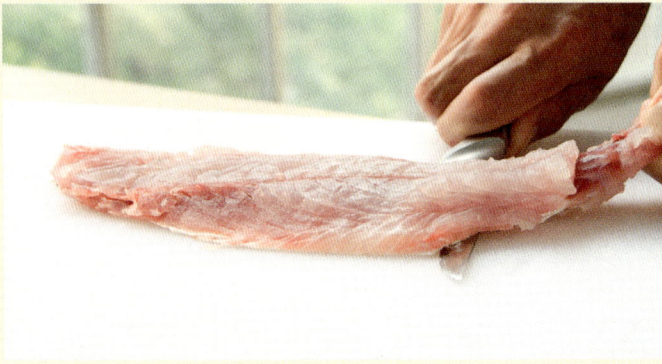

7. To skin the fillets, hold the end of the skin with your fingertips and run the knife just under the flesh.

8. Cut the fillets into individual portions.

LINE FISH IN COCONUT BROTH

SERVES: 8
PREP TIME: 20 MINUTES

HEAT: DIRECT HIGH HEAT 230°–290°C (450°–550°F)
BRAAIING TIME: 4–5 MINUTES

BROTH
    3 tablespoons oil (peanut, canola or sunflower)
    250 ml finely diced carrot
    4 tablespoons finely chopped shallot or spring onion
    1 teaspoon freshly grated ginger
    1 teaspoon finely grated lime zest
    1 can (400 ml) unsweetened coconut milk, stirred
    125 ml water
    3 tablespoons fresh lime juice
    1 tablespoon sugar
    2 teaspoons finely chopped red Thai chilli (birds-eye chilli)
    1 teaspoon fish sauce

8 skinless line fish fillets, each 125–175 g and about 1 cm thick
Peanut or canola oil
Coarse sea salt
Freshly ground black pepper

1. Warm the oil in a small saucepan over medium heat. Add the carrot, spring onion, ginger and lime zest, mix well and cook for 3–5 minutes, stirring often, until the carrots are softened. Add the remaining broth ingredients, mix well and allow to simmer for 2–3 minutes.

2. Prepare the braai for direct cooking over high heat. Lightly brush each fillet on both sides with oil. Season evenly with salt and pepper. Brush the cooking grates clean. Braai over **direct high heat** for 4–5 minutes, with the lid closed as much as possible but turning once with a spatula, until the fish just barely begins to flake when you prod it with the tip of a knife. Meanwhile, warm the broth over medium heat.

3. Spoon equal portions of broth into 8 shallow bowls and place a fillet in the centre of each bowl. Serve warm.

HOW TO USE A GRILL PAN FOR VEGETABLES AND FISH

1. Coat the fish portions generously with marinade on both sides.
2. Preheat the grill pan over medium heat for about 10 minutes to prevent food from sticking.
3. Place the vegetables on the grill pan and cook until they soften and begin to brown.
4. Grill each fish portion flesh side down first, turning with a spatula only when it releases easily from the grill pan.

MEXICAN GRILL-PAN FISH

SERVES: 4
PREP TIME: 15 MINUTES
MARINATING TIME: 30 MINUTES

HEAT: DIRECT MEDIUM HEAT 230°–290°C (450°–550°F)
BRAAIING TIME: 16–20 MINUTES
SPECIAL EQUIPMENT: PERFORATED GRILL PAN

MARINADE
    4 tablespoons extra-virgin olive oil
    4 teaspoons fresh lime juice
    2 teaspoons chilli powder
    1½ teaspoons coarse sea salt
    ½ teaspoon ground cumin
    ½ teaspoon garlic flakes
    ½ teaspoon dried origanum
    ½ teaspoon paprika

    4 line fish fillets (with skin), 180–230 g each and about 1.5 cm thick
    Sea salt

    2 mild to medium-hot chillies, stems and seeds removed, cut into 1-cm rings
    4 ripe tomatoes, cored and cut into 1-cm slices
    8 garlic cloves, peeled
    4 large spring onions, rinsed and trimmed

1. Combine the marinade ingredients in a small bowl. Transfer 2 tablespoons of the marinade to a larger bowl.

2. Arrange the fillets in a single layer on a platter, pour the marinade from the small bowl over the fillets to coat each piece evenly and season with some salt. Cover with clingfilm and marinate at room temperature for 30 minutes.

3. Place the chillies, tomatoes, garlic and spring onions in the bowl with the reserved marinade and toss to coat them evenly.

4. Prepare the braai for direct cooking over medium heat. Brush the cooking grates clean. Preheat the grill pan over **direct medium heat** for about 10 minutes. When hot, grill the vegetables on the pan for 6–8 minutes, with the lid closed as much as possible but turning occasionally, until the chillies and tomatoes soften and the garlic and spring onions begin to brown. Remove the vegetables from the grill pan and set aside. Cook the fish, skin side up, on the grill pan, over **direct medium heat** for 10–12 minutes with the lid closed as much as possible but carefully turning once when the fish releases easily from the grill pan, until the fish is opaque and still juicy.

5. Transfer the fish and vegetables to a serving platter. Serve warm.

WHOLE LINE FISH IN MOROCCAN MARINADE

SERVES: 4–6
PREP TIME: 10 MINUTES
MARINATING TIME: 2–3 HOURS

HEAT: DIRECT MEDIUM HEAT 180°–230°C (350°–450°F)
BRAAIING TIME: 12–15 MINUTES

MARINADE
- 75 ml extra-virgin olive oil
- 4 tablespoons fresh lemon juice
- 4 tablespoons fresh flat-leaf (Italian) parsley, finely chopped
- 4 tablespoons fresh coriander, finely chopped
- 1 tablespoon finely chopped garlic
- 1½ teaspoons sweet paprika
- 1 teaspoon ground cumin
- 1 teaspoon coarse sea salt
- ½ teaspoon freshly ground black pepper
- ¼ teaspoon ground cayenne pepper

2 whole line fish, 700 g–1 kg each, scaled, cleaned and fins removed

1. Combine the marinade ingredients in a bowl. Set aside 5 tablespoons to spoon over the fish after grilling.

2. Cut 3 or 4 slashes about 1 cm deep and 2.5 cm apart on each side of the fish.

3. Place the fish on a roasting tray. Spread the marinade over the fish, inside and out, working it well into the cuts. Cover with clingfilm and refrigerate both the fish and the reserved marinade for 2–3 hours.

4. Prepare the braai for direct cooking over medium heat.

5. Remove the fish from the refrigerator and brush with a little more olive oil. Braai over **direct medium heat** for 12–15 minutes, with the lid closed as much as possible but carefully turning once, until the flesh is opaque near the bone but still juicy. Transfer to a platter and spoon the reserved marinade over the top. If desired, serve with Roasted Pepper, Lemon and Olive Relish (see recipe below).

ROASTED PEPPER, LEMON AND OLIVE RELISH
PREP TIME: 10 MINUTES

- 2 roasted red peppers, peeled, seeded and cut into 5-mm dice
- 1 whole lemon, peeled, white pith removed, segmented, seeded and coarsely chopped
- 125 ml oil-cured black olives, stoned and coarsely chopped
- 75 ml extra-virgin olive oil
- 2 tablespoons fresh lemon juice
- 2 tablespoons chopped fresh coriander
- Coarse sea salt
- Freshly ground black pepper

1. Combine the relish ingredients in a bowl, adding salt and pepper to taste. Keep at room temperature.

HOW TO PREP WHOLE LINE FISH

1. Scale the fish and cut off the pectoral fins with kitchen scissors.

2. Cut the spiny dorsal fins off the backbone.

3. Also cut off the fins along the belly (ventral) side of the fish.

4. Cut 3 or 4 slashes, about 1 cm deep and 2.5 cm apart, on each side of the fish.

HOW TO BRAAI TROUT IN A BASKET

Whole fish can be difficult to braai without their skin sticking to the grate. A fish basket allows you to turn small whole fish easily. Just be sure to oil the basket itself so that the skin of the fish pulls away cleanly after it is cooked.

1. Lining the fish basket with orange slices, lettuce leaves or thick spring onions helps to prevent the skin of the fish from sticking to the basket.

2. In this recipe, the juice of the orange complements the sake marinade on the fish.

3. Lower the moveable section of the basket so that it rests snugly on the top layer of orange slices, preventing the ingredients from shifting.

4. You can braai the fish without the cooking grate. Just wear barbecue mitts or oven gloves and hold the basket over the coals, turning it over as needed for even cooking.

5. If flare-ups do occur, move quickly to rotate the basket away from the flames.

6. The goal is to lightly char the orange and cook the fish all the way to the bone without burning the skin.

SAKE-MARINATED TROUT

SERVES: 4
PREP TIME: 25 MINUTES
MARINATING TIME: 15–30 MINUTES

HEAT: DIRECT MEDIUM HEAT 180°–230°C (350°– 450°F)
BRAAIING TIME: ABOUT 8 MINUTES
SPECIAL EQUIPMENT: FISH BASKET

MARINADE
    75 ml sake or dry sherry
    4 tablespoons soy sauce
    4 tablespoons mirin (sweet rice wine)
    2 tablespoons peeled and finely chopped fresh ginger
    2 tablespoons unseasoned rice vinegar
    2 garlic cloves, finely chopped
    ¼ teaspoon crushed red chilli flakes

    4 whole deboned trout, each about 350 g, cleaned and gutted
    Canola or sunflower oil
    4–6 oranges, cut into 32 slices, each about 5 mm thick

1. Whisk the marinade ingredients together in a bowl. Place the trout in a large, resealable plastic bag and pour in the marinade. Press out the air and seal the bag tightly. Turn to distribute the marinade. Refrigerate for 15–30 minutes. Take care not to over marinate the fish. (Although this marinade isn't highly acidic, the delicate flesh could become overwhelmed by the combination of sake, soy sauce and mirin.)

2. Remove the trout from the bag and transfer to a roasting tray. Strain the marinade into a medium saucepan. Bring to a boil over medium-high heat. Cook for 10–15 minutes, until syrupy and reduced to about 4 tablespoons. Set aside.

3. Prepare the braai for direct cooking over medium heat.

4. Lightly brush the inside of the fish basket with oil. Place 4 orange slices in the basket and place 1 trout on top of them. Then place 4 more orange slices on top of the fish in the same manner. Repeat with the remaining trout, and then close and secure the grill basket (if your fish basket is not large enough to hold 4 whole trout, you will need to cook the fish in 2 batches). Braai the trout over **direct medium heat** for about 8 minutes with the braai lid open, turning every 2 minutes and rotating the basket when needed for even cooking, until the flesh is opaque in the centre and the skin and oranges are lightly charred. Using a fish slice or spatula, carefully remove the trout from the basket and transfer each fish to a dinner plate. Serve hot with the reduced marinade on the side.

HOW TO TRIM TROUT

1. Trim off the collarbone with scissors and cut off the head.

2. Cut off the dorsal fin.

3. Cut off the fins attached to each side of the belly.

4. Cut off the fin near the tail.

5. Trim the very thin edges of the belly.

6. Remove the bit of backbone between the fillets.

HOW TO SEGMENT AN ORANGE

1. Slice off the ends of an orange and stand it upright. Following the curve of the sides, slice off the peel, leaving as much flesh as possible.

2. Cut out individual segments by slicing as close as possible to the membrane on both sides of each segment.

3. Squeeze the remaining orange 'skeleton' to capture all the juices.

4. Use the segments for the salad and the juice for the dressing.

Heat the soaked cedar planks by themselves until they begin to smoke and char. Then turn them over and set the trout on top to cook and smoke simultaneously.

CEDAR-PLANKED TROUT WITH ROCKET, FENNEL AND ORANGE

SERVES: 4–6
PREP TIME: 20–25 MINUTES

HEAT: DIRECT MEDIUM-HIGH HEAT 190°–230°C (375°–450°F)
BRAAIING TIME: 11–18 MINUTES
SPECIAL EQUIPMENT: 2 UNTREATED CEDAR PLANKS, EACH ABOUT 30 CM LONG AND 1.5 CM THICK, SOAKED IN WATER FOR AT LEAST 1 HOUR

2 tablespoons red wine vinegar
1 small spring onion, finely chopped
2 oranges
4 tablespoons grapeseed, canola or sunflower oil
Coarse sea salt
Freshly ground black pepper

4 whole deboned trout, each about 350 g, cleaned and gutted with head, tails and fins removed
Extra-virgin olive oil

175 g rocket
1 fennel bulb, cored and thinly sliced

1. Combine the vinegar and spring onion in a small non-metallic bowl. Remove the zest from one of the oranges, then peel and segment both oranges, reserving the juice. Set aside the orange segments. Whisk the orange juice (there should be about 4 tablespoons) into the vinegar and spring onions. Drizzle in the oil, whisking constantly, and season to taste with salt and pepper.

2. Prepare the braai for direct cooking over medium-high heat. Rinse the trout under cold water and pat dry with roller towels. Lightly brush the inside of the trout with oil and generously season with salt and pepper.

3. Place the soaked planks over **direct medium-high heat** and close the lid. After 5–10 minutes, when the planks begin to smoke and char, turn them over and then place 2 trout, slightly overlapping, on each plank. Braai over **direct medium-high heat** for 6–8 minutes, with the lid closed, until the fish are firm to the touch and cooked through.

4. Using a fish slice or spatula, carefully lift each fish onto an individual serving plate, skin side down and open like a book.

5. Put the rocket in one bowl and the orange segments and fennel in another. Season both with salt and pepper and toss with vinaigrette. Spoon some of the orange-fennel mixture over each fish, top with the dressed greens and garnish with the remaining orange and fennel mixture.

HOW TO PREP SQUID (CALAMARI)

1. Cleaning a whole squid (left) will leave you with a tube-like body and separate tentacles (right).

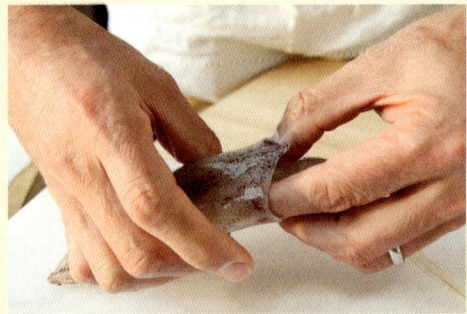

2. To start, pull the tentacles away from the body (tube) of each squid. Then reach inside to grab the end of the hard quill.

3. Pull the plastic-like quill out of the tube and discard.

4. Squeeze the tube to push out and discard the mushy innards.

5. Scratch the surface of the brownish skin and peel it off the tubes. Discard the skin.

6. Cut the tentacles from the head just above the eyes. Discard the eyes.

7. Squeeze the hard mouth (beak) from the tentacles and discard it.

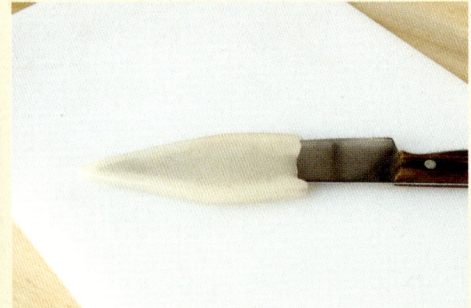

8. Slide a knife into each tube.

9. The knife inside the tube allows you to score each tube without cutting all the way through.

10. As you remove the squid from the marinade, shake off the excess liquid to help browning.

11. Braai the tubes as quickly as possible over very high heat.

12. The tentacles will cook a little faster. Be careful not to lose them through the cooking grate.

THAI SQUID (CALAMARI)

SERVES: 4
PREP TIME: 45 MINUTES
MARINATING TIME: 20 MINUTES

HEAT: DIRECT HIGH HEAT 230°–290°C (450°–550°F)
BRAAIING TIME: 2–3 MINUTES

12 whole, small squid (calamari)

MARINADE
4 tablespoons finely chopped fresh coriander
4 tablespoons fresh lime juice
4 tablespoons fish sauce
2 tablespoons sugar
1 tablespoon very finely chopped garlic
½ teaspoon freshly ground black pepper

1. Hold each squid and gently pull to separate the tube from the tentacles. Pull out and discard any remaining contents from inside the tube, including the plastic-like quill. Peel off the brownish skin that covers the tube. Rinse the inside of the tube and set aside. Slice off the tentacles portion just above the eyes and discard everything except the tentacles. Squeeze out and discard the hard beak found at the base of the tentacles. Remove the gritty 'teeth' on the tentacles (you can feel them) by rubbing them between your fingers under cold running water.

2. Combine the marinade ingredients in a large bowl. Add the squid and toss to coat them evenly. Cover and refrigerate for 20 minutes. Prepare the braai for direct cooking over high heat.

3. Remove the squid from the bowl and discard the marinade. Brush the cooking grates clean. Braai the squid over **direct high heat** for 2–3 minutes with the lid open and turning once, until they are just turning opaque and no longer look wet. Serve warm.

HOW TO BRAAI CALAMARI UNDER BRICKS

1. Separate the tubes from the tentacles on a roasting tray, making sure that everything is well coated with the marinade.

2. Line up the tubes on the braai in groups of 4. Immediately set a foil-covered brick on top of each group, with the smooth side of the foil facing down.

3. Braai the tubes for about 2 minutes. Then carefully roll the bricks onto their sides so that you can turn the tubes over.

4. Braai the tentacles alongside the bricks, turning them once and being careful not to lose them through the grate.

5. For the most flavourful and tender calamari possible, lightly char them over very high heat and remove them from the braai before they overcook.

BRICKYARD CALAMARI SALAD

SERVES: 4
PREP TIME: 25 MINUTES
MARINATING TIME: 30 MINUTES

HEAT: DIRECT HIGH HEAT 230°–290°C (450°–550°F)
BRAAIING TIME: ABOUT 4 MINUTES PER BATCH
SPECIAL EQUIPMENT: 2 FOIL-WRAPPED BRICKS

DRESSING
- 3 tablespoons fresh lemon juice
- 1 teaspoon finely chopped garlic
- ½ teaspoon crushed red chilli flakes
- ½ teaspoon coarse sea salt
- ¼ teaspoon freshly ground black pepper
- 75 ml extra-virgin olive oil

- 12 whole, small squid (calamari), cleaned (see page 224)
- ¼ teaspoon coarse sea salt
- ¼ teaspoon freshly ground black pepper
- 250 g small cherry tomatoes, halved
- 4 tablespoons finely chopped red onion
- 2 large ripe avocados, cubed
- 1½ tablespoons chopped fresh origanum

1. Combine the lemon juice, garlic, chilli flakes, salt and pepper in a bowl and slowly whisk in the olive oil.

2. Season the calamari with the salt and pepper and place on a roasting tray with 2 tablespoons of the dressing. Toss to coat and then allow to marinate at room temperature for about 30 minutes.

3. Prepare the braai for direct cooking over high heat. Brush the cooking grates clean.

4. Place about 4 calamari tubes in 2 rows in a line over **direct high heat** so that they can be weighted under the bricks. Place the bricks on top of the tubes, with the smooth side of the foil facing down, and braai for about 2 minutes, with the lid closed as much as possible, until the tubes easily lift off the cooking grate. Wearing insulated barbecue mitts or oven gloves and using tongs, carefully tilt the bricks onto their sides off the tubes. Turn the tubes over, and set the bricks back in place over the tubes for a further 2 minutes. Transfer the tubes to a platter. Repeat with the remaining tubes, brushing the cooking grates clean after you remove the first batch. Braai the tentacles alongside the bricks for about 4 minutes, turning once.

5. Put the tomatoes and onion into the bowl with the remaining dressing and toss to coat, then spoon over the calamari tubes and add the avocado. Sprinkle with the origanum.

VEGETABLES

TECHNIQUES

230	How to make **POLENTA**
232	How to braai **MEALIES ON THE COALS**
233	How to prep **MEALIES (CORN ON THE COB)**
235	How to braai **PAK CHOI AND SHIITAKE MUSHROOMS**
236	How to braai **PORTABELLO MUSHROOMS**
238	How to braai **PIZZA**
241	How to braai **ONIONS**
242	How to flame-roast **TOMATOES**
244	How to braai **ARTICHOKE HEARTS**
246	How to braai **ASPARAGUS**
248	How to braai **BROCCOLI**
249	How to braai **GREEN BEANS**
250	How to braai **CARROTS**
252	How to braai **TOFU**
254	How to braai **GARLIC**
254	How to prep **BRINJALS**
256	How to braai **SANDWICHES**
259	How to braai **FENNEL**
261	How to braai **SWEET POTATOES**
262	How to make **FLATBREAD**

RECIPES

231	**POLENTA** with Feta and Roasted Tomatillo Sauce
232	**FLAME-ROASTED MEALIES** with Lemon-Curry Butter
233	Ginger and Lime-glazed **MEALIES**
234	Grilled Corn and Mushroom **RISOTTO**
235	Marinated Baby **PAK CHOI AND SHIITAKE MUSHROOMS**
236	**PORTABELLO MUSHROOM SANDWICHES** with Basil and Balsamic Aïoli
237	Marinated **PORTABELLO MUSHROOMS** with Pecorino Cheese
239	**PIZZA** with Mushrooms, Peppers, Garlic and Smoked Mozzarella
240	Roasted Pepper and Bacon **BRUSCHETTA**
241	Roasted Pepper, Grilled Onion and Feta Cheese **SALAD**
242	Flame-roasted **TOMATO SOUP** with Parmesan Croutons
243	**PANZANELLA SKEWERS** with Sherry Vinaigrette
245	**ARTICHOKE HEARTS** with Smoked Tomato and Roasted Garlic Aïoli
247	**ASPARAGUS** and Prosciutto with Lemon Vinaigrette
248	Lemon **BROCCOLI**
249	**GREEN BEANS** with Lemon Oil
251	Orange-glazed **CARROTS**
252	Lemon-Ginger **TOFU** Steaks with Carrot and Cashew Salad
253	**CHILES RELLENOS** with Tomato Salsa and Guacamole
255	Roasted **BRINJAL DIP**
256	**VEGETABLE SANDWICHES** with Sun-dried Tomato Spread
257	Honey and Curry-glazed **BUTTERNUT**
258	Flame-roasted **BEETROOT SALAD** with Pumpkin seeds and Feta
259	**FENNEL** and Fontina
260	**POTATO SALAD** with Pistachio Pesto
261	Coconut-glazed **SWEET POTATOES**
262	Braaied **FLATBREAD** with Three Toppings

HOW TO MAKE POLENTA

1. As soon as the polenta begins to boil, turn the heat to low and stir with a wooden spoon to prevent the hot mixture from splattering out of the saucepan.

2. Cook over low heat until the polenta is thick and no longer gritty. Continue to stir every few minutes to prevent sticking and scorching on the bottom and sides of the saucepan.

3. Scrape the hot polenta into an oiled baking tray and smooth it out with the back of a wet spoon or spatula. Allow the mixture to cool and firm up for a couple hours. Then flip it onto a board and cut it into serving pieces.

4. Tomatillos provide really nice tangy and herblike flavours to the base of the sauce. You will often find them with papery husks still attached. Peel the husks off and rinse each tomatillo under water to remove the sticky coating.

5. Braai the tomatillos over direct medium heat until their skins begin to break, turning occasionally. During the braaiing time, their flavours will turn richer, sweeter and more concentrated.

6. Braai the whole chilli and onion slices at the same time as the tomatillos. Once the chilli has been peeled and seeded, purée the vegetables with some olive oil, fresh coriander, brown sugar and salt for a bold vegetarian sauce to serve with the polenta.

POLENTA WITH FETA AND ROASTED TOMATILLO SAUCE

SERVES: 4
PREP TIME: 40 MINUTES
COOLING TIME: 2 HOURS

HEAT: DIRECT AND INDIRECT MEDIUM HEAT
180°–230°C (350°–450°F)
BRAAIING TIME: 18–22 MINUTES

POLENTA
    2 tablespoons unsalted butter
    125 ml finely chopped onion
    1 litre milk
    125 g polenta
    1 teaspoon chilli powder
    ¾ teaspoon coarse sea salt
    Extra-virgin olive oil

SAUCE
    2 slices onion, each about 1 cm thick
    4 tomatillos, about 250 g total, papery skins removed
    1 medium-hot chilli, 7–10 cm long
    4 tablespoons fresh coriander leaves
    ½ teaspoon brown sugar
    ¼ teaspoon coarse sea salt

    100 g feta or queso fresco cheese, crumbled
    1 ripe avocado

1. Melt the butter in a large saucepan over medium heat. Add the onion and cook for 3–5 minutes, stirring occasionally, until lightly browned. Add the milk, polenta, chilli powder and salt, whisking until the mixture begins to boil. Turn the heat to very low and stir with a wooden spoon almost constantly to prevent splattering or burning. Cook and stir for 15–20 minutes until the polenta is very thick and no longer gritty to the bite.

2. Brush the inside of a 20 cm-square baking tray with 1 tablespoon of oil. Scrape the hot polenta into the tray and spread it into a smooth, even layer. Allow to cool at room temperature for about 2 hours. Prepare the braai for direct and indirect cooking over medium heat.

3. Brush the onion slices, tomatillos and whole chilli with olive oil. Brush the cooking grates clean. Braai the vegetables over **direct medium heat**, with the lid closed as much as possible but turning as necessary, until the onions are lightly charred, the tomatillos soften and begin to collapse, and the chilli is slightly softened and lightly charred. The onions will take 8–10 minutes, the tomatillos about 10 minutes, and the chilli 10–12 minutes. Remove the vegetables from the braai as they are done. Place the chilli in a bowl, cover with clingfilm and allow to steam for 10–15 minutes.

4. When the chilli is cool enough to handle, pull off and discard the skin, stem and seeds. Put the vegetables, the coriander, brown sugar and salt into a food processor or blender. Whirl until evenly puréed. Add more brown sugar and salt to taste.

5. Invert the tray of polenta onto a chopping board, tapping to release the polenta if necessary. Cut the polenta into 4–8 pieces of whatever size and shape you like.

6. Set the pieces of polenta, smooth and oiled side down, over **indirect medium heat**. Carefully pile the crumbed cheese on top of each piece. Braai for 8–10 minutes without turning, with the lid closed, until the polenta is warm and the cheese begins to melt. While the polenta is on the braai, peel and thinly slice the avocado.

7. Transfer the polenta to serving plates. Spoon the tomatillo sauce over the polenta and top with avocado slices.

HOW TO BRAAI MEALIES ON THE COALS

1. Cut off the exposed brownish silk and peel the layers of the husk until you begin to see some kernels showing through the layers. Now the charcoal flavours can penetrate the kernels.

2. Lay the mealies on and alongside the coals, turning them as the husks blacken in spots.

3. Allow the mealies to cool a bit and then peel off the remaining layers of the husk. Finish cooking the mealies in a roasting tray of melted lemon-curry butter.

FLAME-ROASTED MEALIES WITH LEMON-CURRY BUTTER

SERVES: 4
PREP TIME: 10 MINUTES

HEAT: DIRECT MEDIUM HEAT 180°–230°C (350°–450°F)
 FOR CHARCOAL BRAAIS ONLY
BRAAIING TIME: 20–25 MINUTES

BUTTER
 4 tablespoons unsalted butter, softened
 1 tablespoon finely chopped fresh dill
 2 teaspoons finely grated lemon zest
 1 teaspoon curry powder
 ½ teaspoon coarse sea salt
 pinch of freshly ground black pepper

4 fresh sweetcorn mealies, in husks

1. Prepare the charcoal braai as seen on the left. Allow the coals to burn down to medium heat.

2. Mash the butter ingredients together in a bowl with the back of a fork, mixing until the ingredients are evenly distributed.

3. Trim the pointed end of each mealie, cutting off and discarding the fine silk sticking out of the husk. Remove and discard a layer or two of the tough outer leaves of each husk. If you can see some kernels through the transparent leaves, that's good.

4. Carefully place the mealies in a single layer on the charcoal grate, both on and alongside the coals. Cook the mealies for 15–20 minutes, with the lid closed as much as possible but swapping the positions of the mealies and rolling them over a few times for even cooking, until the husks are blackened all over and the kernels are tender. If any kernels are exposed, keep that side away from direct exposure to the coals. If the outer leaves burn, that's okay.

5. Using long-handled tongs, carefully remove the mealies from the braai. Allow to cool for a few minutes or until you can safely hold them in your hands. Carefully peel off and discard the husk and silk from each mealie. Leave the stem ends attached to use as handles.

6. Arrange the mealies in a single layer in a roasting tray that will fit on the braai. Add the butter to the tray. When ready to serve, place the tray on the cooking grate and braai over **direct medium heat** for about 5 minutes, with the lid closed as much as possible but turning occasionally, until the butter melts and the mealies are warm. If desired, keep the mealies warm in the roasting tray over indirect heat while you finish braaiing other parts of the meal.

GINGER AND LIME-GLAZED MEALIES

SERVES: 6
PREP TIME: 15 MINUTES

HEAT: DIRECT MEDIUM HEAT 180°–230°C (350°–450°F)
BRAAIING TIME: 10–15 MINUTES

GLAZE
   75 ml chicken stock
   4 tablespoons unsalted butter
   1 tablespoon sugar
   1 teaspoon finely grated lime zest
   1 teaspoon coarse sea salt
   1 teaspoon grated fresh ginger

   6 ears fresh sweetcorn mealies, in husks

1. Prepare the braai for direct cooking over medium heat.

2. Stir the glaze ingredients together in a saucepan set over a medium-high heat. Bring to the boil and cook for 5–7 minutes until the glaze slightly thickens. Keep the glaze warm.

3. Cut the top off each mealie just above the first row of kernels. Set aside a couple of corn husks to make long strips. Pull the corn husks back, but do not break them off the cobs. Remove and discard the corn silk. Gather the husks together on each mealie, where they narrow towards the ends, and use a strip of husk about 1 cm wide to tie the husks together for a handle. Mix the glaze and brush it over the mealies. Brush the cooking grates clean. Braai the mealies over **direct medium heat** for 10–15 minutes, with the lid closed as much as possible and letting the husks extend over indirect heat so that they do not burn, but turning several times, until they are browned in spots and tender. Transfer the mealies to a platter and baste with the remaining glaze.

HOW TO PREP MEALIES (CORN ON THE COB)

1. Pull the husks back, but leave them attached to the stalk end so that you have handles. Remove and discard the corn silk.

2. Use a couple of long husks from the outer layers to cut long strips for tying up the handles.

3. Brush the exposed corn kernels with some of the glaze.

4. Braai the mealies over direct medium heat, with the handles extending over indirect heat so that they do not burn.

For optimal flavour, fresh mealies should be shucked just before braaiing. Many of the kernels will turn golden brown and crisp-tender over direct medium heat.

GRILLED CORN AND MUSHROOM RISOTTO

SERVES: 4–6
PREP TIME: 50 MINUTES

HEAT: DIRECT MEDIUM HEAT 180°–230°C (350°–450°F)
BRAAIING TIME: 8–10 MINUTES
SPECIAL EQUIPMENT: 30 CM FRYING PAN

- 250 g button mushrooms
- 1 medium hot chilli, about 15 cm long
- 3 fresh sweetcorn mealies, husked
- 1 onion, cut crossways into 1 cm slices
- Extra-virgin olive oil
- 1.2 litres chicken stock
- 2 tablespoons unsalted butter
- 200 g Arborio rice
- ½ teaspoon coarse sea salt
- 100 g finely grated Parmesan-style cheese
- 125 ml feta cheese, crumbled
- 4 tablespoons fresh coriander leaves, chopped

1. Prepare the braai for direct cooking over medium heat.

2. Wipe the mushrooms with a damp cloth or roller towel. Remove and discard any discoloured stem ends. Lightly brush the mushrooms, chilli, mealies and onion slices with oil.

3. Braai the vegetables over **direct medium heat** for 8–10 minutes, with the lid closed as much as possible but turning as needed, until the mushrooms and onion slices are tender, the chilli is blackened and blistered all over and the mealies are browned in spots and tender. Remove the vegetables from the braai and allow them to cool. Coarsely chop the mushrooms and cut the corn kernels off the cobs. Scrape off the loosened bits of skin from the chilli and discard, along with the seeds and stem; finely chop the remaining part of the chilli. Combine the mushrooms, chilli and corn in a bowl. Roughly chop the onion and set it aside. (The vegetables can be left at room temperature for 3–4 hours.)

4. Warm the stock in a large saucepan over a medium heat, until it simmers.

5. Melt the butter in a 30 cm frying pan over high heat. Add the onion and rice and cook for 2–3 minutes, stirring frequently, until the rice is slightly opaque. Pour in 250 ml of the hot stock and stir the mixture often until the stock is absorbed.

6. Continue to add the hot stock, 250 ml at a time, and cook at a simmer for 20–30 minutes, stirring frequently, until the stock is absorbed and the rice is tender. When the rice is fully cooked, the mixture should be creamy but not soupy. At this point, add the remaining grilled vegetables and the salt.

7. Remove the risotto from the heat, add the Parmesan-style cheese and stir until melted. Spoon the risotto into warmed, wide bowls and top with crumbled feta cheese and coriander.

MARINATED BABY PAK CHOI AND SHIITAKE MUSHROOMS

SERVES: 4
PREP TIME: 15 MINUTES
MARINATING TIME: 1–2 HOURS

HEAT: DIRECT MEDIUM HEAT 180°–230°C (350°–450°F)
BRAAIING TIME: ABOUT 5 MINUTES
SPECIAL EQUIPMENT: PERFORATED GRILL PAN

MARINADE
   75 ml low-sodium soy sauce
   4 tablespoons dry sherry
   1 tablespoon light brown sugar
   1 tablespoon dark sesame oil
   4 slices peeled fresh ginger, each 5 mm thick, crushed
   2 garlic cloves, crushed
   ¼ teaspoon crushed red chilli flakes

   4 baby pak choi, larger ones cut in half
   20 large shiitake mushrooms

1. Whisk the marinade ingredients together in a bowl until the sugar has dissolved.

2. Plunge the pak choi into a bowl of water and shake to clean off any dirt trapped between the leaves. Wipe the mushrooms clean with a damp cloth or roller towel and then remove and discard the stalks.

3. Place the vegetables into a large, resealable plastic bag and pour in the marinade. Press the air out of the bag and seal tightly. Turn the bag to distribute the marinade and leave at room temperature for 1–2 hours, turning occasionally.

4. Prepare the braai for direct cooking over medium heat. Preheat a grill pan over **direct medium heat** for about 10 minutes.

5. Remove the vegetables from the bag and reserve the marinade. When the grill pan is hot, place the pak choi and the mushrooms onto the pan, spreading them out in a single layer. Braai over **direct medium heat** for about 5 minutes, with the lid closed as much as possible but turning once or twice and basting occasionally with the reserved marinade, until the pak choi is crisp-tender and the shiitakes are heated through. Serve hot.

HOW TO BRAAI PAK CHOI AND SHIITAKE MUSHROOMS

1. Plunge the baby pak choi into water to remove any dirt trapped between the leaves.

2. Remove and discard the tough stalks from the mushrooms.

3. Cut the larger pak choi in half, keeping the root ends intact.

4. Leave the smaller pak choi whole.

5. Place the vegetables in a large plastic bag and coat with the marinade.

6. Braai the vegetables on a preheated grill pan, basting them occasionally with the marinade.

PORTABELLO MUSHROOM SANDWICHES WITH BASIL AND BALSAMIC AÏOLI

SERVES: 6
PREP TIME: 20 MINUTES
MARINATING TIME: 15–20 MINUTES

HEAT: DIRECT MEDIUM HEAT 180°–230°C (350°–450°F)
BRAAIING TIME: 8–12 MINUTES

AÏOLI
　　5 tablespoons mayonnaise
　　2 tablespoons balsamic vinegar
　　1 teaspoon coarse sea salt
　　½ teaspoon finely chopped garlic

MARINADE
　　175 ml extra-virgin olive oil
　　4 tablespoons red wine vinegar
　　2 tablespoons finely chopped shallot
　　1 teaspoon finely chopped garlic
　　1 teaspoon coarse sea salt
　　½ teaspoon freshly ground black pepper

　　6 large portabello mushrooms, cleaned, stalks and
　　　black gills removed (see photos below)
　　Coarse sea salt
　　Freshly ground black pepper

　　6 hamburger rolls, cut in half
　　Fresh rocket or basil, trimmed, rinsed and dried

1. Combine the aïoli ingredients in a small bowl. Refrigerate until ready to assemble the sandwiches.

2. Whisk the marinade ingredients together in another small bowl. Place the mushroom caps, gill sides down, in a large dish. Brush the mushroom caps generously with the marinade and turn the caps over. Spoon the rest of the marinade over the gill side. Allow the mushrooms to marinate at room temperature for 15–20 minutes.

3. Prepare the braai for direct cooking over medium heat.

4. Remove the mushrooms from the dish and reserve the marinade. Lightly season the mushrooms with salt and pepper. Brush the cooking grates clean. Braai the mushrooms, gill sides down, over **direct medium heat** for 4–6 minutes, with the lid closed as much as possible, until they begin to soften. Brush the cap sides of the mushrooms with some of the remaining marinade from the dish. Turn the mushrooms over and braai them for a further 4–6 minutes, until they are tender when pierced with a knife.

5. Braai the rolls, cut sides down, over **direct medium heat** for about 30 seconds, until lightly toasted.

6. Spread aïoli on the toasted rolls and top each one with a mushroom and some basil or rocket. Serve warm.

HOW TO BRAAI PORTABELLO MUSHROOMS

1. Cut away the stalks and any curled edges around the rims.

2. With a spoon, gently scrape away the dark gills that might be holding dirt.

3. Use a vinaigrette to marinate and baste the mushrooms.

4. Finish braaiing the mushrooms with the stalk side facing up so that the juices stay inside the cap.

MARINATED PORTABELLO MUSHROOMS WITH PECORINO CHEESE

SERVES: 6
PREP TIME: 10 MINUTES
MARINATING TIME: 15–20 MINUTES

HEAT: DIRECT MEDIUM HEAT 180°–230°C (350°–450°F)
BRAAIING TIME: 8–12 MINUTES

MARINADE
    4 tablespoons extra-virgin olive oil
    3 tablespoons balsamic vinegar
    1 tablespoon soy sauce
    1 teaspoon chopped fresh rosemary
      or ½ teaspoon dried rosemary
    ½ teaspoon freshly ground black pepper
    ¼ teaspoon coarse sea salt

6 large portabello mushrooms, each 12–15 cm in diameter
40 g fresh breadcrumbs
1 tablespoon finely chopped flat-leaf (Italian) parsley
150 g Pecorino, Asiago or Parmesan-style cheese, grated
Coarse sea salt
Freshly ground black pepper

1. Whisk the marinade ingredients together in a small bowl.

2. Wipe the mushrooms clean with a damp cloth or roller towel. Remove and discard the stalks. With a teaspoon, carefully scrape out and discard the black gills from the mushroom caps (see photos on opposite page). Place the mushrooms, cap sides up, on a rimmed plate and brush them with the marinade. Turn them over and brush again with the marinade. Allow them to stand for 15–20 minutes at room temperature. Meanwhile, prepare the braai for direct cooking over medium heat.

3. Combine the breadcrumbs with the parsley in another small bowl.

4. Brush the cooking grates clean. Braai the mushrooms, gill sides down, over **direct medium heat** for 4–6 minutes, with the lid closed, until the mushrooms start to soften. Brush the cap sides with the remaining marinade. Turn the mushrooms over, top each one with some of the cheese, close the lid and cook for 4–6 minutes, until tender when pierced with a knife. During the last minute of cooking, put some of the breadcrumb mixture on top of each mushroom. Remove from the braai, add salt and pepper to taste, and serve immediately.

HOW TO MAKE PIZZA ON THE BRAAI

1. A grill pan is a convenient tool for cooking small pizza toppings, like chopped mushrooms and pepper slices. Wrap the garlic in a foil parcel before roasting it.

2. To flatten and stretch dough easily, without it springing back, it needs to be at room temperature. If you buy refrigerated ready-made dough, allow it sit on a work surface for a few hours so it will warm up and relax.

3. A bit of olive oil on your hands and your board will make the dough more pliable. Finish flattening each piece of dough on a sheet of greaseproof paper.

4. The greaseproof paper will help to hold the shape of the dough as you flip it onto the braai. After a minute or so of cooking, you should peel off the paper.

5. The oil will prevent sticking and promote even browning. When the underside is crisp and toasted, transfer the pizza bases to a work surface, with the grilled sides facing up.

6. Arrange the toppings on the toasted sides. Return the pizzas to the braai and continue to cook them until the bottoms of the bases are crisp and the cheese has melted.

PIZZA WITH MUSHROOMS, PEPPERS, GARLIC AND SMOKED MOZZARELLA

SERVES: 8
PREP TIME: 25 MINUTES
RISING TIME: 1½–2 HOURS

HEAT: DIRECT MEDIUM HEAT 180°–230°C (350°–450°F) AND DIRECT MEDIUM-HIGH HEAT ABOUT 230°C (450°F)
BRAAIING TIME: 29–46 MINUTES
SPECIAL EQUIPMENT: ELECTRIC STAND MIXER

DOUGH
- 350 ml warm water
- 1 sachet instant dry yeast
- ½ teaspoon sugar
- 625 g cake flour
- 3 tablespoons extra-virgin olive oil
- 2 teaspoons coarse sea salt

- 4 tablespoons extra-virgin olive oil
- ½ teaspoon coarse sea
- ¼ teaspoon freshly ground black pepper
- 10 garlic cloves, peeled
- 1 large red pepper, cut into 5-mm strips
- 250 g brown mushrooms, stalks removed and quartered
- 225 g grated smoked mozzarella cheese

1. Combine the water, yeast and sugar in the bowl of an electric mixer. Stir briefly and allow to stand for 5 minutes, or until the surface has a thin, frothy layer (this indicates that the yeast is active). Add the flour, oil and salt. Fit the mixer with the dough hook and mix on low speed for about 1 minute or until the dough begins to come together. Increase the speed to medium and continue to mix for about 10 minutes, until the dough is slightly sticky, smooth and elastic. Form the dough into a ball and place in a lightly oiled bowl. Turn it to coat all sides and cover the bowl tightly with clingfilm. Allow the dough to rise in a warm place for 1½–2 hours, until it has doubled in size.

2. Mix 4 tablespoons of oil with the salt and pepper in a large bowl. Place the garlic cloves in the centre of a small sheet of heavyweight foil and pour 1 tablespoon of the oil mixture over the garlic. Fold up the sides to make a sealed parcel, leaving a little room for the expansion of steam.

3. Add all the peppers and mushrooms to the bowl with the remaining oil mixture. Toss to coat the vegetables evenly.

4. Prepare the braai for direct cooking over medium-high heat. Preheat a perforated grill pan over **direct medium-high heat** for about 10 minutes. While the pan is preheating, place the parcel of garlic over **direct medium-high heat** and cook for 15–20 minutes, until the cloves are soft and light brown. Remove the parcel from the braai. When the grill pan is really hot, lift the mushrooms and peppers from the bowl with tongs, and spread them out in a single layer on the pan. Cook for about 6 minutes, stirring once or twice, until they are nicely browned and tender. Wearing braai mitts or oven gloves, remove the pan from the braai and set it down on a heatproof surface.

5. Cut the dough into 8 equal pieces. Lightly brush eight, 25 × 25 cm squares of greaseproof paper on one side with oil. Using your fingers, flatten each piece of dough onto a sheet of greaseproof paper to create 8 rounds, each about 1 cm thick and 15–20 cm in diameter. Lightly brush the tops with oil. Allow the rounds to sit at room temperature for 5–10 minutes.

6. Lower the temperature of the braai to medium heat. Brush the cooking grates clean. Working with 4 rounds at a time, place the dough on the cooking grate with the paper sides facing up. Braai over **direct medium heat** for 2–5 minutes, with the lid closed as much as possible but rotating as needed for even cooking, until the dough is well marked and firm on the underside. Peel off and discard the greaseproof paper. Transfer the pizza bases to a work surface with the grilled sides facing up. Repeat with the other 4 rounds.

7. Spread the cheese evenly over the bases and then arrange some of the roasted garlic, mushrooms and pepper slices on top. Return the pizzas to the braai and cook over **direct medium heat** for 2–5 minutes, with the lid closed as much as possible but rotating the pizzas occasionally for even cooking, until the cheese is melted and the bottom of the bases are crisp. Transfer to a chopping board and cut into wedges. Serve warm.

Go ahead and burn them. Roasting peppers is one technique where it is okay to burn the food... to a degree. Charring the peppers until they are black (see above, left) helps to loosen the skin so that you can peel it away and reveal the sweet flesh beneath (see above, right).

ROASTED PEPPER AND BACON BRUSCHETTA

SERVES: 6 AS AN APPETIZER (MAKES 18 PIECES)
PREP TIME: 15 MINUTES

HEAT: DIRECT MEDIUM HEAT 180°–230°C (350°–450°F)
BRAAIING TIME: 13–17 MINUTES

  3 red peppers
  6 bacon rashers, cooked and finely chopped
  2 tablespoons extra-virgin olive oil, divided
  1 tablespoon red wine vinegar
  Coarse sea salt
  1 loaf Italian or French bread, cut in half lengthways
  2–3 tablespoons finely grated Parmesan-style cheese
  4 tablespoons coarsely chopped fresh basil

1. Prepare the braai for direct cooking over medium heat. Brush the cooking grates clean. Braai the peppers over **direct medium heat** for 12–15 minutes, with the lid closed as much as possible but turning every 3–5 minutes, until blackened and blistered all over. Place the peppers in a bowl, cover with clingfilm and leave to stand for 10–15 minutes. Remove the peppers from the bowl and peel away and discard the charred skins. Cut off and discard the tops and seeds, and then finely chop the peppers. Transfer the chopped peppers to a bowl and toss with the bacon, 2 teaspoons of the oil and the vinegar. Season to taste with salt.

2. Lightly brush or spray the cut sides of the bread with the remaining 4 teaspoons of oil and braai over **direct medium heat** for 1–2 minutes, until toasted. Remove from the braai and cut the bread on the diagonal into 5-cm wide pieces.

3. Just before serving, add the cheese to the pepper mixture. Spoon the mixture on the toasted pieces of bread. Scatter the basil on top and serve at room temperature.

HOW TO BRAAI ONION SLICES

1. Cut off the root and stem ends from each onion. Peel off the papery skin.
2. Cut each onion crossways into 1-cm thick slices.
3. The layers will hold together best if they are evenly sliced.
4. When turning the slices, grip the layers closest to the centre with the tongs.

ROASTED PEPPER, GRILLED ONION AND FETA CHEESE SALAD

SERVES: 6
PREP TIME: 15 MINUTES

HEAT: DIRECT MEDIUM HEAT 180°–230°C (350°–450°F)
BRAAIING TIME: 12–15 MINUTES

VINAIGRETTE
 4 tablespoons extra-virgin olive oil
 2 tablespoons red wine vinegar
 ½ tablespoon finely chopped garlic
 ½ teaspoon coarse sea salt
 ¼ teaspoon freshly ground black pepper

 2 red onions, cut crossways into 1 cm slices
 Extra-virgin olive oil
 2 large red peppers
 350 g rocket, rinsed and dried
 125 ml toasted walnuts, coarsely chopped
 125 g feta cheese, crumbled

1. Prepare the braai for direct cooking over medium heat.

2. Whisk the vinaigrette ingredients together in a small bowl until emulsified.

3. Lightly brush the onion slices with oil. Brush the cooking grates clean. Braai the onions and bell peppers over **direct medium heat**, with the lid closed as much as possible and turning occasionally, until the onions are tender and the skins of the peppers are evenly charred and blistered. The onions will take 8–12 minutes and the peppers, 12–15 minutes. Remove the veggies from the braai. Place the peppers in a bowl, cover with clingfilm, and allow them to steam for 10–15 minutes. When the peppers are cool enough to handle, remove and discard the charred skins, stalks and seeds and cut them into strips about 1 cm wide.

4. Place the peppers and onions in a bowl. Add 2 tablespoons of the vinaigrette and toss to coat.

5. In a salad bowl, toss the rocket with the remaining dressing. Top with the onions and peppers and then add the walnuts and feta cheese. Serve right away.

FLAME-ROASTED TOMATO SOUP WITH PARMESAN CROUTONS

SERVES: 4
PREP TIME: 30 MINUTES

HEAT: DIRECT LOW HEAT 110°–180°C (250°–350°F)
BRAAIING TIME: 8–10 MINUTES
SPECIAL EQUIPMENT: PERFORATED GRILL PAN

1 kg firm, ripe tomatoes
1 red onion, quartered through the root end and peeled
10 garlic cloves, peeled
4 tablespoons fresh thyme sprigs
4 tablespoons extra-virgin olive oil
1 litre chicken stock
1 teaspoon sugar
1 teaspoon coarse sea salt
½ teaspoon freshly ground black pepper
2 tablespoons unsalted butter, softened
8 slices baguette, each about 5 mm thick
50 g Parmesan-style cheese, finely grated
2 tablespoons coarsely chopped fresh basil

1. Prepare the braai for direct cooking over low heat. Preheat a grill pan over **direct low heat** for about 10 minutes.

2. Combine the tomatoes, onion, garlic, thyme and oil in a bowl and toss to coat. Using tongs, arrange all the vegetables and herbs on the grill pan and cook over **direct low heat** for 20–25 minutes with the lid closed as much as possible but turning occasionally, until the tomato skins wrinkle and start to brown. Transfer the tomatoes to a large saucepan. Continue to cook the onions, garlic and thyme for a further 5–10 minutes, until the onions and garlic are lightly charred on all sides. Add the onions and garlic to the saucepan. Discard the thyme.

3. Add the chicken stock to the saucepan. Bring to a boil, reduce the heat, and simmer for 8–10 minutes until the tomatoes have collapsed completely. Transfer the soup to a blender and purée until very smooth. Pour the soup through a mesh strainer to remove all the tomato seeds and skin. Season with the sugar, salt and pepper.

4. If the braai has an infrared burner above the warming rack, preheat the burner on **high**, with the braai lid open. Butter each slice of bread on one side and top with 2 teaspoons of grated cheese. Using tongs, position the bread slices towards the back of the warming rack, just in front of the burner. Cook for about 2 minutes, with the lid open, until the cheese melts and browns, but take care that the cheese doesn't burn. Remove the croutons from the warming rack. If your braai does not have an infrared burner, toast the croutons under a conventional grill.

5. Just before serving, reheat the soup, if necessary, and add the basil. Ladle the soup into bowls and float the croutons on top. Garnish with any remaining cheese. Serve warm.

HOW TO ROAST TOMATOES ON THE BRAAI

1. Coat the tomatoes and other vegetables with oil and place them on a preheated grill pan.

2. Cook over direct low heat until the tomato skins are wrinkled and browned.

3. Turn the vegetables occasionally for even caramelization.

4. Don't be afraid of deep, dark colours on the vegetables. That's where the flavour is.

PANZANELLA SKEWERS WITH SHERRY VINAIGRETTE

SERVES: 4
PREP TIME: 15 MINUTES

HEAT: DIRECT MEDIUM HEAT 180°–230°C (350°–450°F)
BRAAIING TIME: ABOUT 4 MINUTES
SPECIAL EQUIPMENT: 4 BAMBOO SKEWERS, SOAKED IN WATER FOR AT LEAST 30 MINUTES

VINAIGRETTE
    2 tablespoons sherry vinegar
    1 teaspoon Dijon mustard
    ½ teaspoon finely chopped garlic
    90 ml extra-virgin olive oil
    ¼ teaspoon sea salt
    ¼ teaspoon freshly ground black pepper

    1 small loaf focaccia or Italian bread, cut into 2.5 cm cubes
    12 firm but ripe cherry tomatoes
    250 g baby rocket
    2 tablespoons coarsely chopped fresh basil
    2 tablespoons finely grated Parmesan-style cheese

1. Prepare the braai for direct cooking over medium heat.

2. Whisk the vinegar, mustard and garlic together in a small bowl. Slowly drizzle and whisk in the oil until it is emulsified. Season with the salt and pepper.

3. Combine the bread cubes and tomatoes in a large bowl with 2 tablespoons of the vinaigrette and toss to coat. Thread the bread cubes and tomatoes alternately on the skewers.

4. Brush the cooking grates clean. Braai the skewers over **direct medium heat** for about 4 minutes, with the lid open and turning every minute, until the tomato skins are browned and the bread is lightly toasted. (If the bread starts to burn, move the skewers over indirect heat for the remaining time.)

5. Toss the rocket and basil in a bowl with 2 tablespoons of vinaigrette. Brush the skewers with the remaining vinaigrette. To serve, divide the salad greens evenly onto serving plates and top with a panzanella skewer. Sprinkle with the cheese.

HOW TO PREP VINAIGRETTE

1. Whisk the vinegar, mustard and garlic first. The mustard will help to emulsify the oil.

2. Slowly add the extra-virgin olive oil, whisking all the time for a smooth dressing.

HOW TO PREP SKEWERS

Cut the bread cubes just a little bigger than the tomatoes so the cubes will toast nicely before the tomatoes collapse.

VEGETABLES

HOW TO BRAAI ARTICHOKE HEARTS

1. Bend back the dark outer leaves of each artichoke, breaking them just above the base. Stop when you see the pale green and yellowish leaves exposed.

2. Trim the stalk of each artichoke, leaving 1.5 cm or so attached.

3. Use a sharp knife to remove the pale green and yellowish leaves above the base of each artichoke.

4. Use a small spoon to scrape out the fuzzy choke from each artichoke heart.

5. Cut each artichoke heart in half lengthways through its stalk.

6. Using a vegetable peeler or paring knife, trim most of the rough edges from the artichoke hearts and trim off a thin layer of the stalk to expose the softer interior.

7. After blanching the artichoke hearts in boiling water to make them tender, brush them with oil, season with salt, and braai them over direct medium heat until warmed and lightly charred on all sides.

ARTICHOKE HEARTS WITH SMOKED TOMATO AND ROASTED GARLIC AÏOLI

SERVES: 4-6
PREP TIME: 35 MINUTES

HEAT: INDIRECT AND DIRECT MEDIUM HEAT 180°–230°C (350°–450°F)
BRAAIING TIME: 24–26 MINUTES

- 3 ripe red tomatoes, about 125 g each, halved, cored and seeds removed
- Extra-virgin olive oil
- 3 large garlic cloves
- 2 handfuls hickory wood chips, soaked in water for at least 30 minutes
- 200 ml mayonnaise
- 1½ teaspoons balsamic vinegar
- 1 teaspoon coarse sea salt, divided
- ¼ teaspoon freshly ground black pepper

- 6 large artichokes, 300–350 g ounces each
- Juice of 1 lemon

1. Prepare the braai for indirect and direct cooking over a medium heat.

2. Lightly brush the tomatoes with oil. Cut a 20 × 30 cm sheet of heavyweight foil. Put the garlic cloves in the centre of the foil. Drizzle ½ teaspoon of oil over the garlic cloves and fold up all four sides to make a parcel.

3. Drain and add the wood chips directly onto burning coals or to the smoker box of a gas braai, following the manufacturer's instructions. Brush the cooking grates clean. As soon as the wood begins to smoke, place the tomatoes and the parcel of garlic over **indirect medium heat** and cook for about 20 minutes, until the tomatoes are lightly smoked and browned in spots, and the garlic is browned along the edges.

4. Purée the tomatoes and garlic in a food processor until they are smooth. Add the mayonnaise, vinegar, ½ teaspoon of the salt and the pepper. Pour the sauce into individual serving bowls. (Cover and refrigerate if you are not planning to serve the sauce within the next hour, but allow to stand at room temperature for about 30 minutes before serving.)

5. Bring a large pot of salted water to a boil.

6. Prepare the artichokes by snapping off the dark outer leaves until you expose the yellowish leaves with pale green tips. Place each artichoke on its side. Using a sharp knife, cut off the remaining leaves just above the base. With a small teaspoon, scoop out the fuzzy choke. Cut the base of each artichoke in half lengthways, through the stalk, and then trim the stalk, leaving about 1.5 cm attached. Using a vegetable peeler or small knife, trim and smooth the rough greenish areas around the base. Trim a very thin strip all the way around the stalk to expose the tender part of the stalk. As each artichoke heart is trimmed, place it in a bowl of water mixed with lemon juice.

7. Cook the artichokes in the boiling salted water for 10–12 minutes, until you can pierce them easily with a knife, but being careful not to overcook them. Drain the artichokes in a colander and place them in a large bowl. While they are still warm, add 2 tablespoons of oil and the remaining salt and toss gently to coat the artichokes. (They can be prepared up to this point and refrigerated for up to 4 hours, but bring to room temperature before braaiing.)

8. Lift the artichoke hearts from the bowl, letting any excess oil drip back into the bowl. Braai the artichokes over **direct medium heat** for 4–6 minutes, with the lid closed as much as possible but turning them once or twice, until warm and lightly charred. Serve warm or at room temperature with the sauce.

HOW TO BRAAI ASPARAGUS

1. In spring, the peak season for asparagus, look for firm spears with smooth skins and tightly closed heads.

2. Spears of medium thickness do better on the braai than pencil-thin spears. They are less likely to fall through the cooking grate and they usually have fuller flavours. Both purple and green spears will be green when they are cooked.

3. Coat raw, trimmed asparagus spears with vinaigrette dressing to add flavour and promote even browning on the braai. The spears should not be very wet when you place them on the braai as this could cause flare-ups.

4. So that you don't lose spears through the cooking grate, align them so that they lie at right angles to the bars. Roll the spears over every few minutes with tongs to cook them evenly.

HOW TO BRAAI PROSCIUTTO

1. While the asparagus is cooking, lay thin slices of prosciutto over direct heat and braai them until crispy, turning once or twice.

2. It will take only a minute to melt the fat, making the prosciutto golden and delicious. Break the cooled slices into pieces for garnish.

ASPARAGUS AND PROSCIUTTO WITH LEMON VINAIGRETTE

SERVES: 4
PREP TIME: 20 MINUTES

HEAT: DIRECT MEDIUM HEAT 180°–230°C (350°–450°F)
BRAAIING TIME: 6–8 MINUTES

VINAIGRETTE
    2 tablespoons apple cider vinegar
    1 tablespoon finely chopped shallot
    2 teaspoons finely grated lemon zest
    1 teaspoon Dijon mustard
    4 tablespoons extra-virgin olive oil
    ¼ teaspoon coarse sea salt
    ¼ teaspoon freshly ground black pepper

    750 g fresh asparagus
    ½ teaspoon coarse sea salt
    4 thin slices prosciutto or Parma-style ham, about 50 g total

1. Prepare the braai for direct cooking over medium heat.

2. Whisk the vinegar, shallot, lemon zest and mustard together in a bowl. Slowly drizzle and whisk in the oil until it is emulsified. Season with the salt and pepper.

3. Remove and discard the tough bottom of each asparagus spear by grasping each end and bending it gently until it snaps at its natural point of tenderness, usually two-thirds of the way down the spear. If desired, use a vegetable peeler to peel off the outer skin from the bottom half of each spear. Spread the asparagus on a large plate, drizzle with a few tablespoons of the vinaigrette and season evenly with the salt.

4. Brush the cooking grates clean. Braai the asparagus and the prosciutto over **direct medium heat**, with the lid closed as much as possible but turning once or twice, until the asparagus is tender and the prosciutto is crisp. The asparagus will take 6–8 minutes and the prosciutto will take 1–2 minutes.

5. Arrange the asparagus on a serving platter, spoon over the rest of the vinaigrette and crumble the crisp prosciutto on top.

LEMON BROCCOLI

SERVES: 4
PREP TIME: 10 MINUTES

HEAT: DIRECT MEDIUM HEAT 180°–230°C (350°–450°F)
BRAAIING TIME: 4–6 MINUTES
SPECIAL EQUIPMENT: PERFORATED GRILL PAN

2½ teaspoons coarse sea salt
500 g broccoli florets
2 tablespoons extra-virgin olive oil
1 tablespoon finely grated lemon zest
Parmesan-style cheese

1. Fill a large saucepan with water, add 2 teaspoons of the salt and bring to a boil over a high heat. Add the broccoli to the boiling water and cook for 3–5 minutes until bright green and crisp-tender. Remove the florets from the saucepan and plunge into a bowl of iced water to rapidly cool them, then remove the broccoli from the water and drain.

2. Prepare the braai for direct cooking over medium heat. Brush the cooking grates clean. Preheat a grill pan over **direct medium heat** for about 10 minutes.

3. Mix the broccoli, olive oil, lemon zest and the remaining ½ teaspoon salt together in a small bowl.

4. Spread the broccoli on the grill pan in a single layer. Cook over **direct medium heat** for 4–6 minutes, with the lid closed as much as possible but turning occasionally, until the broccoli is warm and just beginning to brown.

5. Remove the broccoli from the braai and garnish with fine shavings of parmesan-style cheese. Serve warm.

HOW TO BRAAI BROCCOLI

1. Cut broccoli florets into even-sized pieces before blanching them.

2. For quick browning, preheat the grill pan before laying out the florets.

3. Turn the florets occasionally with tongs or shake the grill pan while wearing an insulated barbecue mitt or oven glove.

GREEN BEANS WITH LEMON OIL

SERVES: 4
PREP TIME: 20 MINUTES
COOLING TIME: 30–60 MINUTES

HEAT: DIRECT MEDIUM HEAT 180°–230°C (350°–450°F)
BRAAIING TIME: 5–7 MINUTES
SPECIAL EQUIPMENT: PERFORATED GRILL PAN

LEMON OIL
    1 lemon
    4 tablespoons extra-virgin olive oil
    2 large garlic cloves, thinly sliced
    ¼ teaspoon crushed red chilli flakes

    500 g fresh, thin green beans
    2 vitamin C tablets (500 mg each)
    Coarse sea salt

1. Using a vegetable peeler, remove wide strips of yellow zest from the lemon. Put them in a small saucepan with the oil, garlic and red chilli flakes. Cook over low heat until the oil simmers. Allow it to simmer for about 2 minutes, then remove the saucepan from the heat and set aside to cool and steep for 30–60 minutes.

2. Remove and discard the stem ends from the green beans. Pile the beans into a large bowl.

3. Remove and discard the lemon zest and garlic from the oil. Using the sharp blade and the side of a knife, chop and crush the vitamin C tablets into a powder. Add the powder and ½ teaspoon salt to the oil. Mix well.

4. Prepare the braai for direct cooking over medium heat. Preheat the grill pan over **direct medium heat** for about 10 minutes.

5. Pour the oil mixture over the green beans and toss the beans over and over again to make sure they are well coated.

6. Lift the green beans from the bowl with tongs and shake off any excess oil, letting it fall back into the bowl. Spread the green beans on the grill pan in a single layer. Braai over **direct medium heat** for 5–7 minutes, with the lid closed as much as possible but turning occasionally, until they are browned in places and crisp-tender.

7. Remove the green beans from the pan. Season to taste with salt and freshly squeezed lemon juice. Serve warm.

HOW TO BRAAI GREEN BEANS

1. To infuse olive oil with more flavour, heat it with strips of lemon zest, garlic and crushed red chilli flakes.

2. Crushed vitamin C (an antioxidant) in the oil will help to keep the beans bright green as they cook.

3. Spread the beans on a preheated grill pan so that they cook quickly in direct contact with the pan.

HOW TO BRAAI CARROTS

1. I once considered carrots too crunchy to braai. Then I realized that I should just boil them first to make them tender. Now they are one of my favourite side dishes, especially when I find young carrots with their tops still attached. They are so sweet and fabulous.

2. Trim off the stems and leaves to 2 cm or so above the end of each carrot. Next, peel the carrots and blanch them in boiling salted water until they are barely tender.

3. Stop the cooking by plunging the carrots into a bowl of iced water. At this point, you could drain the carrots and set them aside for several hours before braaiing them.

4. When you are ready to braai, place the carrots in a bowl with some melted butter, honey, orange zest and a little balsamic vinegar, and toss gently to coat.

5. Arrange the carrots more or less at right angles to the bars of the cooking grate so that you don't lose any. Braai them over direct medium heat until they develop handsome grill stripes.

6. Finally, return the carrots to the bowl with the glaze and coat them again for extra flavour.

ORANGE-GLAZED CARROTS

SERVES: 4–6
PREP TIME: 8–10 MINUTES

HEAT: DIRECT MEDIUM HEAT 180°–230°C (350°–450°F)
BRAAIING TIME: 4–6 MINUTES

2¼ teaspoons coarse sea salt
12 carrots, each 15–20 cm long, peeled and trimmed
3 tablespoons unsalted butter, melted
2 tablespoons honey or maple syrup
2 teaspoons finely grated orange zest
2 teaspoons balsamic vinegar
2 tablespoons finely chopped flat-leaf (Italian) parsley
Orange wedges, to serve (optional)

1. Fill a large saucepan with water, add 2 teaspoons of the salt and bring to a boil over high heat. Add the carrots to the boiling water and cook for 4–6 minutes, until tender but still crisp. Remove the carrots from the saucepan and plunge them into a bowl of iced water to cool them rapidly, then remove the carrots from the water and drain.

2. Prepare the braai for direct cooking over medium heat.

3. Combine the melted butter, honey, orange zest, vinegar and the remaining ¼ teaspoon of salt in a large bowl. Add the carrots to the bowl and toss to coat them evenly.

4. Brush the cooking grates clean. Remove the carrots from the bowl and let the excess butter mixture drip back into the bowl. Set the bowl aside. Braai the carrots over **direct medium heat** for 4–6 minutes, with the lid closed as much as possible but turning occasionally, until lightly caramelized. Place the carrots back into bowl with the remaining butter mixture. Toss to coat thoroughly. Garnish with the parsley and serve warm with orange wedges for squeezing over, if desired.

HOW TO BRAAI TOFU

1. Tofu 'steaks' can be a delicious alternative to meat. Buy extra-firm tofu so that it holds together well on the braai.

2. To give tofu some added flavour, coat the steaks in a marinade based on lemon juice, fresh ginger and soy sauce.

3. Cooking tofu steaks on sheets of heavyweight foil avoids any risk of sticking. The heat that is conducted through the foil browns the surfaces nicely.

LEMON-GINGER TOFU STEAKS WITH CARROT AND CASHEW SALAD

SERVES: 4
PREP TIME: 20 MINUTES
MARINATING TIME: 3–4 HOURS

HEAT: DIRECT HIGH HEAT 230°–290°C (450°–550°F)
BRAAIING TIME: 6–8 MINUTES

MARINADE
  4 tablespoons fresh lemon juice
  4 tablespoons canola oil or sunflower oil
  4 tablespoons soy sauce
  2 tablespoons freshly grated ginger
  2 tablespoons light brown sugar
  1 teaspoon chilli-garlic sauce, such as Sriracha

850 g extra-firm tofu (not silken-style)

SALAD
  500 ml coarsely grated carrot
  125 ml coarsely chopped cashews
  4 tablespoons finely chopped spring onions, white and light green parts
  4 tablespoons finely chopped fresh coriander or flat-leaf (Italian) parsley
  2 teaspoons fresh lemon juice
  1 teaspoon dark sesame oil
  1 teaspoon soy sauce

1. Whisk the marinade ingredients together in a bowl. Remove the blocks of tofu from their containers, leaving the liquid behind. Cut each block lengthways into slices about 2.5 cm thick. Arrange the slices in a single layer on a rimmed platter or in an ovenproof dish.

2. Pour the marinade over the tofu slices and brush the marinade on all sides. Cover with clingfilm and refrigerate for 3–4 hours, turning the slices over once or twice.

3. Combine the salad ingredients in a bowl and mix well. Set aside at room temperature.

4. Prepare the braai for direct cooking over high heat. Brush the cooking grates clean. Lay a large sheet of heavyweight foil, about 40 × 30 cm, directly on the cooking grate. Lift the tofu slices from the platter and arrange them in a single layer on the foil, reserving the marinade for glazing. Braai the tofu over **direct high heat** for 6–8 minutes, with the lid closed as much as possible but turning once and brushing occasionally with some of the reserved marinade, until both sides are nicely caramelized and the slices are warm. Using a spatula or fish slice, transfer the tofu slices to serving plates. Stack the salad on top. Serve warm or at room temperature.

When roasting, peeling and opening the chillies, be careful that you maintain enough structure in the chillies that they can hold the cheese filling.

CHILES RELLENOS WITH TOMATO SALSA AND GUACAMOLE

SERVES: 6
PREP TIME: 30 MINUTES

HEAT: DIRECT AND INDIRECT MEDIUM HEAT 180°–230°C (350°–450°F)

BRAAIING TIME: 22–31 MINUTES

SALSA
    3 firm, ripe tomatoes, halved and cored
    1 small white onion, cut crossways into 1-cm slices
    Extra-virgin olive oil
    2 tablespoons finely chopped fresh coriander leaves
    1 tablespoon fresh lime juice
    1 teaspoon very finely chopped serrano or jalapeño chilli
    1 teaspoon coarse sea salt

GUACAMOLE
    3 large ripe avocados
    1 medium red onion, finely chopped
    2 tablespoons fresh lime juice
    1 teaspoon coarse sea salt

    6 large medium hot chillies, for stuffing
    100 g Cheddar cheese, grated
    100 g Wensleydale cheese, grated
    65 g fresh goat's cheese, crumbled

1. Prepare the braai for direct and indirect cooking over medium heat. Brush the cooking grates clean.

2. Lightly brush the tomatoes and onion slices with oil. Braai over **direct medium heat** for 6–8 minutes, with the lid closed as much as possible but turning once, until lightly charred all over. Remove from the braai, finely chop and transfer to a bowl. Stir in the remaining salsa ingredients.

3. Using a fork, coarsely mash the avocados in another bowl. Stir in the onion and lime juice, then season with the salt. Cover with clingfilm, placing the plastic directly on the surface of the guacamole to prevent it from browning, and refrigerate until about 1 hour before serving.

4. Braai the large chillies over **direct medium heat**, for 10–15 minutes, with the lid open and turning occasionally, until the skins are blackened and blistered all over. (The goal is to char the skins quickly so that you can peel them without the chillies collapsing. You will need chillies with enough structure, even when roasted, to hold the filling.) Place the chillies in a large bowl, cover with clingfilm, and allow them to steam for about 10 minutes. Gently peel and discard the skin from the chillies, leaving the stems intact. Carefully cut a slit down one side of each chilli and remove and discard the seeds and veins.

5. Combine the cheeses in a bowl and mix together with a fork. Carefully stuff the cheese mixture into the chilli cavities. Brush the chillies with olive oil.

6. Braai the stuffed chillies, seam sides up, over **indirect medium heat** for 6–8 minutes, with the lid closed, until the cheese has melted. Gently remove them from the braai with a spatula. Serve warm with the salsa and guacamole.

HOW TO BRAAI GARLIC

1. Cut off the top of a head of garlic to expose the cloves, and drizzle some oil on the cloves.

2. Wrap the head in foil and braai it over indirect heat until the cloves are soft and beginning to brown.

3. Allow the head to cool and then squeeze out the soft, mellow-tasting garlic cloves.

HOW TO PREP BRINJALS

1. Brinjals (aubergines) should be firm, with glossy, unblemished skins. Look for cylindrical shapes that feel heavy for their size.

2. A male brinjal (left) will often have fewer seeds than a female brinjal (right), making the pulp of the male sweeter and less bitter.

3. Prick the whole brinjals several times with a fork and braai them over direct high heat until the skins are charred and beginning to collapse.

4. Cut the cooled brinjals in half lengthways and scoop out the pulp for the dip. Remove and discard any clumps of seeds that could turn the dip bitter.

ROASTED BRINJAL DIP

SERVES: 8-10 AS AN APPETIZER
PREP TIME: 10 MINUTES

HEAT: INDIRECT AND DIRECT HIGH HEAT 230°–290°C (450°–550°F), DIRECT MEDIUM HEAT 180°–230°C (350°–450°F)
BRAAIING TIME: 40–50 MINUTES

- 1 head garlic
- 1 teaspoon extra-virgin olive oil
- 2 brinjals (aubergines), about 500 g total
- 1 tablespoon fresh lemon juice
- 1 teaspoon fresh origanum leaves
- ½ teaspoon coarse sea salt
- ½ teaspoon freshly ground black pepper

BAGEL CHIPS

- 2 bagels
- 2 tablespoons extra-virgin olive oil
- ¼ teaspoon coarse sea salt

1. Prepare the braai for indirect and direct cooking over a high heat.

2. Remove the loose, papery outer skin from the head of garlic and cut off the top to expose the cloves. Place the garlic on a large square of heavyweight foil and drizzle the oil over the top of the cloves. Fold in the sides to make a sealed parcel, leaving a little room for the expansion of steam. Brush the cooking grates clean. Braai over **indirect high heat** for 40–50 minutes, with the lid closed, until the cloves are soft.

3. Prick the brinjals several times with a fork. Braai over **direct high heat** for 15–20 minutes, with the lid closed as much as possible but turning occasionally, until the skins are charred and they begin to collapse. A knife should slide into the flesh without resistance.

4. Once the garlic and brinjals are cool enough to handle, squeeze the garlic cloves into the large bowl of a food processor fitted with a metal blade. Cut the brinjals in half lengthways and, using a large spoon, scrape away the flesh from the skin. Discard the skin and any large seed pockets. Add the flesh of the brinjals to the food processor and pulse to create a thick paste. Add the lemon juice and origanum and process until the mixture is smooth. Season with salt and pepper. Decrease the temperature of the braai to medium heat.

5. Slice the bagels in half so you have two half-moons. Slice each bagel half lengthways into 5 mm-thick slices.

6. Lightly brush the bagel slices with the oil. Sprinkle with salt and braai over **direct medium heat** for about 2 minutes, turning once, until the chips begin to brown and get crispy.

7. Serve the dip warm with bagel chips and fresh vegetables.

HOW TO BRAAI SANDWICHES

1. Cut the courgettes and brinjals lengthways and evenly into 5 mm-thick slices and braai them over direct medium heat before assembling the sandwiches.

2. Roughly chop the herbs, sun-dried tomatoes and garlic for the spread. Cover one side of each bread slice with the spread.

3. Brush the outside of each slice of bread with oil and braai the sandwiches until toasted on each side.

VEGETABLE SANDWICHES WITH SUN-DRIED TOMATO SPREAD

SERVES: 4
PREP TIME: 20 MINUTES

HEAT: DIRECT MEDIUM HEAT 180°–230°C (350°–450°F)
BRAAIING TIME: 10–14 MINUTES

SPREAD
    250 ml fresh basil leaves
    250 ml fresh flat-leaf (Italian) parsley
    1 garlic clove
    4 tablespoons finely chopped sun-dried tomatoes in oil
    2 tablespoons oil from the jar of sun-dried tomatoes
    1 teaspoon finely grated lemon zest
    1 teaspoon fresh lemon juice
    ¼ teaspoon coarse sea salt

    500 g brinjal, trimmed and cut lengthways into 5-mm slices
    250 g courgettes, trimmed and cut lengthways into 5-mm slices
    Extra-virgin olive oil
    ½ teaspoon coarse sea salt
    ¼ teaspoon freshly ground black pepper
    8 slices sourdough bread, each about 1 cm thick
    4 slices provolone cheese, cut to fit the bread

1. Prepare the braai for direct cooking over medium heat.

2. Finely chop the basil and parsley with the garlic. Place the herb mixture into a small bowl. Add the remaining spread ingredients and mix well to form a paste.

3. Lightly brush both sides of the brinjal and courgette slices with oil. Season with the salt and pepper. Braai the vegetable slices over **direct medium heat** for 8–10 minutes, with the lid closed as much as possible but turning once or twice, until nicely marked on both sides. The courgettes will cook a little faster than the brinjal. Transfer the vegetables from the braai to a platter as they are done.

4. Distribute the spread on one side of each bread slice. Arrange the cheese and braaied vegetables in layers on half of the bread slices, making sure that the cheese is in the centre. Place another slice of bread on top and gently press with your hand to keep the sandwich together. Lightly brush the outsides of the bread with oil.

5. Braai over **direct medium heat** for 2–4 minutes with the lid open but turning once, until the bread is toasted and the cheese has melted. Serve warm.

HONEY AND CURRY-GLAZED BUTTERNUT

SERVES: 4–6
PREP TIME: 15 MINUTES

HEAT: INDIRECT MEDIUM HEAT 180°–230°C (350°–450°F)
BRAAIING TIME: 60–70 MINUTES

   2.5–3 kg butternut (or winter squash, such as acorn or hubbard squash)
   4 tablespoons extra-virgin olive oil
   Coarse sea salt
   Freshly ground black pepper

GLAZE
   4 tablespoons unsalted butter
   4 tablespoons honey
   1 tablespoon cider vinegar
   2 teaspoons mild curry powder
   ¼ teaspoon chilli powder

1. Prepare the braai for indirect cooking over medium heat.

2. Wash the butternut under cold water. Using a heavy, sharp knife, cut the ends off each butternut and cut the butternut into large pieces. Using a tablespoon, scoop out and discard the seeds and pulp. Place the butternut on a baking tray and brush the flesh with the oil and season to taste with salt and pepper.

3. Brush the cooking grates clean. Braai the butternut, skin side down, over **indirect medium heat** for about 30 minutes, with the lid closed.

4. Meanwhile, combine the glaze ingredients in a small saucepan over a medium heat and cook for about 2 minutes, stirring often, until the butter has melted and the glaze is smooth. Remove from the heat.

5. After the first 30 minutes of cooking, return the butternut pieces to the baking tray. Close the braai lid to maintain the heat inside. Brush the flesh with the glaze, return the butternut to the braai and continue to cook over **indirect medium heat**, for 30–40 minutes, with the lid closed as much as possible but glazing every 15–20 minutes, until the butternut is soft and tender. Season with more salt, if desired. Drizzle with the remaining glaze and serve warm.

Braai the butternut pieces over indirect medium heat for about 30 minutes before glazing them. Applying a sweet glaze too early could cause burning. During the final 30–40 minutes of cooking, glaze the butternut every 15–20 minutes, but close the lid as quickly as possible to maintain the correct temperature.

After roasting red and golden beetroot over indirect heat, put them in separate bowls so their colours won't run together. Cover the bowls with clingfilm to help loosen the skins with steam. When peeling beetroot, use a paring knife and wear rubber gloves to avoid staining your hands.

FLAME-ROASTED BEETROOT SALAD WITH PUMPKIN SEEDS AND FETA

SERVES: 4
PREP TIME: 30–40 MINUTES

HEAT: INDIRECT MEDIUM HEAT 180°–230°C (350°–450°F)
BRAAIING TIME: 1–1½ HOURS

    1 kg red or golden beetroots (or a combination of both)
    Extra-virgin olive oil

DRESSING
    2 tablespoons red wine vinegar
    1 teaspoon Dijon mustard
    1 teaspoon honey
    1 teaspoon ground cumin
    ¼ teaspoon crushed red chilli flakes
    125 ml extra-virgin olive oil
    ½ teaspoon coarse sea salt
    ¼ teaspoon freshly ground black pepper

    175 g Cos lettuce leaves, whole or torn into pieces
    4 tablespoons toasted pumpkin seeds (pepitas)
    125 g feta or goat's cheese, crumbled

1. Prepare the braai for indirect cooking over medium heat. Brush the cooking grates clean.

2. If necessary, trim off the leafy tops and root ends from the beetroots and scrub them under cold water. Lightly brush them with oil. Braai the beetroots over **indirect medium heat** for 1–1½ hours, depending on size, with the lid closed as much as possible but turning occasionally, until they are tender when pierced with the tip of a knife. Remove from the braai. Place the red and golden beetroots in separate bowls to prevent the red beetroots from staining the golden beetroots. Cover the bowls with clingfilm and allow to stand at room temperature until cool enough to handle. With a sharp paring knife, cut off the ends and remove the skins. Cut the beetroots crossways into slices (5 mm – 1 cm thick) and keep the slices in their separate bowls until ready to serve.

3. Whisk together the vinegar, mustard, honey, cumin and chilli flakes. (You can do this in a blender or by hand in a bowl.) Slowly drizzle in the oil while whisking, until the dressing has emulsified. Season with the salt and pepper.

4. Divide the lettuce and beetroot slices between 4 plates and drizzle with some dressing. Garnish each plate with pumpkin seeds and cheese. Serve warm.

FENNEL AND FONTINA

SERVES: 4–6
PREP TIME: 10 MINUTES

HEAT: DIRECT MEDIUM-LOW HEAT ABOUT 180°C (350°F)
BRAAIING TIME: 23–28 MINUTES

3 fennel bulbs
3 tablespoons extra-virgin olive oil
1 tablespoon fresh lemon juice
½ teaspoon coarse sea salt
pinch of freshly ground black pepper
125 g fontina cheese, grated

1. Prepare the braai for direct cooking over medium-low heat.

2. If the fennel stalks have the fronds attached, trim off the fronds and chop enough to make 2 tablespoons. Cut off the thick stalks above the bulbs and save the stalks for another use. Cut each fennel bulb into quarters and then remove the thick triangular-shaped core. Cut the fennel vertically into 5-mm thick slices.

3. Pile the fennel on one side of a large sheet of heavyweight foil, about 60 × 20 cm, leaving enough foil to completely cover and envelope the fennel. Pour the oil and lemon juice over the fennel. Season with the salt and pepper. Fold the foil over the fennel and seal the parcel tightly so that no liquid can escape.

4. Braai the parcel over **direct medium-low heat** for 20–25 minutes with the lid closed, until the fennel is barely tender. Carefully open the parcel with tongs. Sprinkle the cheese over the fennel and grill for 2–3 minutes, with the foil parcel open, until the cheese has melted slightly. Carefully remove the parcel from the braai and garnish with chopped fennel fronds. Serve warm.

HOW TO BRAAI FENNEL

1. Cut off the thick stalks and the root end from each bulb, but reserve some of the fronds for garnish.

2. Cut each bulb lengthways into quarters and cut away nearly all of the tough core.

3. Thinly slice the fennel, arrange the slices on a large sheet of foil, and coat them with good-quality olive oil.

4. Braai the fennel in a foil parcel until barely tender. Open the parcel, top the fennel with grated cheese and finish cooking the fennel. Garnish with chopped fennel fronds and serve.

VEGETABLES

Shelled pistachios and garlic are at the heart of a non-traditional but delicious pesto for coating flame-roasted potatoes.

POTATO SALAD WITH PISTACHIO PESTO

SERVES: 4–6
PREP TIME: 20 MINUTES

HEAT: DIRECT MEDIUM HEAT 180°–230°C (350°–450°F)
BRAAIING TIME: 10–15 MINUTES
SPECIAL EQUIPMENT: PERFORATED GRILL PAN

PESTO
    1 garlic clove
    250 ml fresh basil leaves
    4 tablespoons shelled unsalted pistachios
    2½ tablespoons mayonnaise
    2 teaspoons white wine vinegar
    ½ teaspoon coarse sea salt
    ¼ teaspoon freshly ground black pepper

1 kg baby potatoes, scrubbed but not peeled
Coarse sea salt
2 large red or yellow peppers (or 1 of each)
2 tablespoons extra-virgin olive oil
Freshly ground black pepper
Torn fresh basil leaves, optional

1. Chop the garlic very finely in a food processor. Add the basil and pistachios and pulse until they are finely chopped. Transfer the mixture to a large bowl and mix with the remaining pesto ingredients.

2. Cut each potato into halves or quarters and put them into a large saucepan. Cover with water, add 2 teaspoons of salt and bring to a boil over high heat. Reduce the heat to a simmer and cook for 5–10 minutes, until the potatoes are barely tender. Meanwhile cut each pepper in half lengthways. Remove and discard the stem, seeds and large white veins and cut each pepper into 2–3 cm pieces.

3. When the potatoes are barely tender, drain them in a colander and return them to the dry saucepan. Add the pepper pieces, olive oil and ½ teaspoon of salt. Toss gently to coat the vegetables evenly.

4. Prepare the braai for direct cooking over medium heat. Preheat the grill pan over **direct medium heat** for 10 minutes. When the pan is hot, spoon the potatoes and peppers onto the pan, spreading them out in a single layer. Cook over **direct medium heat** for 10–15 minutes, with the lid closed as much as possible but turning occasionally, until the potatoes are tender, and seared with golden brown marks on all sides. Transfer the vegetables to the bowl with the pesto and gently toss to coat the vegetables completely. Allow to cool for at least 5 minutes. Season to taste with salt and pepper and garnish with fresh basil, if desired. Serve warm or at room temperature.

COCONUT-GLAZED SWEET POTATOES

SERVES: 4–6
PREP TIME: 15 MINUTES

HEAT: DIRECT MEDIUM HEAT 180°–230°C (350°–450°F) FOR CHARCOAL BRAAIS ONLY
BRAAIING TIME: ABOUT 1 HOUR
SPECIAL EQUIPMENT: 30-CM CAST-IRON FRYING PAN

4 medium sweet potatoes

GLAZE
  1 can (425 ml) coconut milk
  Finely grated zest and juice of 1 lime
  2 tablespoons brown sugar
  1 tablespoon unsalted butter
  1 jalapeño chilli, very finely chopped
  ½ teaspoon coarse sea salt

4 tablespoons coconut flakes

1. Wash and dry the potatoes and then wrap them individually in sheets of heavyweight foil.

2. Prepare a bull's-eye fire for medium heat (see below). When the coals are ready, place the sweet potatoes directly on the charcoal grate resting on the edge of the charcoal. Close the lid and cook for 45–55 minutes, turning them occasionally, until the potatoes are soft. To check for doneness, squeeze the potatoes with a pair of tongs.

3. Remove the potatoes from the braai and allow them to cool for about 15 minutes before unwrapping them. Slit the skins with a knife and peel off and discard the skin. Cut the flesh into 1-cm cubes. Set aside while you make the glaze.

4. Place a cast-iron frying pan over **direct medium heat**. (You can also do this step on your stove top.) Combine the glaze ingredients in the pan and bring the mixture to a simmer, stirring occasionally, for 5–8 minutes, until reduced by half. The glaze will be slightly thick. Remove the pan from the heat and add the sweet potato cubes, stirring them gently to coat with the glaze, but being careful not to mash them.

5. Toast the coconut flakes for about 2 minutes in a small frying pan over high heat, until they are just light brown.

6. Place the potatoes in a serving bowl and sprinkle the toasted coconut over the top. Serve warm.

HOW TO BRAAI SWEET POTATOES

1. Choose sweet potatoes of similar size and thickness so that they cook evenly.

2. Wrap them in foil and place them against the coals, turning them occasionally.

3. Moisten and flavour the sweet potatoes with a thick glaze based on coconut milk and brown sugar.

4. Garnish with flakes of coconut that have been lightly toasted in a frying pan.

HOW TO MAKE FLATBREAD

1. To make sticky dough easier to handle, add a little oil to the dough and the chopping board.

2. Use a 'bench scraper' (shown here) or a large knife to cut the dough into equal portions.

3. Make 12 individual balls and use your hands to press and stretch each one into whatever shape you like, as long as they are about 1 cm thick.

4. Stack the flattened pieces of dough between sheets of baking paper. Make sure that every piece of dough is coated with oil on both sides to prevent them from sticking to the braai.

BRAAIED FLATBREAD WITH THREE TOPPINGS

SERVES: 4
PREP TIME: 15 MINUTES
RISING TIME: 1½–2 HOURS

HEAT: DIRECT MEDIUM HEAT 180°–230°C (350°–450°F)
BRAAIING TIME: ABOUT 6 MINUTES FOR EACH BATCH
SPECIAL EQUIPMENT: ELECTRIC STAND MIXER

DOUGH
    350 ml warm water (40–45°C)
    1 sachet instant yeast
    ½ teaspoon sugar
    625 g flour
    3 tablespoons extra-virgin olive oil
    2 teaspoons coarse sea salt

1. Combine the water, yeast and sugar in the bowl of an electric stand mixer. Stir briefly and allow to stand for 5 minutes, or until the top surface has a thin, frothy layer. (This indicates that the yeast is active.) Add the flour, oil and salt. Fit the mixer with the dough hook and mix on low speed for about 1 minute or until the dough begins to come together. Increase the speed to medium. Continue to mix for about 10 minutes, until the dough is slightly sticky, smooth and elastic. Form the dough into a ball and place in a lightly oiled bowl. Turn it over to coat all sides and tightly cover the bowl with clingfilm. Leave the dough to rise in a warm place for 1½–2 hours, until it has doubled in size.

2. Prepare the braai for direct cooking over medium heat.

3. Turn the dough out onto a lightly oiled surface and cut it into 12 equal-sized portions, 50–70 g each. Using your fingers and the palms of your hands (oil them, too), stretch the dough to a length of about 20 cm. The first stretch will probably shrink back, but continue to pull and stretch, using gentle pressure, until you achieve the proper length. Add more oil to the surface, as needed, to keep the dough moist and pliable. Stack the pieces of dough between sheets of baking paper.

4. Brush the cooking grates clean. Carefully place the pieces of dough, a few at a time, over **direct medium heat**. Within 1–2 minutes the undersides of the dough should crisp, darken, and harden, and the tops will puff slightly. Turn them over and continue to cook for about 6 minutes total, turning every minute, until both sides are dark brown. If desired, keep warm over indirect heat. Serve warm or at room temperature with the topping(s) of your choice (see opposite page).

WHITE BEAN PURÉE WITH ROASTED GARLIC

MAKES: 375 ML
PREP TIME: 10 MINUTES

HEAT: INDIRECT MEDIUM HEAT 180°–230°C (350°–450°F)
BRAAIING TIME: 45–60 MINUTES

- 1 small head garlic
- 2 tablespoons plus 1 teaspoon extra-virgin olive oil
- 1 can (425 g) cannellini beans, rinsed and drained
- 1 teaspoon finely grated lemon zest
- 2 tablespoons fresh lemon juice
- 1 teaspoon coarse sea salt
- ¼ teaspoon freshly ground black pepper
- 4 tablespoons fresh flat-leaf (Italian) parsley
- 2–3 small fresh sage leaves, coarsely chopped

1. Prepare the braai for indirect cooking over medium heat.

2. Remove the loose, papery outer skin from a head of garlic and cut off the top to expose the cloves. Place the garlic on a large square of heavyweight foil and drizzle 1 teaspoon of the oil over the top of the cloves. Fold up the sides to make a sealed parcel, leaving a little room for the expansion of steam. Braai over **indirect medium heat** for 45–60 minutes, with the lid closed, until the cloves are soft.

3. Squeeze the roasted garlic into the bowl of a food processor, being careful not to include any of the papery skin. Add the cannellini beans, the remaining 2 tablespoons of olive oil, the lemon zest, lemon juice, salt and pepper, and purée the mixture. Add the parsley and sage and pulse until the purée has a consistency that resembles the texture of hummus. If necessary, add more oil to create a smoother consistency.

TOMATO TAPENADE

MAKES: 250 ML
PREP TIME: 10 MINUTES

- 125 ml pitted kalamata olives, drained
- 125 ml oil-packed sun-dried tomatoes, drained
- 1 small garlic clove or several roasted garlic cloves
- 3–4 tablespoons extra-virgin olive oil
- 4 tablespoons fresh basil leaves
- 2 tablespoons capers, drained
- 2 teaspoons balsamic vinegar
- ¼ teaspoon freshly ground black pepper

1. Place the olives, sun-dried tomatoes and garlic in the bowl of a food processor and pulse several times to coarsely chop them. Add 3 tablespoons of the oil and the rest of the ingredients. Continue to purée until the mixture is well combined. Add the remaining tablespoon of oil if the tapenade seems too chunky.

BLUE CHEESE AND WALNUT SPREAD

MAKES: 250 ML
PREP TIME: 10 MINUTES

- 125 g blue cheese, crumbled
- 4 tablespoons unsalted butter, softened
- 125 ml walnuts, lightly toasted and coarsely chopped
- 4 tablespoons very finely chopped shallot
- 1 tablespoon fresh lemon juice
- ¼ teaspoon freshly ground black pepper
- Finely chopped fresh flat-leaf (Italian) parsley

1. Mash the blue cheese and butter with a fork (or blend in a food processor) to form a semi-smooth spread. It's okay if there are still some chunks of blue cheese. Fold in the remaining ingredients, adding parsley to taste.

FRUIT

TECHNIQUES

266	How to braai **PINEAPPLE** upside-down cake
268	How to braai **APPLES**
269	How to braai gingerbread and **APRICOTS**
271	How to braai **BANANA** s'mores
274	How to braai **PEACHES**
276	How to prep **PEAR** and prosciutto

RECIPES

267	**PINEAPPLE** Upside-down Cake
268	**APPLE** Caramel on Puff Pastry
269	Gingerbread with Braaied **APRICOTS**
270	**BANANAS** Foster
271	Braaied **BANANA** S'mores
272	Lemon-Buttermilk Panna Cotta with Braaied **FIGS**
273	Flame-roasted **STRAWBERRIES**
275	**PEACH** Shortcakes
276	**PEAR** and Prosciutto Salad with Champagne Vinaigrette
277	Vine Leaf-wrapped **CAMEMBERT** with Grape Salsa

HOW TO BRAAI PINEAPPLE UPSIDE-DOWN CAKE

1. Trim 2–3 cm from both the top and bottom of a ripe pineapple.

2. Stand the pineapple upright and rotate it as you cut off the tough skin.

3. Go back around the pineapple to trim off the dark 'eyes'.

4. Cut the pineapple crossways into slices about 1 cm thick.

5. Use a paring knife to cut around the core of each slice (on both sides) and remove it.

6. Brush the slices with butter and braai them over direct medium heat.

7. Combine brown sugar, cream and cinnamon in a 30-cm cast-iron frying pan.

8. Melt the brown sugar mixture over direct medium heat.

9. When the mixture bubbles around the outer edge, remove the pan from the heat.

10. Carefully arrange the pineapple slices in the hot mixture and pour the batter on top.

11. Spread the batter evenly to the edge of the frying pan.

12. Cook over indirect heat until a skewer inserted into the centre comes out clean.

PINEAPPLE UPSIDE-DOWN CAKE

SERVES: 6–8
PREP TIME: 30 MINUTES

HEAT: DIRECT AND INDIRECT MEDIUM HEAT 180°–230°C (350°–450°F) **FOR GAS BRAAIS ONLY**
BRAAIING TIME: 46–58 MINUTES
SPECIAL EQUIPMENT: 30 CM CAST-IRON FRYING PAN

TOPPING
    6 slices fresh pineapple, each 1 cm thick, peeled and cored
    2 tablespoons unsalted butter, melted
    125 ml treacle (dark brown) sugar
    4 tablespoons cream
    ½ teaspoon ground cinnamon

BATTER
    250 ml flour
    1 teaspoon baking powder
    ½ teaspoon sea salt
    ¼ teaspoon bicarbonate of soda
    150 ml buttermilk
    2 large eggs
    1 teaspoon vanilla extract
    125 g unsalted butter, softened
    200 ml sugar

1. Prepare the braai for direct and indirect cooking over medium heat. Brush the cooking grates clean.

2. Brush the pineapple rings with the melted butter. Braai them over **direct medium heat** for 4–6 minutes with the lid open and turning once, until nicely marked. Remove from the braai and allow them to cool. Leave one pineapple ring whole and cut the others in half.

3. Combine the brown sugar, cream, cinnamon and any melted butter remaining from brushing the pineapple slices in a cast-iron frying pan over **direct medium heat**. Cook for about 2 minutes until the sugar has melted and the liquid starts to bubble around the edge. Remove the pan from the heat and place on a baking tray. Place the whole pineapple ring in the centre of the pan, then arrange the pineapple halves around it. Set aside.

4. Mix the flour, baking powder, salt and bicarbonate of soda together in a large bowl. Whisk the buttermilk, eggs and vanilla in a separate bowl.

5. Cream the butter and sugar with an electric mixer on medium-high speed for 2–4 minutes, until light and fluffy. With the mixer on low, add the buttermilk mixture and then gradually add the flour mixture. Blend until smooth, scraping down the sides as necessary. Using a rubber spatula, spread the batter evenly over the pineapple slices in the pan.

6. Bake the cake over **indirect medium heat** for 40–50 minutes, keeping the temperature of the braai as close to 180°C (350°F) as possible, with the lid closed, until the top is golden and a skewer inserted into the centre comes out clean. Wearing insulated oven gloves, remove the cake from the braai and allow it to cool at room temperature for about 10 minutes.

7. To remove the cake from the pan, first run a knife around the edge to loosen it. Place a serving platter, large enough to hold the cake, on top of the pan. Wearing gloves, carefully invert both the pan and platter, then slowly remove the pan. Replace any pineapple that has stuck to the bottom of the pan. Let the cake cool briefly before slicing into wedges and serving. Serve warm or at room temperature on the day it is made.

HOW TO MAKE CRÈME FRAÎCHE

1. After standing for 8 hours at room temperature, a bit of buttermilk turns cream into thick crème fraîche.

2. After 24 hours, the same crème fraîche is even thicker and more delicious.

HOW TO BRAAI APPLES

1. Apple slices coated with butter quickly turn brown and tender on the braai.

2. Toss them with caramel sauce before assembling the dessert.

APPLE CARAMEL ON PUFF PASTRY

SERVES: 4
PREP TIME: 20 MINUTES

HEAT: DIRECT MEDIUM HEAT 180°–230°C (350°–450°F)
BRAAIING TIME: 8–10 MINUTES
SPECIAL EQUIPMENT: PERFORATED GRILL PAN

    1 sheet frozen puff pastry, about 23-cm square, thawed

SAUCE
    125 ml light brown sugar
    125 ml cream
    4 tablespoons unsalted butter

    4 Granny Smith apples, peeled, cored and cut into 1-cm thick wedges
    4 tablespoons unsalted butter, melted
    Coarse sea salt, optional
    4 tablespoons crème fraîche (recipe follows) or whipped cream

1. Cut 4 rounds from the pastry sheet using a 10-cm biscuit cutter. Prick each pastry round about 12 times with a fork to prevent the dough from rising too much in the oven. Following the package directions, bake the pastry rounds on a baking sheet until golden brown. Transfer to a wire rack to cool.

2. Combine the sauce ingredients in a small saucepan over medium heat, stirring constantly for 4–5 minutes, until the sugar has dissolved and the butter has melted. Remove the saucepan from the heat and set aside.

3. Toss the apple slices with the melted butter in a large bowl to coat well.

4. Prepare the braai for direct cooking over medium heat. Preheat a perforated grill pan over **direct medium heat** for about 10 minutes. Add the apple slices to the pan and cook them for 8–10 minutes, with the lid closed as much as possible but turning once or twice, until they are well browned and tender. Transfer the apple slices to a bowl. Reheat the sauce over low heat, if necessary, and spoon some of the sauce over the apple slices, gently tossing to coat.

5. To assemble, place each pastry round on a dessert plate. Arrange the apple slices on top of the pastry rounds. Spoon the remaining sauce over the apples, allowing it to run down onto the plates. Sprinkle with a little coarse sea salt, if desired. Finish with a dollop of crème fraîche or whipped cream.

CRÈME FRAÎCHE
MAKES: 275 ML
PREP TIME: 2 MINUTES
STANDING TIME: 8–24 HOURS

    250 ml cream
    2 tablespoons buttermilk

1. Combine the cream and buttermilk in a small bowl. Cover and allow to stand at room temperature for 8–24 hours. It can be kept in the refrigerator for up to 10 days.

GINGERBREAD WITH BRAAIIED APRICOTS

SERVES: 12
PREP TIME: 30 MINUTES

HEAT: INDIRECT AND DIRECT MEDIUM HEAT 180°–230°C (350°–450°F) **FOR GAS BRAAIS ONLY**
BRAAIING TIME: 39–41 MINUTES
SPECIAL EQUIPMENT: 23–25-CM CAST-IRON FRYING PAN

200 g cake flour
1 teaspoon ground ginger
¾ teaspoon ground cinnamon
¾ teaspoon bicarbonate of soda
¾ teaspoon salt
125 g unsalted butter, softened, plus extra for the pan
100 g sugar
1 large egg, at room temperature
125 ml molasses or treacle syrup
125 ml hot water
3 tablespoons chopped crystallized ginger

12 firm but ripe apricots, cut in half and stoned
4 tablespoons unsalted butter, melted
3 tablespoons sugar
1 tablespoon dark rum, optional

12 scoops vanilla ice cream

1. Combine the flour, ginger, cinnamon, bicarbonate of soda and salt in a small bowl. In a separate bowl, beat the butter and sugar with an electric mixer on high speed for about 3 minutes, until light and fluffy. Beat in the egg and then the molasses. With the mixer on low speed, gradually add the flour mixture, scraping down the sides of the bowl with a rubber spatula. Add the water and mix until smooth. Stir in the crystallized ginger. Lightly butter the inside of a 23- or 25-cm cast-iron frying pan. Pour the gingerbread mixture into the pan and spread it evenly.

2. Prepare the braai for indirect cooking over medium heat. Brush the cooking grates clean.

3. Cook the gingerbread over **indirect medium heat** for about 35 minutes, with the lid closed, until a wooden cocktail stick inserted into the centre comes out clean. Keep the braai's temperature as close to 180°C (350°F) as possible. Wearing insulated oven gloves, carefully remove the pan from the braai.

4. Gently toss the apricots with the melted butter, sugar and rum in a large bowl. Lift the apricots from the butter mixture, letting the excess butter fall back into the bowl. Braai the apricots, cut sides down, over **direct medium heat** for 4–6 minutes, with the lid closed as much as possible but turning and brushing with the butter mixture once, until heated through. The cooking time will vary depending on the ripeness of the apricots.

5. Cut the gingerbread into wedges and serve warm with the apricots. Spoon any remaining butter mixture over the top and serve with ice cream.

HOW TO BRAAI GINGERBREAD AND APRICOTS

1. Cook the gingerbread over indirect medium heat until a cocktail stick comes out clean.

2. Cut each apricot in half and remove the stones.

3. Toss the apricots in a bowl with sugar and melted butter.

4. Braai the apricots, cut sides down first, over direct medium heat.

BANANAS FOSTER

SERVES: 6–8
PREP TIME: 10 MINUTES

HEAT: DIRECT MEDIUM HEAT 180°–230°C (350°–450°F)
BRAAIING TIME: 2–3 MINUTES

    4 firm but ripe bananas
    4 tablespoons unsalted butter, melted

SAUCE
    125 g unsalted butter
    100 g dark brown (treacle) sugar
    ¼ teaspoon ground cinnamon
    pinch of ground nutmeg
    125 ml dark rum
    4 tablespoons banana liqueur

    Vanilla ice cream

1. Prepare the braai for direct cooking over medium heat.

2. Cut each banana in half lengthways and leave the skins attached (they will help the bananas hold their shape on the braai). Brush the cut sides with the melted butter.

Braai banana halves in their skins to hold the fruit together. Peel and cut the fruit before adding it to the rum sauce.

3. Brush the cooking grates clean. Braai the bananas over **direct medium heat** for 2–3 minutes, with the lid open and without turning, until warmed and well marked but not too soft. Remove from the braai. Peel the banana halves and cut them into quarters. Set aside.

4. To make the sauce, melt the butter in a large frying pan over medium-high heat. Add the brown sugar, cinnamon and nutmeg and cook for about 2 minutes, stirring constantly, until it bubbles. Stir in the rum and banana liqueur. Allow the liquid to warm for a few seconds and then carefully ignite the rum with a long match or multi-purpose lighter. Allow the flames to die down. Add the banana pieces and cook over medium heat for 2–3 minutes, or until the bananas curl slightly. Spoon the banana mixture over vanilla ice cream and serve immediately.

BRAAIED BANANA S'MORES

SERVES: 8
PREP TIME: 15 MINUTES

HEAT: INDIRECT AND DIRECT MEDIUM HEAT ABOUT 200°C (400°F)
BRAAIING TIME: 15–21 MINUTES
SPECIAL EQUIPMENT: 20 x 20-CM BAKING DISH SUITABLE FOR THE BRAAI

BISCUIT BASE
    250 ml finely crumbled digestive biscuits
    4 tablespoons unsalted butter, melted
    1 egg yolk

    1 tablespoon unsalted butter, melted
    1 teaspoon brown sugar
    2 firm but ripe bananas
    400 g mini marshmallows
    125 ml chocolate chips

1. Prepare the braai for indirect and direct cooking over a medium heat.

2. Combine the crust ingredients in a large bowl and mix well. Firmly and evenly press the mixture into the bottom of a 20 x 20 cm baking dish. Cook the crust over **indirect medium heat** for 6–8 minutes with the lid closed as much as possible, until firm. Remove the crust from the braai and set aside to cool for about 10 minutes. This will allow the crust to set.

3. Meanwhile, combine the butter and brown sugar in a small bowl. Cut each banana in half lengthways and leave the skins attached (they will help the bananas hold their shape on the braai). Liberally brush the cut sides of the bananas with the butter mixture.

4. Braai the bananas, cut sides down, over **direct medium heat** for 2–4 minutes, with the lid open and without turning, until they start to soften. Remove the bananas from the braai and allow them to cool briefly, then score the bananas into bite-sized pieces, cutting through just to the peel.

5. Fill the baking pan with half the marshmallows, making sure they cover the bottom of the crust evenly. Scoop the banana pieces from the skins and distribute them, then top with the remainder of the marshmallows.

6. Cook the pie over **indirect medium heat** for 5–7 minutes, with the lid closed, keeping the temperature of the braai as close to 200°C (400°F) as possible, until the marshmallows have puffed up and start to brown. At this point sprinkle the chocolate chips over the top and continue cooking for about 2 minutes until the chocolate chips appear glossy and melted. Remove the pie from the braai and allow it to cool for 5 minutes. Spoon into small serving bowls and serve warm.

HOW TO BRAAI BANANA S'MORES

1. Pour the biscuit base into a baking pan and press it into place with a spatula.

2. Cook the base until firm. Braai the buttered bananas in their skins so they hold their shape.

3. Cut the bananas into bite-sized pieces and layer them in the baking pan between the marshmallows.

4. During the last couple of minutes, sprinkle chocolate chips on top so that they melt into the sweet, gooey marshmallows.

HOW TO PREP PANNA COTTA

1. Sprinkle gelatin over cold water to soften it.

2. Oil the ramekins to help the panna cotta slide out later.

3. Fill the ramekins and chill the panna cotta for at least 8 hours.

4. Very gently separate the chilled dessert from each ramekin with your thumb.

LEMON-BUTTERMILK PANNA COTTA WITH BRAAIED FIGS

SERVES: 6
PREP TIME: 20 MINUTES
CHILLING TIME: AT LEAST 8 HOURS

HEAT: DIRECT MEDIUM HEAT 180°–230°C (350°–450°F)
BRAAIING TIME: 4 MINUTES
SPECIAL EQUIPMENT: SIX 175-G RAMEKINS OR CUSTARD CUPS

PANNA COTTA
- 2½ teaspoons (1 sachet) gelatine
- 4 tablespoons cold water
- 250 ml cream
- 125 ml sugar
- 500 ml buttermilk, well shaken
- ½ teaspoon vanilla extract
- 1 tablespoon finely grated lemon zest

Sunflower or canola oil

- 9 ripe figs, about 40 g each, stalks removed and cut in half lengthways
- 1 tablespoon honey
- 1 bunch fresh mint, optional

1. Sprinkle the gelatine over the water in a small bowl and allow to stand for about 5 minutes, until the gelatine softens.

2. Bring the cream and sugar to a simmer in a saucepan over a medium-low heat, stirring to dissolve the sugar. Once the mixture is simmering, remove the pan from the heat and add the softened gelatine, stirring constantly for about 2 minutes, until the gelatine has completely dissolved. Stir in the buttermilk and vanilla. Strain the mixture through a fine sieve into a large glass measuring jug, and then stir in the lemon zest.

3. Use roller towel to oil the insides of 6 ramekins. Pour equal amounts of the mixture, about 150 ml, into each ramekin. Place the ramekins on a roasting tray and loosely cover with clingfilm. Refrigerate the panna cottas for at least 8 hours, or up to 1 day, until they are chilled and set.

4. Prepare the braai for direct cooking over medium heat. Brush the cooking grates clean. Lightly brush the cut sides of the figs with oil and cook over **direct medium heat** for about 4 minutes, with the lid closed as much as possible but turning once after 3 minutes, until well marked and heated through.

5. To remove the panna cotta from the ramekin, use your thumb to gently press each pudding around its circumference to pull it away from the sides of the ramekin. You may need to go around a couple of times before it totally releases. This works better than running a knife around the inside of each pudding, which could cut into it. Place a dessert plate on top of the ramekin and invert both the plate and ramekin. Shake firmly, and allow the pudding to fall onto the plate.

6. For each serving, arrange 3 warm fig halves alongside the panna cotta and drizzle a little honey on the plate. Decorate with fresh mint leaves, if desired.

Arrange ripe strawberries snugly in a pan and cook them over direct heat so that their juices bubble and thicken with butter, sugar, vanilla and orange liqueur.

FLAME-ROASTED STRAWBERRIES

SERVES: 6–8
PREP TIME: 10 MINUTES

HEAT: DIRECT HIGH HEAT 230°–290°C (450°–550°F)
    FOR GAS BRAAIS ONLY
BRAAIING TIME: 8–12 MINUTES
SPECIAL EQUIPMENT: 10 × 10 CM BAKING DISH
    SUITABLE FOR THE BRAAI

    20–24 fresh large strawberries, washed and patted dry
    4 tablespoons sugar
    ½ teaspoon vanilla extract
    4 tablespoons orange-flavoured liqueur,
      or 2 tablespoons water and 1 tablespoon lemon juice
    1 tablespoon unsalted butter, softened
    Vanilla ice cream

1. Hull and trim the stalk end of the strawberries so that they are flat. Combine the berries, sugar, vanilla and liqueur in a bowl and toss to coat.

2. Use the softened butter to generously coat the bottom and sides of a 10 × 10 cm ovenproof dish or disposable foil tray. The dish should be just large enough to hold the strawberries in a single layer with their sides almost touching (this allows the strawberries to gently support one another as they begin to soften). Prepare the braai for direct cooking over high heat.

3. Remove the strawberries from the bowl and line them up so they fit snuggly, pointing up, in the prepared dish. Pour the contents from the bowl over the strawberries and cook over **direct high heat** for 8–12 minutes, with the lid closed, until they're bubbling and beginning to slump. Cooking times will vary depending on the variety, size and ripeness of the strawberries. Watch closely to catch them before they collapse.

4. Spoon the pan juices over the strawberries to moisten them, and allow to cool for 5 minutes, then carefully cut them into quarters or leave whole. Ladle the strawberries and their juices over vanilla ice cream.

The woodsy smoke of charcoal doesn't belong in fruit desserts like this one. Cook them over gas instead.

HOW TO MAKE SHORTCAKES

1. Mix the butter with the dry ingredients using the back of a fork to create a crumbly mixture. Leave some pea-sized clumps of butter for flaky shortcakes.

2. Add the cream and gently stir the mixture just until it comes together, but don't toughen the dough by overworking it.

3. Turn the dough out onto a lightly floured work surface and gently pat it to a thickness of about 2 cm.

4. Use a floured biscuit cutter to stamp out smooth rounds.

5. Gently gather the scraps into another single strip of dough.

6. Cut a couple more rounds from the strip.

HOW TO BRAAI NECTARINES AND PEACHES

1. Fill the centres of the nectarine or peach halves with brown sugar and braai until the sugar melts and the flesh is tender.

2. Remove the nectarines or peaches with a spatula. Peel and discard the charred skins, chop the flesh and serve with shortcake biscuits and whipped cream.

PEACH SHORTCAKES

SERVES: 8
PREP TIME: 20 MINUTES

HEAT: DIRECT MEDIUM HEAT 180°–230°C (350°–450°F)
    FOR GAS BRAAIS ONLY
BAKING AND BRAAIING TIME: 23–30 MINUTES

- 300 g cake flour, plus extra for dusting
- 5 tablespoons sugar
- 1 tablespoon baking powder
- ½ teaspoons sea salt
- 125 g cold unsalted butter, cut into small pieces
- 125 ml cream, cold
- 1 tablespoon unsalted butter, melted

- 250 ml cream
- 1 teaspoon vanilla extract
- 2 tablespoons icing sugar
- 4 large firm but ripe cling peaches or nectarines, cut in half lengthways and stones removed
- 4 tablespoons brown sugar
- 8 fresh mint sprigs, optional

1. Preheat the oven to 200°C (400°F).

2. Combine the flour, sugar, baking powder and salt in a large bowl and blend well. Add the butter and mix with a fork or a pastry blender just until the mixture resembles coarse breadcrumbs. Add the cream and gently stir it in (the mixture will be crumbly). Use your hands to mix the dough quickly and gently in the bowl just until it comes together. Turn the dough out onto a lightly floured work surface. Lightly dust your hands with flour and gently pat out the dough to about 2 cm thick. Dip a 6–7-cm round biscuit cutter in some flour and cut out rounds of dough. Gather any scraps of dough and pat out, using a light touch so you don't overwork the dough. Cut out a total of 8 rounds. Place the shortcakes about 5 cm apart on a baking tray lined with baking paper. Brush the tops with the melted butter. Bake the shortcakes in the oven for 15–20 minutes. Set aside to cool.

3. Combine the cream, vanilla and icing sugar in a large bowl and whip to stiff peaks; do not over beat. Cover and refrigerate until serving.

4. Prepare the braai for direct cooking over medium heat. Brush the cooking grates clean. Sprinkle the cut sides of the peach or nectarine halves with the brown sugar. Braai the peach halves, cut sides up, over **direct medium heat** for 8–10 minutes, with the lid closed, until the sugar melts and the peaches are soft. Carefully remove from the braai and pour the melted brown sugar from the peaches into a medium bowl.

5. Pull the charred skin off the peaches and discard. Slice the peaches into bite-sized pieces and add them to the bowl with the melted brown sugar. Gently toss to coat. Split each shortcake horizontally and top each bottom half with equal portions of the peaches and whipped cream. Add the shortcake tops and garnish with mint sprigs, if desired.

PEAR AND PROSCIUTTO SALAD WITH CHAMPAGNE VINAIGRETTE

SERVES: 4
PREP TIME: 20 MINUTES

HEAT: DIRECT MEDIUM HEAT 180°–230°C (350°–450°F)
BRAAIING TIME: 4–6 MINUTES

VINAIGRETTE
    4 tablespoons champagne or white wine vinegar
    2 tablespoons very finely chopped shallot
    1 teaspoon Dijon mustard
    ½ teaspoon sugar
    ¼ teaspoon coarse sea salt
    ¼ teaspoon freshly ground black pepper
    4 tablespoons extra-virgin olive oil
    2 tablespoons toasted hazelnut oil or olive oil

    8 paper-thin slices prosciutto
    2 firm but ripe pears, quartered and cored
    500 g rocket or mesclun greens
    50 g manchego or Parmigiano-Reggiano cheese
    100 g skinned hazelnuts, toasted and coarsely chopped
    Coarse sea salt
    Freshly ground black pepper

1. Whisk the vinegar, shallot, mustard, sugar, salt and pepper in a small bowl. Gradually drizzle in both oils, whisking constantly, until emulsified. Taste, and if the vinaigrette is too acidic, add 1 tablespoon or so of water.

2. Prepare the braai for direct cooking over medium heat. Brush the cooking grates clean.

3. Wrap a slice of prosciutto around each pear wedge, pressing the loose ends of the prosciutto down so the meat stays together. Lightly brush the outside of the wrapped pears with some vinaigrette and braai them over **direct medium heat** for 4–6 minutes, with the braai lid open and turning as needed, until the prosciutto is slightly crispy and golden brown and the pears are warm.

4. Whisk the vinaigrette again to emulsify the ingredients. In a large bowl, toss the rocket with enough vinaigrette to lightly coat the leaves (you may not need all the vinaigrette) and divide among 4 salad plates. Top each salad with 2 warm pear wedges and drizzle with some additional vinaigrette. Using a vegetable peeler, shave wide ribbons of cheese over each salad and thn sprinkle with the hazelnuts. Season to taste with salt and pepper. Serve immediately.

HOW TO PREP PEAR AND PROSCIUTTO

1. Quarter each pear lengthways into halves and then quarters.

2. Trim away the core and seeds.

3. Cut the prosciutto into strips for wrapping around the quarters.

4. Overlap and press each strip of prosciutto on itself so that it stays in place during cooking.

HOW TO WRAP CAMEMBERT IN VINE LEAVES

1. Overlap rinsed and dried vine leaves, vein-side up, and place the cheese in the centre.

2. Pull the edges of the leaves over the cheese, overlapping them on top.

3. Create an 'X' with two long pieces of butcher's string and put the cheese bundle on top.

4. Wrap the string around the bundle a few times, knotting it in the centre each time.

VINE LEAF-WRAPPED CAMEMBERT WITH GRAPE SALSA

SERVES: 4–6 AS AN APPETIZER
PREP TIME: 15 MINUTES

HEAT: DIRECT MEDIUM HEAT 180°–230°C (350°–450°F)
BRAAIING TIME: 4–5 MINUTES
SPECIAL EQUIPMENT: BUTCHER'S STRING

SALSA
    1 tablespoon balsamic vinegar
    ½ teaspoon sugar
    250 ml coarsely chopped seedless red or purple grapes
    1 tablespoon finely chopped fresh mint

    6–8 large vine leaves
    1 whole Camembert or Brie cheese (250 g–500 g)
    1 baguette, cut diagonally into 1-cm thick slices
    1 tablespoon grapeseed oil or olive oil

1. Combine the vinegar and sugar in a small sauté pan over medium heat. Add the grapes and cook for about 2 minutes, stirring occasionally, to soften them. Transfer to a small bowl and cover to keep warm. Add the mint just before serving.

2. Prepare the braai for direct cooking over medium heat.

3. Unroll and rinse the vine leaves. Spread out the leaves on a work surface and pat dry. Cut off and discard the tough stalks. Overlap 4 vine leaves, vein-side up, in a 20-cm circle. Put another leaf in the centre and then place the cheese on top. Cover the cheese with another vine leaf. Wrap the leaves around the cheese, overlapping them to prevent the cheese from leaking out. Knot together two metre-long pieces of butcher's string in the centre and lie them on a work surface in the shape of an 'X'. Place the cheese bundle on top. Bring the string over the top and tie snugly. Wrap the string around the cheese a few more times, like spokes on a wheel, knotting in the centre each time. Tuck in any loose leaf edges. Trim the ends of the string.

4. Lightly brush the cheese bundle and bread slices all over with oil. Brush the cooking grates clean. Braai the cheese over **direct medium heat** for 3–4 minutes, with the lid closed as much as possible but turning once, until each side is soft when gently pressed. Carefully remove the cheese and allow it to rest for about 2 minutes. After you remove the cheese, toast the bread slices over **direct medium heat** for about 1 minute, until they are lightly toasted on one side only. By toasting only one side of the bread it ensures a nice sturdy base for the melted cheese and the salsa.

5. Arrange the cheese and toasted bread on a serving platter or tray. Cut the string and discard it. Pull the vine leaves open to reveal the cheese inside. (Only do this just before serving as the cheese will begin to ooze out as soon as you remove the vine leaves.) Top the cheese with some of the grape salsa or serve it alongside in a bowl. Use spoons to scoop up some of the cheese and salsa, and place on slices of toasted bread.

RESOURCES

BRAAIING GUIDES AND TIPS

292	**RED MEAT**: What you need to know
293	Cuts of **STEAK**
294	How to **FREEZE STEAKS**
296	**BEEF** braaiing guide
297	**LAMB** braaiing guide
298	**PORK** braaiing guide
301	**POULTRY** braaiing guide
302	**SEAFOOD**: Tips to prevent sticking
303	**SEAFOOD** braaiing guide
305	**VEGETABLE** braaiing guide
306	**FRUIT** braaiing guide
307	Braai **MAINTENANCE**
308	Selecting the right **BRAAI**
310	**SAFETY**
312	**TECHNIQUE INDEX**
315	**RECIPE INDEX**

RECIPES

281	**RUBS**
285	**MARINADES**
288	**SAUCES AND SALSAS**

RUBS

A rub is a mixture of spices, herbs and other seasonings (often including sugar) that can quickly give a boost of flavours to foods before braaiing. The following pages provide some good examples, along with recommendations for which foods they complement, but dare to be different. One of the steps toward developing your own style at the braai is to concoct a signature rub recipe or two. Only you will know exactly what ingredients are blended in your special jar of 'magic dust'.

A word about freshness: Ground spices lose their aromas in a matter of months (8–10 months maximum). If you have been holding onto a little jar of ground coriander for years, waiting to blend the world's finest version of curry powder, forget about it. Dump the old, tired coriander and buy some freshly ground. Better yet, buy whole coriander seeds and grind them yourself. Whatever you do, store your spices and rubs in airtight containers away from light and heat, to give them a long, aromatic life.

HOW LONG?

If you leave a rub on for a long time, the seasonings intermix with the juices in the meat and produce more pronounced flavours, as well as a crust. This is good to a point, but a rub with a lot of salt and sugar will draw moisture out of the meat over time, making the meat tastier, yes, but also drier. So how long should you use a rub? Here are some guidelines.

1–15 MINUTES	Small foods, such as cubed meat for kebabs and vegetables, or shellfish
15–30 MINUTES	Thin cuts of boneless meat, such as chicken breasts, chops and steaks, fish fillets, pork fillets
30–90 MINUTES	Thicker cuts of boneless or bone-in meat, such as leg of lamb, whole chickens and beef roasts
2–8 HOURS	Big or tough cuts of meat, such as racks of ribs, whole hams, pork shoulders and turkeys

CLASSIC BARBECUE SPICE RUB

MAKES: ABOUT 5 TABLESPOONS

4 teaspoons coarse sea salt
2 teaspoons chilli powder
2 teaspoons light brown sugar
2 teaspoons garlic flakes
2 teaspoons paprika
1 teaspoon celery seed
1 teaspoon ground cumin
½ teaspoon freshly ground black pepper

CHICKEN AND SEAFOOD RUB

MAKES: ABOUT 4½ TABLESPOONS

4 teaspoons onion flakes
4 teaspoons garlic flakes
1 tablespoon coarse sea salt
2 teaspoons chilli powder
2 teaspoons freshly ground black pepper

CRACKED PEPPER RUB

MAKES: ABOUT 1½ TABLESPOONS

1 teaspoon whole black peppercorns
1 teaspoon mustard seed
1 teaspoon paprika
½ teaspoon garlic flakes
½ teaspoon coarse sea salt
½ teaspoon light brown sugar
pinch of ground cayenne pepper

Using a spice mill or mortar and pestle, crush the black peppercorns and mustard seed. Transfer to a small bowl and combine with the remaining ingredients.

CAJUN RUB

MAKES: ABOUT 3 TABLESPOONS

2 teaspoons finely chopped fresh thyme
1½ teaspoons coarse sea salt
1 teaspoon garlic flakes
1 teaspoon onion flakes
1 teaspoon paprika
1 teaspoon light brown sugar
¾ teaspoon freshly ground black pepper
¼ teaspoon ground cayenne pepper

PORK RUB

MAKES: ABOUT 3 TABLESPOONS

2 teaspoons chilli powder
2 teaspoons freshly ground black pepper
2 teaspoons coarse sea salt
2 teaspoons ground cumin
2 teaspoons dried origanum
1 teaspoon garlic flakes

BEEF RUB

MAKES: ABOUT 4 TABLESPOONS

4 teaspoons coarse sea salt
1 tablespoon chilli powder
1 tablespoon onion flakes
1½ teaspoons garlic flakes
1 teaspoon paprika
1 teaspoon dried marjoram
½ teaspoon ground cumin
½ teaspoon freshly ground black pepper
¼ teaspoon ground cinnamon

FENNEL RUB

MAKES: ABOUT 4 TABLESPOONS

3 teaspoons ground fennel seed
3 teaspoons coarse sea salt
3 teaspoons chilli powder
1½ teaspoons celery seed
1½ teaspoons freshly ground black pepper

LEGEND

- RED MEAT
- PORK
- POULTRY
- SEAFOOD
- VEGETABLES

MORE RUBS

TEX-MEX RUB

MAKES: ABOUT 3½ TABLESPOONS

- 2 teaspoons chilli powder
- 2 teaspoons garlic flakes
- 2 teaspoons paprika
- 2 teaspoons coarse sea salt
- 1 teaspoon ground coriander
- 1 teaspoon ground cumin
- 1 teaspoon freshly ground black pepper

CARIBBEAN RUB

MAKES: ABOUT 5 TABLESPOONS

- 1 tablespoon light brown sugar
- 1 tablespoon garlic flakes
- 1 tablespoon dried thyme
- 2¼ teaspoons coarse sea salt
- ¾ teaspoon freshly ground black pepper
- ¾ teaspoon ground allspice

TARRAGON RUB

MAKES: ABOUT 4½ TABLESPOONS

- 1½ tablespoons dried tarragon
- 2½ teaspoons coarse sea salt
- 2 teaspoons freshly ground black pepper
- 1½ teaspoons dried thyme
- 1 heaped teaspoon dried sage

MAGIC RUB

MAKES: 2 TABLESPOONS

- 1 teaspoon dry mustard
- 1 teaspoon onion flakes
- 1 teaspoon paprika
- 1 teaspoon coarse sea salt
- ½ teaspoon garlic flakes
- ½ teaspoon ground coriander
- ½ teaspoon ground cumin
- ½ teaspoon freshly ground black pepper

ESPRESSO-CHILLI RUB

MAKES: ABOUT 4 TABLESPOONS

- 2 tablespoons dark-roast coffee or espresso beans
- 2 teaspoons cumin seed, toasted
- 1 tablespoon chilli powder
- 1 teaspoon sweet paprika
- 1 teaspoon coarse sea salt
- 1 teaspoon freshly ground black pepper

Pulse the coffee beans and cumin seed in a spice mill until finely ground. Transfer to a small bowl, add the remaining ingredients and stir to combine.

ASIAN RUB

MAKES: ABOUT 4½ TABLESPOONS

- 2 tablespoons paprika
- 2 teaspoons coarse sea salt
- 2 teaspoons ground coriander
- 2 teaspoons Chinese five-spice powder
- 1 teaspoon ground ginger
- ½ teaspoon ground allspice
- ½ teaspoon ground cayenne pepper

LEGEND

- RED MEAT
- PORK
- POULTRY
- SEAFOOD
- VEGETABLES

BABY BACK RIBS RUB

MAKES: ABOUT 8 TABLESPOONS

- 2 tablespoons coarse sea salt
- 2 tablespoons paprika
- 4 teaspoons garlic flakes
- 4 teaspoons chilli powder
- 2 teaspoons dry mustard
- 2 teaspoons freshly ground black pepper

BAJA FISH RUB

MAKES: ABOUT 1½ TABLESPOONS

- 1 teaspoon chilli powder
- 1 teaspoon ground cumin
- 1 teaspoon coarse sea salt
- ½ teaspoon ground cayenne pepper
- ½ teaspoon ground cinnamon

MEXICAN RUB

MAKES: ABOUT 4 TABLESPOONS

- 1 tablespoon ground cumin
- 1 tablespoon brown sugar
- 2 teaspoons coarse sea salt
- 1 teaspoon chilli powder
- 1 teaspoon ground coriander
- 1 teaspoon dried origanum

NEW WORLD RUB

MAKES: ABOUT 2 TABLESPOONS

- 1 teaspoon garlic flakes
- 1 teaspoon onion flakes
- 1 teaspoon paprika
- ½ teaspoon ground cumin
- ½ teaspoon dried lemongrass
- ½ teaspoon dried basil
- ½ teaspoon dried thyme
- ½ teaspoon coarse sea salt
- ¼ teaspoon freshly ground black pepper
- pinch of ground cayenne pepper

BARBECUE CHICKEN RUB

MAKES: ABOUT 2½ TABLESPOONS

- 1 tablespoon smoked paprika
- 2 teaspoons dry mustard
- 1 teaspoon coarse sea salt
- ½ teaspoon garlic flakes
- ½ teaspoon onion flakes
- ¼ teaspoon chilli powder

LEMON-PAPRIKA RUB

MAKES: ABOUT 2 TABLESPOONS

- 2 teaspoons smoked paprika
- 2 teaspoons coarse sea salt
- Finely grated zest of 1 lemon
- ½ teaspoon garlic flakes
- ½ teaspoon freshly ground black pepper

ALL-PURPOSE RUB

MAKES: ABOUT 2 TABLESPOONS

- 1 teaspoon chilli powder
- 1 teaspoon garlic flakes
- 1 teaspoon paprika
- 1 teaspoon coarse sea salt
- ½ teaspoon ground coriander
- ½ teaspoon ground cumin
- ½ teaspoon freshly ground black pepper

PULLED PORK RUB

MAKES: ABOUT 6 TABLESPOONS

- 2 tablespoons chilli powder
- 2 tablespoons coarse sea salt
- 4 teaspoons garlic flakes
- 2 teaspoons freshly ground black pepper
- 1 teaspoon dry mustard

MARINADES

Marinades work more slowly than rubs, but they can seep in a little deeper. Typically, a marinade is made with some acidic liquid, some oil and some combination of herbs and spices. These ingredients can 'fill in the gaps' when a particular meat, fish, or vegetable (yes, vegetable) lacks enough taste or richness. They can also give food characteristics that reflect regional and/or ethnic cooking styles.

If your marinade includes some acidic liquid, make sure you use a non-metallic container (made of glass, plastic, stainless steel or ceramic). A container made of aluminum, or some other metals, will react with acids and add a metallic flavour to food.

HOW LONG?

The right times vary depending on the strength of the marinade and the food you are marinating. If your marinade includes intense ingredients such as soy sauce, alcohol, or hot chillies and spices, don't overdo it. A fish fillet should still taste like fish, not a burning-hot, salt-soaked piece of protein. Also, if an acidic marinade is left too long on meat or fish, it can make the surface mushy or dry. Here are some general guidelines to get you going.

15–30 MINUTES	Small foods, such as cubed meat for kebabs, tender vegetables, shellfish and fish fillets
1–3 HOURS	Thin cuts of boneless meat, such as chicken breasts, chops, steaks and pork fillet, as well as sturdy vegetables
2–6 HOURS	Thicker cuts of boneless or bone-in meat, such as whole chickens, leg of lamb, and beef or pork roasts
6–12 HOURS	Big or tough cuts of meat, such as racks of ribs, whole hams, pork shoulders, and turkeys

BEER MARINADE

MAKES: ABOUT 300 ML

250 ml beer
2 tablespoons dark sesame oil
1 tablespoon finely chopped fresh garlic
1 teaspoon dried origanum
1 teaspoon coarse sea salt
½ teaspoon freshly ground black pepper
¼ teaspoon ground cayenne pepper

JERK MARINADE

MAKES: ABOUT 250 ML

1 onion, roughly chopped
1 jalapeño chilli, roughly chopped
3 tablespoons white wine vinegar
2 tablespoons soy sauce
2 tablespoons canola or sunflower oil
½ teaspoon ground allspice
¼ teaspoon garlic flakes
¼ teaspoon ground cinnamon
¼ teaspoon coarse sea salt
¼ teaspoon freshly ground black pepper
pinch of ground nutmeg

PACIFIC RIM MARINADE

MAKES: ABOUT 300 ML

1 small onion, roughly chopped
5 tablespoons soy sauce
4 tablespoons fresh lemon juice
4 tablespoons vegetable oil
2 tablespoons dark brown sugar
2 tablespoons finely chopped fresh garlic
½ teaspoon ground allspice

LEGEND

- RED MEAT
- PORK
- POULTRY
- SEAFOOD
- VEGETABLES

MOJO MARINADE

MAKES: ABOUT 200 ML

4 tablespoons fresh orange juice
3 tablespoons fresh lime juice
3 tablespoons extra-virgin olive oil
2 tablespoons finely chopped fresh coriander
1 tablespoon finely chopped jalapeño chilli, including seeds
1 tablespoon finely chopped fresh garlic
¾ teaspoon ground cumin
½ teaspoon coarse sea salt

LEMON-SAGE MARINADE

MAKES: ABOUT 250 ML

1 tablespoon finely grated lemon zest
4 tablespoons fresh lemon juice
4 tablespoons extra-virgin olive oil
3 tablespoons finely chopped fresh sage
2 tablespoons finely chopped shallot or small onion
2 tablespoons wholegrain mustard
1 tablespoon finely chopped fresh garlic
1 tablespoon freshly ground black peppercorns

TERIYAKI MARINADE

MAKES: ABOUT 600 ML

250 ml pineapple juice
125 ml soy sauce
1 onion, finely chopped
1 tablespoon dark sesame oil
1 tablespoon grated fresh ginger
1 tablespoon finely chopped fresh garlic
1 tablespoon dark brown (treacle) sugar
1 tablespoon fresh lemon juice

GREEK MARINADE

MAKES: ABOUT 145 ML

6 tablespoons extra-virgin olive oil
3 tablespoons red wine vinegar
½ teaspoon finely chopped fresh garlic
½ teaspoon coarse sea salt
½ teaspoon dried origanum
¼ teaspoon crushed red chilli flakes

MORE MARINADES

MEDITERRANEAN MARINADE

MAKES: ABOUT 60 ML

2 tablespoons extra-virgin olive oil
2 teaspoons paprika
1 teaspoon ground coriander
1 teaspoon ground cumin
1 teaspoon garlic flakes
1 teaspoon coarse sea salt
¼ teaspoon freshly ground black pepper

CHILLI-ORANGE MARINADE

MAKES: ABOUT 250 ML

125 ml fresh orange juice
3 tablespoons extra-virgin olive oil
2 tablespoons red wine vinegar
1 tablespoon finely chopped fresh garlic
2 teaspoons chilli powder
1½ teaspoons dried origanum
1 teaspoon coarse sea salt
½ teaspoon freshly ground black pepper
½ teaspoon ground cinnamon

TEQUILA MARINADE

MAKES: ABOUT 450 ML

250 ml fresh orange juice
125 ml tequila
2 tablespoons fresh lime juice
2 tablespoons light brown sugar
2 teaspoons ground cumin
1 jalapeño chilli, cut into 8-mm slices

BOURBON OR BRANDY MARINADE

MAKES: ABOUT 250 ML

125 ml bourbon or brandy
4 tablespoons tomato purée or tomato sauce
2 tablespoons extra-virgin olive oil
2 tablespoons soy sauce
1 tablespoon white wine vinegar
2 teaspoons finely chopped fresh garlic
½ teaspoon Tabasco or other hot sauce, or to taste
½ teaspoon freshly ground black pepper

HONEY-MUSTARD MARINADE

MAKES: ABOUT 250 ML

125 ml Dijon mustard
4 tablespoons honey
2 tablespoons extra-virgin olive oil
2 teaspoons curry powder
1 teaspoon freshly grated lemon zest
½ teaspoon garlic flakes
½ teaspoon coarse sea salt
¼ teaspoon ground cayenne pepper
¼ teaspoon freshly ground black pepper

TARRAGON-CITRUS MARINADE

MAKES: ABOUT 250 ML

4 tablespoons extra-virgin olive oil
4 tablespoons roughly chopped fresh tarragon
Zest and juice of 1 fresh orange
Zest and juice of 1 fresh lemon
2 tablespoons sherry vinegar
2 teaspoons coarse sea salt
1 teaspoon finely chopped fresh garlic
1 teaspoon grated fresh ginger
½ teaspoon chilli powder
½ teaspoon freshly ground black pepper

LEGEND

- RED MEAT
- PORK
- POULTRY
- SEAFOOD
- VEGETABLES

MONGOLIAN MARINADE

MAKES: ABOUT 300 ML

- 125 ml hoisin sauce
- 2 tablespoons oyster sauce
- 2 tablespoons soy sauce
- 2 tablespoons dry sherry
- 2 tablespoons rice vinegar
- 2 tablespoons canola or sunflower oil
- 1 tablespoon honey
- 1 tablespoon finely chopped fresh ginger
- 1 tablespoon finely chopped fresh garlic
- ½ teaspoon crushed red chilli flakes (optional)

SPICY CAYENNE MARINADE

MAKES: ABOUT 125 ML

- 4 tablespoons extra-virgin olive oil
- 2 tablespoons fresh lemon juice
- 1 tablespoon finely chopped fresh garlic
- 2 teaspoons dried origanum
- 2 teaspoons paprika
- 1½ teaspoons coarse sea salt
- 1 teaspoon celery seed
- 1 teaspoon ground cayenne pepper

CUBAN MARINADE

MAKES: ABOUT 500 ML

- 125 ml fresh orange juice
- 125 ml fresh lemonade
- 1 onion (±65 g), finely chopped
- 4 tablespoons extra-virgin olive oil
- 2 tablespoons finely chopped fresh garlic
- 2 tablespoons dried origanum
- 2 tablespoons fresh lime juice

CHINESE HOISIN MARINADE

MAKES: ABOUT 175 ML

- 125 ml hoisin sauce
- 2 tablespoons red wine vinegar
- 1 tablespoon canola or sunflower oil
- 2 teaspoons finely chopped fresh garlic
- 1 teaspoon grated fresh ginger
- 1 teaspoon Tabasco or other hot sauce, or to taste
- 1 teaspoon dark sesame oil

TANDOORI MARINADE

MAKES: ABOUT 300 ML

- 250 ml plain yoghurt
- 1 tablespoon finely grated fresh ginger
- 1 tablespoon paprika
- 1 tablespoon vegetable oil
- 2 teaspoons finely chopped fresh garlic
- 2 teaspoons coarse sea salt
- 1½ teaspoons ground cumin
- 1 teaspoon ground turmeric
- ½ teaspoon ground cayenne pepper

BARCELONA MARINADE

MAKES: ABOUT 175 ML

- 5 spring onions, cut into 2-cm pieces
- 250 ml fresh basil leaves
- 3 large garlic cloves
- 2 serrano chillies, roughly chopped
- 4 tablespoons extra-virgin olive oil
- 2 tablespoons sherry vinegar
- 1 teaspoon coarse sea salt
- ½ teaspoon freshly ground black pepper

Process the ingredients in a food processor or blender for 1–2 minutes, until a smooth paste forms.

CORIANDER PESTO MARINADE

MAKES: ABOUT 250 ML

- 2 tablespoons coarsely chopped walnuts
- 2 medium garlic cloves
- 375 ml fresh coriander leaves and tender stalks
- 125 ml fresh flat-leaf (Italian) parsley leaves and tender stalks
- ½ teaspoon coarse sea salt
- ¼ teaspoon freshly ground black pepper
- 4 tablespoons extra-virgin olive oil

Chop the walnuts and garlic in a food processor, scraping down the sides of the bowl. Add the coriander, parsley, salt and pepper and continue to process until finely chopped. With the motor running, slowly add the oil to create a smooth purée.

SAUCES AND SALSAS

Sauces open up a world of flavours for braaiers. They offer us almost limitless ways for distinguishing our food and making it more interesting. Once you have learned some of the fundamentals about balancing flavours, and some of the techniques for holding sauces together, you are ready to develop your own. I've included several styles of sauces on the following pages, some of them featuring a braaied ingredient or two for greater depth. Find the sauces that suit you and the kind of food that you like to cook. Return to them a couple times so that you understand how and why they work. Then start pushing the parameters. A little more of this. A little less of that. Maybe a few more minutes simmering over the fire. Sauces are playgrounds for discovery. Learn the basics and build from there.

NECTARINE, RED PEPPER AND ONION SALSA

MAKES: ABOUT 375 ML

- 2 firm but ripe nectarines, about 400 g total, finely chopped
- 1 medium red pepper, finely chopped
- 125 ml finely chopped red onion
- 1 jalapeño chilli, deseeded and finely chopped
- 2 tablespoons finely chopped fresh mint leaves
- 2 tablespoons finely chopped fresh Italian parsley leaves
- 1 tablespoon freshly squeezed lime juice
- 1 tablespoon honey
- ¼ teaspoon dried chilli flakes
- ¼ teaspoon coarse sea salt

Combine all the ingredients in a large bowl. Cover and refrigerate until about 30 minutes before serving.

CLASSIC RED BARBECUE SAUCE

MAKES: ABOUT 350 ML

- 175 ml clear apple juice
- 150 ml tomato purée
- 3 tablespoons cider vinegar
- 2 teaspoons soy sauce
- 1 teaspoon Worcestershire sauce
- 1 teaspoon molasses (treacle syrup)
- ½ teaspoon chilli powder
- ½ teaspoon garlic flakes
- ¼ teaspoon freshly ground black pepper

Combine the ingredients in a small saucepan. Simmer for a few minutes over medium heat, then remove the saucepan from the heat.

BLACK BEAN AND AVOCADO SALSA

MAKES: ABOUT 1 LITRE

- 1 can (400 g) black beans, rinsed and drained
- 1 large avocado, chopped
- 1 red pepper, finely chopped
- 250 ml fresh corn (mealie) kernels
- 1 small red onion, finely chopped
- 125 ml coarsely chopped fresh coriander leaves
- 4 tablespoons freshly squeezed lime juice
- 2 tablespoons extra-virgin olive oil
- 1 teaspoon ground cumin
- 1 teaspoon coarse sea salt
- ½ teaspoon freshly ground black pepper
- ¼ teaspoon ground cayenne pepper

Combine all of the ingredients in a large bowl. Cover and refrigerate if not using immediately.

SASSY BARBECUE SAUCE

MAKES: ABOUT 300 ML

- 125 ml water
- 125 ml tomato purée
- 2 tablespoons molasses or treacle syrup
- 1 tablespoon white wine vinegar
- 1 tablespoon Dijon mustard
- 1 tablespoon light brown sugar
- 2 teaspoons Worcestershire sauce
- ½ teaspoon coarse sea salt
- ¼ teaspoon Tabasco or other hot sauce, or to taste
- ¼ teaspoon garlic flakes
- ¼ teaspoon freshly ground black pepper

Whisk all the ingredients together in a small, heavy-based saucepan and bring to boil over medium heat, then reduce the heat and simmer for 10 minutes, stirring occasionally.

CHERMOULA

MAKES: ABOUT 300 ML

- 80 ml extra-virgin olive oil
- 4 tablespoons freshly squeezed lemon juice
- 4 tablespoons chopped fresh Italian parsley leaves
- 4 tablespoons chopped fresh coriander leaves
- 1 tablespoon finely chopped garlic
- 1-1½ teaspoons paprika
- 1 teaspoon ground cumin
- 1 teaspoon coarse sea salt
- ½ teaspoon freshly ground black pepper
- ¼ teaspoon ground cayenne pepper

Thoroughly mix all the ingredients in a bowl.

LEGEND

- RED MEAT
- PORK
- POULTRY
- SEAFOOD
- VEGETABLES

MORE SAUCES AND SALSAS

CREAMY HORSERADISH SAUCE

MAKES: ABOUT 250 ML

175 ml sour cream
2 tablespoons prepared horseradish
2 tablespoons finely chopped fresh flat-leaf parsley
2 teaspoons Dijon mustard
2 teaspoons Worcestershire sauce
½ teaspoon coarse sea salt
¼ teaspoon freshly ground black pepper

Thoroughly mix the ingredients together in a bowl. Cover and refrigerate until about 30 minutes before serving.

CHIMICHURRI SAUCE

MAKES: ABOUT 350 ML

4 large garlic cloves
250 ml fresh flat-leaf (Italian) parsley
250 ml fresh coriander
125 ml fresh basil
175 ml extra-virgin olive oil
4 tablespoons rice vinegar
1 teaspoon coarse sea salt
½ teaspoon freshly ground black pepper
½ teaspoon hot sauce (Tabasco), or to taste

Finely chop the garlic in a food processor. With the motor running, add the parsley, coriander and basil leaves and pulse to finely chop the herbs. With the motor still running, slowly add the oil in a thin stream, then add the remaining ingredients.

ROMESCO SAUCE

MAKES: ABOUT 175 ML

2 large red peppers
1 garlic clove
4 tablespoons whole almonds, toasted
125 ml fresh flat-leaf (Italian) parsley
2 teaspoons sherry wine vinegar
½ teaspoon coarse sea salt
⅛ teaspoon ground cayenne pepper
4 tablespoons extra-virgin olive oil

Braai the peppers over **direct medium heat** (180°–230°C/ 350°–450°F) for 12–15 minutes, with the lid closed as much as possible but turning occasionally, until they are blackened and blistered all over. Place the peppers into a small bowl, cover with clingfilm and set aside for at least 10 minutes, then remove and discard the skins, stalks and seeds. Finely chop the garlic in a food processor. Add the almonds and process until finely chopped. Add the peppers, parsley, vinegar, salt and cayenne and process to create a coarse paste. With the motor running, slowly add the oil and process until you have a fairly smooth sauce.

GARLIC AND RED PEPPER SAUCE

MAKES ABOUT 150 ML

1 large red pepper
4 tablespoons mayonnaise
2½ tablespoons sour cream
1 tablespoon finely chopped fresh basil
2 teaspoons finely chopped fresh garlic
2 teaspoons balsamic vinegar
¼ teaspoon coarse sea salt

Braai the pepper over **direct medium heat** (180°–230°C/ 350°–450°F) for 12–15 minutes, with the lid closed as much as possible but turning occasionally, until the skin is blackened and blistered all over. Place the pepper into a small bowl, cover with clingfilm to trap the steam and set aside for at least 10 minutes, then remove the pepper from the bowl and peel away the charred skin. Cut off the top, remove the seeds and roughly chop the pepper. Place in a food processor along with the remaining ingredients and process until smooth. Cover and refrigerate until about 20 minutes before serving.

LEGEND

- RED MEAT
- PORK
- POULTRY
- SEAFOOD
- VEGETABLES

COOL GREEN CHILLI SAUCE

MAKES: ABOUT 350 ML

- 3 jalapeño chillies
- 3 spring onions, root ends discarded and the rest roughly chopped
- 1 tablespoon fresh coriander leaves and tender stems
- 1 small garlic clove
- 125 ml sour cream
- 125 ml mayonnaise
- Finely grated zest and juice of 1 lime
- ¼ teaspoon coarse sea salt

Braai the chillies over **direct high heat** (230°–290°C/450°–550°F) for 3–5 minutes, with the lid open but turning occasionally, until they are blackened and blistered in spots all over. Remove the chillies from the braai. When cool enough to handle, remove and discard the stalk ends. Using a sharp knife, scrape off and discard nearly all the blackened skins. Roughly chop the remaining parts of the chillies and drop them into a food processor or blender. Add the spring onions, coriander and garlic. Process to make a coarse paste, scraping down the sides once or twice. Add the remaining ingredients and process for a minute or two to create a smooth sauce. If it seems too thick, add a little water. Adjust the seasonings. Cover and refrigerate until about 30 minutes before serving.

NECTARINE & RED PEPPER SALSA

MAKES: ABOUT 500 ML

- 2–3 firm, ripe nectarines, finely chopped
- 1–2 tablespoons freshly squeezed lime juice
- 1 red pepper, seeds removed and finely chopped
- 1 red onion, finely chopped
- 1 jalapeño chilli, seeds removed and finely chopped
- 2 tablespoons finely chopped fresh mint
- 2 tablespoons finely chopped flat-leaf parsley
- 1 tablespoon honey
- ¼ teaspoon red chilli flakes
- ¼ teaspoon coarse sea salt
- Freshly squeezed lime juice, to taste

Squeeze some lime juice over the chopped nectarines, to prevent them from discolouring. Combine the nectarines with the rest of the ingredients in a bowl, adding extra lime juice to taste. Allow the salsa to stand at room temperature for about 1 hour, to enable the flavours to merge.

RÉMOULADE

MAKES: ABOUT 175 ML

- 125 ml mayonnaise
- 1 tablespoon capers, drained and minced
- 1 tablespoon sweet pickle relish
- 1 tablespoon finely chopped fresh tarragon
- 2 teaspoons finely chopped shallot or small onion
- 1 teaspoon tarragon vinegar
- 1 teaspoon finely chopped fresh garlic
- ½ teaspoon Dijon mustard
- ¼ teaspoon paprika
- ⅛ teaspoon coarse sea salt

Whisk the ingredients together in a bowl. If not using right away, cover and refrigerate for up to 24 hours.

BALINESE PEANUT SAUCE

MAKES: ABOUT 300 ML

- 175 g smooth peanut butter
- 125 ml coconut milk, stirred
- 2 tablespoons fresh lime juice
- 2 teaspoons garlic-chili sauce (such as Sriracha)
- 2 teaspoons fish sauce

Combine the ingredients in small saucepan over very low heat and cook for 3–5 minutes, whisking occasionally, until the sauce is smooth. (Do not let the sauce simmer; keep the heat very low.) If the sauce seems too thick, whisk in 1–2 tablespoons of water.

TOMATO SALSA

MAKES: ABOUT 500 ML

- 300 g ripe tomatoes, finely chopped
- 1 medium onion, finely chopped and rinsed in a sieve under cold water
- 2 tablespoons finely chopped fresh coriander
- 1 tablespoon extra-virgin olive oil
- 2 teaspoons fresh lime juice
- 1 teaspoon finely chopped jalapeño chilli (with seeds)
- ¼ teaspoon dried origanum
- ¼ teaspoon coarse sea salt
- ¼ teaspoon freshly ground black pepper

Mix the ingredients together in a bowl. Allow the salsa to stand at room temperature for about 1 hour. Drain in a sieve just before serving.

RED MEAT

WHAT YOU NEED TO KNOW

TASTE AND TENDERNESS ARE TRADE-OFFS

When you pay more for steak, usually you are paying for tenderness. That's why a fillet steak is more expensive than a flank steak, even though the flank steak has more flavour. The pricey and tender steaks, like the porterhouse, T-bone, fillet and sirloin, come from the loin area of a cow, which gets very little exercise while the cow lumbers around. Other steaks, like the flank and the rump, come from parts of the cow that get more of a workout.

FEED MATTERS

It's natural for cows to eat grass. But feeding them grass their whole lives is expensive. It requires moving the animals from pasture to pasture as the seasons change. It's cheaper to herd them into one place and feed them a grain-based diet, which fattens them up faster than grass, and makes them more tender. Grass-fed cattle are usually leaner and free of the added hormones and antibiotics that grain-fed animals often receive, but the meat is a little tougher and stronger in flavour.

BE A SMART SHOPPER

Whether you shop at a supermarket or at a butcher, it is up to you to know what to look out for when buying meat. Be selective, and choose cuts with a coarse marbling of milky white fat. The flesh should be a rich pink or light cherry colour. If you see any with a deep red or brown colour, it could mean the meat comes from older, tougher animals. And the surface should be moist, but not wet or sticky. When you get your purchase home, immediately place it at the bottom of the refrigerator, where there isn't any chance of the meat cross-contaminating cooked or ready-to-eat foods.

BROWN IS BETTER

Whichever cut of meat you choose, and whatever its grade or quality might be, you'll get the most flavour from it when the surface is cooked to a deep brown colour. When sugars and proteins in the meat are heated by the braai, they produce literally hundreds of flavours and aromas. That's why so many recipes in this book involve searing over direct heat. A lot of people will tell you that searing seals in moisture, but that theory has been debunked. Instead, searing develops a layer of incredible flavour and also some nice texture.

Wet meat doesn't sear, it steams, so be sure to pat the surface of the meat dry with roller towel before braaiing. Salt can also affect searing. I recommend waiting to salt red meat until 20–30 minutes before braaiing because, over a longer period of time, salt pulls blood and juices from inside the meat, making the surface wet. Salt does, however, need to go on before braaiing. Salt added afterwards doesn't penetrate very well.

CUTS OF STEAK

RIB-EYE
A rib-eye steak's abundant internal fat melting into the meat creates one the juiciest steak-eating experiences imaginable. Do yourself a favour; before braaiing, trim the fat around the perimeter to about 5 mm. That will reduce the chance of flare-ups.

SIRLOIN
This is known in other parts of the world as a New York strip, strip loin, top loin, shell steak, club steak and ambassador steak… it all depends on where you are and who's talking. Regardless of the name, the sirloin is a relatively lean cut with a firmer texture than a rib-eye or fillet, but the flavour is great.

FILLET
Pricey and velvety soft, fillets make a nice splurge for special guests, though it's really the tenderness of the meat that you are buying. The flavour can be a little underwhelming unless you lightly char the outside over a blazing hot fire.

PORTERHOUSE
This classic steakhouse steak features both a sirloin steak and a fillet, separated by a bone. Start these steaks over high heat and finish them on a cooler section of the braai so that you don't blacken the bone or the meat beside it.

T-BONE
This is just like a porterhouse, except that the piece of fillet is not as big, because this steak is cut a little further forwards on the animal.

RUMP
These flat, firmly grained steaks bring kebabs quickly to mind because it's so easy to cut them into solid cubes. Pick out rump steaks with visible marbling and don't braai them beyond medium rare.

TRI-TIP
Not widely available, a tri-tip is taken from the sirloin area. It's not so much a steak as it is a skinny roast, but you can braai it like a thick steak. The meat is affordable and very flavourful. Just don't overcook it.

FLANK
You can quickly spot this steak by its flat oval shape and its long, clearly defined grain. Once the steak of choice for the dish known as London broil, flank steak now stars in all kinds of braai recipes. Minimize the chewy effect of the grain by slicing across it.

SKIRT
Like the flank steak, the coarsely grained skirt steak is cut from the chest area of the animal, so chewiness is an issue. Even so, after braaiing, it tends to be juicier and richer in flavour than flank steak, especially if you marinate it first.

FEATHER
Normally you would expect a steak cut from the shoulder to be tough, but the feather steak (flatiron or top blade steak), is nestled into a tender pocket of the shoulder area, so it's a surprisingly soft exception to the rule. In some cases you'll need to remove a thin vein of gristle that runs down the centre.

TYPES OF RED MEAT FOR THE BRAAI

Tender cuts for braaiing	Moderately tender cuts for braaiing	Bigger cuts for searing and grill-roasting	Tougher cuts for braaiing
Beef fillet	Beef rump steak	Beef whole fillet	Brisket
Beef rib steak/rib-eye steak	Beef flank steak	Beef rib roast (prime rib)	Beef ribs
Beef porterhouse steak	Beef hanger steak	Beef strip loin	
Beef T-bone steak	Beef skirt steak	Beef tri-tip roast	
Sirloin strip	Beef feather steak	Rack of veal	
Lamb loin chop	Veal shoulder chop	Rack of lamb	
Veal loin chop	Lamb shoulder chop	Leg of lamb	
	Lamb loin chop		

HOW TO FREEZE STEAKS

Cutting steaks from a big piece of meat like a sirloin or a boneless rib roast allows you to make steaks just the right thickness. Braai some of the steaks now and freeze the remaining ones for another day. Here's how: The key to freezing a steak properly is to prevent air from touching the surface of the meat. Wrap each steak individually with clingfilm, not foil, and seal it as tightly as possible. Place the individually wrapped steaks in a resealable freezer bag and set the freezer as low as it will go. The colder, the better. Steaks packaged this way will keep very well for about 3 months. Remember to label and date the steaks so that you know when to braai them!

WHEN IS IT DONE?

Recognizing the moment when a big piece of red meat has reached the degree of doneness you want is actually quite simple. Stick the probe of an instant-read thermometer into the thickest part of the meat. When the internal temperature is a few degrees below what you want to eat, take the meat off the braai. That's because large pieces of meat, such as a leg of lamb, retain quite a bit of heat as they 'rest' at room temperature and they continue to cook.

International recommendations are that for safety, red meat should be cooked to an internal temperature of at least 63°C (145°F), bearing in mind that the interior of a thick cut of meat will rise in temperature by 3–5°C if it is allowed to rest for a few minutes after being removed from the heat source. Burgers and sausages should reach 70°C (160°F). Most chefs consider 55°–60°C (130°–140°F) as medium rare. The chart below gives an indication of the optimal internal temperatures for beef and lamb steaks and roasts. Ultimately though, it is up to you to choose your own degree of doneness.

Checking for the doneness of steaks and chops is a little more difficult with an instant-read thermometer because you need to position the sensing 'dimple' of the probe right in the centre of the meat. It's easy to miss the centre and get an inaccurate reading, so I recommend learning to use the 'touch test'. Most raw steaks are as soft as the fleshiest part of your thumb when your hand is relaxed. As they cook, the steaks get firmer and firmer. If you press your index finger and thumb together and press the fleshiest part of your thumb again, the firmness is very close to that of a rare steak. If you press your middle finger and thumb together, the firmness on your thumb is very close to that of a medium-rare steak.

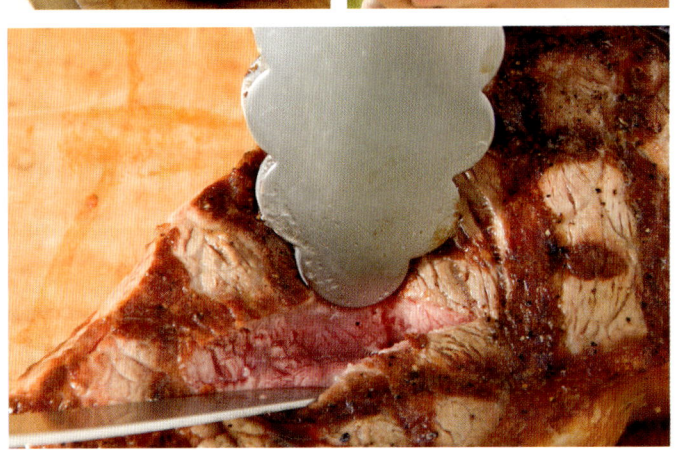

If you are still not sure of the doneness, take the steak off the braai and put the best-looking side (presentation side) face-down on a chopping board. With the tip of a sharp knife, make a little cut in the middle so that you can see the colour of the meat inside. If the colour is still too red, put it back on the braai. If the colour is right, take the rest of the meat off the braai and pat yourself on the back. Before you serve the steaks, feel their firmness and remember that for the next time you use the touch test.

DONENESS	BEEF AND LAMB STEAKS AND ROASTS
Rare	50°–55°C (122°–130°F)
Medium rare	55°–60°C (130°–140°F)
Medium	60°–65°C (140°–150°F)
Medium well	65°–69°C (150°–156°F)
Well done	70°C (158°F)

BEEF BRAAIING GUIDE

The following cuts, thicknesses, weights and cooking times are meant to be guidelines rather than hard and fast rules. Cooking times are affected by factors such as altitude, wind, outside temperature and desired doneness. Two rules of thumb: Braai steaks and kebabs using the direct method for the time given on the chart or to your desired doneness, turning once. Braai larger joints and thicker cuts using the indirect method for the time given on the chart or until an instant-read thermometer reaches the desired internal temperature. Allow joints, larger cuts of meat and thick steaks to rest for 5–10 minutes before carving. The internal temperature of the meat will rise during this time.

BEEF	THICKNESS/WEIGHT	APPROXIMATE BRAAIING TIME
Steak: sirloin, porterhouse, rib-eye, rump, T-bone and fillet	1.5 cm thick	**4–6 minutes** direct high heat
	2.5 cm thick	**5–8 minutes:** sear 4–6 minutes direct high heat, braai 1–2 minutes indirect high heat
	3 cm thick	**8–10 minutes:** sear 6 minutes direct high heat, braai 2–4 minutes indirect high heat
	3.5 cm thick	**10–14 minutes:** sear 6–8 minutes direct high heat, braai 4–6 minutes indirect high heat
	5 cm thick	**14–18 minutes:** sear 6–8 minutes direct high heat, braai 8–10 minutes indirect high heat
Skirt steak	5 mm–1 cm thick	**4–6 minutes** direct high heat
Flank steak	750 g–1 kg, 1.5 cm thick	**8–10 minutes** direct high heat
Kebabs	2.5–3.5 cm cubes	**4–6 minutes** direct high heat
Fillet, whole	1.75–2 kg	**35–45 minutes:** sear 15 minutes direct medium heat, braai 20–30 minutes indirect medium heat
Beef burger (minced beef)	1.5 cm thick	**8–10 minutes** direct high heat
Rib roast (prime rib), deboned	2.5–3 kg	**1¼–1¾ hours** indirect medium heat
Rib roast (prime rib), with bone	4 kg	**2½–3 hours:** sear 10 minutes direct medium heat, braai 2⅓–3 hours indirect low heat
Deboned sirloin roast	2–2.5 kg	**50–60 minutes:** sear 10 minutes direct medium heat, braai 40–50 minutes indirect medium heat
Tri-tip roast	900 g–1.25 kg	**30–40 minutes:** sear 10 minutes direct medium heat, braai 20–30 minutes indirect medium heat
Veal loin chop	2 cm thick	**5–8 minutes:** sear 4–6 minutes direct high heat, braai 1–2 minutes indirect high heat

Note: All cooking times are for medium-rare doneness, except minced beef (medium).

LAMB: THE OTHER RED MEAT

When buying lamb, look for meat that is light red (not too dark) and finely grained (not coarse). The fat should be white (not yellow). Lamb chops cut from the rack are quite flavourful and tender. Be sure to trim the fat close to the meat so that you don't have flare-ups. The lamb loin produces very nice braai chops, with a little bone in the middle of each one, just like a miniature T-bone steak. Chops from the shoulder areas are also tender enough for braaiing, because the animals are almost always younger than one year-old when they are brought to market. A leg of lamb opens up lots of possibilities, including roasting it over indirect heat or cutting the meat into cubes for kebabs.

LAMB BRAAIING GUIDE

The following cuts, thicknesses, weights and braaiing times are meant to be guidelines rather than hard and fast rules. Cooking times are affected by factors such as altitude, wind, outside temperature and desired doneness. Two rules of thumb: Braai lamb chops using the direct method for the time given on the chart or to your desired doneness, turning once.

Braai roasts and thicker cuts using the indirect method for the time given on the chart or until an instant-read thermometer reaches the desired internal temperature. Allow joints, larger cuts of meat and thick chops to rest for 5–10 minutes before carving. The internal temperature of the meat will continue to rise during this time.

LAMB	THICKNESS/WEIGHT	APPROXIMATE BRAAIING TIME
Chop: loin, rib or shoulder	1.5–3 cm thick	**8–12 minutes** direct medium heat
Leg of lamb, deboned, rolled	1.25–1.5 kg	**30–45 minutes:** sear 10–15 minutes direct medium heat, braai 20–30 minutes indirect medium heat
Leg of lamb, butterflied	1.5–1.75 kg	**30–45 minutes:** sear 10–15 minutes direct medium heat, braai 20–30 minutes indirect medium heat
Rib crown roast	1.5–2 kg	**1–1¼ hours** indirect medium heat
Lamb burger (minced lamb)	1.5 cm thick	**8–10 minutes** direct medium heat
Rack of lamb	500–750 g	**15–20 minutes:** sear 5 minutes direct medium heat, braai 10–15 minutes indirect medium heat

Note: All cooking times are for medium-rare doneness, except minced lamb (medium)

PORK

PORK BRAAIING GUIDE

The following cuts, thicknesses, weights and braaiing times are meant to be guidelines rather than hard and fast rules. Cooking times are affected by factors such as altitude, wind, outside temperature and desired doneness. Two rules of thumb: Braai pork chops and sausages using the direct method for the time given on the chart or to your desired doneness, turning once. Braai joints and thicker cuts using the indirect method for the time given on the chart or until an instant-read thermometer reaches the desired internal temperature. Allow joints, large cuts of meat and thick chops to rest for 5–10 minutes before carving. The internal temperature of the meat will continue to rise during this time.

PORK	THICKNESS/ WEIGHT	APPROXIMATE BRAAIING TIME
Sausages, fresh		**20–25 minutes** direct medium heat
Sausages, pre-cooked		**10–12 minutes** direct medium heat
Pork chop, deboned or bone-in	1 cm thick	**5–7 minutes** direct high heat
	1.5 cm thick	**6–8 minutes** direct high heat
	2.5 cm thick	**8–10 minutes** direct medium heat
	3–3.5 cm thick	**10–12 minutes:** sear 6 minutes direct high heat, braai 4–6 minutes indirect high heat
Fillet	500 g	**15–20 minutes** direct medium heat
Loin roast, deboned	1.25 kg	**40–50 minutes** direct medium heat
Loin roast, bone-in	1.5–2.5 kg	**1¼–1¾ hours** indirect medium heat
Pork shoulder, deboned	2.5–3 kg	**5–7 hours** indirect low heat
Pork burger (minced pork)	1 cm thick	**8–10 minutes** direct medium heat
Ribs, baby back	750 g–1 kg	**3–4 hours** indirect low heat
Ribs, spareribs	1.25–1.75 kg	**3–4 hours** indirect low heat
Ribs, country-style, deboned	750g–1 kg	**12–15 minutes** direct medium heat
Ribs, country-style, bone-in	1.5–2 kg	**1½–2 hours** indirect medium heat

WHEN IS IT DONE?

General recommendations are that pork should be cooked to well done 70°C (158°F), but most chefs cook it to 65°–67°C (150°–153°F), when it still has some pink in the centre and all the juices haven't been driven out. Of course, the degree of doneness you choose is entirely up to you. The pork chop on the left, with raw meat in the centre, is clearly undercooked. The chop on the right, with a dry, grey appearance, is overcooked. The chop in the middle, with a little bit of pink in the centre, is cooked to 65°C (150°F), which is just right in my opinion. Notice how the meat gives a little under pressure.

BABY BACK RIBS VERSUS SPARERIBS

Despite the big differences in the size of baby back ribs and spareribs, they are really just two pieces of the same slab of meat. Baby back ribs (bottom of photo) are cut from the top of the ribcage, near the backbone. Spareribs (top of photo) are cut from the bottom of the ribcage, and sometimes they include the brisket, which is a bony piece of meat that hangs from the bottom. The further down the ribcage you go, the meatier the ribs get. That is essentially why spareribs take longer to cook.

WHAT IS A SHINER?

A shiner is an exposed bone on a rack of ribs. It is what unfortunately happens when a butcher cuts too close to the bone. Ribs should be meaty all over, so if you see a rack with shiners at the butcher or supermarket, look for something better. Also avoid all ribs with dry edges or yellowish fat. And know that fresh ribs will almost always yield better results than previously frozen ribs.

TYPES OF PORK FOR THE BRAAI

Tender cuts for braaiing	Moderately tender cuts for braaiing	Bigger cuts for searing and roasting	Tougher cuts for braaiing
Rib chop Loin chop Centre-cut chop Fillet (whole or medallions)	Sirloin chop Shoulder blade steak Ham steak	Rack of pork Loin roast Centre rib roast Centre loin roast Cured gammon Country-style ribs	Baby back ribs Spareribs Shoulder (butt)

POULTRY

WHAT TO LOOK FOR IN CHICKEN

Chicken is chicken, right? Not exactly. Most supermarkets carry big national brands, or put their own brands on these mass-produced birds raised in cages. They are low in fat, they cook quickly and they are tender, but their flavour is pretty darn bland. Fortunately the braai provides just what they need. With a little oil, some seasonings and maybe a sauce, they are very good on the braai.

Today we are seeing more premium chickens available, and usually they are worth their higher price, though not always. Typically, these chickens are from old-fashioned breeds known more for their flavour than their plump breasts and perfectly even shape. Often called 'free-range chickens', they have access to the outdoors, or at least the freedom to wander indoors. The exercise contributes to firmer, more flavoursome meat. Check them out.

Any chickens you buy should have skins that fit their bodies well, not spotty or shrivelled or too far overlapping. The colour of the skin says little about quality, but the smell of a chicken will tell everything you need to know about freshness. If it smells funny, don't buy it.

How chickens are processed can also affect their quality. Some producers submerge their chickens in chlorinated iced water to chill them, which works quickly, but often the process means that the chickens absorb some water. Another process involves spraying the chickens with chlorinated water and sending them through long tunnels filled with cold air. The air-chilled chickens absorb less water, which is good. Who wants to pay extra for iced water?

Some chickens, even when they have been properly chilled, carry upsetting bacteria like salmonella. There is no sense in rinsing raw chickens prior to cooking. That would only raise the chances of spreading bacteria around your kitchen. Simply cook your chickens properly, and all the dangerous bacteria will be killed.

WHEN IS IT DONE?

It is generally recommended that poultry is cooked until the internal temperature reaches 70°C (158°F), however my recipes give you an internal temperature of 74°C (165°F) with tender, succulent results. Keep in mind that in whole birds. the internal temperature will rise 5–10 degrees during resting. Check the thigh meat by inserting the probe of a thermometer into the thickest part (but not touching the bone). If you don't have a thermometer, cut into the centre of the meat. The juices should run clear and the meat should no longer be pink at the bone.

POULTRY BRAAIING GUIDE

The following cuts, weights and braaiing times are meant to be guidelines rather than hard and fast rules. Cooking times are affected by factors such as altitude, wind and outside temperature. Two rules of thumb: Braai deboned poultry pieces using the direct method for the time given on the chart, turning once. Braai whole poultry and bone-in poultry pieces using the indirect method for the time given on the chart or until an instant-read thermometer reaches the desired temperature. Cooking times are for an internal temperature of 74°C (165°F). Allow whole poultry to rest for 5–10 minutes before carving. The internal temperature of the meat will continue to rise during this time.

POULTRY	WEIGHT	APPROXIMATE BRAAIING TIME
Chicken breast, deboned, skinless	175–250 g	**8–12 minutes** direct medium heat
Chicken thigh, deboned, skinless	125 g	**8–10 minutes** direct high heat
Chicken breast, bone-in	300–375 g	**30–40 minutes** indirect medium heat
Chicken pieces, bone-in leg/thigh		**30–40 minutes** indirect medium heat
Chicken wing	50–75 g	**18–20 minutes** direct medium heat
Chicken, whole	1.5–2 kg	**1–1½ hours** indirect medium heat
Poussin	500–750 g	**30–40 minutes** indirect high heat
Turkey breast, deboned	1.25 kg	**1–1¼ hours** indirect medium heat
Turkey, whole, unstuffed	5–6 kg (10–12 lb)	**2½–3½ hours** indirect low heat
	6.5–7.5 kg (13–15 lb)	**3½–4½ hours** indirect low heat
Duck breast, deboned	300–350 g	**9–12 minutes:** braai 3–4 minutes direct low heat, braai 6–8 minutes indirect high heat
Duck, whole	2.5–3 kg	**40 minutes** indirect high heat

SEAFOOD

TIPS TO PREVENT STICKING

CLEAN COOKING GRATES
Use a stainless-steel bristle brush to get the grates really clean.

A LITTLE OIL
Coat the fish on all sides with a thin layer of oil, but don't oil the grates.

HIGH HEAT
Fish comes off the grate after a delicate crust of caramelization develops between the flesh and grate. That requires heat, usually high heat.

A LOT OF PATIENCE
Leave the fish alone. Caramelization happens faster when the fish stays in place on the hot grate. Keep the lid down as much as possible and turn the fish only once.

GOOD TIMING
The first side down on the grates will be the side that eventually faces you on the plate. Braai it a few minutes longer than the second side and it will release more easily and look fabulous on the plate, with perfect grill marks.

HOW TO REMOVE FISH FROM THE COOKING GRATES
If the fillets have skin attached, braai the skin side last. When each fillet is ready to serve, slide a spatula between the skin and flesh, and then lift each fillet off the grate, leaving the skin behind.

WHAT TO LOOK FOR IN FISH

The first thing to know is that firm fish and seafood are easiest to braai. The meatier they are, the better they hold together as they cook and as you turn them over. Many tender fish work nicely, too, although they require a little more care.

The chart below features some widely available choices. Feel free to substitute within the categories. If you find two fish with similar sizes and textures, just replace one for the other.

TYPES OF FISH FOR THE BRAAI

Firm fillets and steaks	Medium-firm fillets and steaks	Tender fillets	Whole fish	Shellfish
Yellowtail	Hake	Gurnard	Hottentot	Prawns
Snoek	Kingklip	East Coast Sole	Sardines	Black mussels
Yellowfin Tuna	Cape Salmon (Geelbek)	Rainbow Trout	Mackerel	Crayfish (Rock Lobster)
Dorado (Mahi-mahi)	Horse Mackerel (Maasbanker)		Rainbow Trout	Oysters
Atlantic Salmon	Kob			Scallops
Calamari (Squid)	Angelfish			Clams

WHEN IS IT DONE?

Overcooking fish is a crime. With almost every kind of fish, you should get it off the braai before it flakes by itself. You are looking for an internal temperature of 52°–55°C (125°–130°F), but that's tough to measure with fish fillets or steaks, so rely on the internal appearance (the whitish colour of the flesh should be opaque all the way to the centre), as well as the times given in the recipes, and in the chart below.

SEAFOOD BRAAIING GUIDE

The following types, thicknesses, weights and braaiing times are meant to be guidelines rather than hard and fast rules. Cooking times are affected by factors such as altitude, wind, outside temperature and desired doneness. The general rule of thumb for braaiing fish portions is to allow 4–5 minutes cooking time per 1 cm thickness and 8–10 minutes per 2.5 cm thickness.

FISH	THICKNESS/ WEIGHT	APPROXIMATE BRAAIING TIME
Fish, fillet or steak Includes yellowtail, snoek, dorado, salmon, swordfish and tuna	5mm–1 cm thick	**3–5 minutes** direct high heat
	1–2.5 cm thick	**5–10 minutes** direct high heat
	2.5–3 cm thick	**10–12 minutes** direct high heat
Fish, whole	500 g	**15–20 minutes** indirect medium heat
	1–1.2 kg	**20–30 minutes** indirect medium heat
	1.5 kg	**30–45 minutes** indirect medium heat
Prawns	40 g	**2–4 minutes** direct high heat
Scallops	40 g	**4–6 minutes** direct high heat
Mussels (discard any that do not open)		**5–6 minutes** direct high heat
Clams (discard any that do not open)		**6–8 minutes** direct high heat
Oysters		**2–4 minutes** direct high heat
Crayfish (Rock Lobster) tail		**7–11 minutes** direct medium heat

VEGETABLES

COOK WHAT'S GROWING AT THE TIME
Vegetables in season locally have big advantages over whatever has been shipped from across the world. They are riper, so they taste better. That means you can cook them simply with great results.

EXPOSE AS MUCH SURFACE AREA AS POSSIBLE
Cut each vegetable to give you the biggest area to put in contact with the cooking grates. The more direct contact, the better the flavours will be. For example, choose peppers with flat sides that you can easily slice off the core. Flatter sides mean a greater surface area that will caramelize on the hot cooking grates.

USE THE GOOD OIL
Vegetables need oil to prevent sticking and burning. Neutral oils like canola or sunflower oil will do the job, but extra-virgin olive oil provides the added benefit of improving the flavour of virtually every vegetable. Brush on just enough to coat each side thoroughly but not so much that the vegetables would drip oil and cause flare-ups. Season the vegetables generously with salt and pepper (some of it will fall off). For more flavours, marinate the vegetables at room temperature for 20 minutes to an hour in olive oil, vinegar, garlic, herbs and spices.

WHEN IS IT DONE?
I like firm vegetables, such as onions and fennel, to be somewhere between crisp and tender. If you want them softer, cook for a few minutes longer, but watch them carefully for burning. The braai intensifies the sweetness of vegetables quickly and that can lead to burning. Cut vegetables as evenly as you can; about 1 cm thickness is right for most of them.

VEGETABLE BRAAIING GUIDE

Most vegetables, from artichokes to zucchini (courgettes), cook best over direct medium heat. The temperature on the braai's thermometer should be between 180° and 230°C (350°–450°F). If any parts get too dark, turn the vegetables over. Otherwise turn them as few times as possible.

VEGETABLES	THICKNESS/SIZE	APPROXIMATE GRILLING TIME
Artichoke (300–375 g)	whole	**14–18 minutes:** boil 10–12 minutes; cut in half and braai 4–6 minutes direct medium heat
Asparagus	1-cm diameter	**4–6 minutes** direct medium heat
Beetroot (175 g)		**1–½ hours** indirect medium heat
Brinjal (Aubergine)	1-cm slices	**8–10 minutes** direct medium heat
Butternut and Pumpkin	halved	**40–60 minutes** indirect medium heat
Carrots	2-cm diameter	**7–11 minutes:** boil 4–6 minutes, braai 3–5 minutes direct high heat
Chillies	5-mm slices	**6–8 minutes** direct medium heat
Courgette (Baby marrow)	1-cm slices	**3–5 minutes** direct medium heat
	halved	**4–6 minutes** direct medium heat
Fennel	5-mm slices	**10–12 minutes** direct medium heat
Garlic	whole	**45–60 minutes** indirect medium heat
Mushroom (portabello or black)		**10–15 minutes** direct medium heat
Mushroom (shiitake or button)		**8–10 minutes** direct medium heat
Onion (red or white)	whole or halved	**35–40 minutes** indirect medium heat
	1-cm slices	**8–12 minutes** direct medium heat
Peppers (green, red, yellow)	whole or halved	**10–15 minutes** direct medium heat
Potato	whole	**45–60 minutes** indirect medium heat
	1-cm slices	**14–16 minutes** direct medium heat
Potato, baby	whole or halved	**15–20 minutes** direct medium heat
Spring onions	whole	**3–4 minutes** direct medium heat
Sweetcorn mealies, without husk		**10–15 minutes** direct medium heat
Sweetcorn mealies, with husk		**25–30 minutes** direct medium heat
Sweet potato	whole	**50–60 minutes** indirect medium heat
	5-mm slices	**8–10 minutes** direct medium heat
Tomatoes	halved	**6–8 minutes** direct medium heat
	whole	**8–10 minutes** direct medium heat

FRUIT

Braaiing fruit is much like braaiing vegetables. Select fruit that's ripe (or almost ripe) and firm, because it will soften on the braai. Because of its texture, it's a good idea to watch fruit carefully while cooking and to turn it occasionally. The sweet succulence of most fruits turns golden brown and delicious on the braai, but if left too long in one place, golden brown can quickly turn to black and bitter. To check the colour and doneness, slide a thin spatula gently under the fruit and slightly lift.

Warm fruit off the braai needs only a scoop of ice cream or frozen yoghurt to seal a meal with style. Or use braaied fruit to accompany a shortbread biscuit, a wedge of gingerbread or a slice of Madeira cake. Fruit served like this shows your guests that you've developed the techniques to braai almost anything, from starters to desserts.

FRUIT BRAAIING GUIDE

The following types, thicknesses and cooking times are meant to be guidelines rather than hard and fast rules. Cooking times are affected by factors such as altitude, wind and outside temperature. Braaiing times will depend on both the ripeness and the size of the fruit.

FRUIT	THICKNESS/SIZE	APPROXIMATE BRAAIING TIME
Apple	whole	**35–40 minutes** indirect medium heat
	1-cm thick slices	**4–6 minutes** direct medium heat
Apricot	halved, stone removed	**6–8 minutes** direct medium heat
Banana	halved lengthways	**6–8 minutes** direct medium heat
Nectarine	halved lengthways, stone removed	**8–10 minutes** direct medium heat
Peach	halved lengthways, stone removed	**8–10 minutes** direct medium heat
Pear	halved lengthways	**10–12 minutes** direct medium heat
Pineapple	peeled and cored, 1-cm slices or 2.5-cm wedges	**5–10 minutes** direct medium heat
Strawberry		**4–5 minutes** direct medium heat

BRAAI MAINTENANCE

A little TLC is all it takes to ensure that you get years of use from your braai. Maintenance is the key (consult the owner's manual that came with your braai). Each time you use the braai, remember to clean the cooking grates. With the braai on high (either just before cooking or just afterwards) brush the cooking grates with a long-handled stainless-steel brush. Make sure you get in between the grates with your brush, too.

MONTHLY MAINTENANCE PLAN FOR GAS BRAAIS

1. When your braai is warm, but not hot, use a wet, soapy sponge or cloth to wipe the inside of the lid. This will help keep natural carbon build-up from accumulating inside the lid.

2. Remove the grates and brush the metal bars that shield the burners. A good brush, like the one you use to brush the cooking grates, will work well. This will help to eliminate flare-ups. (If you braai often, like I do, you may need to do this more than once a month.)

3. Gently clean the burner tubes with a steel brush. Brush side-to-side along the burner tubes, but take care not to damage the burner openings by brushing too hard.

4. Use a plastic putty knife or spatula to scrape the grease from the bottom of the braai. If your braai has a collection tray, scrape the bits into it. Then dispose of the contents of the collection tray.

5. Wash the inside of the braai with warm, soapy water, taking care not to get any water into the burner tubes.

6. Reassemble. Repeat after a month.

MONTHLY MAINTENANCE PLAN FOR CHARCOAL BRAAIS

1. When the braai is cold, remove the ash from the bowl. Because the ash naturally contains a small amount of moisture, it is important to get the ash out of the bowl each time you use it and before storing your braai. If your braai has an ash catcher, empty it after each use.

2. Wipe the inside of the bowl with a warm, wet sponge or cloth. This will help to keep natural carbon build-up from accumulating inside your braai.

MONTHLY MAINTENANCE PLAN FOR ELECTRIC BRAAIS

1. When your braai is warm, but not hot, use a wet, soapy sponge or cloth to wipe the inside of the lid. This will help to keep natural carbon build-up from accumulating inside the lid of the braai.

2. Remove the grates. Use a plastic putty knife or spatula to scrape the grease from the bottom of the braai. If your braai has a collection tray, scrape the bits into it, then dispose of the contents of the collection tray.

3. Wipe the inside of the braai with a warm, damp sponge or cloth, being very careful not to get the heating element wet.

SELECTING YOUR BRAAI

One of the most valuable skills a good cook learns is the art of substitution. Dorado, for instance, can substitute for tuna steaks, and a T-bone steak will cook the same way as a porterhouse. However, when it comes to choosing a braai, there simply is no substitute for quality. After all, the one thing that every meal you prepare from this book will have in common is your braai.

WHAT TO LOOK FOR IN A
GAS BRAAI

1. Check out the construction and durability.
A braai is an important purchase and you will own it for years to come. Since most braais are kept outside and exposed to the elements, they need to be well made and durable. If you choose a stainless steel braai, look for heavy-gauge construction that will ensure the braai will last more than a season or two. A porcelain-enamel finish will also hold up well. Carefully check out the corners to make sure that there are no sharp edges. Size up the fit and finish. If the doors or frame are misaligned, it may be a reflection of poor design.

2. Lift the lid and kick the tyres. The inner workings and construction of a braai are more important than how it looks on the outside. Lift the lid to see how the braai opens and closes. It should be a tight fit and the braai shouldn't feel wobbly when you open it. Look for heavy-duty cooking grates that will hold up to years of regular use.

3. Look at burner placement. Uneven heat is a cook's worst nightmare. A well-designed gas braai will have burners placed evenly across the cooking box. Angled metal bars will cover the burners, directing drippings away from the flames and minimizing flare-ups. These bars also distribute the heat evenly across the entire cooking surface.

4. Give yourself space. The cooking grate needs to be big enough to handle the amount food you like to cook. Remember, many recipes call for both direct and indirect heat. Ensure you have space to move your food from direct to indirect heat any time.

5. Don't be blinded by BTUs. It's a common belief that more is better when it comes to BTUs. Not necessarily so. BTU stands for British Thermal Unit, an international standard that measures how much heat it takes to raise one pound of water by one degree Fahrenheit. A gas braai burning 35,000 BTUs per hour should reach a searing temperature of around 290°C (550°F) without any problem. Unless your cooking area is large, you should be fine with a braai with a rating of 35,000–40,000 BTUs. More than that, and you may be wasting energy.

6. Don't overlook the basics. One of the most important things you should consider when buying a gas braai is where the grease and debris will go. Grease is combustible and if it is not channelled away from the inside of your braai, it could lead to some serious flare-ups. A well-designed system should include a removable grease tray that is accessible from the front of the braai. The drip tray should be a couple of centimetres deep and should come with disposable liners to make clean-up easier.

7. Be critical of the bells and whistles. These days, many braais come with nice added features such as a side burner or a rotisserie. These options can improve your braaiing experience, if they are done well. Make sure the side burner has adequate power to do the job, or it may be a waste of money. It should also have a hinged cover so that you don't lose valuable cooking space when the burner is not in use. An added benefit of a hinged cover is that it can act as a windshield, improving the burner's performance. If you are buying a braai with a rotisserie, check out the motor. An ineffective motor will lead to poor performance. You will need a heavy-duty motor to turn large items, like a turkey or leg of lamb. And check out the strength of the spit; it needs to be strong enough to hold large items and should have strong forks to hold the meat in place. Finally, look at the position of the rotisserie. If the motor or the spit is over the side burner, you'll limit your ability to use it when you are rotisserie cooking.

WHAT TO LOOK FOR IN A CHARCOAL BRAAI

1. Go for one with a lid. Open braais, such as hibachis, are fun to use but their design limits your flexibility. Buying a braai with a lid broadens your options. When you buy a charcoal braai, make sure it has a well-fitting lid, with top and bottom vents for airflow. The lid effectively turns the braai into an outdoor oven capable of both direct and indirect cooking. The vents allow you to control the temperature inside.

2. Make sure it's built to last. A good charcoal braai should last for years. Look for solid construction and a durable porcelain-enamel finish over thick gauge metal.

3. Look for great grates. Your charcoal braai should have thick, durable grates. Either heavy wire or stainless steel work well. For the serious cook, I recommend a hinged cooking grate that allows you to add more coals while cooking. My favourite way to prepare the Christmas turkey is on my charcoal braai, and a hinged cooking grate allows me to easily add coals each hour to maintain even heat.

4. Make sure cleanup is easy. Charcoal is going to produce ash, which can be a mess to clean up. I recommend that you choose a charcoal braai that is designed with a system to push ash from the bottom of your braai into a removable ash catcher. After all, the easier it is to clean your braai, the more you're going to use it.

ELECTRIC BRAAIS

Until recently, if you lived in a townhouse complex or flats that didn't allow gas or charcoal braais, your only option was an electric braai or an indoor countertop grill. I'm happy to report that technology has improved and now there are new options with much improved performance. Like its gas and charcoal counterparts, an electric braai should be solid, stable and built to last.

SAFETY

GENERAL NOTES

1. Always read your owner's manual prior to use.

2. Braais radiate a lot of heat, so always keep the braai at least 1.5 m (5 feet) away from any combustible materials, including the house, garage, deck rails and so on. Combustible materials include, but are not limited to, wood or treated wood decks, wood patios or wood porches. Never use a braai indoors or under a covered patio.

3. Keep the braai in a level position at all times.

4. Use proper tools with long, heat-resistant handles.

5. Don't wear loose or highly flammable clothing when braaiing.

6. Do not leave infants, children or pets unattended near a hot braai.

7. Use insulated braai mitts or oven gloves to protect hands while cooking or adjusting the vents.

GAS BRAAI SAFETY

1. Always keep the bottom tray and grease catch-pan of your braai clean and free of debris. This not only prevents dangerous grease fires, it deters visits from unwanted animals. (A sprinkle of cayenne pepper is a safe way to discourage animals.)

2. If a flare-up occurs, turn off all burners and move food to another part of the cooking grate. Any flames will quickly subside. Then light the braai again. Never use water to extinguish flames on a gas braai.

3. Do not line the funnel-shaped bottom tray with foil. This could prevent grease from flowing into the grease catch-pan. Grease is also likely to catch in the tiny creases of the foil and start a fire.

4. Never store gas tanks indoors (that means the garage, too).

Keep a fire extinguisher handy in case of a mishap.

5. For the first few uses, the temperature of a new gas braai may run hotter than normal. Once your braai is seasoned and the inside of the cooking box becomes less reflective, the temperature will return to normal.

CHARCOAL BRAAI SAFETY

1. Charcoal braais are designed for outdoor use only. If used indoors, toxic fumes will accumulate and cause serious bodily injury or death.

2. Do not add charcoal starter fluid or charcoal impregnated with charcoal starter fluid to hot or warm charcoal.

3. Do not use petrol or other highly volatile fluids to ignite charcoal. If using charcoal starter fluid, remove any fluid that may have drained through the bottom vents before lighting the charcoal.

4. Do not use a braai unless all parts are in place. Make sure that the ash catcher is properly attached to the legs, beneath the bowl of the braai.

5. Remove the lid from the braai while lighting and getting the charcoal started.

6. Always put charcoal on top of the charcoal grate and not directly into the bottom of the bowl.

7. Do not place a chimney starter on or near any combustible surface.

8. Never touch the cooking or charcoal grate or the braai's surface to see if they are hot.

9. Use the hook on the inside of the lid to hang the lid on the side of the bowl of the braai. Avoid placing a hot lid on carpet or grass. Do not hang the lid on the bowl handle.

10. To extinguish the coals, place the lid on the bowl and close all of the vents (dampers). Make sure that the vents on the lid and the bowl are completely closed. Do not use water, as it will damage the porcelain finish.

11. To control flare-ups, place the lid on the braai and close the top vent about halfway. Do not use water.

12. Handle and store hot electric starters carefully. Do not place starters on top of or near any combustible surfaces.

13. Keep electrical cords away from the hot surfaces of the braai.

FOOD SAFETY TIPS

1. Wash your hands thoroughly with hot, soapy water before starting any meal preparation and after handling fresh meat, fish and poultry.

2. Do not defrost meat, fish or poultry at room temperature. Defrost in the refrigerator.

3. Use different utensils and preparation surfaces for raw and cooked foods.

4. Wash all plates and/or cooking utensils that have come into contact with raw meats or fish with hot, soapy water and rinse.

5. When resting meats at room temperature before braaiing, remember that 'room temperature' is regarded as 18°–20°C. Do not place raw food in direct sunlight or near any heat source.

6. Always cook minced meats and poultry to at least 70°C (160°F), the recommended temperature for medium (well-done) doneness.

7. If a sauce is to be brushed on meat during braaiing, divide the sauce, using one part for brushing and the other for serving at the table. Vigorously boil any marinades that were used for raw meat, fish or poultry for at least 30 seconds before using as a baste or sauce.

PROPER BRAAIING FORM

1. Trim excess fat from steaks and chops, leaving only a scant 5-mm of fat, which is sufficient to flavour the meat. Less fat is a virtual guarantee against flare-ups and makes cleaning up easier.

2. A light coating of oil will help to brown your food evenly and keep it from sticking to the cooking grates. Always brush or spray oil onto your food, not the cooking grates.

3. Keep a lid on it! A Weber® braai is designed to cook foods with the lid down. Keeping the lid on allows heat to circulate, cooking food evenly and without flare-ups. Every time you lift or open the lid, except when instructed to in a recipe, you add extra cooking time.

4. Take the guesswork out of braaiing. Use a thermometer and a timer to let you know when it's time to take food off the braai. Checking meats for internal temperatures is the best way to determine when food is properly cooked or when done is about to become overdone.

5. Use the right utensils. Long-handled tools and long insulated braai mitts (oven gloves) protect you from the heat. Use forks only to lift fully cooked foods from the braai and tongs or turners to turn them (forks will pierce the food and all the flavourful juices will be lost).

6. Remember that cooking times in charts and recipes are approximate, and based on 20°C weather with little or no wind. Allow a little more cooking time on cold or windy days, or at higher altitudes, and less cooking time in extremely hot weather.

INDEX

TECHNIQUES

A

Air vents, how to work 16
Apples
   grating apples 98
   prepping and braaiing apples 268
Apricots, how to prep and braai 269
Artichoke hearts, how to prep and braai 244
Asparagus, how to braai 246
Avocados, how to stone and chop 156

B

Bananas, how to braai 270, 271
Banana leaves, braaiing in 214
Basil-Garlic oil, how to make 80
Basket, fish 31, 220
Basting brush 27
Beef
   See also Beef fillet; Beef ribs; Beef roast;
      Beef steak; Burgers; Meat loaf
   braaiing guide for beef 296
   checking doneness 49, 295
   choosing beef for the braai 292, 293
Beef fillet
   prepping beef fillet 88
Beef ribs
   braaiing beef ribs 84
   cutting beef short ribs 82
Beef roast
   braaiing brisket 92
   butchering rib roast 52, 58
   butchering sirloin 45
   prepping and smoking rib roast 90
Beef steak
   basics of braaiing 44
   best cuts for the braai 293
   bistecca, carving 65
   braaiing really thick steaks 44, 64
   checking doneness 49, 295
   flank steak, slicing 69
   flank steak, stuffing and rolling, 70
   making cross-hatch marks 62
   porterhouse steak, carving 65
   rib-eye steak, prepping 52
   rib-eye steaks, cutting from rib
      roast 52, 58
   rump flap steak, prepping 68
   sirloin, cubing 72
   sirloin, cutting 45
   sirloin, escalopes, making 51
   sirloin, prepping and braaiing 46–47
   skirt steak, prepping 66
   steaks, freezing 294
Beetroot, how to peel after braaiing 258
Bok Choy see Pak Choi
Boning see Deboning
Braai basics: Q and A 8–25
Braai brush 26

Braai gloves 28
Braaiing and smoking 22–25
   braaiing beef ribs 84
   braaiing brisket 92
   braaiing chicken 151
   braaiing meat loaf 42
   braaiing pork ribs 120, 121, 122,
      126, 128
   braaiing pork shoulder 114
Braais
   See also Charcoal braais; Gas braais
   buying tips 21, 308–309
   cleaning and maintenance 19, 307
   safety tips 310–311
Bratwurst, how to braai 96
Brinjals, how to prep 254
Briquettes 9, 10
Broccoli, how to braai 248
Browning, value of 292
Brushes 26, 27
Bull's-eye arrangement of coals 14
Burgers
   basics of braaiing beef burgers 34, 40
   making 'outside in' cheeseburgers 38
   planking turkey burgers 174
Butter, how to flavour 62
Butterflying
   leg of lamb 86
   turkey breast 168
   whole chicken 166

C

Cabbage, how to shred 175
Calamari, how to braai under bricks 226
Camembert, how to wrap in grape
   leaves 277
Carrots, how to braai 250
Cast-iron frying pan 30
Charcoal 9–10
   arranging the coals 12–14
   how much to use 11
   lighting 10
   versus wood 9
Charcoal braais 9–16
   air vents, how to work 16
   buying tips 21, 309
   cleaning 19, 307
   direct heat 12, 13, 14
   heat level in, how to judge 15
   indirect heat 12, 13, 14
   lids, why to use 20
   lighting the fire 10
   maintaining heat 16
   maintenance 19, 307
   safety tips 310–311
   smoking in 22–23, 121
Chicken
   See also Chicken breasts; Chicken
      legs; Chicken thighs; Chicken wings;
      Chicken, whole and cut-up

   braaiing guide for chicken 301
   checking doneness 136, 301
   choosing chicken for the braai 300
Chicken breasts
   braaiing chicken escalopes 136
   braaiing chicken involtini 134
   checking doneness 136
   making chicken skewers 143
   prepping chicken breasts 144
Chicken legs
   braaiing chicken pieces 151
   prepping whole chicken legs 148
Chicken thighs
   braaiing boneless chicken thighs 154
   braaiing chicken pieces 151
   planking chicken thighs 152
Chicken, whole and cut-up whole
   braaiing butterflied chicken 166
   cooking rotisserie chicken 162
   roasting whole chicken 164
   smoking beer can chicken 160
   trussing 162, 164
Chicken wings
   braaiing chicken drumettes 147
   braaiing whole chicken wings 146
Chillies
   braaiing chillies 230, 240
   making roasted chilli and avocado
      sauce 186
   prepping dried chillies for salsa 54
   prepping whole chillies for stuffing 253
Chimney starters 10, 27
Chops
   braaiing pork chops, basics 100
   cutting a rack of lamb into chops 78
   prepping lamb shoulder (braai)
      chops 80
   prepping veal chops 75
Clambake, how to prep for 191
Coals see Charcoal
Corn see Mealies
Cornish game hens see Poussin
Crab
   how to prep and braai whole crabs 196
   judging freshness 198
Crayfish tails, how to prep and braai 194
Cross-hatch marks, how to make 62
Cucumbers, how to grate 74
Cutting techniques for fruit
   cutting mangoes 139
   prepping fresh pineapple 266
   stoning and chopping avocados 156
Cutting techniques for pork
   prepping baby back ribs 121
   prepping St. Louis-style spareribs 126
Cutting techniques for poultry
   butterflying turkey breast 168
   butterflying whole chicken 166
   carving whole turkey 172
   cutting chicken drumettes 147

prepping whole chicken legs 148
splitting poussins 158
Cutting techniques for red meat
butchering rib roast 52, 58
butchering sirloin 45
butterflying leg of lamb 86
carving bistecca 65
cubing sirloin or rump steak 72
cutting rack of lamb into chops 78
cutting short ribs 82
frenching rack of lamb 76
slicing flank steak 69
Cutting techniques for seafood
cutting up whole crab 196
filleting whole line fish 216
prepping squid (calamari) 224
prepping whole line fish 219
skinning dorado 208
skinning hake 207
trimming trout 222
Cutting techniques for vegetables
cutting artichoke hearts 244
cutting corn from the cob 175
cutting onions into wedges 180
cutting vegetables for the braai 304
shredding cabbage 175
trimming fennel 204, 259

D
Deboning salmon steaks 204
Direct heat 12, 13, 14, 18
Dorado portions, how to skin 208
Drip pans 14
Duck
braaiing guide for duck 301
checking for doneness 301
prepping duck breasts 140
roasting duck legs 150

E
Eggplant *see* Brinjal
Electric braais
buying tips 309
maintanance 307
Escabèche, how to make 213
Escalopes, how to prep and braai
beef 51
chicken 136
pork 102

F
Fennel, how to prep and braai 204, 259
Fish
basics of braaiing 200
braaiing fish in banana leaves 214
braaiing guide for fish 303
checking doneness 200, 206, 303
choosing fish for the braai 302
dorado portions, skinning 208
escabèche, how to make 213
hake, prepping 207
line fish, filleting 216
preventing fish from sticking 302
salmon, braaiing 201
salmon, planking 203
salmon steaks, deboning 204
trout, braaiing in a basket 220

trout, planking 223
trout, trimming 222
tuna, smoking in cedar papers 211
whole line fish, prepping 219
Fish basket 31, 220
Flare-ups 20, 47
Flatbread, how to make 262
Food safety 311
Frenching and braaiing a rack of lamb 76
Fruit
apples, braaiing 268
apples, grating 98
apricots, braaiing 269
avocados, stoning and chopping 156
bananas, braaiing 270, 271
braaiing guide for fruit 306
choosing fruit for the braai 306
lemons, zesting and juicing 138
mangoes, cutting 139
nectarines, braaiing 274
oranges, segmenting 222
peaches, braaiing 274
pears, wrapping in prosciutto 276
pineapple, prepping and braaiing 266
plums, braaiing and simmering for sauce 140
strawberries, flame-roasting 273

G
Garlic
braaiing garlic 254
making basil-garlic oil 80
making garlic paste 58
Gas braais 17–18
buying tips, 21, 308–309
cleaning 19, 307
direct heat 18
indirect heat 18
lids, why to use 20
maintenance, 19, 307
safety tips 310, 311
smoking in 23
starting 17
Ginger root, how to skin 87
Grape leaves, how to wrap around Camembert cheese 277
Grater, microplane 31
Green beans, how to braai 249
Grill pan 26
how to use 218

H
Hake, how to prep 207
Heat level of charcoal, how to judge 15

I
Indirect heat 12, 13, 14, 18

K
Kosher salt *see* Salt

L
Lamb
braaiing guide for lamb 297
butterflying leg of lamb 86
checking doneness 295
choosing lamb for the braai 293, 297

cutting rack of lamb into chops 78
frenching and braaiing rack of lamb 76
prepping lamb shoulder (braai) chops 80
Leeks, how to prep 102
Lemons, how to zest and juice 138
Lids, value of in braaiing 20, 309
Lighter fluid 11
Lighting the fire 10
Line fish, how to fillet 216
Lobster *see* Crayfish

M
Maintaining heat 16
Mangoes, how to cut 139
Mealies
braaiing mealies on the coals 232
cutting kernels from cobs 175
prepping 233, 234
sautéing corn for salsa 208
Meat loaf, how to braai 42
Mitts *see* Braai gloves
Mushrooms
browning mushrooms 61
prepping and braaiing portabello mushrooms 236
prepping and braaiing shiitake mushrooms 235
sautéing mushrooms for salsa 208
Mussels, how to clean 190

N
Nectarines, how to braai 274

O
Onions
braaiing onions 48, 241
cutting onions into wedges 180
grating onions 36
pickling onions 43
Oranges, how to segment 222
Oysters, how to char-grill 192

P
Paella, how to make 188
Pak Choi, how to prep and braai 235
Pans *see also* Trays
grill pan 26
using a grill pan 218
Peaches, how to braai 274
Pears, how to prep and wrap in prosciutto 276
Pineapple, how to prep and braai 266
Pizza, how to braai 238
Planking
chicken thighs 152
salmon 203
scallops 180
trout 223
turkey burgers 174
Plastic bags 30
Plums, how to braai and simmer for sauce 140
Polenta, how to make 230
Pork
See also Bratwurst; Pork chops; Pork fillet; Pork ribs; Pork roast

INDEX

braaiing guide for pork 298
checking doneness 100, 299
choosing pork for the braai 298, 299
Pork chops
   basics of braaiing pork chops 100
   making and braaiing escalopes 102
Pork fillet
   preparing fillet medallions 108
   preparing pork fillet 106
Pork ribs
   baby back versus spareribs 299
   basics of braaiing pork ribs 120
   braaiing stacked baby back ribs 124
   cooking spareribs in a smoker 128
   prepping and braaiing baby back ribs 121, 122
   prepping St. Louis-style spareribs 126
   using the 'Texas crutch' 126
Pork roast
   braaiing bone-in pork loin 112
   braaiing pork shoulder 114
   making porchetta 116
   preparing rotisserie pork loin 110
   seasoning and braaiing a pork joint 118
Poultry
   See also Chicken; Duck; Poussin; Turkey
   braaiing guide for poultry 301
   checking doneness 301
Poussin
   braaiing guide for poussins 301
   checking for doneness 301
   splitting poussins 158
Prawns
   braaiing prawn pops 184
   peeling and deveining 183
   size 181
   skewering 186
Prosciutto, how to braai 246

Q
Quesadillas, how to braai 156

R
Rib rack 31
Ring of fire 14
Rotisserie
   attachments for the braai 21, 30, 309
   cooking rotisserie chicken 162
   preparing rotisserie pork loin 110

S
Safety tips 310–311
Salmon
   braaiing salmon 201
   deboning salmon steaks 204
   planking salmon 203
Salsa
   making pan-roasted chilli salsa 54
Salt
   importance of 7
   salting meat as it cooks 44
   smoked sea salt 140
Sandwiches, how to braai 256
Scallops
   checking doneness 180
   prepping scallops for braaiing 178, 179

Scones, how to make 99
Seafood *see* Fish; Shellfish
Searing 44, 292
Shallots, prepping 68
Shellfish
   braaiing guide for shellfish 303
   calamari, braaiing under bricks 226
   checking doneness 180, 303
   choosing shellfish for the braai 302
   clambake, prepping for 191
   crayfish tails, prepping and braaiing 194
   mussels, cleaning 190
   oysters, char-grilling 192
   prawn pops, braaiing 184
   prawns, peeling and deveining 183
   prawns, size 181
   prawns, skewering 186
   preventing shellfish from sticking 302
   scallops, checking for doneness 180
   scallops, prepping for braaiing 178, 179
   squid (calamari), prepping 224
   whole crab, prepping and braaiing 196
Shiner 299
Shortcakes, how to make 274
Shovel 29
Shrimp *see* Prawns
Skewers 28
   preparing skewers in advance 155
   skewering chicken wings 146
   skewering prawn pops 184
   skewering prawns 186
Skillet *see* Cast-iron frying pan
Smokers 24–25, 114, 128
Smoking and braaiing 22–25
   smoking beer can chicken 160
   smoking in a charcoal braai 121
   smoking pork shoulder 114
   smoking pork spareribs 128
   smoking rib roast 90
   smoking tuna in cedar papers 211
   smoking turkey burgers on planks 174
   smoking whole turkey 171
   woods for 22
Spatulas 28
Squid *see also* Calamari
   braaiing calamari under bricks 226
   prepping squid 224
Strawberries, how to flame-roast 273
Sweet potatoes, how to braai 261

T
Texas crutch 126
Thermometers 27, 29
Three-zone fire 13
Timer 29
Tofu, how to braai 252
Tomatillos, how to braai 230
Tomatoes
   grill-roasting tomatoes 178, 213, 242
   pan-roasting tomatoes 54
Tongs 26
Tools for braaiing 26–31
Trays
   disposable trays 30
   drip tray 14
   roasting tray 27

Trout
   braaiing trout in a basket 220
   trimming trout 222
Trussing whole chicken 162, 164
Tuna, how to smoke in cedar papers 211
Turkey
   basics of cooking whole turkey 170
   braaiing bacon-wrapped turkey breast 168
   braaiing guide for turkey 301
   carving whole turkey 172
   checking doneness, 170, 301
   planking turkey burgers 174
   prepping turkey in advance 171
   smoking whole turkey 171
Two-zone fire 13

U
Utensils for braaiing 26–31

V
Veal
   checking doneness 295
   choosing veal for the braai 293
   prepping veal chops 75
Vegetables
   artichoke hearts, braaiing 244
   asparagus, braaiing 246
   beetroot, peeling 258
   bok choy *see* pak choi
   braaiing guide for vegetables 305
   brinjals, prepping 254
   broccoli, braaiing 248
   cabbage, shredding 175
   carrots, braaiing 250
   checking doneness 304
   chillies, prepping dried ones for salsa 54
   chillies, prepping whole ones for stuffing 253
   chillies, roasting 186, 230, 240
   choosing vegetables for the braai 304
   corn *see also* mealies
   corn on the cob, prepping 233, 234
   corn, removing kernels from cobs 175
   corn, sautéing for salsa 208
   cucumbers, grating 74
   cutting vegetables for the braai 304
   fennel, prepping and braaiing 204, 259
   garlic paste, making 58
   garlic, roasting 254
   green beans, braaiing 249
   leeks, prepping 102
   mealies, braaiing on the coals 232
   mushrooms, browning 61
   mushrooms, prepping and braaiing portabellos 236
   mushrooms, prepping and braaiing shiitakes 235
   mushrooms, sautéing for salsa 208
   onions, braaiing 48, 241
   onions, cutting into wedges 180
   onions, grating, 36
   onions, pickling 43
   pak choi, prepping and braaiing 235
   roasting vegetables on the braai 242
   shallots, roasting 68
   sweet potatoes, braaiing 261

tomatillos, braaiing 230
tomatoes, grilling 213
tomatoes, grill-roasting 178, 242
tomatoes, pan-roasting 54
Vinaigrette, how to prepare 243

W
Water smoker 24–25, 114, 128
Wood
    best choices for smoking 22
    cutting wood chunks for smoking 90
    hardwood briquettes 10
    wood versus charcoal 9

RECIPES

A
Aïoli 193, 236 245
All-purpose Rub 283
Apples
    Apple Caramel on Puff Pastry 268
    Apple-Tarragon Slaw 98
    Cider-brined Pork Chops with Grilled Apples 101
    Cider-simmered Brats with Apples and Onions 97
Apricots
    Gingerbread with Braaied Apricots 269
Argentine Beef Skewers with Chimichurri Sauce 72
Artichoke Hearts with Smoked Tomato and Roasted Garlic Aïoli 245
Asian Black Bean Sauce 108
Asian Butter Sauce 193
Asparagus
    Asparagus and Prosciutto with Lemon Vinaigrette 247
    Sesame-Ginger Flank Steak with Asparagus and Gomashio 69
Avocados
    Black Bean and Avocado Salsa 67
    Brickyard Calamari Salad 227
    Crab and Avocado Quesadillas 198
    Guacamole 157, 253
    Guacamole Mayonnaise 36
    Layered Mexican Chicken Salad 154
    Roasted Chilli and Avocado Sauce 187

B
Baby Back Ribs Rub 283
Bagel Chips 255
Balinese Peanut Sauce 291
Bananas
    Bananas Foster 270
    Braaied Banana S'Mores 271
Barbacoa Sauce 85
Barbecue-baked Beans alla Contadina 65
Barbecue Chicken Rub 283
Barbecue Sauce with Beer 288
Barbecue sauces
    See also Sauces
    Barbacoa 85
    Classic Red 289
    Orange 87
    Red-eye 47
    Sassy 289
    Sofrito 105
    Soo-Wee 122
    Sweet-and-Sour 129
    Triple Play 151
Barcelona Marinade 287
Basil-Garlic Oil 81
Beans
    Barbecue-baked Beans alla Contadina 65
    Black Bean and Avocado Salsa 67
    Green Beans with Lemon Oil 249
    Layered Mexican Chicken Salad 154
    White Bean Purée with Roasted Garlic 263
Beef 34–39, 42–73, 82–84, 87–93
    See also Beef fillet; Beef mince; Beef ribs; Beef roast; Beef steak
    braaiing guide for beef 296
Beef fillet
    Beef Kebabs with Finadene 73
    Herb-crusted Beef Fillet with White Wine Cream Sauce 89
    Tea-rubbed Fillet Steaks 61
Beef mince
    Braaied Meat Loaf 42
    Brie and Shallot Parisian Burgers 38
    Cabernet Burgers with Rosemary Focaccia 37
    California Burgers with Guacamole Mayonnaise 36
    Classic Burger Melts on Rye 35
    Kofta in Pita Pockets 39
Beef ribs
    Beef Ribs with Barbacoa Sauce 85
    Korean Beef Barbecue 83
Beef roast
    Smoked Brisket 93
    Tropical Tri-Tip Roast with Orange Barbecue Sauce 87
    Wood-smoked Boneless Rib Roast with Shiraz Sauce 91
Beef Rub 281
Beef steak
    Argentine Beef Skewers with Chimichurri Sauce 72
    Bistecca alla Fiorentina 65
    Bistro Steaks with Mustard Cream Sauce 68
    Carne Asada with Black Bean and Avocado Salsa 67
    Flank Steak with Roasted Pepper and Feta Stuffing 71
    Garlic-crusted Rib-eye Steaks 59
    Panzanella Steak Salad 50
    Porterhouse Steaks with Red Wine-Shallot Butter 63
    Rib-eye Steaks with Espresso-Chilli Rub 53
    Rib-eye Steaks with Pan-roasted Chilli Salsa 55
    Sesame-Ginger Flank Steak 69
    Skirt Steaks with Baby Potatoes and Feta 66
    Steak and Gorgonzola Piadini 56
    Steak Sandwiches with Braaied Onions and Creamy Horseradish Sauce 48
    Sirloin Steak Escalopes 51
    Sirloin Steaks with Red-eye Barbecue Sauce 47
Beer Marinade 285
Beetroot
    Flame-roasted Beetroot Salad with Pumpkin Seeds and Feta 258
Bistecca alla Fiorentina 65
Bistro Steaks with Mustard Cream Sauce 68
Black Bean and Avocado Salsa 67, 299
Blue Cheese and Walnut Spread 263
Bok choy see Pak choi
Bombay Tomato Sauce 207
Bourbon or Brandy Marinade 286
Braaied Banana S'mores 271
Braaied Flatbread with Three Toppings 262
Braaied Meat Loaf 42
Braaied Tuna Poke 210
Bratwurst
    Cider-simmered Bratwurst with Apples and Onions 97
Breads
    Buttermilk Scones 99
    Flatbread 262
    Piadini 56
    Pizza crust 239
Brickyard Calamari Salad 227
Brinjal
    Ratatouille Salad 81
    Roasted Brinjal Dip 255
    Vegetable Sandwiches with Sun-dried Tomato Spread 256
Broccoli
    Garlic-crusted Rib-eye Steaks with Braaied Tenderstem Broccoli 59
    Lemon Broccoli 248
Bruschetta
    Roasted Pepper and Bacon Bruschetta 240
Burgers see Sandwiches
Buttermilk Scones with Chilli Jam-glazed Ham 99
Butternut
    Honey and Curry-glazed Butternut 257

C
Cabernet Burgers with Rosemary Focaccia 37
Cajun Rub 281
Cajun-style Clambake 191
Cakes
    Pineapple Upside-down Cake 267
Calamari
    Brickyard Calamari Salad 227
    Thai Squid (Calamari) 225
California Burgers with Guacamole Mayonnaise 36
Camembert
    Vine Leaf-wrapped Camembert with Grape Salsa 277
Caribbean Citrus Marinade 212
Caribbean Rub 282
Carne Asada with Black Bean and Avocado Salsa 67

Carrots
    Carrot and Cashew Salad 252
    Orange-glazed Carrots 251
Cedar-planked Chicken Thighs with Soy-Ginger Glaze 153
Cedar-planked Salmon with Hazelnut Sauce 203
Cedar-planked Scallops with Grilled Corn Salad 180
Cedar-planked Trout with Rocket, Fennel and Orange 223
Cedar-planked Turkey Burgers 174
Char-grilled Oysters 193
Chermoula 289
Chicken 134–139, 143–149, 151–157, 160–167
    See also Chicken breasts; Chicken drumsticks; Chicken thighs; Chicken, whole and cut-up whole; Chicken wings
    braaiing guide for chicken 301
Chicken and Seafood Rub 281
Chicken and Vegetable Quesadillas with Guacamole 157
Chicken breasts
    Chicken Escalopes with Tomato and Olive Relish 137
    Chicken Involtini with Prosciutto and Basil 135
    Jerk Chicken Skewers with Honey-Lime Cream 143
    Lemon-Origanum Chicken Breasts 138
    Tandoori Chicken Breasts with Mango-Mint Chutney 139
    Tunisian Chicken with Parsley Pesto 145
Chicken drumsticks
    Provençal Marinated Chicken Legs 149
    Triple-play Barbecued Chicken 151
Chicken thighs
    Cedar-planked Chicken Thighs with Soy-Ginger Glaze 153
    Chicken and Vegetable Quesadillas with Guacamole 157
    Layered Mexican Chicken Salad 154
    Persian Chicken Kebabs 155
    Provençal Marinated Chicken Legs, 149
    Triple-play Barbecued Chicken 151
Chicken, whole and cut-up whole
    Huli-Huli Chicken 159
    Nutmeg Chicken under a Cast-iron Pan 167
    Orange-Tarragon Roasted Chicken 165
    Rotisserie Buttermilk Chicken with Apricot Glaze 163
    Smoked Beer Can Chicken 161
Chicken wings
    Hickory Drumettes with Bourbon-molasses Glaze 147
    Honey-Garlic Chicken Wings 146
Chiles
    Chiles Rellenos with Tomato Salsa and Guacamole 253
Chilli-Orange Marinade 286
Chilli Verde Country-style Ribs 131
Chimichurri Sauce 72, 290
Chinese Hoisin Marinade 287
Chipotle-Lime Slaw 206

Chopped Salad 41
Chutney
    Mango-Mint Chutney 139
Cider-brined Pork Chops with Grilled Apples 101
Cider-simmered Bratwurst with Apples and Onions 97
Clams
    Cajun-style Clambake 191
Classic Barbecue Spice Rub 281
Classic Red Barbecue Sauce 289
Coconut
    Bombay Tomato Sauce 207
    Coconut-Curry Mussels 190
    Coconut-glazed Sweet Potatoes 261
    Peanut Sauce 185, 291
    Red Curry-Coconut Sauce 202
    Line Fish in Coconut Broth 217
Cool Green Chilli Sauce 291
Coriander Pesto Marinade 287
Corn
    Cajun-style Clambake 191
    Chicken and Vegetable Quesadillas with Guacamole 157
    Corn and Mushroom Salsa 209
    Flame-roasted Mealies with Lemon-Curry Butter 232
    Ginger and Lime-glazed Mealies 233
    Grilled Corn and Mushroom Risotto 234
    Grilled Corn Salad 180
    Polenta with Feta and Roasted Tomatillo Sauce 231
    Pork Fillets with Creamy Corn 106
Courgette
    Chicken and Vegetable Quesadillas with Guacamole 157
    Ratatouille Salad 81
    Vegetable Sandwiches with Sun-dried Tomato Spread 256
Crab
    Crab and Avocado Quesadillas 198
    Whole Crabs with White Wine-Garlic Butter 197
Cracked Pepper Rub 281
Crayfish Rolls 195
Creamy Horseradish Sauce 48, 290
Crème Fraiche 268
Cuban Marinade 287
Cucumbers
    Chopped Salad 41
    Cucumber and Tomato Salad 39
    Cucumber-Yoghurt Sauce 74
    Watermelon Salsa 181

D

Desserts 268–275
Dorado with Corn and Mushroom Salsa 209
Duck
    Duck Breast Tacos with Sour Orange and Onion Salsa 142
    Duck Breasts with Port Wine and Plum Sauce 141
    Slow-roasted Duck Legs with Hoisin-Orange Glaze 150

E

Eggplant see Brinjal
Espresso-Chilli Rub 53, 282

F

Fennel
    Cedar-planked Trout with Rocket, Fennel and Orange 223
    Fennel and Fontina 259
    Fennel and Olive Salad 205
    Fennel Rub 281
    Orange-Fennel Prawns over Watercress 183
    Seafood Zuppa 199
Figs
    Lemon-Buttermilk Panna Cotta with Braaied Figs 272
Finadene 73
Fish 199–223
    See also Specific fish
    Braaied Tuna Poke 210
    Cedar-planked Salmon with Hazelnut Sauce 203
    Cedar-planked Trout with Rocket, Fennel and Orange 223
    Dorado with Corn and Mushroom Salsa 209
    Fish Wraps with Chipotle-Lime Slaw 206
    Ginger and Miso Line Fish in Banana Leaves 215
    Grilled Hake in a Caribbean Citrus Marinade 212
    Hake with Bombay Tomato Sauce 207
    Line Fish in Coconut Broth 217
    Mexican Grill-pan Fish 218
    Sake-marinated Trout 221
    Salmon with Fennel and Olive Salad 205
    Salmon with Nectarine Salsa 201
    Salmon with Red Curry-Coconut Sauce 202
    Seafood Zuppa 199
    Smoked Tuna Salad with Grilled Mango 211
    Swordfish Escabèche 213
    Whole Line Fish in Moroccan Marinade 219
Fish Rub 206, 283
Fish Wraps with Chipotle-Lime Slaw 206
Flame-roasted Beetroot Salad with Pumpkin Seeds and Feta 258
Flame-roasted Mealies with Lemon-Curry Butter 232
Flame-roasted Strawberries 273
Flame-roasted Tomato Soup with Parmesan Croutons 242
Flank Steak with Roasted Pepper and Feta Stuffing, 71
Flatbread with Three Toppings 262
Fruit 264–277
    See also Specific fruits
    braaiing guide for fruit 306

G

Garlic
    Basil-Garlic Oil 81
    Garlic and Red Pepper Sauce 291

Garlic-crusted Rib-eye Steaks with Braaied Tenderstem Broccoli 59
Garlic paste 59
Garlic-Thyme Butter 193
Smoked Tomato and Roasted Garlic Aioli 245
White Bean Purée with Roasted Garlic 263
White Wine-Garlic Butter 197
Ginger and Lime-glazed Mealies 233
Ginger and Miso Line Fish in Banana Leaves 215
Gingerbread with Braaied Apricots 269
Gomashio 69
Gorgonzola-Tomato Sauce 193
Grape Salsa 277
Grapefruit-Basil Aioli 193
Greek Marinade 285
Green Beans with Lemon Oil 249
Grilled Hake in a Caribbean Citrus Marinade 212
Ground Beef *see* Beef Mince
Ground Pork *see* Pork Mince
Guacamole 157, 253
Guacamole Mayonnaise 36

H
Hake
   Fish Wraps with Chipotle-Lime Slaw 206
   Grilled Hake in a Caribbean Citrus Marinade 212
   Hake with Bombay Tomato Sauce 207
Ham
   Buttermilk Scones with Chilli Jam-glazed Ham 99
Hazelnut Sauce 203
Herb-crusted Beef Fillet with White Wine Cream Sauce 89
Hickory Drumettes with Bourbon-Molasses Glaze 147
Hickory-smoked Turkey with Bourbon Gravy 172
Honey
   Honey and Curry-glazed Butternut 257
   Honey-Garlic Chicken Wings 146
   Honey-Lime Cream 143
   Honey-Mustard Marinade 286
Hot Dogs with Pickled Onions 43
Huli-Huli Chicken 159

J
Jerk Chicken Skewers with Honey-Lime Cream 143
Jerk Marinade 285
Juicy Prawns with Roasted Chilli and Avocado Sauce 187

K
Kebabs
   See also Skewers
   Argentine Beef Skewers 72
   Beef Kebabs 73
   Lamb Souvlaki 74
   Persian Chicken Kebabs 155
Kofta in Pita Pockets with Cucumber and Tomato Salad 39
Korean Beef Barbecue 83

L
Lamb, 40–41, 74, 76–81, 86
   Lamb Burgers with Tapenade and Goat's Cheese 40
   Lamb Chops in Uzbek Marinade 79
   Lamb Chops with Indian Spices 78
   Lamb Meatballs with Chopped Salad and Minted Yoghurt, 41
   Lamb Shoulder Chops with Ratatouille Salad and Basil-Garlic Oil 81
   Lamb Souvlaki with Cucumber-Yoghurt Sauce 74
   Leg of Lamb with Moroccan Spices 86
   Rack of Lamb with Orange-Pomegranate Syrup 77
Latino Pork Roast 119
Layered Mexican Chicken Salad 154
Leeks
   Pork Escalopes with Romesco Sauce 103
Leg of Lamb with Moroccan Spices 86
Lemon
   Lemon Broccoli 248
   Lemon-Buttermilk Panna Cotta with Braaied Figs 272
   Lemon-Curry Butter 232
   Lemon-Ginger Tofu Steaks with Carrot and Cashew Salad 252
   Lemon Oil 249
   Lemon-Origanum Chicken Breasts 138
   Lemon-Paprika Rub 283
   Lemon-Sage Marinade 285
   Lemon Vinaigrette 247
Lentil Salad 179
Line Fish
   Ginger and Miso Line Fish in Banana Leaves 215
   Grilled Hake in a Caribbean Citrus Marinade 212
   Line Fish in Coconut Broth 217
   Mexican Grill-pan Fish 218
   Whole Line Fish in Morrocan Marinade 219
Lobster *see* Crayfish

M
Magic Rub 282
Mangoes
   Mango-Mint Chutney 139
   Smoked Tuna Salad with Grilled Mango 211
Marinades, 284–287
   Barcelona 287
   Beer 285
   Bourbon or Brandy 286
   Caribbean Citrus 212
   Chilli-Orange 286
   Chinese Hoisin 287
   Coriander Pesto 287
   Cuban 287
   Finadene 73
   Greek 285
   Honey-Mustard 286
   Huli-Huli 159
   Jerk 285
   Lemon-Sage 285
   Mediterranean 286
   Mojo 119, 285
   Mongolian 287
   Moroccan 86, 219
   Pacific Rim 285
   Provençal 149
   Sake 221
   Spicy Cayenne 287
   Tandoori 139, 287
   Tarragon-Citrus 286
   Tequila 286
   Teriyaki 285
   Uzbek 79
Marinated Baby Pak Choi and Shiitake Mushrooms 235
Marinated Portabello Mushrooms with Pecorino Cheese 237
Mealies *see* Corn
Meat Loaf 42
Mediterranean Marinade 286
Mexican Grill-pan Fish 218
Mexican Rub 283
Mojo Marinade 119, 285
Mongolian Marinade 287
Moroccan Marinade 86, 219
Mushrooms
   Corn and Mushroom Salsa 209
   Grilled Corn and Mushroom Risotto 234
   Marinated Baby Pak Choi and Shiitake Mushrooms 235
   Marinated Portabello Mushrooms with Pecorino Cheese 237
   Pizza with Mushrooms, Peppers, Garlic and Smoked Mozzarella 239
   Porcini-rubbed Veal Chops with Herbed Mascarpone 75
   Portabello Mushroom Sandwiches with Basil and Balsamic Aioli 236
   Swordfish Escabèche 213
   Tea-rubbed Fillet Steaks with Buttery Mushrooms 61
Mussels
   Coconut-Curry Mussels 190
   Paella 189

N
Nectarines
   Nectarine, Red Pepper and Onion Salsa 288
   Nectarine Salsa 201
New World Rub 283
Nutmeg Chicken under a Cast-iron Pan 167

O
Olives
   Fennel and Olive Salad 205
   Roasted Pepper, Lemon and Olive Relish 219
   Tapenade 40, 263
   Tomato and Olive Relish 137
Oranges
   Cedar-planked Trout with Rocket, Fennel and Orange 223
   Orange Barbecue Sauce 87
   Orange-Fennel Shrimp over Watercress 183
   Orange-glazed Carrots 251
   Orange-Tarragon Roasted Chicken 165

Sake-marinated Trout 221
Sour Orange and Onion Salsa 142
Oysters; Char-grilled Oysters 193

P

Pacific Rim Marinade 285
Paella 189
Pak choi
    Marinated Baby Pak Choi and Shiitake Mushrooms 235
Panna Cotta 272
Pan-roasted Chilli Salsa 55
Panzanella Skewers with Sherry Vinaigrette 243
Panzanella Steak Salad 50
Parsley Pesto 145
Peaches
    Peach Shortcakes 275
Peanut Sauce 185, 291
Pear and Prosciutto Salad with Champagne Vinaigrette 276
Persian Chicken Kebabs 155
Pesto
    Coriander Pesto Marinade 287
    Pistachio Pesto 260
Piadini 56
Pineapple Upside-down Cake 267
Pistachio Pesto 260
Pizza with Mushrooms, Peppers, Garlic and Smoked Mozzarella 239
Plums
    Port Wine and Plum Sauce 141
Polenta with Feta and Roasted Tomatillo Sauce 231
Porchetta-style Pork Shoulder 117
Porcini-rubbed Veal Chops with Herbed Mascarpone 75
Pork 94–131
    See also Bratwurst; Ham; Pork chops; Pork fillet; Pork ribs; Pork roast
Pork chops
    Cider-brined Pork Chops with Grilled Apples 101
    Pork Escalopes with Romesco Sauce 103
    Pork Loin Chops with Sofrito Barbecue Sauce 105
    Pork, Roasted Pepper and Cheddar Sandwiches 104
Pork fillet
    Pork Medallions with Asian Black Bean Sauce 108
    Pork Fillets with Creamy Corn 106
    Pork Fillets with Smoked Paprika Rouille 107
Pork Loin with Cherry-Chipotle Glaze 109
Pork Mince
    Pork Burgers with Apple-Tarragon Slaw 98
    Vietnamese Prawn Pops with Peanut Sauce 185
Pork ribs
    Chilli Verde Country-style Ribs 131
    Slow Good Baby Back Ribs with Soo-Wee Sauce 122
    Slow-smoked Spareribs with Sweet-and-sour Barbecue Sauce 129
    Stacked Baby Back Ribs 125
    Sweet Ginger and Soy-glazed Spareribs 127
    Tamarind-glazed Country-style Ribs 130
Pork roast
    Latino Pork Roast 119
    Porchetta-style Pork Shoulder 117
    Pork Loin with Cherry-Chipotle Glaze 109
    Pulled Pork Sandwiches 115
    Rotisserie Pork Loin with Red Wine and Prune Sauce 111
    Smoke-roasted Pork Loin with Redcurrant Sauce 113
Pork Rub 281
Port Wine and Plum Sauce 141
Porterhouse Steaks with Red Wine-Shallot Butter 63
Potatoes
    Potato Salad with Pistachio Pesto 260
    Skirt Steaks with Baby Potatoes and Feta 66
Poultry 132–175
    See also Chicken; Duck; Poussin; Turkey braaiing guide for poultry 301
Poussins
    grilling guide for 301
    Poussins Marinated in Bourbon, Honey and Soy 158
Prawns
    Cajun-style Clambake 191
    Grilled Hake in a Caribbean Citrus Marinade 212
    Juicy Prawns with Roasted Chilli and Avocado Sauce 187
    Orange-Fennel Prawns over Watercress 183
    Paella 189
    Prawn Rolls with Creole Rémoulade 182
    Seafood Zuppa 199
    Thai Prawns with Watermelon Salsa 181
    Vietnamese Prawn Pops with Peanut Sauce 185
Provençal Marinated Chicken Legs 149
Pulled Pork Rub 115, 283
Pulled Pork Sandwiches 115

Q

Quesadillas
    Chicken and Vegetable Quesadillas with Guacamole 157
    Crab and Avocado Quesadillas 198

R

Rack of Lamb with Orange-Pomegranate Syrup 77
Ratatouille Salad 81
Redcurrant Sauce 113
Red Curry-Coconut Sauce 202
Red-eye Barbecue Sauce 47
Red Wine and Prune Sauce 111
Red Wine-Shallot Butter 63
Relishes
    Roasted Pepper, Lemon and Olive Relish 219
    Tomato and Olive Relish 137
Rémoulade 182, 291
Rib-eye Steaks with Espresso-Chilli Rub 53
Rib-eye Steaks with Pan-roasted Chilli Salsa 55
Ribs See Beef ribs; Pork ribs
Rice
    Grilled Corn and Mushroom Risotto 234
    Paella 189
Roasted Brinjal Dip 255
Roasted Chilli and Avocado Sauce 187
Roasted Pepper and Bacon Bruschetta 240
Roasted Pepper, Grilled Onion and Feta Cheese Salad 241
Roasted Pepper, Lemon and Olive Relish 219
Roasted Tomatillo Sauce 231
Roasted Tomato Sauce 178
Romesco Sauce 103, 290
Rotisserie Buttermilk Chicken with Apricot Glaze 163
Rotisserie Pork Loin with Red Wine and Prune Sauce 111
Rouille 107
Rubs 280–283
    All-Purpose 283
    Asian 282
    Baby Back Ribs 283
    Barbecue Chicken 283
    Baja Fish 283
    Beef 281
    Cajun 281
    Caribbean 282
    Chicken and Seafood 281
    Classic Barbecue Spice 281
    Cracked Pepper 281
    Espresso-Chilli 53, 282
    Fennel 281
    Fish 206, 283
    Lemon-Paprika 283
    Magic 282
    Mexican 283
    New World 283
    Pork 281
    Pulled Pork 115, 283
    Tarragon 282
    Tex-Mex 282

S

Sake-marinated Trout 221
Salads
    Apple-Tarragon Slaw 98
    Brickyard Calamari Salad 227
    Carrot and Cashew Salad 252
    Chipotle-Lime Slaw 206
    Chopped Salad 41
    Cucumber and Tomato Salad 39
    Fennel and Olive Salad 205
    Flame-roasted Beetroot Salad with Pumpkin Seeds and Feta 258
    Grilled Corn Salad 180
    Layered Mexican Chicken Salad 154
    Lentil Salad 179
    Panzanella Skewers with Sherry Vinaigrette 243
    Panzanella Steak Salad 50
    Pear and Prosciutto Salad with Champagne Vinaigrette 276

Potato Salad with Pistachio Pesto 260
Ratatouille Salad 81
Roasted Pepper, Grilled Onion and Feta Cheese Salad 241
Salsa Slaw 175
Smoked Tuna Salad with Grilled Mango 211

Salmon
- Cedar-planked Salmon with Hazelnut Sauce 203
- Fish Wraps with Chipotle-Lime Slaw 206
- Salmon with Fennel and Olive Salad 205
- Salmon with Nectarine Salsa 201
- Salmon with Red Curry-Coconut Sauce 202

Salsa Slaw 175

Salsas
- See also Sauces
- Black Bean and Avocado 67, 289
- Chermoula 289
- Corn and Mushroom 209
- Grape 277
- Nectarine 201
- Nectarine and Red Pepper 291
- Nectarine, Red Pepper and Onion 289
- Pan-roasted Chilli 55
- Sour Orange and Onion 142
- Tomato 253, 291
- Watermelon 181

Sandwiches
- Braaied Meat Loaf 42
- Brie and Shallot Parisian Burgers 38
- Buttermilk Scones with Chilli Jam-glazed Ham 99
- Cabernet Burgers with Rosemary Focaccia 37
- California Burgers with Guacamole Mayonnaise 36
- Cedar-planked Turkey Burgers 174
- Chicken and Vegetable Quesadillas with Guacamole 157
- Cider-simmered Bratwurst with Apples and Onions 97
- Classic Burger Melts on Rye 35
- Crab and Avocado Quesadillas 198
- Crayfish Rolls 195
- Duck Breast Tacos with Sour Orange and Onion Salsa 142
- Fish Wraps with Chipotle-Lime Slaw 206
- Hot Dogs with Pickled Onions 43
- Kofta in Pita Pockets 39
- Lamb Burgers with Tapenade and Goat's Cheese 40
- Lamb Meatballs with Chopped Salad and Minted Yoghurt 41
- Pork Burgers with Apple-Tarragon Slaw 98
- Pork, Roasted Pepper and Cheddar Sandwiches 104
- Portabello Mushroom Sandwiches with Basil and Balsamic Aioli 236
- Prawn Rolls with Creole Rémoulade 182
- Pulled Pork Sandwiches 115
- Steak and Gorgonzola Piadini 56
- Steak Sandwiches with Braaied Onions and Creamy Horseradish Sauce 48
- Turkey Burgers with Salsa Slaw 175
- Vegetable Sandwiches with Sun-dried Tomato Spread 256

Sassy Barbecue Sauce 289

Sauces 288–291
- See also Barbecue sauces; Salsas
- Agro Dolce see Red Wine and Prune Sauce
- Aioli 193, 236, 245
- Asian Black Bean 108
- Asian Butter 193
- Balinese Peanut Sauce 291
- Bombay Tomato 207
- Chilli Verde 131
- Chimichurri 72, 290
- Cool Green Chilli 291
- Creamy Horseradish 48, 290
- Cucumber-Yoghurt 74
- Finadene 73
- Garlic and Red Pepper 290
- Garlic-Thyme Butter 193
- Gorgonzola-Tomato 193
- Guacamole Mayonnaise 36
- Hazelnut 203
- Honey-Lime Cream 143
- Lemon Vinaigrette 247
- Parsley Pesto 145
- Peanut 185, 291
- Port Wine and Plum 141
- Redcurrant 113
- Red Curry-Coconut 202
- Red Wine and Prune Sauce 111
- Rémoulade 182, 291
- Roasted Chilli and Avocado 187
- Roasted Tomatillo 231
- Roasted Tomato 178
- Romesco 103, 290
- Rouille 107
- Shiraz 91
- Soo-Wee 122
- Tapenade 40
- Tarator see Hazelnut
- White Wine Cream 89

Scallops
- Cedar-planked Scallops with Grilled Corn Salad 180
- Prosciutto-wrapped Scallops with Lentil Salad 179
- Scallops with Roasted Tomato Sauce 178
- Seafood Zuppa 199

Scones
- Buttermilk Scones 99

Seafood 176–227
- See also Fish; Shellfish
- grilling guide for seafood 303
- Seafood Zuppa 199
- Sesame-Ginger Flank Steak with Asparagus and Gomashio 69

Shallots
- Bistro Steaks with Mustard Cream Sauce 68
- Red Wine-Shallot Butter 63

Shellfish 178–199, 224–225
- See also Specific shellfish

Shiraz Sauce 91

Shortcakes
- Peach Shortcakes 275

Shrimp see Prawns

Skewers
- See also Kebabs
- Argentine Beef Skewers 72
- Jerk Chicken Skewers 143
- Juicy Prawns with Roasted Chilli and Avocado Sauce 187
- Lamb Meatballs 41
- Panzanella Skewers 243
- Salmon with Red Curry-Coconut Sauce 202
- Vietnamese Prawn Pops 185

Skirt Steaks with Baby Potatoes and Feta 66

Slaws see Salads

Slow Good Baby Back Ribs with Soo-Wee Sauce 122

Slow-roasted Duck Legs with Hoisin-Orange Glaze 150

Slow-smoked Spareribs with Sweet-and-Sour Barbecue Sauce 129

Smoked Beer Can Chicken 161

Smoked Brisket 93

Smoked Tuna Salad with Grilled Mango 211

Smoke-roasted Pork Loin with Redcurrant Sauce 113

Sofrito Barbecue Sauce 105

Soo-Wee Sauce 122

Soups
- Flame-roasted Tomato Soup with Parmesan Croutons 242
- Seafood Zuppa 199

Spicy Cayenne Marinade 287

Squash, summer see Courgette

Squash, winter see Butternut

Squid see Calamari

Stacked Baby Back Ribs 125

Steak
- See Beef steak

Strawberries
- Flame-roasted Strawberries 273
- Sirloin Steak Escalopes 51
- Sirloin Steaks with Red-eye Barbecue Sauce 47

Sweet-and-Sour Barbecue Sauce 129

Sweet Ginger and Soy-glazed Spareribs 127

Sweet potatoes
- Coconut-glazed Sweet Potatoes 261

Swordfish
- Seafood Zuppa 199
- Swordfish Escabèche 213

T

Tacos
- Duck Breast Tacos with Sour Orange and Onion Salsa 142

Tamarind-glazed Country-style Ribs 130

Tandoori Chicken Breasts with Mango-Mint Chutney 139

Tandoori Marinade 139, 287

Tapenade 40, 263

Tarator Sauce see Hazelnut Sauce

Tarragon-Citrus Marinade 286

Tarragon Rub 282

Tea paste 61

Tea-rubbed Fillet Steaks with Buttery Mushrooms 61
Tequila Marinade 286
Teriyaki Marinade 285
Tex-Mex Rub 282
Thai Prawns with Watermelon Salsa 181
Thai Squid (Calamari) 225
Tofu
   Lemon-Ginger Tofu Steaks with Carrot and Cashew Salad 252
Tomatillos
   Roasted Tomatillo Sauce 231
Nectarine and Red Pepper Salsa 291
Tomatoes
   Bombay Tomato Sauce 207
   Cucumber and Tomato Salad 39
   Flame-roasted Tomato Soup with Parmesan Croutons 242
   Pan-roasted Chilli Salsa 55
   Panzanella Skewers with Sherry Vinaigrette 243
   Panzanella Steak Salad 50
   Roasted Tomato Sauce 178
   Smoked Tomato and Roasted Garlic Aioli 245
   Sun-dried Tomato Spread 256

Tomato and Olive Relish 137
Tomato Salsa 253, 291
Tomato Tapenade 263
Triple Play Barbecued Chicken 151
Tropical Tri-Tip Roast with Orange Barbecue Sauce 87
Trout
   Cedar-planked Trout with Rocket, Fennel and Orange 223
   Sake-marinated Trout 221
Tuna
   Braaied Tuna Poke 210
   Smoked Tuna Salad with Grilled Mango 211
Tunisian Chicken with Parsley Pesto 145
Turkey 168–175
   Bacon-wrapped Turkey Breast with Herb Stuffing 169
   Burgers with Salsa Slaw 175
   Cedar-planked Turkey Burgers 174
   grilling guide for turkey 301
   Hickory-smoked Turkey with Bourbon Gravy 172
Turkey Burgers with Salsa Slaw 175

U
Uzbek Marinade 79

V
Veal
   Porcini-rubbed Veal Chops with Herbed Mascarpone 75
Vegetables, 228–263
   See also Specific vegetables
   Vegetable Sandwiches with Sun-dried Tomato Spread 256
Vietnamese Prawn Pops with Peanut Sauce 185
Vinaigrette
   Champagne 276
   Lemon 247
   Sherry 243
Vine Leaf-wrapped Camembert with Grape Salsa 277

W
Watermelon Salsa 181
White Bean Purée with Roasted Garlic 263
White Wine Cream Sauce 89
White Wine-Garlic Butter 197
Whole Crabs with White Wine-Garlic Butter 197
Whole Line Fish in Moroccan Marinade 219
Wood-smoked Boneless Rib Roast with Shiraz Sauce 91

GENERAL CONVERSIONS: METRIC TO IMPERIAL					
TEASPOONS		TABLESPOONS		CUPS	
METRIC	IMPERIAL	METRIC	IMPERIAL	METRIC	IMPERIAL
2 ml	¼ tsp	15 ml	1 Tbsp	60 ml	¼ cup
3 ml	½ tsp	30 ml	2 Tbsp	80 ml	⅓ cup
5 ml	1 tsp	45 ml	3 Tbsp	125 ml	½ cup
10 ml	2 tsp	60 ml	4 Tbsp	160 ml	⅔ cup
15 ml	3 tsp	75 ml	5 Tbsp	200 ml	¾ cup
20 ml	4 tsp	90 ml	6 Tbsp	250 ml	1 cup